A STUDY IN ST MARK

70
———
542

A STUDY IN
ST MARK

BY

AUSTIN FARRER

DOCTOR OF DIVINITY AND FELLOW OF TRINITY COLLEGE
OXFORD

dacre press
westminster

FIRST PUBLISHED 1951

DACRE PRESS: A. AND C. BLACK LTD
4, 5 AND 6 SOHO SQUARE LONDON W.I

MADE IN GREAT BRITAIN
PRINTED BY UNWIN BROTHERS LIMITED
WOKING AND LONDON

PREFACE

In writing the body of his book an author identifies himself with his thesis and presses his argument. But when he comes to add a preface he may detach himself somewhat and take an outside view. It is true, indeed, that willingness to undergo publication convicts him of believing himself right in the main. No protestation of detachment can disguise the implications of considered action. And I for my part am committed to the claim that I have found in St Mark's Gospel a pattern of which St Mark was in some measure conscious, and which in any case shaped his story as he wrote it. I take so much to be a true discovery and not a speculation. But I am free to say and do sincerely say that it is not possible to know exactly where this pattern of St Mark's ends, or in what degree of detail it can be profitably worked out. I make my readers the judges. I do not withhold from them everything which admits of reasonable doubt, because I want their assistance in dividing the region of the doubtful into two territories, the improbable and the probable. I have done my best to make the division for myself, but the estimate of probabilities is a matter of judgement, not of dead reckoning, and on points of judgement many heads are better than one. I hope my readers will exercise the pruning-knife if I have anywhere run into undue elaborations. But I also hope that the stock and main branches of the argument will flourish all the better for being pruned.

My first chapter is one of the parts which can be retrenched without serious prejudice to the whole. It is not the root from which the development really springs. It merely seeks to mark out on the map of contemporary studies a plot of ground in which I may be free to plant. It describes the state of Gospel-criticism in such a way as to show how there is room for an enterprise like mine. One cannot write summarily about the state of the question without superficiality, and hardly without some injustice. The most one can hope to do is to indicate an attitude towards the problem in hand.

The main thesis of the book is expounded in II–VI, with VII as

v

a sort of note appended. It is in these chapters that the pattern of
St Mark's inspired thinking is analysed and described. It is shown
that St Mark's book is a unity and that, whatever his materials or
sources, he dominated them. The healing miracles as narrated by
him are found to fall into a firm pattern, which can be used as
a clue to the rhythm of his continuous thought. He is found to
travel on a circular path through a limited round of themes and
images, over and over again. With fresh variation and steadily
increasing clarity each successive phase of Christ's ministry
displays the same essentials of redemptive action, until in his
passion and resurrection they are consummated.

The thesis I have outlined is continued and extended in XIII–XV,
but the matter of those chapters is more speculative and the
substance of the argument could stand without them. For that
reason I have placed them at the end as though in an
appendix, cut off from the main body by the intervention
of VIII–XII.

Chapters VIII–XII are designed to afford the reader some relief,
and even, perhaps, some reassurance. After enduring six chapters
of symbolism, he might like to convince himself that history has
not dropped out of sight. So in VIII–IX the historical sense is discussed and defended. In the last part of VIII I ran into a dilemma.
I could not renounce the desire to show how the historical
reasonableness of the Marcan Passion may be upheld; but neither
could I treat it on such a scale as the matter demanded, or I should
have overbalanced my book entirely. The result is more like a
specimen of a discussion than like an adequate discussion.

Chapter X shows how the analysis of the Gospel given in
II–VI enables us to deal with the venerable problem of Messianic
secrecy. I should like to lay some stress on the evidential value
of this chapter. If my reader finds it convincing I would ask him
to consider how much of the thesis expounded in II–VI is bound
up with it. In XI–XII I turn from the general topic of secrecy to
the special case of the secret teaching about the Son of Man.

Since XIII–XV have been mentioned already, there remains only
XVI. There I discuss the date of the Gospel, in so far as the argu-

ment of my book casts light upon it. I add some general remarks
by way of conclusion and so make an end.

Here, then, the book is, an essay in literary analysis, not in
historical learning. It enters on topics of history here and there,
but they are not its principal business. Its concern is with the
sentences St Mark writes and the mental process they express.
I shall put my reader to the trouble of keeping St Mark beside him
and often turning the page, unless he knows the sacred text by
heart already. I hope he will not be mystified by the form in which
quotations from the Old Testament will sometimes appear. It will
be a close English version of the Septuagintic Greek, as being our
nearest guide to the dress in which Scripture was most familiar to
St Mark himself. But all references will follow the order of the
English Bible and not (where it diverges) that of the Septuagint.

My chief personal debt is to Fr. Peter Jones, O.S.B., of Nashdom
Abbey. He read the manuscript with a care and a discretion which
I do not know how to praise. He weeded a cartload of tares out of
my field. He made many suggestions, and hardly one that did not
convince me. My wife also made valuable suggestions about the
manner of presentation. Dr. Lowe, Dean of Christ Church and
present Vice-Chancellor of the University, called my attention to
Dr. Arnold Meyer's work on St James (see p. 320 below). On
p. 212 I have plundered an excellent paper sent me by Mr Michael
Moreton just as I was revising what I had written on John v.
Mr Robert Milburn, Fellow of Worcester College, established for
me the text of the excerpts from Papias which I discuss in my first
chapter. Mr Robin Anstey has made the indices, and how could
a pupil testify more *pietas* to his former tutor than by undertaking
so discouraging a labour?

OXFORD, *February* 1951.

CONTENTS

CHAPTER I

INTRODUCTION

The study of St Mark has held a special position in New Testament scholarship ever since the day when learned opinion arrived at the well-grounded conviction that St Mark's is the earliest written of the Gospels, and that the other three (two of them more particularly) knew and used his work. It may be that there are many things to be learned from the Gospels beside the bare history of Christ's life, death, and resurrection; and each of the four Evangelists may be supreme in some one province. But bare history is of inestimable importance, and when we are thinking about that, we are bound to allow the greatest weight to the written authority which is both prior in date and prior in the actual series through which tradition was handed down.

It is therefore surprising and somewhat disconcerting to hear the unique historical importance of St Mark either questioned or qualified, as happens here and there nowadays. On the first hearing it may sound very Christian and very believing to be told that all the Gospels are historical and all of them interpretative too, so that St Mark is not essentially different from the rest. But if we reflect, we shall see that the tendency of such a remark is ultimately sceptical. For the Four Gospels do not tell the same story, and no one now proposes to reconcile them by the old 'harmonistic' method, that is, by dovetailing them into one another. So to say that all are equally historical really amounts to saying that none of them is very historical, if by history we are meaning a correct account of the whole pattern and order of Christ's public life. If four witnesses are all equally but no more than equally historical and give narratives which differ in plan, we have less confidence about what actually occurred than we should have if we could show that three of them were dependent on one, and that they knew no other plan of the events than that which they derived from him; especially if we had some grounds for thinking that he stood close to the events themselves. There are, of course, cases in which a plurality of differing witnesses supply the kind of evidence enabling a skilled interpreter to construct an account of the course of events; an account which is not what any of the witnesses gives, but which is the best explanation of how their several differing narratives should have come to be what they are. Such situations are common enough both in historical and in legal enquiry. But I do not think that Gospel-criticism presents a situation of that kind, and those who have endeavoured to make a free construction of a supposed history lying behind the differing accounts of, let us say, St Mark and St John, have not produced anything which commands our assent.

Historical facts are not the servants of our interests. The convenience of being able to attach a unique historical value to St Mark is no ground whatever for the claim that his work possesses such a value. But though our interests do not determine facts, they determine the questions we are impelled to ask about the facts. If we were not concerned about the Christian Faith, we should not spend our lives on the interpretation of four little first-century narratives. But being concerned for our faith, we do; and being concerned to know whether St Mark may not hold a peculiar treasure of historical truth, we do not let the question about his uniquely historical character pass without a careful examination.

Why is it, then, that less is made in some quarters nowadays of the special value of St Mark as a history of the life of Christ? It is not that people have changed their minds either about St Mark's priority in time, or about the dependence of the other Evangelists upon him. It is that the attempt to interpret St Mark historically has met with great difficulties, whereas a different and apparently non-historical interpretation of him seems to promise better success.

To interpret St Mark historically means to interpret him in the way in which an historian, or scientific biographer, interprets biographical material. If we possess a pile of anecdotes about an historical person, we have not yet got a history of him, however veracious all or most of the anecdotes may be. His history is his continuous story, and it must be continuous in theme as well as in time. Mere continuity of time does not yield history; if, for example, each anecdote started from the place where the last left off, we might still not have a history; for the chain of anecdotes might still fail to reveal the ground-plan of their subject's life, what external circumstances principally influenced his destiny, or by what intelligible and developing policy of action he met and mastered his circumstances. They might fail to give us a balanced account of his thought and teaching; even if they gave us a fair assortment of his sayings, they might fail to show us where his dominant conceptions lay, what was centre and what was periphery in his mind. Even a well-articulated account of his ideas would not be history if it were statically presented. To make history of it we should want to show how his ideas unfolded, and in what relation the process of thought stood to the sequence of circumstances and the policy of action.

To interpret St Mark historically may mean either of two things. It may mean that with good will and intelligence we can read him as history, that is, as actually exhibiting the sort of continuity and development which we have been talking about. Or it may mean that he supplies the sort of discontinuous evidence from which our historical wisdom can reconstruct an historical continuity not set forth by St Mark. On the first view, St Mark himself is an historian; on the second view, he is not that but something else; let us say an adequate source-book for history. (Such language may sound insulting, but let us remember that we are talking only of the historical aspect of St Mark's work. If we called St Mark's Gospel an adequate source-book for history rather than a history, we should not be denying that, as a dramatic presentation of saving truth, it was an inspired masterpiece.)

It was historical interpretation in the first of our two senses which was first tried upon St Mark after his priority to the other evangelists had been established. Scholars tried to construe his

3

Gospel as a ready-made history; they tried to see the sequence between one episode and the next as an historically significant sequence. Admittedly the evangelist had done little to underline the meaning of his transitions, but it was hoped that, with good will, his intention could be divined. Such hopes were destined to disappointment. It is the common opinion of the learned now that the historical continuity which early modern scholarship thought to find in St Mark's narrative was in fact foisted upon it.

It is natural for men whose interests are primarily historical to fall back from the most hopeful historical hypothesis to the next most hopeful. If an historian has to renounce the belief that a document is a history, he will be likely to try next the hypothesis that it is virgin historical material. If St Mark has not given us an account of the continuous process of events, let us hope that he has given us a collection of authentic reminiscences, which we can organize for ourselves. If he is not an historian, let us trust that he is a traditionalist, chronicler or compiler. On this supposition it would be best for us if he has obtruded himself and his own views to the minimum extent possible; if he has been content to collect materials, and merely string them together with 'and' or 'then' into some semblance of a narrative. All we have to do, then, is to unpick his work, and we shall have the virgin material, learnt orally (let us dare to hope) from actual eye-witnesses.

It may be observed that, on this hypothesis, the special historical value of St Mark as compared with the other evangelists is greatly diminished. For we have abandoned his continuous history, and betaken ourselves to the separate anecdotes and sayings which are its component parts, and these we hope to find authentic. But the other Gospels surely contain many authentic anecdotes from other sources. The advantage of St Mark will merely be that he stands somewhat nearer to the fountain-head from which tradition flows, so that we may expect him to receive it in a somewhat purer form. In a purer form, and also, perhaps, in a less rubbed-down form. The longer anecdotes circulate, the more they tend to lose those marks of particular time and

4

circumstance by which an historian may hope to fix their place in the history of his subject; the hooks and eyes, so to speak, by which they allow of being hitched together in their true order.

It is mortal rashness to generalize about the unconscious hopes of a whole class of people, but perhaps it would not be more misleading than such a statement is bound to be, to say that many if not most well-equipped students of St Mark have their historical hopes set in the direction we have last indicated. They may not be over-confident of success, but what they hope for, so far as they hope, is to find in St Mark *disjecta membra* of simple un-adulterated tradition, which it may be possible for historical wisdom to reassemble into an organic whole of history. And anything that tells against such hopes they accept only when they cannot help it, and then with sadness.

If we settle down to work with historical interpretation of the sort we have been last describing, two subsidiary enquiries are bound to open up. The first and more obviously relevant is, what was the history of the *disjecta membra*, the anecdotes and sayings, while they circulated orally and before St Mark strung them together in writing? Did they undergo much modification and, if so, of what sort? Did oral tradition introduce a characteristic bias, for which we must be on the watch? Form-criticism under-takes this difficult enquiry, looking at the form or shape of the traditional elements, and guessing at the forces which have thus shaped them. The second line of enquiry is less obviously relevant, or rather, its relevance may seem to be negative. We want to see the Gospel as a compilation of virgin tradition, and so we want to reduce the role of the evangelist to that of a compiler, a contributor of 'ands' and 'thens'. But we cannot take this reduc-tion for granted; we cannot let ourselves off looking at the principles of arrangement that he does appear to follow. For it may be that his constructive activity goes further than we wish to allow; that (let us say) in making the traditional anecdotes illustrate theological topics under which he has grouped them, he has had to modify their traditional wording a good deal, so as to make their connexion with those topics more evident.

5

And in that case we shall not be able to use the anecdotes as 'virgin tradition', unless we can first correct the bias introduced by the evangelist.

We see, then, that the enquiry into the principle of whatever arrangement the evangelist does use could not be avoided. But once opened up, it has spread and developed alarmingly; there seems to be no end to the strength and subtlety of the evangelist's own pattern, and it bites deeper and deeper into the substance of his paragraphs the more we look at it. Although this result may have surprised us, a little reflection will show that there is nothing intrinsically surprising in it. For if we had got it into our heads that the paragraphs of the Gospel were only loosely strung together it was merely because we had been looking for a type of connexion between them which they did not exhibit, that is to say, historical connexion. We could not find the order we were looking for, and so we declared that there was little order of any kind. But now, at a later stage, we have set out to look for whatever order there may happen to be, and we find plenty of it. Why? Merely because we are in a more docile state of mind, and are willing to examine the pattern that is there, instead of looking for a preconceived type of pattern which is not there.

The sort of pattern which is there, and which the newer type of research has unearthed, may be called theological or symbolical: that is to say, it is something like the sort of pattern which has for long been recognized as the grand principle of unity in St John's Gospel. And so we frequently hear it said that St Mark's and St John's Gospels are not so different in essential nature and aim as we used to think. Such is the conclusion we are likely to form after reading those two classics of the new method, Dr R. H. Lightfoot's *History and Interpretation in the Gospels*, and his *Locality and Doctrine in the Gospels*.

But meanwhile, what has happened to the historian and his hopes? Some of Dr Lightfoot's readers may have felt that under his guidance they were rediscovering the evangelist and losing the facts of the evangel. Whatever the loss may be, the gain is solid and unmistakable—by Dr Lightfoot's aid we find ourselves in touch with St Mark, a living Christian mind, and a mind of great power. And this discovery comes like water in the desert to men who have been trained to see in his gospel a row of impersonal anecdotes strung together by a colourless compiler. There is the gain; but what of the loss? Are we to say that the force of the evangelist's theological inspiration has so remodelled the material which came to him, as to efface the traditional outlines and to make the recovery of the historical facts impossible? Must we let go the history of Christ and content ourselves with St Mark's inspired and dramatic presentation of the meaning of Christ and of his saving acts?

It does not seem that we are really shut up to so painful a conclusion. The theological interpretation of St Mark, as Dr Lightfoot develops it, fences up or at least obstructs one line of historical advance, but promises to open another. What the theological interpretation makes it difficult for us to do is to shoulder St Mark out of the way and lay our hands on his materials. We can no longer be sure of getting past or behind the evangelist; he stops us, and makes us listen to what he himself chooses to tell us. If we cannot learn what we want to know from St Mark's personal communication, we shall not learn it anyhow else. But is this so evident a disaster? Perhaps we have a further lesson in docility to learn; perhaps if we allow the evangelist to tell us his story in his own 'theological' or 'symbolical' way, and do not interpose with premature questions based on our own ideas of historical enquiry, we may be able to discern a genuine history which is communicated to us through the symbolism and not in defiance of it.

The solid gain of the theological interpretation is that it restores to us the unity of the Gospel. The Gospel is a genuine, and profoundly consistent, complex act of thought. This means that we are no longer reduced to making what we can of the parts. We may hope to make something of the whole, for there is a whole after all. Not at first sight what we should call an historical whole; the unity seems rather to be one of doctrinal and symbolical development. But if we sift this complex unity to the bottom, and master it as fully as we can, we may find that it speaks history to us.

It may be useful here to break off and start at the other end. Let us boldly postulate what we hope to prove, describe the sort of symbolical-historical activity which our hypothesis ascribes to St Mark, and then ask what line of study or enquiry on our part would be appropriate, on the supposition that St Mark did the sort of thing we have described.

Primitive Christianity was, and indeed living Christianity remains, a concord between the testimony of Jesus Christ and the testimony of the Holy Ghost. The Redeemer had acted and spoken among the Jews, the Spirit spoke and worked in the Church. The two activities and the two voices were one; Christ had given the Spirit to continue his redeeming work, and to unfold his saving gospel. An evangelist, therefore, was caught between two forces and subject to a double control. He was controlled by the traditional facts about Jesus Christ and he was controlled by the interpreter Spirit who possessed his mind. It could not occur to him to resist the motions of the Spirit in his presentation of the facts, as though he feared that the Spirit might do violence to them. For to entertain such a fear would be to apostatize from the Christian Faith.

Now we are Christians too; we share St Mark's belief in St Mark's inspiration, and we do not set Jesus against the Holy Ghost any more than he did. We approach his work in the confidence our faith bestows, to learn the truth of Christ divinely interpreted. As scholars we endeavour to understand and to distinguish the effects of the two controls in the evangelist's work; and as historians we shall refer the working of the Spirit to the story of the Church, but the facts about Christ to the story of our redemption.

We assume that St Mark is subject to the two controls of fact and inspiration; we wish to distinguish the two and to see how they operate. The problem of method, then, will be the problem of deciding which control to investigate first. And it seems obvious on a little reflection that we must begin with the control of the Spirit. For the facts about Christ's life and teaching are not known to us in any detail from any source which goes behind St Mark himself. We cannot therefore begin from them, and see how they shaped St Mark's narrative. On the contrary, it is only by the right analysis of St Mark's narrative that we are to arrive at the simple facts. Whereas the control of the Spirit is visible and evident; it issues in precisely that shaping and patterning, that unfolding of symbol and doctrine, which the Gospel exhibits. We must, therefore, begin by examining the control of the Spirit, and when we have grasped that, we may hope to be able to see upon what matter of presupposed fact the process of inspired interpretation is exercised.

Our first business, then, is the attempt to grasp the process of St Mark's inspired thinking, and here we have a task which will fully occupy one book, indeed, many books. We shall, nevertheless, give a sketch or provisional report of such a pattern of historical fact as we seem to be able already to see through the web of inspired interpretation. Such a provisional report, however faulty, may serve to illustrate the sort of way in which the two controls co-operated in shaping the evangelist's paragraphs. It may help us to see what, as historians, we may fairly hope for.

To grasp St Mark's inspired thinking as a whole and as a unity means to see his thinking from inside, to *become*, as far as that is possible, St Mark in the act of gospel-writing, through an effort of carefully guided imagination. That this is a risky and almost presumptuous undertaking, who can deny? Yet there are some tasks which cannot be attempted at all without incurring risks, and this is one of them. We cannot understand St Mark the inspired thinker without thinking his thoughts after him, and a safety-first policy will never arrive at doing it. If the first consideration with us is to be sure of not getting lost in the wood, we shall stand back from the Gospel and look at it from outside and content ourselves with particular observations. Here, we will say, there are traces of such and such a symbol, and there we can observe the expression of such and such an article of doctrine. Such observations may command a wide range of respectful assent and we may compile a large number of them. But still we shall not understand how St. Mark's book grew under his pen, which of the symbolical elements were dominant and which subsidiary, or what as a living whole his thinking was. To know these things we must once for all let go our safe hold upon the bank, plunge into the deep and rapid waters of the Evangelist's mind, and swim with the current of his inspiration. Heaven forbid the arrogance of any claim to success in such an undertaking. We should be well content to have shown a way which others may effectively explore.

The object of our study will be to follow out the symbolical and interpretative element in the Gospel to the farthest point. We shall not talk about the historical sense until afterwards, but we beg our readers not to suppose meanwhile that it is being crushed out by the abundance of symbolical activity. Inspired thinking is a process in itself almost infinitely complex, we can never reach the end of it; but that is no reason for supposing that it is not being exercised upon, and sustained by, historical fact, or that it does not respect the articulations of fact with careful delicacy. There is a great deal to be said about the vital power, the muscular and nervous system of a flying eagle, but that is no reason for denying that he is sustained by the air, or that he adapts his motions with fine appropriateness to its currents and pressures. If we ask whether his flight is upheld rather by his wings than by the atmosphere, or rather by the atmosphere than by his wings, we are talking nonsense. And should we suggest that if the atmosphere plays so large a part, the part played by the wings can hardly be so elaborately subtle as bird-physiologists pretend, the nonsense would be no less.

We have now said as much as we can usefully say about our undertaking in general terms. But before we proceed with it there are two obstacles to be removed from the path. Is not such an attitude to St Mark's work in conflict with a venerable tradition about him coming to us through Papias and Eusebius from 'the

Elder John'? And again, has not the science of Form-Criticism proved that St Mark's Gospel is essentially a traditional compilation, not a freely inspired work? We will take these two questions in order. We will endeavour to show that it is possible to decide exactly what the Papian tradition means, and that what it means is nothing about which we need trouble our heads. And we will claim that the issue with form-criticism turns upon a point of method. It is the form-critic who has to wait for the interpreter of St Mark, not the interpreter of St Mark who has to wait for the form-critic.

The Church historian Eusebius reports to us the words of Papias on the composition of the Gospels. Papias, he says, was a man of very limited intelligence. He was, however, a man of venerable antiquity, near enough to apostolic times to give us hope of genuine tradition. He was, indeed, self-devoted to the task of collecting the echoes of the living apostolic voice, before they died away; and he wrote somewhere about the middle of the second century. If only we could believe Eusebius about his limited intellectual gifts! It would inspire us with a good deal more confidence in him as a simple traditionalist. What he tells us, as we shall presently see, is too clever by half.

There is, in fact, no need to pay any attention to Eusebius's depreciation of Papias's ability. Papias's reputation is simply made the victim of Eusebius's anti-millenarian polemics. Eusebius and his Origenist friends were confronted with a simple-minded form of Second-Adventism called millenarianism, and they had decided that millenarianism was an error. They had distinguished the literal from the spiritual interpretation of scripture and had determined that some passages had both senses, some only one. There must be no literal sense attached to the millenarian passage or passages in the Apocalypse, those, that is, which appeared to place a future reign of Christ on earth within the scope of human history. The Holy Ghost had not so intended it and the sacred author had not so understood it.

But the Origenist construction was a bold defiance of history. Not only did the Apocalypse naturally require to be interpreted both in the letter and in the spirit, but the immediate continuators of the Johannine tradition had in fact so interpreted it. St Irenaeus was a Father of assured position and undoubted orthodoxy, and his voluminous writings left no doubt about his opinion. He had not himself, of course, heard St John of Ephesus, but he had heard Polycarp, who gave many unmistakable testimonies of St John, and he quotes Papias, a man perhaps a little younger than Polycarp, but one that had specially devoted himself to the careful collection of Christian tradition and was able to quote with assurance the sayings of 'the Elder John'.

Against this formidable array of evidence the Origenists deliver a double attack. First they drive a wedge between the Johannine writings and their first known interpreter. Papias, they say, was a collector of traditions, but 'his intellectual capacity was very limited' and so, confusing the literal and spiritual senses, he became the heresiarch of millenarianism, and even St Irenaeus, himself capable of better things, deferred to his opinion. Second, they drive a wedge into the Johannine corpus itself. The Elder John, even though Papias quotes him right, is not, they say, the venerated and apostolic Evangelist; and even if Papias and he are right about the sense of the Apocalypse, that is itself a work very doubtfully attributed to the Evangelist, and indeed it might be a fair conjecture to assign it to the Elder himself.

This elaborate piece of polemic contains some elements of historical and literary analysis that deserve respect, as even the most biased constructions of learned men frequently do. But no modern historian is going to accept the Alexandrines' principal thesis. The generation of St John of Ephesus and its immediate successor were unashamedly millenarian. The 'highly mythical' saying which Papias's Elder attributed to the Lord himself concerning the fertility of the eschatological Canaan in corn and wine, would not offend them in the least. They would see in the fertility both a fact and a sacrament, and Papias's sponsoring of the saying is no evidence of silliness in him especially, nor does it undermine the value of his testimony to the words of the Elder

John. The saying has an undoubtedly Hebraic form, it has a foundation in Apocalyptic writing preserved to us, and there is no absurdity in the Elder's supposing that Our Lord had himself authenticated it.

The Eusebian disparagement of Papias, therefore, amounts to this, that he was not clever enough to be an Origenist before Origen; and the weight of the attack upon him, and the casting of him for the ridiculous part of a millenarian heresiarch, merely go to show that he was in fact an important traditionalist, respected by Irenaeus and others. We are free, then, to re-examine the testimonies about the composition of the Gospels upon their own merits.

These testimonies concern the first two Gospels only. It is safe to assume that Papias, or the Elder he quoted, had nothing to say about St Luke or St John. Otherwise Eusebius's silence is unaccountable. For even if Papias had reported about these evangelists a tradition which Eusebius disliked, it would not have served Eusebius's turn simply to ignore it. For he assumes that Papias's writings are available to his readers, and had they contained notices about St Luke or St John unfavourable to Eusebian orthodoxy, Eusebius would have pilloried them along with those 'mythical' elements in Papias's book, to which he takes open exception.

If Papias reports traditions about St Matthew and St Mark only, it cannot be because they alone, in his time, were reckoned to have authority. It can scarcely be doubted that St Luke and St John were current and authoritative in Papias's Asia. If he had nothing to say about them, it will be because nothing needed to be said. Why write a preface to St Luke, when he had written a preface himself? St Luke, the companion of St Paul, makes it quite clear that he is not himself an eye-witness, but depends on eye-witnesses; in part, at least, through sources already written. While as for St John's Gospel, it is reasonable to suppose that Papias and his Asian contemporaries were aware that this Asian book was a 'spiritual' gospel, later written, and presupposing the other three. In St John we have a 'spiritual' gospel, perhaps apostolic; in St Luke a 'literal' gospel, confessedly non-apostolic. But what of the Gospel both apostolic and 'literal'? St Luke presupposes the existence of written tradition in 'several' forms; of this mysterious plurality, two examples survived and were accepted as authoritative, St Mark and St Matthew. But why should there be two forms side by side, and how account for the discrepancies between them? Surely apostolic testimony should agree.

If we compare St Matthew and St Mark, certain things strike us immediately. St Matthew covers almost everything that St Mark contains, but St Mark omits a great deal that is in St Matthew. Moreover, there is a certain amount of difference in arrangement. The Papian traditions about the two Gospels explain exactly these facts; they also explain why there should be two Gospels, to start with. Why were there two Gospels? Because there were two languages. All the eye-witness apostles, indeed, spoke Aramaic. But whereas St Matthew wrote in his own Aramaic tongue, St Peter did not write for himself at all. Being transplanted into the Greek world, he taught by the aid of an interpreter; and this interpreter, St Mark, having got St Peter's instructions by heart through often interpreting for him, wrote them down in Greek after his master's death. So St Mark was read to the Greeks, and presently St Matthew was being read to them, too; but since his book was in Aramaic, every Greek reader had to make the best *targum*, or interpretation, that he could. This, one may presume, was the state of affairs when St Luke took in hand to write. The excellent Theophilus could not be expected to read an Aramaic Matthew, and to one who, like St Luke, knew the Matthean Gospel, St Mark must seem an insufficient account to put into Theophilus's hands. St Luke might have translated St Matthew, but he did not; he preferred to compose a new book, based on all the available evidence. Soon after St Luke wrote, Papias would presume, the Greek *targum* of St Matthew was put into writing, and displaced the Aramaic original completely.

We see, then, why there were two apostolic Gospels, and what was their relation to St Luke, and what their subsequent history.

But the same hypothesis which so conveniently covers these points, will also cover the discrepancies between the two Gospels. If St Peter's Gospel was not written by himself, but subsequently committed to writing by his interpreter, there is no difficulty in understanding why it was (by comparison with St Matthew's) both incomplete, and partly incorrect in order. For St Peter had never delivered himself of a gospel at all, either orally or in writing; he had given his teaching about the Lord's words and deeds piecemeal, as the occasion appeared to require. Such being St Mark's material, it is no fault in him, but rather a sign of his fidelity, that he did not round off his narrative with what St Peter had never had occasion to deliver; nor can he be blamed for imperfections in order, since he was piecing fragments together.

Here are Papias's own words: 'Mark was Peter's interpreter, and what he remembered he accurately wrote, but not in order (*taxei*) either the sayings or the actions of Christ. For he had neither heard the Lord nor been his companion, but in after time Peter's, as I said; and Peter gave his instructions upon occasion, and not as making a concatenation (*syntaxis*) of the Lord's divine teaching (*logia*). So Mark committed no fault in writing certain things just as he had memorized them. For he made it his sole care to leave out none of what he had heard, and to misrepresent no part of it. But Matthew concatenated (*synetaxato*) the divine teaching (*logia*) in Jewish speech; and every reader' (among us Greeks) 'gave a rendering according to his skill.'

All of this, with the possible but very improbable exception of the last sentence, was given by Papias on the authority of 'the Elder', generally presumed to be the Elder John. But the question remains, how much is the Elder's, and how much Papias's interpretation of him. The wording, at least, is unmistakably Papian. Papias's own purpose, revealed in the title of his book, is to give 'an exposition of the Lord's divine teaching' (*logia*). *Logia* means 'oracles' or 'revelations'; it is one of the possible Greek equivalents for *torah*. Papias appears to regard the New Testament as a new *torah*, the *logia* of the Lord; and so the natural phrase for 'to compose a gospel' is 'to concatenate the *logia*', 'to make a concatenation of the Lord's *logia*'. We might suppose that such an undertaking would exclude narrative. But, it appears, this is not so; just as the *torah* of Moses included sacred history, so did the *logia* of the New Covenant; and had St Peter given his teaching more in the form of a concatenation of the Lord's *logia*, St Mark would have been in a position to give a more truly concatenated account as well of the sayings as of the actions of Christ. So, when we are told that St Matthew, in contrast to St Peter, did 'concatenate the *logia*', nothing is meant but that he wrote a gospel.

Such a turn of phrase appears likely to be Papias's own, and we should hesitate to attribute it to the Elder. But how much else is Papias's? Is it he who pulled together the tradition into that exceedingly neat hypothesis, which so exactly covers all the phenomena, as Papias's age viewed them? Did the Elder perhaps tell him no more than that St Mark had been St Peter's disciple, and that St Matthew had written in the Jewish speech? or is the neat hypothesis itself what the Elder had contributed? In that case we may perhaps acquit Papias of being too clever by half, and accept Eusebius's estimate of his powers.

It is quite useless to conjecture what belongs to Papias, and what to his Elder. The whole thing as we have it is so neat and single that we are obliged to take it as it is; it is futile to guess at earlier states of the tradition underlying it. It is not at all evident that anything underlies it, except the wit of the man who conceived it. And he, in any case, was wrong. The whole hypothesis turns on the supposition that St Matthew's Gospel, as we have it, is a translation from an Aramaic original. But learned opinion is dead against this supposition, and I, for my part, do not think it to be worth discussing.

If we look at the Papian excerpt with an historical eye, it falls easily into its place in patristic tradition, and takes on a disappointingly conventional air. The Church accepted the names traditionally attached to the Gospels as the names of their actual authors, from which it quite simply followed that St Matthew was given pride of place among the three synoptists; for he alone of the three was an apostle and eye-witness. This line of reasoning was the more willingly followed, because his Gospel had many excellences of style and arrangement which recommended it for general use. The Papian excerpt conforms to the common opinion. For while it allows two apostolic Gospels, it denies to St Mark the immediacy of apostolic authorship it asserts of St Matthew, and in consequence exalts the completeness and orderliness of St Matthew at the expense of St Mark.

Papias has not always been read in this sense. It has often been supposed that both Matthew and Mark are being disparaged, for the advantage either of St Luke or St John. This conclusion is obtained by putting a false interpretation on the sentence about St Matthew's Gospel. It is taken to mean that St Matthew's book having been written in Aramaic, and every (Greek) having made such a shot at translating it as he could, our Greek Matthew is the imperfect result of these various and amateurish efforts. So we have no better evidence for St Matthew's teaching than we have for St Peter's, even though St Matthew himself wrote.

This cannot be what Papias means. To begin with, it ought to be assumed, apart from strong evidence to the contrary, that an ecclesiastical writer will be doing his best, not his worst, for the Gospels. Would Papias go out of his way to say that the only surviving Greek translation of St Matthew was quite unreliable? Why accuse divine providence of suffering it to be so? The Greek-speaking Church, to which Papias belonged, was dependent on a Greek version for its knowledge of the Hebrew Scriptures, and to that version it ascribed a providential and inspired character. The Greek of St Matthew was read out with reverence in the Churches, and treated as divine. How could Papias so casually raise the scandal of impugning its accuracy? Doubtless God had at length inspired some competent scribe to translate St Matthew faithfully. It made no difference to this that there had been a time when, as Papias says, every Greek reader had to make his own *targum* according to his ability, just because no such translation yet existed.

The erroneous interpretation of Papias, to which we are objecting, springs from a misunderstanding of the word 'rendered' (*hermeneuse*) in the phrase 'everyone *rendered* it according to his ability'. If Papias were talking here about the imperfect renderings of Greek *scholars*, then his purpose in so doing would presumably be to reflect upon the scholarship which lay behind the existing Greek text of Matthew. But he is not talking about scholars, he is talking about church-readers, as follows unmistakably from the parallel drawn between the interpretation of St Peter and St Matthew respectively. Both were Aramaic speakers, who needed to be *interpreted* to Greek congregations. But whereas St Peter had been orally interpreted to them in his lifetime by his *interpreter* (*hermeneutes*), Mark, and this interpretation subsequently written down, St Matthew had written in Aramaic, and was orally *interpreted* from the Aramaic letter according to the Greek reader's ability. We see, then, that Papias is simply describing the standing of the two Gospels in the Greek Church at an imaginary time before St Matthew had been translated; and his object is not to disparage the Greek St Matthew, but rather to explain how St Mark held his own against the competition of a fully apostolic Gospel; and (very likely) also, why St Luke should have written a new Gospel, instead of simply enclosing to Theophilus a copy of St Matthew's book.

We said just now that it ought to be assumed that Papias would do his best for the Gospels. But this is no mere general assumption. He has, in fact, done his very best for St Mark. St Mark is St Mark, he is not St Peter; there is no unsaying that. But Papias's account goes so far as it is possible to go in the direction of minimizing the difference. St Mark is not St Peter, but he is St Peter's voice translated into Greek; St Mark, through acting as interpreter, had the whole body of Petrine teaching so by heart that he was able simply to recall it and write it down. The only hypothesis that could be conceived more favourable than this, would be the hypothesis that St Peter had been in the habit of preaching gospel-courses in historical order, so that St Mark had the whole thing in his head as a continuous story.

In that case we could be rid of St Mark altogether; St Peter would, to all intents, have written the Gospel. But Papias is not prepared to hazard this. Partly, perhaps, it strikes him as simply absurd; partly he shrinks from it, because it would leave the contradictions of order between St Mark and St Matthew unresolved. St Mark must be set free enough to introduce a few inversions, and make a few omissions. Nevertheless, Papias has done all for St Mark's Gospel that he dared to do, and it is most improbable that he so betrayed St Matthew's as gratuitously to impugn the only version in which it was known.

We will further object to the line of argument which we are criticizing, that it is needlessly hypothetical. Eusebius had quoted Papias's testimony about the Gospels as something sufficiently self-contained for citation; and we have no right to assume that there was any more of it. It contains a contrast between the lack of order in St Mark, and something else. It is gratuitous to find that something else outside the Papias-testimony, when it can perfectly well be found in it, and, indeed, demands to be recognized within it. St Mark could not write in perfect order, because St Peter had not given his instructions as a continuous course on the Lord's divine teaching; whereas St Matthew did make a continuous book of the divine teaching, being himself, of course, just as much an apostle and eye-witness as St Peter was. Nothing could be plainer than this comparison.

But if it is gratuitously hypothetical to look for the order with which St Mark's is contrasted outside the Papian excerpt, is it not just as gratuitously hypothetical to see a reference to St Luke's reasons for addressing Theophilus in the Papian phrase about the Aramaic Matthew requiring translation for the benefit of Greek congregations? I do not think so. For if one singles out the two oldest Gospels for discussion, one is in any case inevitably suggesting the state of affairs existing before St Luke wrote, and in view of which he wrote. St Luke stands ready to take up the pen, he hovers somewhere in the wings of the stage while such a discussion holds the centre. But the reference to him which we see in Papias's words is a mere allusion. It is no necessary part of the logical sense of the passage; if it is missed, we can still understand what the Elder is telling us. The untranslated state of the Aramaic Matthew explains the hold of the Greek Mark on the Grecian Churches; it explains why the state of affairs before St Luke wrote was what it was. If it also helps to explain why St Luke wrote at all, so much the better.

Let us turn from the interpretation of Papias to assess what, if anything, we can learn from him. The outlook is discouraging. For we have seen that the whole substance of what he gives us is neither more nor less than an ingenious but false historical hypothesis; and we have confessed that it is hopeless to try to disentangle from it older or more genuine elements. The whole thing must be given up together with its neat machinery: the assumption that Galilean Apostles can never have learnt to speak Greek; St Mark the interpreter of St Peter's speech; the many church-readers the interpreters of St Matthew's writing. Papias or his Elder had not, of course, been the first to suggest a special relation of discipleship between St Mark and St Peter. Scripture itself makes the suggestion to our minds. In Acts xii St Peter is at St Mark's house; in Acts xv he, and his apostolic colleagues, send a letter by Silvanus and another. In I Peter v, 12 the apostle once more sends a letter by Silvanus, and in the same breath names 'Mark his son' as apparently his chief assistant in 'Babylon', i.e. Rome. These facts can easily prompt the conjecture that, as it is St Peter who addresses us through Silvanus in I Peter, so it is he who addresses us through Mark in Mark's Gospel, even though it be somewhat less directly. It is not absolutely necessary to suppose that Papias's Elder had any other evidences available to him about the Mark–Peter relationship than the scriptural evidences which are available to us.

The Papian tradition must be simply given up, as someone's ingenious but false construction. But we can still learn something from the assumed facts which the hypothesis was intended to explain. The hypothesis was an invention, but it was invented to account for something. The hypothesis supposes anyhow that the first Gospel in Greek to obtain authority in the Greek Churches was Mark's. It was only later that a Greek Matthew appeared, by which time St Mark was firmly entrenched. So much is presupposed as fact. The fact is, on the face of it, awkward for the tradition of genuine Matthean authorship. One would expect the apostolic Gospel to appear before the non-apostolic, or anyhow to enjoy prevailing authority as soon as it did appear. The awkward fact is explained by Papias's Elder, and by us, in different ways. He says that St Matthew's Gospel remained for some while untranslated; we deny the personal Matthean authorship, and regard the Gospel as an amplified re-writing of St Mark's own book. If we prefer our own theory, then we have nothing to derive from Papias's, except the implied confirmation of our own beliefs, that St Mark was the original Greek Gospel, and that it bore some special relation to St Peter's testimony.

It is clear, then, that Papias's words do not place any obstacle in the way of a free attempt to investigate the process and order of St Mark's writing. Papias has given us neither a prescription to be followed nor an oracle to be interpreted, but only a false theory to be set aside. And so we are free to turn to our other task, and see whether the obstacle apparently set up by form-criticism is any more solid.

Form-criticism is rather misleadingly so called, because the name suggests an attempt to appreciate the form of a complete literary unit, say St Mark's Gospel. Whereas what form-criticism studies is the form of the small constituent parts of the Gospels; anecdotal paragraphs, for example, or even such small details as apparently self-contained gnomic sentences. The reason why it does this is that it is not properly concerned with the Gospels as such, but with the form in which the traditions about Christ may have existed in oral tradition before the Gospels were written. We have here a laudable, though speculative, line of enquiry, and one with which we have no quarrel at all. All that we are concerned with here is a question of priorities. Has the man who wishes to understand the unity of thought and plan in the Gospels to wait for the form-critics to do their work, and to go on from there, or is it they, on the contrary, who have to wait for him, and take the question up as he leaves it?

If the student of the whole Gospel has to wait for the form-critics, the effect on his work may be extremely cramping. For the form-critics sometimes seem to be showing, or trying to show, that the evangelist is stitching together and only slightly modifying set pieces of traditional oral recitation. And if this is so, the evangelist's own inspiration, his own conception and unitary grasp of the story he is telling, is reduced to small proportions, and any interpretation of the Gospel as a living and self-unfolding movement of free inspiration is barred from the outset. But our contention here is that the question of priority has to be settled the other way about: it is not we who have to wait for the form-critics, it is the form-critics who have to wait for us.

Form-criticism is concerned with small patterns, the patterns of the parts; we are concerned with a large pattern, the pattern of the whole. What is the relation between the large pattern and the small? The study of the large has the priority. For literature is not, obviously, like physical nature. In physical nature the small patterns—those of the atom and the molecule, for example—come first and are a law to themselves, and when they are organized by larger-scale patterns into larger wholes, for example, into organic bodies, their own minute patterns are not disturbed nor overruled. And so a science which takes these minute and basic patterns for its province can proceed without fear of being overruled from above. Biology does not trench upon physics. In the literary realm there is nothing in the least like this. The pattern of the whole comes first. Every sentence of a book is formulated by the mind which writes the whole. The parts, of course—the paragraphs, let us say—have a sort of independence and interior life of their own, for otherwise the book will be unreadable; indeed the failure of some authors to make their paragraphs relatively self-contained is one reason why some books are unreadable. But we clearly cannot go on to say: 'Therefore in the case of a well-written book we can practise the wholly autonomous art of paragraph-criticism; we can examine the form of any given paragraph in and by itself, confident that no stroke of arrangement in it is due to the pattern of the whole work, or to what the author wants in the end and in general to say. The pattern of the whole merely arranges the paragraphs, it does not in any way constitute them.'

To talk like this would be absurd. It is patently false that paragraph-criticism is autonomous. Paragraph-criticism and book-criticism do not even exist side by side; book-criticism must precede paragraph-criticism. No one can usefully set about paragraph-criticism until he has got the plan and purpose of the whole book into his head. Otherwise he will be in an absurd predicament, always trying to interpret features which relate principally to the whole as relating simply to the constituent part. Indeed he will be in what Spinoza accounted the typical situation of human error. The book of truth, he thought, was the content of the divine mind. Our minds are only paragraphs of it, and by trying to interpret themselves as self-contained they fall into their manifold mistakes.

It will be objected here that our argument is misdirected. 'All that you say could be applied to form-criticism on the supposition that St Mark is a freely composed poetical unity, but you know perfectly well that this is what is denied. It is outrageous to discuss the form-critics as though they were practising their ingenious art on *Paradise Lost* or even *The Pilgrim's Progress*. That St Mark was a mere compiler or chronicler putting together "the gospel tradition" is a perfectly tenable hypothesis; that Milton or Bunyan was such a writer is not tenable at all. But if St Mark was just compiling, then autonomous paragraph-criticism is a proper method. He did not compose the paragraphs at all with a view to the whole, he just wrote them as he found them already formulated in oral memory, adding a few "links" or "editorial touches" to produce some semblance of continuity. By examining the interior requirements of the paragraphs we can reject the editorial material and retain the old traditional units.'

Just so; but it is this hypothesis of St Mark the compiler which we call in question; and our objection is that the form-critics

have begged their case. What we wished to show in the somewhat overdriven argument we have just employed was that the
whole validity of the method depends upon the correctness of
the question-begging assumption; that if St Mark is in fact after
all a living whole, then the work of the form-critics is, every
line of it, called in doubt. So far from its then being probable that
their detailed conclusions will stand, it is more likely that an
appreciation of the form of the whole will place their premature
examinations of the separate parts in an unfavourable light.
Above all, nothing that the form-critics have done must be
allowed to preclude or prejudice any revision of Gospel criticism
from the point of view of the whole, for their conclusions only
stand upon the assumption that there is no whole at all which
really penetrates and organizes its parts.

But are we not going too far? It may be not proven that St
Mark is a traditionalist and compiler. But it is surely evident
that he is not an imaginative creator writing the parts for the
sake of the whole in the way that an epic poet or historical
novelist would do. After all, the applicability of an hypothesis is
some evidence of its truth; if St Mark's paragraphs were not in
a remarkable degree self-contained, and remarkably like the
anecdotes preserved by verbal memory, the whole attempt of
the form-critics would have broken down at the start. Form-
criticism has surely proved something.

Yes, but exactly what has it proved? It has proved that St
Mark uses the anecdotal form. It has not proved that the anecdotes
existed in such form before he wrote them, only that he wrote
them in that form. There is nothing surprising in it, if a man
who was certainly a preacher and narrator before he was a
writer should adopt the oral form when he came to write. But
that would by no means prove that the anecdotes were formulated
without reference to the place they were to occupy, and afterwards accommodated to it by 'editorial touches'. Each may have
been formulated for its place, though in anecdotal form. No
doubt it is right to suppose that the anecdotal form was recommended to St Mark because it was the form in which the oral

tradition already lived. It was fairly inevitable that the first written Gospel should appear as some sort of combination of anecdotes; but this admission prejudges nothing as to the strength of the combination or the degree to which it penetrates and masters the anecdotes themselves.

'Perhaps not; but what is the likeliest supposition? Surely, that St Mark left the anecdotes much as he and others had always preached them; this, after all, can claim to be the most economical hypothesis.' The argument from 'economy' is of very dubious force. Is it 'economy' to assume that in a period when sonnet-writers as a class were publishing their poems in various sorts of arranged sequence, the sonnets of X, newly discovered, were written in no sequence at all? 'No sequence' appears to be economy of supposition, but on the other side it may be an offence against economy of explanation if we have to assume some cause, at present unknown, which made the writer X impervious to a generally prevailing fashion. It is not 'economy' if we have to throw up a strong hypothetical dyke to keep the floods of a force known to have been operating in the environment from overflowing the plot of ground which we have chosen as the field of our enquiry.

Now there was a mighty force operative in the Church of the middle first century with which we have to reckon before we can treat St Mark as a simple traditionalist, and that force was prophetic inspiration. What dykes could contain it? Where would it not go? Was St Mark an inspired man or not? The Church has always supposed he was. Primitive Christianity was traditionalist, it was also inspired; both characteristics can be copiously illustrated from St Paul. He and his contemporaries saw no conflict of principle between the two, in spite of occasional prophetic vagaries. On the contrary, the combination of factual tradition with the interpreter-Spirit sent down from Heaven, this *was* Christianity. Shall we then make parties for either the 'traditionalist' or 'inspirationalist' view of St Mark? It seems, on the face of it, a stupid thing to do. St Mark was writing out of tradition; he was also writing at the dictation of the Spirit.

This is a fine phrase, but what precise consequence will it have for our critical enquiry? Had inspiration one literary form rather than another? Perhaps not one rather than another, but anyhow some. For prophetic inspiration, though in its essence it is nothing else but the invisible fact of the moving of the prophet's mind by God, has something akin to poetry in its visible expression; it fuses its material into a living unity. This says nothing as to the extent of the units thus created, and it might still remain that the parts of St Mark's book were each poetically one, and the whole not so. Yet against this supposition we have this to set, that inspiration makes unities of the units it takes. Isaiah did not see his book as a unit, but only the several visions and oracles, and so his book, perhaps, is not a unity at all. But St Mark set out to write what had a beginning, middle and end, and moved steadily to an overwhelming climax; and if his mind was warmed by inspiration at all, it is only to be expected that it would break down the isolation of the parts, and draw them into the movement of the whole.

It is sometimes thought that a strong negative argument against the significance of St Mark's total pattern can be drawn from its treatment by St Matthew and St Luke. If St Mark's garden were so delicately and symmetrically laid out, could they be such philistines as to drive their ploughshares ruthlessly across it? And if they failed to appreciate the subtleties of Marcan order, is there much hope of our being able to recover them? Can what appeared of such small importance to them have been of any great consequence to St Mark?

This argument is of no real force; and thus it may be answered. The more carefully and intricately planned a garden is, the more it forces on us the dilemma that we must either leave it virtually as it is or very drastically replan it. Now neither St Matthew nor St Luke was proposing to write out St Mark as he stood. St Mark had no monopoly of inspiration; the others had their own visions of the wholeness of the Gospel, into which some of the features of St Mark's planning could be, and were, fitted, but others could not possibly be. Their destruction of much

Marcan planning is no certain evidence that they failed to understand it; it may merely show that they could not use it.

Even if we conceded that several Marcan subtleties eluded the other two evangelists, it would still be no arrogance on our part if we hoped to appreciate what they neglected. For the very force of their creative inspiration would fix their attention on what they were making, and would blind them to what they could not use. Creative inspiration is a handicap from which the modern critic is signally free. He can aspire to get inside the mind of St Mark, and think his thoughts after him, in a way St Matthew or St Luke would never have dreamed of. After all, the modern historical attitude is good for something.

Another, and in a sense, contrary argument from synoptic studies may be brought to bear against our contention. The refashioning of St Mark by the other two was not so drastic, after all. They changed his order and omitted his redundancies, but the paragraphs they used they did not for the most part at all radically recast. Ought we not then to suppose that St Mark's attitude to previous tradition was equally conservative, his freedom of composition equally small? The conclusion would be quite unwarranted. For St Mark, in our belief, had no written original, nor continuous oral repetition even to guide him. His book had to be made, and he fell under the hand of inspiration in the making. It is very arguable that St Matthew and St Luke are equally free, where they have nothing but oral traditions to work upon; and it might even be contended that, from a purely literary point of view, they were hampered in their Marcan passages by the possession of that embarrassing asset, a written source-book. Perhaps it was the greatness of St John to obtain as much detachment from written, as St Mark had enjoyed from oral, materials, and to recover the freedom of primitive inspiration.

But, it will be urged, the systematic continuity of St John's Gospel is evident, whereas St Mark's book does fall very easily into self-contained paragraphs. It is surely contrary to common sense to suggest that there is anything like the same dominating unity here, overmastering the parts. It might be contrary to common sense if the inspiration of Biblical writers had nowhere else taken the form of combining apparently self-contained units into larger wholes. But, in fact, this very process is a characteristically Biblical art.

The traditional form of prophetic vision was a self-contained unit. The prophet sees some single object, and is taught the lesson of it in a brief oracle. But already in Amos such self-contained units are strung together, in such a fashion as leaves us in little doubt that the first are only there for the sake of the approach they provide towards the last. In spite of their apparent self-containedness, they do not exist for their own sake simply.

I

Thus the Lord God shewed me: and, behold, he formed locusts in the beginning of the shooting up of the latter growth; and lo, it was the latter growth after the king's mowings. And it came to pass that when they made an end of eating the grass of the land, then I said, O Lord God, forgive, I beseech thee: how shall Jacob stand? for he is small. The Lord repented concerning this: It shall not be, saith the Lord.

2

Thus the Lord God shewed me: and, behold, the Lord God called to contend by fire; and it devoured the great deep, and would have eaten up the land. Then said I, O Lord God, cease, I beseech thee: how shall Jacob stand? for he is small. The Lord repented concerning this. This also shall not be, saith the Lord God.

3

Thus he shewed me: and, behold, the Lord stood beside a wall made by the plumbline, with a plumbline in his hand. And the Lord said unto me, Amos, what seest thou? And I said, A plumbline. Then said the Lord, Behold, I will set a plumbline in the midst of my people Israel; I will not again pass by them any more: and the high places of Isaac shall be desolate, and the sanctuaries of Israel shall be laid waste; and I will rise against the house of Jeroboam with the sword.

Who can read this simple sequence without seeing that the prophet's intercession is twice accepted only to throw into relief the terrible necessity that it should be at length excluded?

Amos, then, understood how to build apparently complete units into an ampler structure; he knew the art of stringing beads with effect. But Amos had been seven hundred years dead when St Mark wrote; did the art survive? Certainly it did. The Apocalypse of St John is an immensely more elaborate essay in Amos's art. It is made up of single visions, each a rounded whole, but each existing only for its place in a series running into climax. St John the Divine knew all about stringing beads. So perhaps St Mark knew something about it, too; though his beads were not the same sort of beads—not visions, but episodes—and his string a different sort of string—not apocalyptic climax simply but some thread or other more elusive and variable. What it was, it will be the purpose of this book to show.

CHAPTER II

THE HEALING MIRACLES

In St Mark's Gospel the paragraphs are mostly self-contained. They are strung together like beads on a string. But perhaps they are strung with art; perhaps each bead is carved by the jeweller for the place it is to occupy in the row. The supposition is worth exploring; it is worth trying to find out what the principle or pattern is, upon which the paragraphs are arranged.

St Mark's book is neither a treatise nor a poem, but it is more like a poem than a treatise. Now a poem of any extent has a rhythm, not in the sound only, but also in the sense. Themes and symbols recur, not monotonously, but not chaotically either. The reader's imagination responds to their pattern, without being necessarily aware of it; the critic shows his discernment in discovering and analysing it. There may be several overlapping systems of symbolic or thematic rhythm in any one poem. Perhaps one or more of them was consciously devised by the poet, while others were unconsciously shaped by the movement of his imagination. Some system or other expresses the direction of his conscious intention, other systems spontaneously arise in the working out of his plan; the shapely mind of itself produces shapely works. To ask what is *the* shape or rhythm of an inspired work is a question wrongly put. Anyone is at liberty to point out any shapeliness he can find in it; and if the critic says 'My analysis lays bare *the* form' he may fairly be accused of egotism. How many contrary dogmatisms have been propounded, each claiming to state the *real* plan of some Shakespearean tragedy!

It is nevertheless quite sensible to ask, which elements of order the poet consciously formulated; or from which he took his start. For he started with something already in mind, surely; he set out to write some sort of a work rather than another. The playwright at least proposes a piece in a manageable number of scenes, arranged in five acts or in three, and written on a certain plot. He would not even have resolved on the plot, unless he had seen more than the bare bones of it. He must have conceived the characters and incidents far enough to grasp how they are to play towards a particular *dénouement*. He begins to write, and many further elements of form and rhythm work themselves in; some the objects of the author's conscious intention, others the by-products of it.

If we want to pick out among all apparent schemes or patterns the design with which the author started, we have two sorts of criterion available to us, one external and the other internal. The external criterion is historical probability. We ask on what kind of project a writer of that sort, time and nation was likely to go to work. If it is Shakespeare with whom we are concerned, we can use this criterion fruitfully, since we know something of the playwright's task in his day. We know the sort of stage-piece he was expected to produce, and the sort of excellence which the critics of the day looked for, and the playwrights of the day supposed themselves to strive after. We know what sources were used for plots, and how one set about adapting them for the stage. From such considerations as these we can reach a fair idea how the poet is likely to have gone about his task, and what sort of project or design he is likely to have set before his eyes.

The external criterion which we have hitherto described is employed to show which of the patterns in a poem is a *probable* claimant to be the author's original and conscious project. But no argument based on the external criterion alone would ever be thought convincing. The project probable on external grounds must be shown to be on internal grounds both basic and fertile. It must be proved that the project we have taken is presupposed by other schemes and rhythms discernible in the poem, and that it is conceivable or indeed natural that they should arise in the working out of the assumed project. If we can exhibit these things, we have successfully applied the internal criterion.

To turn now to St Mark, we must agree, surely, that the external criterion is difficult to apply, because his gospel-writing was, on the face of it, the production of a new sort of book. The difficulty is not that he will have written without models, or even that he was necessarily conscious of the novelty of his enterprise. He may have thought of himself as writing 'a so-and-so', for example, a sacred history, like the story of Elijah in the Books of Kings. Very likely, but our difficulty is that we do not know what sort of 'a so-and-so' he would feel himself to be writing. It would certainly be a great mistake to say, 'He was so simple and so uncultured a writer that the question of literary models does not arise.' For the simpler and more uncultured one is, the stronger is likely to be the influence of a fixed model. Our first efforts with the pen are servile imitations. It requires much experience and exercise of writing before we can write like ourselves, and not like our favourite author, the newspaper, a Government form, or the advertisement on the outside of a cereal packet.

St Mark was surely more fortunate in his models, and so far as phrasing goes, his debt to the Greek Old Testament is, of course, obvious. Equally obvious is the debt of the *Pilgrim's Progress* to the Authorized English Bible. But merely to recognize that debt does not set us on the track of understanding Bunyan's design. Bunyan is writing a very Biblical book, full of detailed Biblical allegories, but his general pattern does not come from the Bible. It comes from a popular late medieval strain of allegorized pilgrimage story, crossed with a Calvinist account of the plan of salvation and the stages of spiritual progress. In much the same way, we may recognize St Mark's debt to Scripture, and still be in the dark about the origin and nature of his principal design. Perhaps he, like Bunyan, for all his biblicism, had his plan from what was being written in his own time, or shortly before it; perhaps we ought to ransack the Jewish Pseudepigrapha for the missing indications. But nothing we see there leaps to the eye as being what we want, and we must understand St Mark profoundly before we even know what to look for.

It would be a comfort, certainly, if we could discover after the event that our interpretation of St Mark attributed to him a sort of literary design not wholly strange to the world he knew. That would be to use the external criterion for subsequent confirmation. But it seems clear that we shall have to begin by trusting in the internal criterion. That is, we must look at the forms or patterns which appear in St Mark's writing, and look for the one which appears both basic and fertile.

As he listens to our account of Marcan rhythm, no one need feel that to accept it is to deny the genuineness of intuitions he may have about other rhythms in St Mark. If he sees one rhythm and I see another, both may be there, and both may be important. I make no exclusive claim for mine, except that it looks like being the basic one. Even this I do not ask the reader to believe, I merely ask him to entertain it as a hypothesis, and see whether the subsequent exposition sufficiently verifies it or not. Let me give an example of a sort of rhythm or order which I shall not discuss in this book, but which is perfectly compatible, for all I know, with what I shall discuss. Many people suspect that St Mark wrote his book with a view to church-reading, and that it contains (let us say) short lessons for all the weeks in a year. In St Mark's time it is reasonable to suppose that the Christians were still influenced by the sacred calendar of the Jews, with its holy days and fasts and the scripture-lessons attached to each. And so if St Mark had his eye on the calendar, his book might be expected to reflect the order and topics of the Jewish year.

Now I am not going to discuss this sort of order, but neither do I in any way exclude it. It may be genuinely Marcan, but it is not sufficient of itself to supply St Mark with the design he requires. For it must be obvious that there are dozens of ways in which a Christian Gospel might be accommodated to the Jewish festal scheme. One can see no reason *a priori* why St Mark and St John might not both be in step with the same calendar; yet their rhythms and principles of composition are very different. To say that they both wrote on the pattern of the calendar leaves unexplained why they did not both write the same Gospel. The writing of a lectionary book in accordance with the calendar may be compared with the writing of an heroic tragedy in five acts. We have still to find a plot, in either case. The plot, once found, must conform to the presupposed pattern, but must be of an origin independent from it.

The type of pattern which I propose to explore is something in its essence more simple and elementary than a lectionary pattern. It is a quite short recurrent cycle of topics. Christ's action, according to our evangelist, constantly expresses the essentials of the Gospel, and the essentials of the Gospel are always the same. Having expressed them once within quite a narrow compass of events, Christ re-expresses them with different emphases and in different ways, and so on again until he reaches his passion and resurrection, in which he expresses these things perfectly once and for all. We are not going to show that the *history* of Christ circles round and round. The history goes steadily forward to the inevitable end. What circles round and recurs is a series of topics which the forward march of the history constantly re-expresses.

St Mark, we have agreed to assume, places an interpretation on the history which, for want of a better word, it is customary to call 'theological'. If we suppose that his 'theological interpretation' is cyclic, we are attributing to him the simplest possible form of interpretation, not the most complicated. His system of ideas is not so complex and extended as to span the whole Gospel; it is so brief and simple as to be covered in a few pages; and then it recurs.

The cyclic order is the natural order for setting forth theological truth for anyone who is proceeding artlessly and not striving for effect. The artless speaker does not save up the main point for the end, and gradually work towards it. He gives us the whole matter 'in a nutshell' at the very start, and then goes over it again and again, developing, varying and explaining his theme as many times as he thinks fit and necessary. St Mark, indeed, is not giving a theoretical exposition of saving truth, he is showing how Christ's life was a visible enactment of it. But the cyclic form can still apply; the pattern of saving act can be gone through again and again in the action of Christ.

Everyone, in fact, who has paid the most casual attention to the sequence of topics in St Mark's Gospel has been struck by traces of cyclic recurrence. Christ calls Simon and his companions from the midst of their trade beside the sea, eats in Simon's house, and heals a man with paralysed legs, causing indignation in the

34

Pharisees (I, 16–II, 12). Christ calls Levi from the midst of his trade beside the sea, eats in Levi's house and heals a man with an atrophied arm, to the indignation of the Pharisees (II, 13–III, 6). Christ feeds five thousand men, and then voyages over the lake; his disciples show themselves uncomprehending about the mystery of the loaves which they have just witnessed on shore (VI, 30–52). A couple of chapters later we read of a similar feeding of four thousand, another voyage, and similar uncomprehension about the loaves (VIII, 1–21). The Lord's prophecy of his own passion rings like a refrain at spaced intervals from VIII, 31 to X, 33. These are just a few of the most familiar examples of cyclic recurrence.

The object of the chapters that follow will be not simply to make lists of recurrent features, but to try to seize the actual cyclic movement of the evangelist's thought which produced them. Simply to list recurrent features is to approach the Gospel from without, to treat it like a collection of external phenomena in physical nature, and to content oneself with making diagrams of one's observations. But a book is the expression of a living mind like our own, and we can never be satisfied until we have understood from within the movement of thought which produced it.

But before we endeavour to plunge into the stream of St Mark's mind we will make one limited external survey, for fear that when we do plunge in, we should get lost. We will take one single recurrent feature which is most steady and invariable through all the cycles of the narrative, and examine it by itself. This feature is the healing miracle. The sequence of healing miracles does not span the whole of the Gospel, but it spans precisely that part of it which we are inclined to give up as formless, the Galilean Ministry (chapters I–X). And it has a sort of objectivity about it, for we have only to put the healings in a list to see the simplicity and force of their formal grouping.

The first thing to be remarked about the Marcan healings is that they are all of single persons. This is true of the narratives which are in any degree particular. There are, of course, summary statements about the healing of indefinite numbers of sick folk. But there is nothing like the healing of two blind men in St

Matthew, or of a company of ten lepers in St Luke. The nearest parallel in St Mark to such stories as these would be the double narrative of the woman twelve years diseased and the girl twelve years old. Christ is on his way to raise the girl, when he is touched by the woman. But the two healings remain distinct. One is inserted in the other, but either is capable of standing by itself. The two diseases are different diseases, and the healings are separate.

The simple distinction between unity and plurality puts a difference between the healing miracles and all other miracles which this evangelist records. All the beneficiaries of the healings are single persons; none of the beneficiaries of the other miracles are. All twelve disciples are rescued in the two miracles at sea, thousands of men on either occasion eat the supernatural bread. The other miracles do not have beneficiaries in the same obvious sense. The Transfiguration, the withering of the fig, the fetching of the ass and the finding of the supper-room relieve nobody's need; but they all have a plurality of witnesses or instrumental agents.

Since we have been talking of Bunyan, let us borrow one of his tricks and use a feigned dream for an expository purpose. It was a warm evening, and I was sitting in my favourite chair and working (as I called it) on my favourite study. If I had been more serious about working, I should have sat upright, but in fact I was relapsing deeper and deeper into the cushions. I was treading a path through St Mark's history, then back to the beginning, and through it again. I could do it now (so I told myself) just as well in my head; the book slipped through my fingers and fell. I had a special eye, as I went up that Marcan path, for certain of the features I encountered. The stories of healings attracted my notice; they were, so to speak, lit up and vivid; everything else had a way of effacing itself into the shadows. Rather as though—as though—and here I began to dream in earnest.

I was walking up an actual street now, looking for a shop. What shop? I could not tell; my wife had asked me to buy something; what was it? If I walked up the street watching the shops, I should remember, when I came to the right one. The shops were not continuous, there were houses between. But I had no eye for the houses, I was watching the shops. Four shops, then some houses, then a lonely shop and more houses. Three shops, houses, a lonely shop, more houses. Two shops, houses, a lonely shop, more houses. One shop, houses, a lonely shop . . . 'I must have missed what I was looking for', I said to myself, with the mad logic of a dreaming man. 'Four and one, three and one, two and one, one and one—and then it stops: the next below one is nought.' I walked a little farther on to make sure. There were no more shops in the street. 'I must have passed the shop I wanted', I said to myself. 'I must go back and look again.' You might suppose that I did the looking as I walked back, but no; my dream put me at the place where I had begun before, and I took the shop windows in the same order again. This time I did not wait to be reminded of what I sought by encountering it; I looked carefully at each of the shops, and made a note of what it was. No wonder I couldn't find what I wanted; for what a monotonous series! Chemists, ironmongers, restaurants, nothing else. And even the ironmongers' display lacked variety; it consisted of nothing but brushes and cleaning-materials. Ironmongers indeed! 'Soapmongers I shall call them', said I to myself; and did.

It was not only that the sorts of shops were restricted; that was not the only monotony. There was also a monotony of arrangement. I scribbled it down on a page of my diary, putting each group of shops, and each lonely shop, on a separate line; so that the houses, in which I took no interest, must be understood to intervene between the lines. And this was the result:

Chemist, A's Restaurant, Soapmonger, B's Restaurant.
　　　Annexe to B's Restaurant.
Chemist, Soapmonger, C's Restaurant.
　　　Annexe to C's Restaurant (closed).
Chemist, D's Restaurant.
　　　Annexe to D's Restaurant.
Chemist and E's Restaurant (double shop).
　　　Annexe to E's Restaurant.

'How awkward for the restaurant-keepers', I said to myself,

'never to have their annexes next door, but always several doors down, with three houses or more in between. Still, there it is, and it's no more curious than several other things about this street.'

I had complained of the monotony in the order of the shops, but when I looked at the list in my notebook, I saw something beside monotony: a sort of musical theme. Whoever arranged the shops (for someone must, surely, have arranged them) was working out a pattern. True, the even lines in my list presented flat uniformity, nothing but annexes to restaurants. But the odd lines were interesting. The basic idea in the choice of shops appeared to be a simple division of the needs of the human body into negative and positive. Negative: chemist's drugs to exorcize disease, cleansing materials to remove dirt. Positive: restaurants to revive the forces of the body with needful diet. There were two sorts of negative, and only one sort of positive, but in the mere formality of the arrangement of shops, the positive received a compensation for only having one kind: it was permitted to exist in duplicate. Restaurants had annexes.

For the moment, however, my interest was concentrated on the odd lines in my notebook. and I took the annexes for granted. I wrote a new table of the odd lines only, adding N for negative and P for positive.

Chemist (N) Restaurant (P) Soapmonger (N) Restaurant (P)
Chemist (N) Soapmonger (N) Restaurant (P)
Chemist (N) Restaurant (P)
Chemist-Restaurant (NP)

Suppose I wrote N for Chemist and N^1 for Soapmonger. Then I could leave out the words, and see the pattern in all its austerity:

N P N^1 P
N N^1 P
N P
NP

Odd that the planner should have been so attached to his basic duality that he could only finish his design by putting a chemist and a restaurateur into the same shop.

I wanted to put everything into my diagram before I had done. If P stands for 'Restaurant', why should not P¹ stand for 'Restaurant-Annexe'? I would not this time put the symbols for the annexes on separate lines, for that would mean rewriting the diagram. I would add them to the lines I had, but at a good distance along to remind myself that there were gaps between the restaurants (P) and their annexes (P¹).

N	P	N¹	P		P¹
N	N¹	P			(P¹)
N	P			P¹	
NP			P¹		

I conscientiously bracketed the second P¹, because the annexe to Mr C's restaurant was shut.

With the reader's kind permission I shall now wake up; we will stop shop-gazing and look at St Mark's paragraphs instead. The houses between the shops are the paragraphs which are not concerned with the healing of particular persons. We are not interested for the present in these paragraphs; they represent to us nothing but gaps between the stories of healing. The healings are the shops, and the arrangement of the shops applies to them perfectly.

Before we approach the Gospel text, let us interpret the classification of healings we shall use. It is based on a distinction of the needs of the human person into negative and positive. Man's negative need is for purification, his positive need is for life, health or vigour. St Mark sees two sorts of purification which are strikingly different: the expulsion of demons, and the removal of defiling sicknesses such as made the Jew ritually unclean. We will call the two sorts simply 'exorcisms' and 'cleansings'. Christ exorcised Legion, he cleansed the leper. The exorcisms correspond to the chemist's wares in our table, and the cleansings to the soaps and brushes. There is no such sharp division of the positive acts of healing into two sorts (or more); we will call them all restorations; they appeared as restaurants in our dream. Christ restored the paralytic's power of walking, blind Bartimeus's sight, and life itself in Jairus's child.

The restaurants had annexes in the dream; what corresponds to that in the Gospel? An act of restoration is said to have an annexe, when it is followed by another such act, which is its direct pair or complement. In Mark II Christ restores to a *paralysed* man the use of his *legs,* he follows it up in III by restoring to an *atrophied* (withered) man the use of his *arm.* In VII he restores a deaf mute the use of tongue and ears, and in VIII he restores a blind man's use of his eyes. In such cases as these we say that the second healing is annexed to the first. And it is in the Gospel as it was in the visionary street: no annexed miracle is next door to the miracle of which it is the pair. Several 'blank' paragraphs always intervene, paragraphs, that is, which do not describe the healing of particular persons.

We remember that the annexe to Mr C's restaurant was shut. He had shut it (if I may be allowed to doze off again, and dream a further useful point) because he had so enlarged his main premises that they could cater for any conceivable need. Confident in the perfection of our dream, let us apply this detail also to the Gospel text. Let us walk up the street, counting as we go. First there is the exorcism in the synagogue (I, 21–28), corresponding to our first chemist's shop. A's restaurant is the restoration of Peter's wife's mother to the enjoyment of ordinary health (I, 29–31). The first shop with cleansing materials is the cleansing of the leper (I, 40–45). B's restaurant is the restoration of paralysed legs (II, 1–12) and B's annexe is the restoration of an atrophied arm (III, 1–6). The second chemist's shop is the exorcism of Legion (V, 1–20), the second soap shop is the healing of the impure woman (V, 21–34), and C's restaurant is the raising of Jairus's child (V, 35–43).

Mr C's main restaurant was so complete that there was nothing for his annexe to do, and the raising of the dead is so complete a restoration that nothing can be added to it, no pair can be annexed to it. We can say 'walking and handling', 'hearing and seeing', but not 'life and' anything, for life includes all the vital powers. We nowadays sometimes treat 'life' as a minimum, as bare life; and then we may say 'life and consciousness', 'life and health'. But that was not the language of the Bible. Life included consciousness and health. No pair can be annexed to resurrection.

As we walked on up the street we found a vestigial annexe to Mr C's shop, an annexe closed and empty. And as we travel on through St Mark's text from the raising of Jairus's child, we shall find a vestigial annexe, a passage, that is to say, which has all the promise of introducing a particular healing-story, but disappoints us and does not introduce it. The shop is shut and empty. Just what this means in terms of Marcan narrative we are not yet in a position to explain, but will do so in due course.

There is one more point in the dream which still lacks its interpretation, and when we have cleared it up we will have done with the dream for good. The last shop but one was a double shop, a chemist's on one side and restaurant on the other. The last healing miracle but one in the Gospel is that of the so-called epileptic boy (IX, 14–29) and it unites in one healing act St Mark's two types, the negative and the positive. It is an exorcism, and in so far negative or purgative. But it is also a restoration of natural powers, for the demon cast out is a demon of deafness and dumbness. I should agree that it is fanciful to make so much of the attributes 'deaf and dumb spirit'—should agree that the healing is, after all, just an exorcism—were it not for one curious fact. The sequence of shops, or of healings, we remember, ends 'two—one, one—one'. St Mark expresses in the 'one—one' exactly the same qualities of healing as he does in the 'two—one'; the only difference is, that the 'two' of the 'two—one' are compressed into a single healing of a single person in the 'one—one'. The pattern is this:

Exorcism of child at parent's prayer, and healing of a deaf mute;
Healing of a blind man (VII, 24–30, 31–37; VIII, 22–26).
Exorcism of deaf and dumb child at parent's prayer;
Healing of a blind man (IX, 14–29; X, 46–52)

In VII we have two healings, one an exorcism and the other a restoration; in IX the two are fused into one. Nothing could be more emphatic: the last exorcism is also a restoration.

After these preliminaries, we are in a position to write down a table of the Marcan healings, adding to each a letter to mark its quality: E for exorcism, C for cleansing, and R for restoration. The restorations in the *even* lines are all 'annexed restorations'. We will put an empty bracket for the one 'vestigial annexed restoration', the 'closed shop'.

Demoniac (E), Peter's mother (R), Leper (C), paralysed feet (R):
  withered hand (R).
Legion (E), impure woman (C), Jairus's child (R):
  (————————).
Syrophoenician's child (E), deaf-mute Decapolitan (R):
  blind villager (R).
Epileptic deaf mute (ER):
  blind Bartimeus (R).

We shall see the pattern more easily, perhaps, if we substitute the general descriptions represented by the letters for the particular descriptions represented by the words. And in so doing we will take occasion to introduce a refinement which we have hitherto neglected. When we were counting St Mark's healing miracles at the begininng of this chapter we saw that two of them were uniquely coupled by one being enclosed in the other. The healing of the impure woman is a parenthesis in the story of the raising of Jairus's child. We will indicate this fact by actually writing the word describing the one as a parenthesis breaking into the word which describes the other. We will also distinguish 'annexed restorations' from others by adding (*a*) to them.

Exorcism, restoration; cleansing, restoration: restoration (*a*).
    Exorcism, re-(cleansing)-storation: (————————).
                Exorcism, restoration: restoration (*a*).
                Exorcisive restoration: restoration (*a*).

I am sorry to keep serving up the same diagram in one form after another, but some persons of literary education find difficulty with diagrams, and I do want the reader to grasp this one. A critic whose good opinion I should especially like to deserve has (if I understand him) suggested in print that a literary analysis which cannot be stated without diagrams is self-condemned. He may well be right about many sorts of analysis, but about the analysis of rhythm, surely not. How can one set out the rhyme-pattern of a sonnet without the use of a's and b's?

The special point which the latest form of my diagram is intended to bring out is the strength of the influence exercised by the basic duality of negative and positive, purification and restoration. The blocks of healings—for the present I neglect the annexes—are four, three, two, and one. But St Mark does his best to treat all these numbers as forms of two, a negative plus a positive. (1) The four is treated simply as two pairs of negatives and positives, and a pause is placed between them. I have indicated the pause by a semicolon in the diagram, and I will explain what it is presently. (2) The three is not treated as 1 + 1 + 1. It is treated as 1 (a negative, exorcism) + 1 (a positive, restoration); and then another negative (cleansing) is tucked into the forepart of the positive story by way of parenthesis. So the basic two is expanded into a three without altogether losing its fundamental 'twoness'. A man and a woman are a pair; and if the woman carries a little boy in her arms, we still feel them to be a pair. (3) The next block is a simple two; all St Mark need do is to omit the parenthesis from the previous block, and he has the form of this one. 'Cleansing' disappears, and leaves us with exorcism + restoration. (4) As we have seen, the basic duality remains even in the *one*. In the place of exorcism + restoration we have an exorcism which is at the same time a restoration. To put the whole thing in terms of the sexes: The four is two pairs of men and women, the three is a man, and a woman carrying a little boy: the two is a man and a woman, and the one is an artificial figure of double sex. (I have used the sexes simply as illustration, and to stand for the negative and positive. It has nothing to do with the actual distribution of healings between the two sexes in the Gospel.)

I said that I would explain the pause between the two pairs which make up the first four. Explanation is needed, because the whole ground for counting any block, whether four, three, or two, as a single block is that there are no gaps in it. And what is a pause if it is not a gap? Here is the answer. The second miracle of the first pair is the raising of Peter's wife's mother from her bed. The incident is so short and so slightly narrated that it has not the weight of a paragraph. It is the first of three little episodes composing a complex paragraph. The whole describes Jesus as a guest in Peter's house. He (a) healed the mistress of it; (b) healed many people at the door after sundown; (c) rose before dawn and went out to pray (I, 29–31, 32–34, 35–39). The second and third little episodes therefore intervene between the actual healing of the woman and the cleansing of the leper which the next paragraph contains. But if we treat both paragraphs as wholes, we must say that the paragraph containing the cleansing of the leper follows direct upon the paragraph containing the healing of the woman. I hope I have now explained what I mean by a pause which is not a gap. The pause is of slight extent, but it is well marked in the sense. For in the episode of Jesus praying before dawn, we learn that the exclusive mission to Capernaum has ended, and a wider mission to Galilee begins (I, 38–39). Thus the first pair of healings are set by themselves as belonging to the day of the Capernaum mission, whereas the two which follow are assigned to the period of a wider Galilean mission.

So much for a first account of the pattern of healings. Perhaps the analysis we have made is undiscerning. In any case it requires a great deal more development before it can appear either meaningful or convincing. The question I would ask the reader to put to himself at the present stage is no more than this, whether there is a pattern there or not? Is, for example, the gradual condensation of the healing theme in the successive blocks of miracles the effect of chance, or is it a symptom of design? We have not yet got to the heart of the design, of that we may be certain. Whatever St Mark was doing, he was not arranging formal arabesques for their own sake.

If anyone wishes to explode the whole story about a pattern, his best line of attack will be to fasten upon our use of formal classification. 'Such and such healings', he will object, 'are alleged to be *cleansings*, and such and such others to be *restorations*. It is you who call them so, St Mark does not. Take away the classifying terms and the rhythm of the pattern becomes perfectly invisible. Once you have proposed such a classification, we admit that it is applicable. But that is not enough for your purpose; you have got to claim that St Mark himself employed it. For if he did not, he cannot have seen the pattern as you see it; indeed he can have seen no pattern at all. But surely in fact you are not going to maintain that the evangelist said to himself as he wrote, "Now we must have a *catharsis*", or "The next healing act will have to be an *apocatastasis*".'

The objection is full of weight, and it ought to be met. It contains two points. The first is this, that the healings do not require the classification we use, but merely admit of it; they might as well, perhaps, be classified under a different set of distinctions. And the second objection is this, that the pattern would be no pattern for St Mark unless he were classifying in his own mind the healings he described, and it seems absurd to suppose that he was.

To take the second point first, we must agree that we are attributing to St Mark something like classification. We must also agree that it is very unlikely that he used to himself such terms as cleansing (*catharsis*) and restoration (*apocatastasis*). The very suggestion of it is in the vein of parody. But it is not at all difficult to supply him with more credible terms. He begins his Gospel by making the Baptist confess that he comes with water, but not with spirit. Christ's baptism shows that he comes not only with water but with spirit also. St Mark goes on to show Christ performing two pairs of miracles, an exorcism and a restoration, a cleansing and a restoration. Is it not likely that he thought of what we have called two sorts of purification, the exorcism and the cleansing, as 'two manifestations of the power of water'? And that he similarly thought of the restorations to fuller life as manifestations of the power of spirit? This is no more than a suggestion; we are merely showing that there is no difficulty in supplying St Mark with plausible terms. These terms, or terms like these, are all the abstract classification we need attribute to him. As he goes over the ground again in the second line he does not need to say to himself 'That was a cleansing of defilement, and so here is another'. All he needs to do is to supply the closest parallel he can in his second line to the healing he had recorded in his first. He need not say, 'That was a cleansing of defilement and this is a cleansing of defilement'. He may say, 'Leprosy is cleansed by the power of water, for water plays a large part in the ritual for its purification. (The ritual is in Leviticus XIII–XIV, a text actually referred to in Christ's command to the leper, that he should offer *what Moses had commanded*.) The pair to the cleansing of leprosy is the cleansing of sexual issue. It too is expiated with water, and occupies the next place in Moses (Leviticus XV, where the case of morbid issue referred to by St Mark is separately prescribed for in verses 25–30). Indeed Moses treats leprosy and issue as the two typical conditions which defile and are purified by water.'

We can in fact (to take point one of the objection we are answering) dispense with abstract classification and substitute the more concrete notion of self-developing series. The cleansings are such a series; there are only two of them. All we need to claim is that the first easily evokes the second in the mind of a Bible-reading Jew. The sequence of restorations is longer and more elaborate than the simple pair of cleansings, but it is no less evidently a self-developing series.

If St Mark was viewing cleansing as miracles of 'water', it would be natural for him to view restorations as miracles of 'spirit'. Spirit is the power of resurrection, an association made indelible in the Jewish mind by Ezekiel's vision of dry bones. In that vision, it is when Spirit or breath is invoked by the prophet that the dead live and arise. The first three miracles of Spirit in St Mark are bound together by the gradual emergence in them of the theme of 'raising up'. It is the slightest suggestion of raising up from death, when Peter's mother-in-law is raised up from her bed by the hand of Christ. But when the paralytic is raised up from his, the symbolism of resurrection is strongly marked. The man is carried by four bearers, like the dead going to burial. Unable to come at Christ otherwise, they *dig out* (St Mark's word) a hole and lower him as into his grave. Thus descending, he falls in the presence of the Son of God, and 'stands up on his feet', like the dead man whom his bearers dropped into the sepulchre of Elisha (II Kings XIII, 21. St Mark may have even had the text in mind, for he had just finished with the healing of the leper, which could scarcely fail to remind him or II Kings v, Elisha's cure of Naaman).

The miracle of the paralytic carries the symbolism of resurrection almost as far as it will go. The raising of Jairus's daughter presents us with resurrection itself. It develops in a straight line from the cure of the paralytic. But at the same time it reaches back over the paralytic and establishes direct connexions with the healing of Peter's wife's mother. Jesus enters the house of sickness, accompanied in the one case by four, in the other by three, chosen disciples; he takes the woman in one case, and the girl in the other, by her hand and lifts her up. No one surely will deny that Peter's mother-in-law, the paralytic and Jairus's child form a closely written series, with a steadily developing theme. The theme appears to be exhausted in the raising of Jairus's child: resurrection can go no further. But the series of restorations does not end there. St Mark continues it by picking up and elaborating another theme, the theme of the vital powers. The theme has already made its appearance in the Marcan design, but it has not yet received much emphasis. It arose in the relation of the first annexe to the first block. The first block ends with the paralytic. But for the fresh indications offered by the annexe we should have no reason to pay much attention to the members of the paralytic's body inhibited by his disease. The symbolical interest of his cure lies, as we have said, in its being a 'raising up'. But what he previously lacked, and by Christ's help regained, was in fact the use of his feet. And St Mark calls our attention to it, when he adds the healing of a withered *hand* in the annexe-position. Withering or atrophy is a natural pair to paralysis, as the hand is a natural pair to the foot.

47

As we read of the restoration of foot and hand, we feel ourselves to be touching upon a familiar Old Testament list of the vital powers. The most complete example, perhaps, is in Psalm cxv. The gods of the heathen lack the real exercise of the vital powers. 'They have mouths and speak not, eyes have they and see not, they have ears and hear not, noses have they and smell not, they have hands and handle not, feet have they and walk not.' Such are the idols, and such too are their worshippers. 'They that make them are like unto them.' 'But', the Psalmist continues, 'thou, House of Israel, put thy trust in the Lord.' He it is who bestows the effective use of the vital powers on man, for they are the lowly similitudes of his own powers.

The restorations of foot and hand are presented in the first block and first annexe of St Mark's design; the theme of the powers is picked up and completed in the third block and the third annexe. The Decapolitan's tongue receives power to speak plain, and his ears to hear (vii). The blind villager's eyes recover sight (viii). And so the whole of the Psalmist's list is completed, apart from the power of scent. Scent has its importance in the psalm, but it could have none in the Gospel. It is a serious loss to the idolaters, that their deities cannot smell the steam of their sacrifices. It is no serious loss to the servants of the true God that they cannot tell the scent of a pink from the scent of a rose. Having completed the list of vital powers in this third movement, St Mark is content with repetition in the fourth. Another deaf mute and another blind man are healed. Why St Mark should wish to make the repetition is a question we will reserve. That he does make it is obvious enough.

St Mark did not leave his interest in the list of vital powers to be inferred from his miracle pattern alone. He introduced it into the discourses also. The first healing of the blind is the healing which completes the list, and St Mark introduces it by a paragraph in which Jesus thus addresses his slow-hearted disciples. 'Do ye not yet perceive nor understand? Have ye eyes and see not, ears, and hear not?' (viii, 18). Here are the sensitive powers. The active powers have clearly no place in such a context. They make their appearance, however, in a discourse belonging to the next chapter. 'If thy *hand* offend thee, cut it off; it is better for thee to enter into life maimed, than having two hands to go into hell ... Or if thy *foot* offend thee ... or thine *eye*...' (IX, 43–47). It is most striking that a Gospel based upon the scheme of the healing of the whole man in all his members should thus provide its own antithesis. Supernature perfects the whole of nature; but natural powers must on occasion be sacrificed for supernatural good.

The discourse in IX is of peculiar interest to us, because it is based on the contrast between the vigour of the particular powers and the resurrection of the whole person. (To 'enter into life' means, of course, to enter into resurrection-life, the life of the world to come.) This contrast is of interest to us, because we have already used it to interpret the relation of St. Mark's second movement to his first. Feet being healed in the first movement are supplemented by the healing of the hand; but the second movement presents us with the resurrection of the whole person, which admits of no supplementing. In the third movement St Mark returns to the list of particular powers, and achieves development or climax by ascending from the less noble (motive powers) to the more noble (sentient powers). And in the course of this movement he insists, as we have seen, on the necessity that men should be able to hear and see with the ears and eyes they have. In the fourth movement he repeats the sensitive powers, but now he is pressing the other side of the truth. The vigour of the powers is not an end in itself; hand, foot or eye must be sacrificed for resurrection. Just as the motive powers in the first movement give place to the resurrection of Jairus's child in the second, so the sentient powers in the third and fourth are to give way to the resurrection of Jesus which crowns the whole Gospel.

How does St Mark graft the theme of the sensitive powers in his third movement on to the stock of healing themes which runs on into the third movement from the second? The third movement carries a block of two healings (VII, 24–37). St Mark condenses all the old themes into the first one of these two, thus leaving himself free to devote the second of the two to the new theme of sentience. The healings of the previous block were: (1) the exorcism of Legion; (2) the cleansing of an impure woman who thrust herself on Christ; (3) the raising of Jairus's child at Jairus's prayer. The first of the two miracles in the new block (VII, 24–30) does justice to all three themes. For (1) it is anyhow an exorcism, and (2) it is wrought for an impure woman who has the courage to thrust herself on Christ (impure because a Gentile, and the point receives much emphasis: 'It is not meet to take the children's bread and cast it to the dogs'); and (3) it is the healing of a child at the prayer of a parent. Christ visited Jairus's house; he healed the child in the Syrophoenician's without even visiting it. The contrast between visiting and not visiting saves St Mark's narrative from bathos. For though it is a less thing to exorcise than to resuscitate, it is a greater thing to heal from a distance than to heal by contact.

All the old themes having been thus condensed into one of the two miracles in VII, its successor is left free for new treatment. We observe the novel features—comparatively elaborate manipulation by the healer, and the use of spittle; features which recur in the pair supplied to it by the annexe (VII, 31–37, VIII, 22–26).

We have now said something about 'cleansings' and 'restorations' to show that they form strong self-developing series, and so hold together quite apart from the use of artificial terms to classify them. We have given no similar demonstration about exorcisms, because it is surely needless to prove that they form a class by themselves. To cast out a demon is to cast out a demon. Such an act cannot be confused with any other sort of act. Every block begins with an exorcism, and no exorcism is found elsewhere than at the beginning of a block.

Another feature which appears in every block is the relative who intercedes. On Simon's (and Andrew's) prayer Simon's mother-in-law is healed, Jairus's daughter at her father's, the Syrophoenician's daughter at her mother's, the 'epileptic' son at his father's. The formality of this series is remarkable. St Mark records the story of Simon's mother-in-law as it stands because it is obviously of historical importance. But the sequel suggests that he saw it on the background of the Old Testament type for all such stories. Son-in-law and mother-in-law remind him of mother and son: of how Elijah had raised the son of the widow for his mother's sake, and Elisha likewise the son of the Shunammite. True, the story of Simon's mother-in-law reverses the scriptural relation: son(-in-law) intercedes for mother(-in-law), not mother for son. The evangelist cannot help it; the story is important and must be told as it stands. But as he advances to the later movements of his pattern, he obtains greater freedom, and is able to select those traditions of Christ's healing acts which exactly ring the changes on the theme of parent and child. In working out the permutations, he bases himself on the perfect scriptural type (son healed for mother) and not on the imperfect antitype provided by the cure in Simon's house. Here is a table of the result:

1st block: Son requests healing for mother-in-law
2nd block: Daughter healed at request of father
3rd block: Daughter healed at request of mother
4th block: Son healed at request of father.

The pattern adds to its other beauties the beauty of climax. The male sex is considered superior by the ancients, so where both intercessor and patient are males, the healing is 'noblest'. Moreover, the healing of 'the son of the father' prepares our minds most directly for what the climax of the Gospel is to reveal, the resurrection of the Father's only Son. It is directly after being proclaimed Only Son by the Father's voice that Jesus descends the mountain to heal the son of the father (IX, 7, 17).

It is indeed the function of the healing at the mountain's foot to draw together all the themes of healing in the previous signs. To begin with, it fuses exorcism with restoration of sensitive powers, for the demon exorcised is a spirit of deafness and dumbness. It completes the theme of parental intercession, and revives the theme of resurrection. For the boy being exorcised falls as dead, and must be raised by the hand like Jairus's child before he can enjoy his new and purified life.

We are now in a position to take the decisive step of our whole exposition, and to appreciate the meaning of the gradual condensation of the healing themes from four to three, from three to two, and from two to one. The evangelist's purpose is to exhibit Christ's many healing works as types and anticipations of the one great healing work performed on the cross and in the Easter sepulchre. The final expulsion of the demon is through the going forth of Christ's spirit, the effective cleansing is the death of the perishable in Christ's flesh, Christ's resurrection is the vivification of man and carries with it the restoration of all his vital powers. The use of the many healing miracles is to exhibit the richness and diversity of the one saving act, much as the many creatures exhibit the multiform fecundity of the one creative power. Therefore the evangelist begins from multitude. But in order to apply multitude to unity he condenses it as he proceeds. The themes of the many miracles, concentrated at length into a single sign, point on through it into the heart of the reality signified, which is the passion and resurrection of Christ.

That is the only true conclusion of the pattern: Jesus is the last and fourteenth person healed. Even from a formal point of view the pattern is incomplete without its fourteenth term. The principle of the pattern is a movement towards unity, but without the fourteenth healing unity is not achieved. The fourth line of the pattern unifies the healings within the block, but the duality of block and annexe still remains. The healing of the epileptic boy absorbs many healings into itself, but not the healing of blind Bartimeus; that much remains obstinately independent alongside of the other, an annexe paired with its block, a healing of the eyes set over against a healing of the ears. Jairus's daughter has already shown us how the unification we look for is to be achieved: resurrection, being the life of the whole person, draws into itself all dualities of partial powers. The resurrection of Jesus is all things together, it is seeing eyes, open ears and a praising tongue, for it is the life of the world to come.

CHAPTER III

FIRST DOUBLE CYCLE

We cannot be content with picking out a pattern in St Mark's book, however clear, striking or important it may be. He cannot have written the healing miracles to a pattern, and all the other paragraphs just as they came. The pattern of healings must find its place in the whole rhythm of St Mark's mind, as he writes his way straight on from one sentence to the next. The readiest way to indicate the rhythmic character of his thinking is to do what we have done already, and to pick out the most visible and impressive recurrences or correspondences we can find in it. But such a way of proceeding is artificial. We cannot be content until we succeed in following the actual movement of the evangelist's mind straight through his Gospel. It is a formidable undertaking, but unless we attempt it we can achieve really nothing. Let us begin, then, from the beginning.

The first phrases of the first chapter look like a formal heading and nothing more. 'Beginning of' (i.e. Here beginneth) 'the joyful message of Jesus, Messiah and Son of God. . . .' We should probably expect a full stop after these words, and a fresh beginning to the actual story: something like 'In the days of Pontius Pilate the governor it came to pass. . . .' St Mark does not do anything like this, and the reason why he does not do it is that he is writing under inspiration.

Inspiration, as dogmatic theology understands it, is a purely theological fact. It consists of a man's mind being specially moved by God, by whatever means it may please God to move it. The man need not necessarily be aware of his inspiration, and his psychological or mental processes need not be of one kind rather than another. But some inspired men are conscious of inspiration, or even seek it; and the sacred writers of the New Testament age were mostly such men. One of the principal evidences of the new and supernatural dispensation under which they lived was the visible and wide diffusion of special inspiration in the Church. The motions of the Pentecostal Spirit were too plain to be overlooked. To prophesy and to teach divine truth were acts which men performed under the impulse of the Holy Ghost. It would have been strange if St Mark had written what he wrote without looking for inspiration, and his book shows that in fact he did not.

Inspiration as such may be invisible and without any necessary symptoms, but when belief in inspiration co-operates with inspiration, there is a psychological fact, and one that is no more or less invisible than any other psychological fact. What can we say about the practical effects of belief in inspiration? The man who believes in his inspiration expects what he is saying to be 'given to him', to 'come' or to 'grow'. He is not to be the master of his discourse, he is not going to decide what it is good for his hearers to learn, and how he will present it to them. His discourse is to 'grow'; but if so, from what seed? From a stock of sacred truth already accepted, certainly; from the inspired writings of former prophets. But if it is to have any continuity, the discourse must also grow out of itself, like any living thing. There must be a fertility, a gentle necessity, arising out of what has been written or said, and determining what must be said or written next.

So St Mark's first phrase is no mere title, it is a seed out of which the following sentences are to grow. His own control over the Gospel he is writing goes no farther than the formal phrase, 'Beginning of the joyful message of Jesus, Messiah and Son of God'. The rest is what grows from that, and St Mark's business is not creation but obedience. He is moved first to develop the inspired suggestion arising out of 'joyful message' (*evangelion*). 'Even as it is written', he continues, 'in Isaiah the prophet, Behold, I send my messenger (*angelos*) before thy face, who shall prepare thy way; The voice of one crying in the wilderness, Prepare ye the way of the Lord, make straight his paths.'

There is much compression of thought here; let us pause to unravel it. The fortieth chapter of Isaiah, which St Mark quotes, is indisputably the *locus classicus* of the Old Testament for the proclamation of divine advent as a joyful message. The passage which begins 'The voice of one crying', continues 'Ascend the high mountain, thou who bearest the joyful message to Sion' (*evangelizomenos Sion*); 'uplift thy voice with strength, thou who bearest the joyful message to Jerusalem'. It is natural, then, that St Mark should connect the joyful message of Christ with Isaiah's prediction, and should plunge into Isaiah's fortieth chapter.

But the Jew was used always to refer the sentences of the prophets to sentences of the Law. The prophets were not read in synagogue except as comments upon the Law, and St Mark, obedient to the custom, places in front of Isaiah's text the text of Moses with which it most simply corresponds, and on which it may be taken to be the comment. God had said through Moses: 'Behold, I send my messenger before thy face, to keep thee in the way' (Exod. XXIII, 20). He had been speaking of divine leading in the return from Egyptian bondage to the Promised Land. Isaiah in chapter XL is predicting a new return to Canaan from a second bondage, a new Exodus like the old, and so it is very proper that Isaiah's text should be applied to the Exodus text. Needless to say, St Mark, like all Christians, sees our salvation through Jesus as a spiritual exodus, and a conquest of the true Promised Land.

But complication does not end here. St Mark does not merely quote as 'Isaiah' a text of Moses together with its Isaianic comment. He colours the wording of the Mosaic text with the wording of a text in Malachi. It will be best to put down Exodus, Malachi, and Mark one after the other.

Exodus XXIII, 20. Behold, I send my messenger before thy face, to keep thee in the way.

Malachi III, 1. Behold, I send forth my messenger, and he shall look to (i.e. prepare) a way before my face.

Mark I, 2. Behold, I send my messenger before thy face, who shall prepare thy way.

Exodus sends the messenger before Israel, Malachi before the Lord, and Mark before Jesus. If Mark can fuse Exodus and

Malachi, he must see in Jesus both Israel and the Lord. The equation of 'Lord' and 'Israel' is assisted, no doubt, by the fact that the *leader* of Israel who will bring them into the promised land according to Exodus, is Jesus (Joshua the Son of Nun). He bears the person of Israel by virtue of his office, and, to a Christian mind, he bears the person of the Lord by virtue of his name.

The Malachi text has a special value to St Mark. It is rich in suggestions of what is coming, because the last verses of Malachi's prophecy appear to interpret the 'messenger' as Elijah returning to earth; and St Mark is going to cast the mantle of Elijah on the 'messenger' he describes; that is, on John Baptist.

We have rationalized the relations between St Mark's Exodus, Malachi and Isaiah texts; whether he worked them out as carefully as we have suggested is a question no one can answer. Still less can we guess how much of the close thought involved in the use of such intertwined citations went on in St Mark's mind when he was writing his Gospel. He may have done the thinking on previous occasions, when he was expounding the scriptures; he may have taken his cluster of texts ready-made from other expositors, or even (if you like to think so) from a little handbook of 'Christian Evidences'.

However that may be, St Mark uses his composite citation to draw out the suggestion contained in 'joyful message'. 'Beginning of the joyful message of Jesus, Messiah and Son of God, even as it is written in Isaiah the prophet: Behold, I send my messenger before thy face, who shall prepare thy way; The voice of one crying in the wilderness, Prepare ye the way of the Lord, make straight his paths.'

St Mark has started by simply naming his subject, the 'gospel' or 'joyful message'. It was, by his time, a well-established name for the Christian preaching and nothing particular might seem to arise out of his use of it. But 'joyful message' readily suggests a messenger other than him of whom the message tells. The *evangelion* of a royal advent is not proclaimed by the king; the gospel of Christ's coming was not proclaimed to the Roman subject of St Mark's day by Christ, but by a Christian gospeller. Moreover, the text from Isaiah XL, with the composite text supporting it, sketches the typical picture of *evangelizing*. The messenger, the voice, is distinct from the Lord who comes. Thus by simply developing the normal associations of the word *evangelion*, and calling in the help of Old Testament texts, St Mark is found to have adumbrated the figure of the forerunner.

The next move is inevitable. The prophetic adumbration must be translated into historical flesh and blood. And it is notable that St Mark makes the historical application in about as many phrases as the adumbration has taken.

(i)

Beginning of the joyful *message* of Jesus Christ, Son of God, as it is written in Isaiah the prophet: Behold, I send my *messenger* before thy face, who shall *prepare* thy way; the voice of one crying in the *wilderness*, *Prepare* ye the way of the Lord, make straight his paths.

(ii)

John came, who *baptized* in the *wilderness*, and preached *baptism* of repentance unto remission of *sins*. And there went forth to him all the country of Judea and all the men of Jerusalem, and were *baptized* by him in the river Jordan, making confession of their *sins*.

An interlocking pattern of refrain-words emphasized the continuous drawing out of the sense, and how the matter grows under the evangelist's pen out of the suggestions contained in what he has written already. As 'message' is taken up in 'messenger', so is the first 'prepare' in the second; the voice in the wilderness suggests John in the wilderness, and so on. St Mark's tendency is to write short passages which are rounded and complete, and yet provide rich material for further development. The second of the two little paragraphs we have transcribed above gives us a general description of John and his activity which could stand by itself. But it is not left to do so; St Mark writes another paragraph of equal length, starting again from the name of John.

(iii)

John was wearing camel's hair,[1] and eating locusts and wild honey; and preached, saying: A mightier than I comes after me, whose sandal-string I am not worthy to stoop and loose. I have baptized you with water; he shall baptize you with the Holy Ghost.

The third paragraph puts together the lessons of the first and second. The second has revealed John as a preacher of baptism, while the first had prophesied a forerunner. The third shows us that John's baptism is a forerunner's baptism, because it is with water only. John's being a forerunner is also hinted at in the description of his ascetic dress and habits. These things suggest Elijah, and Elijah is the Lord's forerunner according to the prophecy of Malachi which St Mark has glanced at in his composite citation.

Let us recapitulate. St Mark began with 'evangel of Jesus the Anointed, Son of God', took up 'evangel', and developed from it the 'evangelist' or forerunner. He has now reached the point where the 'forerunner' idea must be completed by the introduction of the king whose forerunner he is. We already know him: he is 'Jesus, the Anointed, the Son of God'. St Mark proceeds to bring the three descriptions alive; the first quite simply; *Jesus* comes to John. Next the *anointing*. David was anointed with oil, but Christ is anointed with the Spirit of the Lord, as Isaiah had foretold in one of the most famous of his prophecies (XI, I ff.). The spiritual anointing is revealed when John baptizes Jesus, for then the Holy Ghost descends visibly upon him. Thus *baptism* is taken up into *anointing*. According to St Mark's first line or title, Jesus is not Anointed only, he is also *Son of God*. Therefore the descent of the Holy Breath is joined with that of the Heavenly Voice, 'Thou art my Son'.

(iv)

And it came to pass in those days, Jesus came from Nazareth of Galilee and was baptized by John in the Jordan. Then ascending

[1] Omitting with some MSS. the Matthaean insertion: 'and a leather girdle about his loins'.

from the water he saw the skies parted and the Spirit as a dove descending on him. And a voice came from the skies: Thou art my beloved Son, in thee I am content.

St Mark has now written two paragraphs on John, and one on Jesus. The one on Jesus appears to be complete. It fully shows him to be the Lord whom John came to proclaim—Jesus, Anointed, Son of God, Spirit-bringer. But there is another and quite different way in which John foreshewed Jesus, and so there is matter for a second paragraph on Jesus, to balance the second paragraph on John. This other way of foreshewing is foreshewing by deed. John's activity is the type of that of Jesus; we are to see how Jesus becomes a second and a greater John.

The active foreshewing of Jesus in John is implied in John's recorded words: 'There comes after me a mightier than I, whose shoe-string I am not worthy to stoop and loose. I have baptized you with water; he shall baptize you with the Holy Ghost.' The words suggest something foreign to the typical relation between a bearer of good tidings and a king whose happy advent he announces. In the typical case messenger and king are quite unalike in their attributes and functions. It is one thing to proclaim a royal advent, quite another thing to make a royal progress. The Baptist steps out of the lines of the traditional picture when he draws a direct comparison between his own activity and his king's. 'I baptized, he will baptize; I with water, he with Spirit.' Jesus is to be a greater baptist, and it is an easy step from such an idea to the thought of his being a greater John Baptist. Anyhow, it is a thought which plays a large part in St Mark's Gospel.

The next paragraph begins to show us Jesus 'fulfilling' John; he, like John, endures the rigours of the desert. But here is a greater John. God does greater things for him. John fed on locusts and wild honey; Jesus goes forty days in the strength of supernatural bread. That is what Elijah had done, when an angel so ministered to him, that he had the force to go forty days, and reach the Mount of God. Jesus is a new Elijah; the Christian, whether it be St Mark or we, inevitably understands, 'a better Elijah'. This too is all part of his being a better John. For John is the returning Elijah, the forerunner Malachi promised. St Mark has already hinted that much to us broadly enough.

(v)

Thereupon the Spirit drove him into the wilderness. And he was in the wilderness forty days, being tempted by Satan. And he was with the wild beasts, and the angels ministered to his need.

We have now had two paragraphs on John, and two on Jesus as fulfiller of John. And now the narrative overflows into the description of Christ's active ministry, and begins to take an ampler sweep. But that which overflows still wells up out of the already written page; that is what we have by now come to expect. The first two acts of Christ's public ministry are but the transposition of two hidden mysteries just recorded. One of the paragraphs about Jesus told us how he came up out of the water and was commissioned by the divine voice, the other told us how he wrestled with Satan in the desert alone. We are now going to be told how Jesus, calling disciples out of the water, commissions them by his own word; and how he wrestles with Satan no longer alone, but publicly in synagogue.

Henceforward the evangelist begins to use an ampler scale. He employs three little paragraphs, not one, for the calling of the disciples, and again three for the exorcism of Satan. And the three little paragraphs of each group so grow together as to form a single longer paragraph. The longer paragraph thus formed becomes the standard unit throughout the rest of the Gospel. The transition from the small paragraph to the greater takes place before our eyes, if we will but apply them to the text.

(vi)

And after John had been committed to prison Jesus came into Galilee preaching the evangel and saying, The time is fulfilled and the kingdom of God is at hand. Repent and believe the evangel.

(vii)

And passing by the sea of Galilee he saw Simon and Andrew the brother of Simon casting a net in the sea, for they were fishers. And Jesus said to them, Hither after me, and I will make you fishers of men. And thereupon leaving their nets they followed him.

(viii)

And going a little on he saw James the son of Zebedee and John his brother, them also in their boat, fitting the nets. And thereupon he called them, and leaving their father Zebedee in the boat with the journeymen, they went after him.

(ix)

And they came to Capernaum. And as soon as it was Sabbath he went to synagogue and taught. And they were amazed at his teaching, for he was teaching them as possessed of authority, and not as their scribes.

(x)

Thereupon there was in their synagogue a man with an unclean spirit, and cried saying, Away from us, Jesus of Nazareth; thou art come to destroy us. I know who thou art, Holy One of God. And Jesus rebuked him, saying, Be silent and come out of him. And the unclean spirit, tearing him and crying with a loud voice, came out of him.

(xi)

And all marvelled, so that they disputed with one another, saying, What is this? Strange teaching. He commands even the unclean spirits and they obey him. And thereupon the fame of him went forth everywhere in the whole district about Galilee.

We have transcribed six little paragraphs in two sets of three. We see at a glance that the three parts of the first set are much more equal, and more distinct from one another, than the three parts of the second. The second is, indeed, one story, with a top and a tail, and all the weight is in the middle. Whereas the first contains two exactly parallel narratives of equal weight, the call of Simon and Andrew, and the call of the sons of Zebedee; the third part being an introductory section which has hardly less weight and is capable of standing by itself, for it describes how Christ entered on his public mission. The first set is really a set of three little paragraphs, the second is really a single paragraph with the classic threefold structure, beginning, middle and end. In passing from the form of the first to the form of the second, St Mark deserts the small unit he has hitherto used and begins to employ a greater.

We will now treat the two sets of three each as a whole and consider the subject-matter of each rather than the form. For we said above that the first set corresponds to the narrative of Christ's baptism, and the second to the narrative of his sojourn in the wilderness. We wish now to show how this is so.

Christ's baptism is a story of fulfilment. We have just heard John's prophecy, 'There cometh one after me mightier than I. . . . I have baptized you with water; he will baptize you with the Holy Ghost'. When therefore 'Jesus comes from Nazareth of Galiee and is baptized of John' and when he sees 'the Spirit as a dove descending on him' we recognize that this is he. John's prediction is so far fulfilled, that the Mightier has come, and has been marked out as the Spirit-Giver. But another part of the prediction, 'He shall baptize you with the Holy Ghost', remains unfulfilled. Jesus has as yet made no movement towards being the active successor of John in his mission. He has been baptized himself; he has not yet baptized others.

But when John 'was committed to prison', then Jesus began to act as his successor; then he returned to the *Galilee* from which he had come, and preached *fulfilment*: 'The time is made full and the Kingdom of God is at hand; repent and believe the Gospel.' Jesus was visible now as a second John preaching repentance. If a second John, then a second Elijah too, for John is an Elijah. Jesus had already shown himself a new Elijah by his sojourn in the desert, sustained with angels' bread. He continued to act in the character of the ancient prophet when he called disciples suddenly from the midst of their trade and from their father's side. For this was the first thing Elijah had done when he returned from those forty days in the wilderness: he found Elisha ploughing, and cast his mantle upon him. The disciple left his father and his trade, and came (I Kings XIX). But was Elisha 'baptized with Spirit' by the master who called him? He was, but not at the time of his calling. It was not until Elijah had ascended, and Elijah's mantle became Elisha's permanent possession, that 'a double portion' of the master's spirit came upon the disciple (II Kings II). When Elijah threw the mantle on him as he ploughed, it was no more than the promise and the foretaste of this. So with the disciples of Christ: their baptism with Spirit awaits the day when their Master ascends. Their call is no more than the promise of such a baptism. It is prefigured, nevertheless, in the circumstance of their call. For they came up out of the water, as Christ himself had done, to receive a divine commission. When Christ came up out of the water, he was baptized with the Holy Ghost. They are not yet so baptized, but they will be hereafter.

The supernatural baptism of Jesus was a secret between his Father and himself. In the call of the disciples some effects of it began to be more publicly manifested. The victory over Satan in the wilderness was no less secret; in the exorcism in synagogue its effects too began to appear. This exorcism is what the second of our sets of three little paragraphs describes. The demon in synagogue speaks for the whole host of Satan, who knew themselves defeated in the overthrow of their chief. 'Away from *us*,' he cries, 'Jesus of Nazareth; thou art come to destroy *us*. *I* know thee. . . .' What Satan had met in the wilderness was Christ fresh from his baptism, visibly hallowed with the Spirit of Holiness, the Spirit of the Lord. What the unclean spirit in synagogue acknowledges is 'the Holy One of God'.

The exorcism of the unclean spirit caused a general amazement, and Christ's fame went forth into the whole neighbourhood of Galilee. The name of Galilee carries us back from the end of our second threefold paragraph to the beginning of our first;

63

we are reminded of Christ's entry into Galilee with the gospel of the kingdom, when he came to call his four earliest disciples. If our minds circle back to that former mention of Galilee, we are in step with St Mark. For he is about to go over the ground again from that very point. That is to say, he goes over the matter of his two triple paragraphs in two new paragraphs (29–39, 40–45). The new pair correspond to the old pair in form as well as in substance.

As to form, we remember that the first triple paragraph was really a sequence of three little paragraphs, whereas the second was a single paragraph with beginning, middle, and end. The same is true of the two new sections. The first is a sequence of three little paragraphs, Jesus healing indoors at noon, Jesus healing by the door at dusk, Jesus praying out-of-doors at dawn (29–31, 32–34, 35–38). The second is the continuous story of the leper. We naturally take it as one; perhaps if we look hard at it, we can distinguish three acts; the leper cleansed, the leper charged, the leper disobedient (40–42, 43–44, 45).

So much for the formal correspondence between the two new sections and the two old ones. The material correspondence is no less unmistakable. We have first to compare 29–39 with 14–20. The one is the direct continuation of the other: 21–28, the exorcism in synagogue, which intervenes between them, may be regarded as a parenthesis disturbing the continuous story of Christ's dealings with his new disciples. In 14–20 he called Simon and Andrew, James and John. In 29 he enters the house of Simon and Andrew, accompanied also by James and John; and 29–39 gives the story of Christ in Simon's house, and how he came to leave it. Simon and those with him, that is, no doubt, the other three, sought him and found him praying in a desert place, and learnt something of the width of the sphere into which Christ's call had brought them. They must be ready to follow him throughout Galilee, and so they do (39). 'Throughout Galilee' acts as a sort of rubrical mark, and brings the section we are discussing to a close. For it echoes the phrase with which the previous section ended. In 28 the fame of Jesus went throughout

Galilee; in 39 Jesus himself goes where his fame had gone before.

Jesus now goes 'preaching in their synagogues throughout Galilee, and casting out the demons'. The phrase simply tells us that he set about to do everywhere in the district what he had done in the principal town. For this is what Christ had done in the synagogue of Capernaum: he had taught, and he had cast out a demon. So our minds are carried back to the scene in 21-28, and we are ready for what St Mark proceeds to give us—an antitype to the exorcism in synagogue. St Mark's antitype for exorcism is not exorcism but cleansing; a variation on the common theme, the purging out of defilement. The parallel is emphasized by harping on the words clean, cleanse, unclean. The demon of 21-28 is never called a demon, but twice an 'unclean spirit', and in the conclusion the description is generalized (He commandeth even the unclean spirits and they obey him). Not that St Mark is already preparing the ground for the cleansing of the leper when he writes of the unclean spirit by that name. He is providing the perfect verbal antithesis to the Holy Spirit, wherewith the Holy One of God is hallowed. 'A man with an unclean spirit . . . cried out, saying, Away from me . . . Holy One of God' (23-24). But when St Mark comes to provide an antitype to the demoniac in the person of the leper, he echoes the 'unclean, unclean, unclean' of 23, 26 and 27 in the 'cleanse, cleansed, cleansing' of 40, 41-2, 44. We may observe also that the leper, like the demon, is 'driven out' and 'rebuked' (43). Strange expressions, which have caused commentators much difficulty. But whatever ought to be said about them, this much is clear: they strengthen the parallel between the leper and the demon, the unclean man and the unclean spirit.

St Mark seems now to have established the custom of writing each new paragraph on the model of the last but one. In passing from the leper to the paralytic (II, 1-12) he does not desert the custom. He writes the paralytic on the model of the paragraph preceding the leper; we are back again 'home', presumably, that is, in Simon's house at Capernaum (II, 1), where Jesus had raised

Simon's mother-in-law from her bed (29–31). Now, in the same place, he raises the paralytic from his. Since he is not a member of the household, he is carried in, bed and all.

We have allowed ourselves to speak of St Mark as composing his paragraphs in pairs, in such a way that the first member of one pair corresponds to the first member of another, and the second member of the one pair to the second member of the other. When we talk like this, need we mean that St Mark thought in pairs? Did he ever say to himself, 'That is the end of one pair; now for another?' If he did not say it, did he even feel it? The irreducible fact which we have encountered is not pairing but alternation. The evangelist keeps reviving the theme of the last paragraph but one. To acknowledge this fact is not to attribute anything very elaborate to the evangelist. We are assigning him the very simplest of all rhythms. A, A, A, A is no rhythm at all; the beginning of rhythm is A B, A B, A B. Even these symbols are not simple enough for what we are trying to symbolize; for if we say A B, A B we are suggesting something beside mere alternation. We are suggesting that the A's are intrinsically prior to the B's, and that A B, A B, A B is a more proper division than A, B A, B A. . . . We feel that way about A's and B's, we do not feel it about noughts and crosses: A's are prior to B's, but O's are not prior to X's, but just different. Let us use O and X to express the alternation of themes in so much of the Gospel as we have analysed, and write out a table.

1	X	Gospel-prophecies	I, 1–3
2	O	John's baptism	4–5
3	X	John's desert life and prophecy	6–8
4	O	Christ baptized and called	9–11
5	X	Christ in the desert, tempted by Satan	12–13
6	O	Christ calls Simon and others	14–20
7	X	Christ exorcizes unclean spirit	21–28
8	O	Christ raises up Simon's mother-in-law	29–39
9	X	Christ cleanses a leper	40–45
10	O	Christ raises up paralytic in Simon's house	II, 1–12

In our previous talk about 'pairs' we were coupling the lines of the above table in the order O–X. The reason for this was that we started our coupling in the region of lines 2–5, and it felt natural to treat 2–3 and 4–5 as pairs. For 2–3 described John's ministry, and 4–5 Christ's fulfilment of it. But if we shift our ground and look at 5–10 without prejudice, we may feel the X–O order to be more natural and more illuminating. Christ, after receiving the divine sign, must repeat the destiny of the people of God: first he must endure trial in the wilderness (5), and then enter the inhabited country with the declaration that the time is fulfilled for the kingdom to come (6). He must first exorcise in the Jewish synagogue (7), then raise to newness of life in the house of the Christian disciple (8). He must first cleanse the flesh (9), then forgive the sins of the will, once more in the disciple's house, and once more to the accompaniment of a 'raising up' (10).

'First the synagogue, then the disciple's house.' Here surely is a point which the original readers of the Gospel would appreciate immediately, for it was the ordinary rhythm of the Christian mission. The Acts of the Apostles gives us all the evidence we need. The missionary comes to a new town. He finds the synagogue, preaches there on Sabbath, and has a mixed reception. He withdraws into the house of his first or chief convert, the 'firstfruit of the city', and there exercises an effective and less impeded ministry. The house becomes the local church, and the householder leader, *prohistamenos*, ultimately bishop.

With such a model before our eyes, we see the one-day mission to Capernaum (1, 21–39) as absolutely typical. Jesus begins in the synagogue on Sabbath, performs one cure, and 'shocks' or 'amazes' the congregation. He withdraws to the house of Simon, his first and chief convert, and there performs not one cure only but a multitude of cures. He goes on to preach elsewhere, but Simon's house remains his headquarters, and Simon becomes Peter, the rock on whom the Church is built. The Petrine texts in Matthew XVI make the point explicit. St Mark, as his manner is, leaves it to be understood.

Desert and Promised Land, synagogue and house-church, cleansing and resurrection—such, then, is the rhythm into which St Mark settles as he writes I, 12–II, 12. When we were previously examining the pattern of healing by itself, we observed that the first four healing miracles appeared as two pairs, containing variations on the same theme, purification and restoration. Later on we said that we could not be content to see the healing pattern as a thing by itself; we must see it as arising naturally out of the whole rhythm of St Mark's writing. We may now venture modestly to claim that we have executed part of our programme. We have seen how the two pairs of miracles in I, 21–II, 12 arise naturally out of the general alternating rhythm of the first chapter. We have shown how that rhythm makes the second pair cover the same ground as the first, or, to put it otherwise, makes it develop variations on the same theme.

So far, so good. But what are we going to find next? Alternating rhythm has brought us so far; will it carry us any farther? Let us pause, and consider probability and reason. In a previous chapter we laid bare a healing pattern having some complexity of structure. The healing pattern, we have confessed, is not the whole pattern of the book, but the healing pattern has got to find a place in the total pattern. The total pattern, therefore, cannot be less complex than the healing pattern, or how is the healing pattern to find a place in it? The total pattern, then, cannot consist of anything so elementary as mere alternating rhythm.

Alternating rhythm has carried St Mark so far; it has thrown up four healings arranged in two pairs. To judge by the way in which he manages the rest of his Gospel, it would seem that he became aware of the four as a four as soon as he had completed it. Here were four healings in two pairs, matching the four apostles, the two pairs of brethren, whose calls he had narrated earlier. The persons called thus balanced the persons healed; he would tell of no more healing until he had described some further calling.

Such a balance between calling and healing may seem to us perfectly senseless, but that is to prejudge the significance St

Mark attached to callings and healings. Christ would, in the end, call twelve apostles. It is not St Mark who records how he promised them thrones over the twelve tribes of Israel (Matthew XIX, 28, Luke XXII, 30), but we shall see reason to allow that he was well aware of the symbolism of their number. If St Mark tells off persons healed against apostles called, is he not showing us that Christ has a mission to all Israel, and that he heals all Israel from every sort of disease? There is nothing absurd or far-fetched in such a suggestion. We shall develop it when we have collected a little more evidence. For the present let it stand by way of hypothesis.

Whatever the value of the hypothesis may be, there is no disputing the fact. After narrating four callings and a block of four healings, St Mark proceeds to narrate a single calling (of Levi) and a single healing (of the withered hand). The old ground he has to cover (the four callings and the four healings) occupies five full paragraphs, and the new development in which he covers it takes five paragraphs as well (II, 13–III, 12). A cycle of five matching a cycle of five—here is something more ambitious than alternating rhythm, for alternating rhythm matches two against two.

But the five new paragraphs do not cover the five old paragraphs one by one. It is easy to see why they do not. The five old paragraphs are made up as follows: one is devoted to the call of the four, and one each to each of the four healings. If the new cycle covered the old cycle paragraph by paragraph, we should have four healings again. But the plan of the new cycle is that we shall have only one. It looks, in fact, as though the first two paragraphs of the old five would give St Mark all the model he needs to work upon: one call-story and one healing. But that would mean leaving three paragraphs of the old five unused, and the last of the three at that. What he has written in these three last paragraphs should be freshest in St Mark's mind, and it is not very likely that what he writes next will fail to be coloured by what he has just written. If he writes with his eyes on the first two paragraphs of the old five, he will see them *through* the three later paragraphs, in the sense in which one sees the farther part of the aquarium through the nearer part. And it will be easy for him to do this, because the old alternating rhythm has matched the third and fourth of these five paragraphs with the first and second; so he can easily see the first through the third, and the second through the fourth: he can see the call of Simon through the story of Christ in Simon's house, and the exorcism of the unclean spirit through the cleansing of the leper.

Perhaps the language of seeing an earlier paragraph 'through' a later is not particularly useful. Let us say more simply that St Mark fuses two models into one, and writes a single antitype to them. That is to say, he writes a new narrative which reflects both the first and third paragraphs, and another which reflects both the second and fourth. But what about the fifth? It is added in with the second and fourth, for good measure. We may illustrate the relations between model and antitype in the following figure:

Call of Simon
Sabbath exorcism   Call of Levi; in Levi's house
In Simon's house
Leper cleansed   Sabbath-Law and sabbath healing;
Paralytic raised   the withered hand

St Mark reduces his model to two points, but he does not treat the two points in two paragraphs. He expands the first point into two paragraphs, and the second point into three, and so the antitype is as long as the model.

This sounds rather mystifying in the abstract description: the concrete facts are clear enough. Does II, 13–22 reflect both I, 16–20 and I, 29–39? Does II, 23–III, 12 reflect both I, 21–28 and I, 40–II, 12? It is plain that the answer to both questions is 'yes'.

To take the first question first. Does the story of Levi reflect both Simon's call and Simon's entertainment of Jesus? Plainly it does. We read how Jesus goes 'again' by the sea; he was last there when he called Simon and his three companions. This time he calls Levi, and he calls him from the midst of his trade, as he had called those other four from the midst of theirs. He bids him follow, and he follows at a word. All this in a couple of verses; the substance of the paragraph begins with the transference of the scene to Levi's house. Jesus eats in Levi's house, as he had eaten in Simon's. In Simon's house Jesus had acted as physician to the very person who got him his dinner. In Levi's house the same thing is said to happen, but in a spiritual manner. Levi has made Jesus a feast, and many more like Levi, publicans and law-breakers, share it. The Pharisees criticize his eating with publicans and sinners, and Jesus gives the defence: 'It is not the whole who need the physician, but the sick.' This part of the saying carries us no farther than Levi's house, or its prototype, Simon's. But a second part is added, which carries us out to the shore, where both Simon and Levi were called: 'I came not to *call* the righteous, but sinners.'

Jesus answers the Pharisaic criticism, but it is interesting that it is addressed not to him but to his disciples. The Pharisees see a strange new community round Levi's table, and they attack it. 'And it came to pass that Jesus sat to meat in Levi's house, and many publicans and sinners sat with Jesus and with his disciples; for his disciples were numerous, and they went about with him.' To the Christian mind, the new fellowship is there in germ when Christ sits down to eat in Simon's house with four companions. In Levi's house the fellowship begins to manifest its peculiar marks and draw upon itself the criticism of the orthodox. Jesus and his disciples feast with the wrong people—we have heard the answer to that. But they also feast on the wrong days, and a new paragraph is required to set forth the answer to that (II, 18–22).

It is a Monday or a Thursday, and John's disciples keep the customary fast no less carefully than the Pharisees; Jesus and his disciples do not. Jesus's reply deals first with the particular point, and then generalizes the debate. The new society has its own life, and is different from the old. The new cloth cannot be patched on the old garment, nor the new wine contained in the old

leather. Such is the summing up of the fact that Jesus has called
disciples, and formed them into a table-fellowship.

We pass on to the second part of the Levi-cycle (II, 23–III, 12).
The transition is perfectly smooth. We are still reading of
Pharisaic criticism against the new fellowship, and the criticism
still has something to do with eating. But the scene has changed
from the set meal indoors to the casual plucking of ears in a
cornfield; and the criticism is not on the disciples' eating what
they pluck, but on their plucking what they eat. For it is Sabbath,
a good day on which to feast, but a bad day on which to gather
food. A negligent attitude to Sabbath rule is the real point. We
are no longer on the ground of Christ calling Simon and eating
in his house, we are approaching the ground of Christ exorcizing
in synagogue on Sabbath day (I, 21–28). In I a single paragraph
describes how (a) Jesus entered synagogue on Sabbath and
taught with a degree of personal authority surpassing that of
the scribes presiding there; (b) how, still on Sabbath and in
synagogue, he exorcised. In II–III the matter is distributed between
two paragraphs. (a) The first paragraph tells us how Christ, on
Sabbath but not yet in synagogue, used the authority of the Son
of Man to override the Sabbath rule of the scribes, citing the
example of David. David had done more: he had overridden the
authority, not of scribes in synagogue, but of priests in the
temple. (b) A second paragraph shows us Christ imitating the
example of David: he enters the synagogue on Sabbath, and
overrules the scribes by healing a man with a withered hand in
spite of their critical attitude.

The subject of the privileges of the Levitical priesthood is
drawn into the cornfield story by way of comment and analogy.
And so the cornfield paragraph combines the subject of Sabbath
with the subject of priestly privilege; that is to say, it combines
the theme of exorcism on Sabbath (I, 21–28) with the theme of
the cleansing of the leper (I, 40–45). As the exorcism on Sabbath
challenged Sabbath rule, so the cleansing of the leper challenged
priestly privilege, for Moses had given the cleansing of the leper
to the priests (Lev. XIII–XIV). When Jesus cleansed the leper,

he was careful to respect the priests' rights. He sent him to make his offering and register his cure; there was no conflict there between the priestly law and the merciful aims of God's Anointed; both could be upheld. It had been otherwise when God's Anointed had wanted bread for himself and his hungry friends: he had gone into the temple in the days of Abiathar and taken the shewbread (I Sam. xxi). There was a conflict between law and need; and so there is when Christ desires food for his disciples or healing for the sick on Sabbath day.

The sequel to the cleansing of the leper was that Christ 'could no more openly come into town, but was without in desert places; and they came to him from every quarter'. The sequel to the withered hand greatly enlarges on this model, and makes a paragraph of itself (III, 7–12). Christ withdraws once more, though for a more urgent reason. He is threatened with death, and not merely with mobbing. But when he has withdrawn, he is mobbed as well, for once more 'they came to him from every quarter'. The 'quarters' are now particularized: Galilee, Judaea, Jerusalem, Idumaea, Transjordan, Phoenicia. And the mobbing is such that Jesus has recourse to the expedient of the boat. It stands off-shore, ready to remove him in case of need.

We have said nothing so far about the special quality of the miracle in III, I–6, the restoration of the hand; and this is where the third of St Mark's models, the paragraph of the paralytic, makes its influence most obviously felt. Our whole analysis of the healing pattern showed the importance of the pairing of atrophied hand with paralysed feet; the one is the natural complement of the other, just as blind eyes are the natural complement of deaf ears. Such a link between II, I–12 and III, I–6 is strong enough by itself, but it is reinforced by two additional points of comparison. Each miracle is wrought as an open sign of Christ's authority in face of Pharisaic criticism; and each miracle both follows and illustrates a saying about the authority or lordship of the Son of Man. He has the authority to forgive sins, therefore he sets the paralytic on his feet; he is lord of Sabbath, therefore he heals the withered hand.

St Mark profits by the division of II, 23–III, 12 among several paragraphs, and distributes the unwieldy bulk of the paragraph about the paralytic into a more comfortable form. The dispute which leads up to the first saying about the Son of Man is actually packed into the heart of the paragraph of the paralytic (II, 6–10). A corresponding dispute leading up to the second saying about the Son of Man is more happily managed in II, 23–III, 6: it stands by itself in a distinct paragraph preceding the paragraph about the withered hand.

There is a very generally accepted analysis of the paragraph of the paralytic which illustrates the principles of form-criticism in a truly classical manner, and it seems right to pay attention to it, if only to make clear by contrast the principles on which we are proceeding. The form-critical analysis is made in terms of standard types of story, assumed to be characteristic of the primitive Christian tradition. There is a proper and shapely form of healing story, of which several perfect specimens are preserved in the Gospels; the student may cut them out, and paste them in his note-book side by side. Again, there is the type of dispute story, in which the narrative setting is restrained within suitable limits; of this type also rows of specimens can be found, and placed in the student's note-book. Judged by the standard of these two types, the paragraph of the paralytic is a manifest hybrid. A complete healing miracle has been distended to embrace a complete dispute within its womb. It cannot have grown there; it must have been artificially inserted by editorial violence.

Such form-criticism places the paragraph of the paralytic in an hypothetical series of pre-Marcan oral paragraphs, and complains that it does not fit. We would prefer to see it placed in the actual series of St Mark's paragraphs, where we find that it fits perfectly. We cannot study the evolution of pre-Marcan oral stories because we have not got them. But we can study the evolution of the Marcan written story, for it evolves under our very eyes, as one paragraph elaborates upon another and the antitype improves upon its model.

74

We find no special difficulty with the paragraph of the paralytic. St Mark does not glue it together out of the healing story type and the dispute story type, because up to this point the dispute story type has no literary existence. The story of the paralytic contains the first dispute story in gospel literature. Here the new type is born, and we are permitted to assist at the birth.

From the very beginning the Marcan healing story has carried the germ of dispute within it, but it has been no more than a germ. Christ exorcizes in synagogue, and the congregation are shocked or amazed, they do not know what to make of it. Christ cleanses the leper, and a dispute with priestly privilege threatens but is averted. Christ forgives the sinful paralytic, and the dispute unfolds fully grown. The result is, if you like to say so, a strained paragraph; but this is the birth of a new form and birth is a thing of strain. There is nothing unnatural or morbid about it, however, so long as the process of delivery is not unduly prolonged. It would be unnatural, if St Mark went on writing paragraphs like the paralytic; but he does not. Having brought the dispute story to the birth, he gives it separate existence; it proceeds to show its independent vitality in a series of paragraphs. (Eating with sinners, eating on fast-days, plucking the ears of corn.) And so, when his cyclic rhythm brings him round to the composition of an antitype to the paralytic, he writes it in two parts, first the dispute, then the healing.

But we have yet to meet what is to many the most serious of the form-critical arguments, the grammatical argument. It is claimed that the syntax is so outrageous at the point where dispute ends and healing resumes, that anyone can detect a clumsy editorial suture. The passage complained about is as follows: 'Why reason ye thus in your hearts? Which is easier: to say to the paralytic, Thy sins are forgiven thee, or to say, Arise, take up they bed and walk? But that ye may know that the Son of Man hath authority on earth to forgive sins—he saith to the paralytic, I say unto thee, Arise, take up thy bed and go to thy house. And he arose, and straightway taking up his bed, went forth.'

What is there to complain of here? The effect is magnificent, and could not be bettered. Such is my judgement, and I claim to follow St Matthew and St Luke. Those two evangelists are commonly and rightly credited with sharp eyes for detecting St Mark's primitive roughnesses, but they knew better than to touch this one. Perhaps they realized that if they did they would not be able to stop there, but would have to extend their reforming zeal to the wording of a famous Old Testament text, Exodus IV, 4–5. How was Moses to accredit himself to the elders of Israel? God gave him a sign to work, bidding him throw down his staff. It became a serpent on the ground. Then 'the Lord said to Moses, Put forth thy hand, and take it by the tail. So he put forth his hand, and took it by the tail, and it became a staff in his hand—that they may believe that the Lord God of their fathers has appeared to thee'.

Both in Exodus IV and in Mark II a 'that' (*hina*) clause concerned with belief in divinely given authority is made to have its grammatical dependence not upon a statement, but on an attesting action. Exodus does not say: 'I bid you take up the snake, and I make it a staff again in your hand, that they may believe. . . .' Nor does Mark say, 'That ye may know . . . I command the paralytic to arise, and enable him to do so'. It is superfluous to talk, when action supplies the place of words. A boy says to me, 'To show you whether I can jump three feet' and jumps a three-foot-six hurdle. Or he jumps first, and adds, 'Just to show if I can jump three feet'. Exodus places the action first, and the 'to show' clause second; St Mark has things the other way about. Both in St Mark and in Exodus the action which 'shows them' is complex: it consists of a divine command and its fulfilment. 'The Lord said to Moses, Put forth thy hand and take it by the tail. So he put forth his hand, and took it by the tail, and it became a staff in his hand—*that they may believe*. . . .' And in the Gospel: '*That ye may know* . . . —he saith to the paralytic: I bid thee arise, take up thy bed, and go to thy house. And he arose and took up his bed straightway and went forth.'

Needless to say, St Mark is not, in our view, writing in independence of Exodus. On the contrary, he is writing a Gospel parallel to the incident of Moses's staff. The sign of the staff was the first of several signs given by God to Moses; the purpose of them was to convince the elders of the congregation that he had authority to deliver from bondage. St Mark's text describes the first sign given by Jesus explicitly as a sign; and the purpose of it is to convince the elders of the congregation that he has authority to deliver from sin. The parallel between Moses and Jesus becomes presently open and unmistakable, when Jesus gives a second sign, and precipitates an exodus like that which Moses led out of Egypt (III, 3-12).

The critical digression which we made in examining a well-known analysis of the cure of the paralytic has proved useful to our own argument after all. For our present business is to show in how many ways the withered hand is the pair to the paralysed feet. And our critical digression, by referring us to Exodus, has revealed a fresh and very striking way in which the one healing pairs with the other. They are a pair, for they are the two signs shown by a greater than Moses to the elders of Israel in warrant of his authority. The crawling staff was the first of Moses's signs, and the second was the sign of the hand. As soon as the Divine Voice had finished teaching Moses the sign of the staff, in the words we have just been discussing, it proceeded to teach him the sign of the hand. He was to make his own hand leprous, and then restore it. 'And,' said the Divine Voice, 'if they will not believe thee nor hearken to the message of the first sign, they will believe the message of the latter sign' (Exodus IV, 8). And, in the case of Moses, so it proved. But Jesus showed the elders of Israel a second sign, the sign of the hand restored, and they believed neither the second sign nor the first. Moses convinced the elders, it was Pharaoh he could not convince. But the elders of Israel, the Pharisees, were Pharaoh to Christ; they it was whose hardened heart turned Mercy from them hot with anger, they who practised with the royal power against his life (Mark III, 5-6, cf. Exodus X, 27-28, XI, 8).

The sign of the hand in Exodus was the sign of the *leprous* hand. One of St Mark's models for the withered hand is the healing of the leper. It is as though the one Mosaic sign were divided and made to furnish two gospel signs: 'the leprous hand restored' becomes (a) the leper cleansed (like Naaman), and (b) the hand restored (like Jeroboam's, I Kings XIII, 6). The point is not of great importance, and the web of associations is so thick that we do not know which to single out for mention.

To return to a more important point, the second Mosaic sign having been refused by the hardened heart, Christ makes his exodus. 'He withdrew', a word not elsewhere used by St Mark, but current in his time for a whosesale withdrawal of population; when for example the Egyptian peasants abandoned their fields and took to the mountains in strike against the taxes. Jesus, then, withdrew, followed by a great multitude; and his withdrawal, like Moses', was towards the sea; and he used the water, as Moses had done, to bar pursuit. His next act will be to make a covenant on a mountain (III, 13–19). But that is to anticipate.

The last sentence of the exodus scene, with all the demons on their knees acknowledging the Son of God, rings like a doxology and fitly closes the cycle. The previous cycle ended with a doxology also. 'All were amazed and glorified God, saying, We never saw the like' (II, 12).

We have now followed St Mark through two changes of rhythm. We have seen an alternating rhythm of little paragraphs (I, 1–15) develop into an alternating rhythm of paragraphs three times as long (I, 16–II, 12). Then we have seen alternating rhythm give place to cyclic rhythm (II, 13–III, 12), a theme of calling and healing in five paragraphs being gone over again with variations in five new paragraphs. St Mark's total rhythm is now in step with the rhythm of the healing pattern which we studied in a chapter by itself. It looks as though each block of healings, and each annexed healing, is going to be the heart of a separate cycle. If so, we may reasonably hope that the rest of our task will not be so puzzling. If the beat of the rhythm does not keep changing, but goes on steadily in one cycle after another, we shall have a more straightforward phenomenon to describe.

CHAPTER IV

SECOND AND THIRD DOUBLE CYCLES

There is no impression I should be so sorry to convey as that St Mark's Gospel is a sort of learned acrostic. We are analysing the rhythm of a living process. The analysis is, of course, analytical, but the process is alive. St Mark used certain symbolical conventions, but they were his instruments and not his masters. He could use them without any painful labour of building them up, because they were current in his world. We reconstruct them with pain, but that is because we are men of a different generation. Even so we can recognize how simple and how fundamental the ideas are which his symbolism expresses. The elements of his cyclic movement, as we have so far experienced it, are calling and healing. And what could be closer to the heart of the Gospel than these things? They concern the relation of every Christian man to Christ. But the call of the Christian, and the healing of the Christian, are not private to him alone. He is called as a member of the Israel of God, and God's Israel is a mystical person, a body of Christ, healed in all its members by the divine physician. Christ had expressed this by giving a first and special calling to twelve men, as it were his twelvefold Israel in germ. And St Mark continues and deepens that divine symbol, by setting persons healed in comparison with apostles called. In this way it is to be shown that all Israel is not only called but healed.

His method for making the comparison is the fundamentally simple one of numerical equivalence. Simon and his three companions are called in one group, Simon's mother-in-law and three other persons are healed in a corresponding group, and that makes St Mark's first cycle. Levi is called alone, and the man with the withered hand is healed alone, and that makes his second cycle. We have now to see what the third is like. Will it show us another small group of callings, followed by a small and equal group of healings? Are we going to read, let us say, of Philip, Bartholomew and Matthew called from the cornfield or the vineyard, and then of three healings to correspond—Legion, the impure woman, and Jairus's child? Surely it is not necessary for the evangelist to inflict upon us such monotony. By balancing four healings against four callings, and one healing against one calling, has he not done enough to make the balance of healings and callings plain?

There is, after all, something that he must want very much to say, as soon as the ground is well enough prepared for him to say it. The very meaning of his numerical symbolism is the twelvefold wholeness of Israel, both Israel called and Israel healed; and this meaning cannot be effectively expressed by the calling of the Twelve in small groups or by instalments. It is necessary to describe their corporate vocation, and that is what St Mark does at the beginning of his third cycle (III, 13–19). The name-list of the whole twelve is given. If we force the new call narrative into the forms of the old, and try to regard it as a call of new disciples additional to those already called, we shall have to say that it adds eight new apostles; for the names of Simon, James, John and Andrew are old. St Mark spills out all his eight remaining apostolic names at a single throw; but the healings of the eight persons who are to correspond with them are not similarly recounted one after another in a single group. We have already described how St Mark distributes them: three in chapter V, two in VII, one in VIII, one in IX, and one in X.

The name of Levi is not in the apostolic list. If it were, there would be thirteen apostles. But as Levi's call has a healing to correspond with it, there are thirteen healings, one for each of the twelve, and one for Levi. Levi's name is, as it were, cancelled by omission from the apostolic list, but the corresponding healing, the restoration of the withered hand, is not cancelled; there it stands on an equal footing with all the other healings the evangelist records. So there are twelve apostles, and thirteen healings. Anomalous, perhaps, but no more anomalous than the Biblical reckoning of the Israelite tribes. There were twelve tribes by conventional reckoning, but one of them, Joseph, counted as two, both in fact and in right; Joseph was 'Ephraim and Manasseh.' So the number of Israel was both twelve and thirteen. If St Mark has twelve apostles and thirteen persons healed, he has represented Christ's mission to all Israel in a very balanced way.

By recording in III, 13–19, the call of the whole twelve rather than the call of a further small apostolic group, St Mark develops the suggestions of the context. Let us recall what that context is. After giving the sign of the withered hand to hardened hearts, Jesus made an exodus, like Moses, towards the sea. After the Red Sea Moses came to Mt Sinai. The next scene of the Gospel must be a Sinai covenant. Jesus, like Moses, goes up into the mountain (III, 13). If Jesus's covenant is to be like Moses's, it must embrace a whole twelvefold Israel, at least in symbol. He must call to him a whole twelve, and constitute them the germ and token of the people of God. 'He called to him whom he would, and they went to him. And he made twelve, that they might be with him, and that he might send them to preach, and to have authority to cast out demons.'

So far we have studied the unlikeness of the new Marcan cycle to the old, rather than the similarity. Nevertheless, a call-story is a call-story, and the calling of the Twelve holds in the new cycle the place held by the call of Levi in the cycle before it, and by the call of Simon and his companions in the cycle before that.

The immediate sequel to Levi's call was Levi's feasting of Christ, and Levi's feasting of Christ stood on the background of Simon's entertainment of Christ. The immediate sequel to the call of the Twelve is a return 'home' (to Simon's, presumably) for a meal. But this time the meal is never eaten, so besieged they are by the crowds (III, 20). It seems as though nothing Christ does can please his critics. He eats, and they take exception to the company and the day (II, 13–22). He puts his work before his food, and people say he is unbalanced by his enthusiasm; his family come to save him from himself, and scribes from Jerusalem pronounce his 'madness' to be downright possession: it is the Satan in him that masters the demons in his patients.

Jesus answers both the malice of the scribes and the misdirected zeal of his family. The answer to the family is of particular interest in the present connexion, because it brings out a new aspect of the fact that Christ's table (had he but leisure to sit down to it) is in Simon's house. He has migrated from Nazareth to a new family, and he resists pressure put upon him to return. But the meaning of his migration is not simply that he has adopted the hearth of Simon at Capernaum instead of the hearth of Mary at Nazareth. The new family is of a new kind. 'Who are my mother and my brethren?' he said. 'And looking round upon those who sat about him, Behold, he said, my mother and my brethen. Whoever does the will of God is my brother or sister or mother' (III, 33–35). We remember that James and John sacrificed family connexion for the gospel (I, 20). We now perceive that Jesus himself has made the same sacrifice.

We are trying to see how far St Mark's new cycle (III, 13–VI, 6) follows the model of his last (II, 13–III, 12). So far we have compared the call of the Twelve with the call of Levi, and Christ criticized for not eating in Simon's house with Christ criticized for eating in Levi's house. The next piece of the old is the cornfield incident (II, 23–28) and the next piece of the new is the cornfield parable, with all the teaching which is made to hang upon it (IV, 1–34). The theme of the cornfield comes from the model in II, but it takes a completely fresh direction in obedience to the requirements of its immediate context. Christ has been answering the scribes 'in parables' (III, 23). He has also been adopting as his family those who sit to hear his word, and fulfil it as the will of God (III, 34–35). He uses the image of the cornfield to show what it is for men to hear his word and do it, and what it is for the truth to be uttered in parables. We are not here concerned to examine the cornfield discourses, but merely to point out that being cornfield discourses they answer to the acted lesson of the cornfield in II.

The next piece of the old cycle is the healing of the withered hand in synagogue. Now when we were examining the healing miracles by themselves, in an earlier chapter, we saw that they came in alternate 'blocks' and 'annexes', and that one block appeared to be modelled on the block before it. This ought to mean that the model for the block we have in front of us (V) is to be found in the previous block (I, 21–II, 12) and not in the annexe of that block, which is the withered hand (III, 1–6). That is to say, that whereas the directly previous cycle (II, 13– III, 12) has served St Mark so far as the model for his new cycle (III, 13 ff.), when he comes to the healing miracles of the new cycle he must desert his model, and go a cycle back to find the model he requires. He is going to write three healings as a condensation of the four he wrote in I—II. We will presently turn to see how he does it; but for the present we will observe how, after having done it, he returns to the model he had temporarily deserted and brings the conclusion of his new cycle into line with the conclusion of its direct predecessor. The result of the healing of the withered hand was a rejection in synagogue, and a withdrawal of Christ (III, 6–12). After describing the three healings in V, St Mark appends another scene of rejection in synagogue and of withdrawal elsewhere (VI, 1–6). It belongs to the healing of the withered hand to be performed in synagogue, and directly to occasion the rejection of Christ by the Pharisees. It belongs to the last miracle of the three in V to be performed secretly, and not in synagogue; it is the raising of Jairus's child. St Mark has recourse to a favourite device and supplies a double antitype to a single model. In the model, Christ heals in synagogue and is rejected. In the antitype, Christ heals in the house of the ruler of synagogue (there is something synagogal about the place after all, then) and afterwards enters a synagogue, teaches, and is rejected. The synagogue is that of his native town. His own fatherland rejects him, a premonition of his rejection by the Jewish people.

We must turn now to St Mark's treatment of his other model I, 21–II, 12, in the great miracles of IV, 35–V, 43. When we were analysing the pattern of healing miracles by itself, we pointed out that the three healings in V are not arranged as a simple three, 1 + 1 + 1. There are three miracles, indeed, but they are arranged as an expanded pair, the second member of the pair having a third miracle inserted into it by way of a parenthesis. We begin with the exorcism of Legion, and proceed direct to the story of Jairus's child. But while Jesus is following Jairus to his house, the cleansing of the impure woman intervenes. Then he goes on, and raises the child. So much we observed before. Let us now consider what the curious arrangement of the three as an expanded pair involves in the matter of St Mark's use of his model.

It seems obvious that the first pair of miracles in I—II is the model for the basic pair in v. The exorcism of Legion corresponds to the exorcism in synagogue, and Christ entering Simon's house with Simon, Andrew, James and John to take Simon's mother-in-law by the hand and raise her up is the model of Christ entering Jairus's house with Simon, James and John to take Jairus's daughter by the hand and raise her up. There is even a significant parallel between Simon's house, the house of the 'firstfruit' convert who becomes ruler of the Church, and the house of Jairus, ruler of the Jewish synagogue.

If so, what does St Mark do with the latter pair of miracles in I—II, the leper and the paralytic? It appears that he sets them *both* in parallel with the second of the former pair. The story of Jairus's child has both a single model (Peter's mother-in-law) and a double model (the leper and the paralytic). Regarded as the antitype to the single model, it is one story, how Jesus raised Jairus's child (with a halt on the way). Regarded as the antitype to the double model, it is two stories: how Jesus cleansed the impure woman (in antitype to the leper) and raised the dead girl (in antitype to the paralytic). We remember how strongly the symbolism of death and funeral was expressed in the story of the paralytic. When Jesus enters Jairus's house, there has been an actual death, and an actual funeral has begun. Another feature which the Jairus story takes up from the cure of the paralytic is the part played by the faith of relatives or friends. Seeing the faith of the paralytic's bearers Christ said to him first 'Thy sins are forgiven thee' and at length 'Rise up and walk'. Similarly all he required for the raising of Jairus's daughter was the faith of Jairus himself: 'Fear not,' he said to him, 'only believe.'

Shall we say, reverting to a previous language, that St Mark sees the raising of Simon's wife's mother 'through' the pair of miracles which directly follow it? Shall we even say that the pair of subsequent miracles split the image of Peter's wife's mother herself, so that she reappears in two distinct antitypes? In so far as she is the adult woman healed by Christ, she appears as the woman twelve years afflicted with impurity: in so far as she is the relative raised from bed at the intercession of her family, she reappears in the twelve-year-old daughter of Jairus. But to talk like this is to say we know not what.

In any case it seems harmless to say that a single model, the story of Peter's wife's mother, receives a double antitype. What we have now to show is that St Mark balances his narrative by giving a double antitype also to the predecessor of the miracle in Peter's house, the exorcism in synagogue. But, we may protest, if there are two antitypes to the miracle in the synagogue and two to the miracle in the house, we shall have four antitypes in all; whereas the cycle with which we are concerned has only three healings, and its position in St Mark's whole pattern allows for no more. Certainly; but the awkward consequence can be avoided if one of the antitypes is not a healing at all, but a miracle of a different kind. And so it proves; the two antitypes to the exorcism in synagogue are the exorcism of the wind (IV, 35–41) and the exorcism of Legion (V, 1–20). And the exorcism of the wind is not a healing.

The parcelling out of the features of the exorcism in synagogue between the exorcism of the wind and the exorcism of the Legion is anyhow unmistakable. The first point to be grasped is that 'wind' and 'spirit' are one thing to the Biblical mind. The demon in synagogue was exorcised under the name of 'unclean spirit', that is to say, 'unholy breath'. It is no great step from this to the exorcising of the rugged breath which the storm lets loose on the sea. All we need do is to compare the actual texts.

(A man possessed by an unclean spirit) cried, saying. . . . Thou art come to destroy us. . . . And Jesus rebuked it (the spirit), saying, Be muzzled. . . . And it came out. . . . And they were all dumb-founded, so that they questioned one with another, saying, What is this? . . . He commands even the unclean spirits and they obey him (I, 24–27).

(The disciples overmastered by the wind) say to him. . . . Carest thou not that we are destroyed? And . . . he rebuked the wind and said. . . . Be muzzled. And the wind ceased. . . . And they feared a great fear, and said one to another: Who then is this, that the wind and the sea obey him? (IV, 38–41).

And straightway there was a man with an unclean spirit . . . and he cried, saying, What have we to do with thee, Jesus . . . Holy One of God? And Jesus said . . . Come out of him. And he came out of him. . . . And the fame of him (Jesus) went forth into all the neighbourhood of Galilee (I, 23–28).

And straightway there met him a man with an unclean spirit . . . and crying with a loud voice he said, What have I to do with thee, Jesus, Son of God most High? . . . For he said to him, Come out . . . of the man. . . . And the unclean spirit came forth. . . . And the man went out and began to proclaim in Decapolis what Jesus had done for him, and all marvelled (V, 2–20).

The exorcism in synagogue appears actually to call for the elaborations it receives in the exorcisms of the wind and of the Legion. For the exorcism in synagogue contains two confusions of identity and the two new exorcisms clear them up. The confusions of identity are (a) between the possessed man and the spirit possessing him, (b) between the spirit possessing the man, and the host of Beelzebul in general. Let us observe these two confusions one by one, and show how the new exorcism stories clear them up.

(a) It is apparently the *man* who cries out in synagogue; but what he says in his cry is not the utterance of the man, but of the demon, and it is the demon, not the man, who is rebuked. Nevertheless the evangelist does not want to say that possession leaves its victim personally unaffected, or that man himself does not shrink with fear, and doubt the issue, when Christ and the Holy Ghost intervene for him against the tyranny of evil. The point can be made clear if we take a different case, where the breath of evil is not maddening men's thoughts, but beating down their sails. In such a case it is unambiguously the voice of man himself which cries 'We are destroyed'. Here as there Christ saves man by 'muzzling' the breath of evil. But in the case of the storm it can be clearly seen that man himself earns rebuke for lack of confidence in the presence of divine power. 'Why are ye fearful? Have ye not yet faith?' And still 'they feared a great fear, and said one to another, Who is this?'

(b) The demon in synagogue says, 'Away from *us*, Jesus of Nazareth, thou art come to destroy us', as who might say, 'Hands off the servants of Beelzebul'. He goes on to speak in his own name, '*I* know thee who thou art, Holy One of God'. The story of the Legion clears up the equivocation between the one and the many. The demoniac cries out, as the other had done, when he sees Christ, but unambiguously in the single number: 'Away from *me*, Jesus, Son of God Most High: I conjure thee by God, torment *me* not.' In answer Christ constrains the demon to confess his name, and in naming himself he throws off the mask of unity and confesses himself to be a multitude. 'Legion is my name, for we are many.' So long as the demons possess one man, their number is concealed, and they pass under a single name. But when, in their vain attempt to escape destruction, they allow themselves to be distributed among two thousand swine, a regiment of Satan's host is visibly displayed.

When the legion of demonic swine are lost in the waters, the story of the demoniac is brought into a fresh relation with the story of the storm. The host of the wicked perish in the waves, through which divine intervention has brought the disciples safely. We may recall the waters of the Red Sea, through which Israel was wonderfully brought, and in which the Egyptians drowned. The new exodus delivers not from political, but from spiritual oppression; the enemy is Satan and not Pharaoh. And the waters which have to be passed are not the waters of the Red Sea but the waters of the Passion; then it is that Christ supremely shows his divine tranquillity and brings the ark of the Church through, while his disciples panic; and in the Passion the whole power of Satan is destroyed. The waters of the Passion are the waters of baptism, where men are initiated into Christ's death. By that initiation they put the sea of eternal death behind them, and leave their demonic enemies drowning in the font. They put off madness and oppression; they are clothed with holiness and made vocal in thanksgiving to God.

Thus to allegorize may be to bring out the spiritual sense of what St Mark writes, and to clarify the relation between exorcism and baptismal water as he sees it. But in St Mark's narrative the things we have been speaking of are concrete symbols and not allegories, and it would be a gross error to suppose that he began with doctrine, advanced to allegory, and incarnated allegory into factual narrative. He begins, of course, from fact, from the traditions of Christ's mighty works; but under the breath of his inspiration, and in the building up of his Gospel, the facts fall into such a pattern that, like true works of God, they become expressive, and are no less words than deeds.

We cannot speak of the tradition as it existed before St Mark wrote; we can speak only of the way in which the literary form takes shape in the writing. For that is open to our inspection. And from the point of view of such a study, we have been assisting at the birth of a fresh story-type, the miracle at sea. We have seen it spring like a side-shoot from the stock of the exorcism narrative. In much the same way we saw at an earlier point how the dispute story arose like a child ripe for birth within the bosom of the restoration narrative. The dispute story, once born, began to enjoy an independent existence in a whole series of examples. The miracle at sea also has a subsequent and independent history, but in a single example only, the walking on the water (VI, 45–52). The walking on the water is of immediate and peculiar interest to us, as we will now proceed to show. But first of all we must make the transition from the cycle we have been discussing (III, 13–VI, 6) to a new cycle (VI, 7–56).

The new cycle is much shorter than the old, but that is not surprising, since it is an 'annexe' cycle and the old was a 'block' cycle. It may be shorter than its predecessor, but it is longer than either of the cycles before that. Like those two first cycles, it consists of five paragraphs, but some of the paragraphs are longer than those in I, 14–II, 12 or II, 13–III, 12.

The new cycle is modelled on its predecessor, with certain

notable omissions; of which the most striking is the omission of all particular healing miracle whatever. It was this strange fact which was symbolized in our dream by the statement that the annexe to the third restaurant was shut. In the imagery of the dream, we were only concerned with shops, not with the houses between them, and shops stood for healing miracles. This shop was shut: that is to say, there was no healing miracle in that place. But if so, why did the dreamer see a closed shop, and not just no shop at all? The closed shop is at least like enough to a working shop to hold its place in the row of buildings, and make up the rhythm of the street, that 'four-one, three-(one), two-one, one-one' series of shops which we found so interesting. Can it be that St Mark had at his command a literary feature which, though not a healing miracle, might be felt to do duty for one?

The answer is to be found in that new offshoot from the stock of healing, the miracle at sea. We have seen that the block of miracles in IV, 35-V, 43 is a single closely knit system of four mighty acts, the stilling of the storm, the exorcism of Legion, the cleansing of the impure woman, and the raising of Jairus's child. In VI, 45-56 St Mark comes to write an antitype to these miracles. What the rest of his Gospel would lead us to expect would be a single healing, in antitype to the raising of Jairus's child, and, in the special sense we have given to the words, by way of 'pair' or 'annexe' to it. But a 'pair' or 'annexe' has to to be a supplement, as the restoration of the hand supplements that of the feet, or the restoration of sight supplements the restoration of hearing. And there is no supplement to the restoration of the whole person. And so, out of the complex of mighty acts in IV, 35-V, 43, St Mark selects the act which is not a healing, and provides it with a particular antitype; the walking on the water answers the stilling of the storm. The healing miracles of V receive no particular antitypes, but a specially impressive general antitype, the account of a great healing mission (VI, 53-56). It is worthy of note that a striking feature from one of the stories in V is embodied in it. The impure woman said, 'if I touch but his garments, I shall be saved', and Christ said to her, 'Thy faith hath saved thee'. And this is the climax of the general description of healing in VI, 56: 'They besought him that they might touch but his garment's hem; and so many as touched him were saved.'

We have now seen how St Mark manages to finish a cycle without a particular healing, and without our too much feeling the absence of it; how he manages to close the shop without pulling it down. We must now turn back and follow the cycle through in order, showing how it is based on the cycle preceding it.

The first thing we look for in a new cycle is a scene of apostolic calling. Our cycle begins with such a scene: Christ calls the Twelve to him, and sends them out on mission (VI, 7–13). It is both the perfect counterpart and the direct sequel of the beginning to the preceding cycle. In III, 13–19 the Twelve were instituted on the mountain, and a great part of the purpose of their institution was that Christ might send them preaching, and with authority to cast out demons. In VI the intention is fulfilled. Jesus begins to send forth the Twelve, and gives them authority over unclean spirits. Being thus sent forth they preach, and cast out many devils.

The institution of the Twelve in III ends with a phrase of which it is easy to miss the great importance. Jesus instituted Simon Peter, James, John and the rest, and last of all Iscariot, 'the man who betrayed him'. It is the first open reference to the passion which the Gospel contains. Christ institutes among the apostles his own betrayer, as though his betrayal were necessary to the fulfilment of their apostolate. Or is that to force the sense somewhat? It would be so, if the saying about Judas stood alone. But in fact St Mark seems to be at pains to show that no Christian preaching is possible except on a background of betrayal or death.

(1) It is only when John Baptist has been betrayed that Christ himself begins to preach, and calls Simon and his three companions into association with his work (I, 14–20).

(2) In appointing the twelve preaching apostles Jesus institutes his own betrayer (III, 13–19).

(3) But it is not until John Baptist, already betrayed, has been actually done to death, that Jesus sends them out to begin their preaching (VI, 7–29).

Even without further indications, the Christian reader would be aware that the series must find its completion and its meaning in:—

(4) It is not until Jesus has himself been betrayed and killed, that the apostles can be sent with the gospel into the whole world.

We should see (4) in (1)–(3) without further indications. But there are, in fact, further indications. St Mark handles (3) in such a way as to make it prefigure (4). He tells us of the comment aroused by the mission of the Twelve in Galilee. Why, men ask, is the name of Jesus so mighty to work miracles? Because, they reply, it is the name of a martyr who has risen from the dead; for Jesus is as it were a John Baptist returning (VI, 14). How can the Christian read this, without reflecting that the power of the Saving Name hereafter on the lips of the apostles will derive from the actual death and resurrection of Jesus in his own person?

Other suggestions are offered by the populace: that Jesus is Elijah or a prophet equal to any of the prophets of old. These suggestions both help to hint at what St Mark wants to say. For John Baptist was 'a prophet as one of the prophets', an authentic member of the great succession, and in particular he was the promised Elijah. In so far as Jesus can be called John Baptist returning from the dead, he can be called a true prophet, and especially an Elijah; for the Baptist was both. The name of Elijah gives special support to St Mark's real theme. For it was only when Elijah had been taken up in the fiery chariot, when he was dead to the world, and yet not dead, that Elisha received a double portion of his spirit and began to perform the mighty works of his master, or works even mightier still. So what St Mark is really saying is something to this effect: 'They said that the power of the disciples to work with Jesus's name showed Jesus to be John Baptist departed yet living. John was a true Elijah in this: he liberated the power of new Elishas by a departure which was no real death; no real death, for his mission continued mightier in Jesus than it had been in himself. To speak of John returning from the dead in Jesus is, indeed, to speak the exaggerated or superstitious language of popular rumour. But the time would come when Jesus would die and return in his own person, and in the reality of fact. Then the mystery of Elijah departed and living would be truly fulfilled, and a double portion of the master's Spirit would spread the wonderful acts of his disciples to the ends of the world.'

St Mark proceeds to give the story of John's martyrdom in such a way as to bring out its similarities with the sufferings of Elijah on the one side, and with the passion of Christ on the other. The Baptist attacks the association of a new Ahab with a new Jezebel. Herod, like Ahab, 'goes softly' under rebuke and pays the prophet some measure of respect (I Kings XXI, 27–29). Herodias is as implacable as Jezebel and plots his death (I Kings XIX, 2). What the old Jezebel intended, the new achieves, and the prophet dies.

But the story is equally applicable to the coming passion of Christ. Herod is a Pilate, embarrassed by the emissary of God, but willing to spare him if he can. In a season of feast he binds himself to grant a boon, and is tricked. As the priests afterwards incite the people to save Barabbas and crucify Jesus, so Herodias incited her daughter to ask for the Baptist's head, rather than for the princely gift her husband had intended.

The narrative of the Baptist's martyrdom appears to spill into the story like an overgrown historical footnote, but its real importance and appropriateness reveal themselves when we look closer. In raising the daughter of Jairus Jesus showed the emblem of his own resurrection; by suffering rejection in his native town he anticipated his rejection by the Jewish people; by sending out the apostolic mission he foreshadowed Pentecost. Those who witnessed the mission attributed its power to the death of the messenger of God and his return from the dead; and a passion history is recalled, John's in fact, but Christ's in prefigurement.

We have interpreted VI, 7–29 as an antitype of III, 13–19. Let us see how the next part of the cycle we are studying responds to the next part of its model. After the phrase about Judas the traitor in III, 19 we read how Christ returns home with his newly instituted apostles, but they find no leisure to eat their meal, such is the pressure of the crowds. They withdraw at length by means of their boat, and lie off shore; Christ gives the parable of the corn to the multitude, after which they put out and cross the lake (III, 20–IV, 34). In the antitype, the disciples reassemble with their Master after their mission, but there are so many 'coming and going' that they find no leisure to eat a meal. They withdraw by boat along the shore in search of solitude. The multitude nevertheless pursues them, and receives from Christ no mere parabolic 'bread' as in the corn parable, but miraculously real bread through the multiplication of the loaves. Then they put out to cross the lake (VI, 30–45).

The multiplication of the good corn in the parable is expressed by numerical proportion: one seed yields thirty, sixty, or a hundred. So with the multiplication of the bread: five cakes satisfy not five but five thousand men. Both proportions express the fertility of divine grace in the building up of the Church. The two symbols of the spiritual harvest and of the heavenly bread lay very close to one another in the primitive Christian mind, however hard we may find it to work out a logical relation between them. In John IV, 30–36 Christ's supernatural nourishment is to do his Sender's will, and complete the task he assigns; the task is the harvest of souls, and even to labour upon it is to be sustained with the food of eternal life which it produces. (The same association of ideas probably underlies John VI, 26–29. To earn the food of eternal life a man must do God's field-work; to do God's field-work is to put himself into the hands of the field-master whom God commissions.)

There is no reason to suppose that St Mark would have worked out the connexion between the harvest of grace and the bread of heaven in the way St John does. All it concerns us to know is that he passes easily from the one to the other, feeling them to be in some manner equivalents. When he passes from the spiritual harvest of the corn-parable to the supernatural feast of the five thousand, he is merely retracing in an opposite direction a path he has already trodden. For he passed to the corn parable of IV, 1–8 from the cornfield of II, 23–28, where the point had not been the growth of the crop, but the disciples' enjoyment of the fruit, made free to them by Christ as the shewbread was made free to his companions by David. If the evangelist can pass from the eating of corn (whether raw or baked) to the fertility of corn scattered in the field, he can easily turn back again from the fertility of the corn to the eating of the bread; especially if the bread, by supernatural blessing, borrows the natural fertility of the corn, and multiplies a thousandfold.

The discourses on the corn parable in IV are directly followed by the stilling of the storm, and the miracle of bread in VI leads direct to the walking on the water. We have already commented on the equivalence between the two rescues at sea. So our examination of the 'annexe' cycle VI, 7–56 is now complete. We have traced its reflection of its predecessor from beginning to end.

We turn to a fresh cycle, and to an important alteration of the cyclic form. Indeed the form changes with every cycle, for St Mark is not writing to a fixed prescription. We have no thesis to make out about what is essential to the Marcan cycle and what is not. All we claim is that the cycle develops gradually enough to remain recognizable through its transformations; it is more like child, boy, man than larva, pupa, moth. Even in the growth of children, however, there are stages of more rapid modification, and St Mark's cyclic form passes through an analogous stage between VI and VII.

Hitherto the cycle has been based on the duality, apostolic calling and regenerative healing. But St Mark's thought now begins to revolve round another pair, healing and feasting. Healing corresponds to baptism throughout the Gospel; it expresses the power of Water and Spirit. Similarly the miraculous feast which Christ offers to the people is a foreshadowing of the Eucharist. The means by which the miracle is performed are simply the eucharistic acts, blessing, breaking, distribution (VI, 41).

Healing reaches its most impressive exposition in the great miracles of V, and the first miracle of feasting is in the next chapter. The two mysteries are close enough together to be felt as a pair, even though, formally speaking, they are in distinct cycles. For reasons which we have discussed above, there is no

94

particular narrative of healing in the cycle which contains the feast; and so looking back over the cycles III, 13–VI, 6 and VI, 7–VI, 56, we are all the more likely to distinguish them from one another as the cycle of the great healing, and the cycle of the great feast. Taken together, they make up the pair of the two greater sacraments, baptism and eucharist. And it is natural to take them together, even on formal grounds. For the second is the 'annexe' to the first, and it is no less natural to think of a 'block' and an 'annexe' as forming one complex cycle, than to think of them as forming two linked cycles.

Let us call III, 13–VI, 56 one complex cycle, and interpret VII–VIII as another complex cycle conceived as a whole, and composed on the model of the other. The controlling idea of the new cycle is the extension of privilege and sacrament to the Gentiles. It is this that distinguishes the new cycle from the old. In the old a most correct of Israelites, a ruler of synagogue, intercedes for his child and obtains her resuscitation. It is a Gentile mother who obtains the cure of her child in the new. There is not much, perhaps, which emphasizes the Jewish character of the five thousand recipients of miraculous bread, but when we reach the four thousand in VIII, we are made to feel that the four thousand are, or stand for, Gentiles, while the five thousand were still only Jews.

The new cycle retains and repeats from the old those features alone which belong to the pattern of the two sacraments, or which can be made relevant to the contrast between Jew and Gentile. What is taken is taken in order, but much is let go. The most surprising omission is that of the customary first feature, the apostolic calling. Yet, on reflection, perhaps, not so surprising after all, for two reasons. St Mark's attention has shifted from 'calling and healing' to 'healing and feeding'; and the theme of calling has, in a sense, been worked right out and exhausted. It began with particular callings (I, 17–20, II, 13–14) and advanced to the comprehensive call and institution of all the apostles (III, 13–19). It remained only that they should be actually sent forth on the divine mission to which they had been called (VI, 7–13). That looks like being the end of the series. Even if it is not, still it seems that no further extension of the series is relevant to the transition St Mark makes in passing from his old complex cycle to his new, that is, in passing from vi to vii. For the transition is from Jew to Gentile, and both Jew and Gentile are within the scope of the apostolic mission. Once instituted and sent forth, the apostles need no more instituting or sending; all they need is to learn that the Spirit of their commission is 'no respecter of persons', and that Gentiles must be evangelized as well as Jews.

So the new complex cycle contains nothing to match the scene of apostolic institution which began the old (iii, 13–19). But it takes up the next paragraph of the old, Pharisaic criticism (iii, 20-30). In iii Christ's many exorcisms have been newly and particularly emphasized (iii, 11, cf. 15). So it is natural that the criticism of the scribes should fasten on that point: 'He hath Beelzebul, and casts out demons by the prince of demons.' In the last verse of vi, on the other hand, we have a summary of healing in which demons are not mentioned, and the accent falls on Christ's willingness to let all and sundry touch him to obtain their cures. And so it is natural that the scribal criticism should now attack Christ's disregard of the customary ritual precautions against defilement by contact with the impure. The verbal continuity between vi, 56 and vii, 1–4 is worth observing. 'Wherever he entered village, town, or country, they laid the sick in the *markets* and besought him that they might but touch the border of his garment, and those who touched were saved. And he was waylaid by the Pharisees and certain scribes who had arrived from Jerusalem and had seen his disciples eat bread with profane—that is, unwashed—hands. For the Pharisees and Jews in general, except they wash their hands, eat not ... and returning from *market* eat not unless they have bathed.'

The subjects of Pharisaic criticism in iii and vii, then, are different; but taken together, they form one of St Mark's firmest pairs of ideas. We have seen that his miracle pattern is based on the division of healing into purification and restoration, and the further division of purification into exorcism and cleansing, the expulsion of demons and the expulsion of (ritual) defilements. Christ expels demons because he is the temple of the Holy Ghost, and they say, He hath Beelzebul. Christ expels defilements because his divine purity overflows and sanctifies those whom he touches, or those who touch him; and they say he is negligent in matters of cleanness. The verse we have just quoted about those who touched the hem of his garment and are saved directly evokes the memory of the unclean woman in v about whom the same words are used; so that the theme of defiling sicknesses is scarcely less present at the beginning of vII than the theme of exorcism is in III.

It is remarkable that in both texts the same mysterious personages appear in the role of critics, visiting scribes from Jerusalem. They are nowhere else to be found in this Gospel. It is no less remarkable that the discourse which begins with Christ's answer to them in VII, 6 follows the general pattern of the whole range of discourse beginning with Christ's answer to the same people in III, 23 and continuing through his teaching in the boat (IV, 1–34). In both cases there is first an answer to the Pharisees (III, 23–30, VII, 6–13), then a single 'parable' addressed to the crowds, introduced by the word 'Hearken' and concluded with the formula, 'He that hath ears to hear, let him hear' (IV, 1–8, VII, 14–16).[1] Then, when Jesus is in private again, the disciples 'demand of him the parable', are reproached for incomprehension, and answered (IV, 9–34, VII, 17–23).

In III an answer given by Christ to his mother and brethren intervenes between his reply to the Pharisees and his instruction of the people. In VII there is of course no such intrusive episode. But the reply to the Pharisees is divided into two halves by the formula, 'Moreover, he said to them', and the second half is concerned with Pharisaic evasion of the command to honour parents.

---

[1] 'He that hath ears to hear', etc., is omitted by ℵ and B. But there is plenty of good evidence on the other side, and in my view the verse should be retained. An interjectory sentence like this is easily dropped out by error, because the general sense is unaffected by its loss. And the influence of the parallel text in Matthew would tend to banish it. See Matt. xv, 10–12.

H

The point has nothing material to do with the subject of discussion: filial duty is not a case of ritual cleanness. Christ has widened the issue and taken the Pharisees up on the general ground of the law and tradition. Almost any illustration of corrupt tradition would do, but it is interesting that the illustration chosen forms a striking companion-piece to the corresponding paragraph in III. Neither Christ nor the Pharisee, in fact, is willing to treat family duty as in all circumstances an unchallengeable claim. Christ has left mother and brethren that he may espouse the Church, that is, for a greater and more universal good. 'Who are my mother and my brethren?' he says, and then, looking round upon his hearers, 'Behold my mother and my brethren. For whoever doeth the will of God . . .' Whereas the Pharisees are prepared to inhibit the operation of the commandment to honour parents out of formal respect for the force of an oath, though the oath be frivolous or unjust.

The parabolic discourses of III–IV are followed by the great miracles of IV, 35–V, 43. Those miracles find their antitype in the miracles of VII, 24–37. We have discussed elsewhere the way in which the dyad of healings in VII is related to the triad in V, how Legion, the impure woman and the child of Jairus are 'condensed' into the child of the Syrophoenician and the deaf stammerer from Decapolis. We will not repeat what we have said, but dwell upon a different point: how the two miracles in VII are made to show the practical bearings of the discourses which lead up to them. If Christ attacks the Pharisaic way of fencing the table from defilement, it is that he may extend the 'children's bread' to the 'Gentile dogs', which is his own manner of describing what he does, when he exorcizes the Syrophoenician's child. If Christ calls upon the hearers of his 'parable' to hear and understand and to use what ears they have, if he reproaches his own disciples for lack of comprehension, it is with a merciful will to quicken the functions he invokes and help the faults he blames. He himself corrects the vice of the unhearing ear and the tongue that stammers for an answer when his 'Effatha' restores the Decapolitan. Then indeed tongues break loose, and a doxology is heard which marks the end of the cycle: 'He hath done all things well; he makes both the deaf to hear, and the dumb to speak' (VII, 37).

The doxology marks the end of the cycle, of the single cycle, that is, but we remember that we are concerned with a double cycle, and we keep straight on, and take the next piece of the model. After the miracles of V comes the rejection of Christ by his countrymen (VI, 1–6), which can have no antitype in a cycle devoted to his acceptance by the Gentiles. Then comes the sending forth of the apostles with its appended material (VI, 7–29). We have already considered why this feature also is passed over. And so we come to the feeding of the five thousands of which the antitype is the feeding of the four (VI, 30–44, VIII, 1–10). The result of the omissions St Mark makes is to draw together healing and feeding into immediate proximity and allow the full force of the combination to be felt. If Christ exorcizes the Gentile as though by the power of water, if he restores tongue and ears as though by the gift of the Spirit, he has already in principle given the children's bread to the dogs, for those who are baptized in water and spirit proceed to the table of the Lord and communicate there; it is the completion of their initiation.

The parallel with VI continues. Both feedings of the multitude are followed by voyages over the lake in which the disciples earn rebuke for failing to understand concerning the loaves. 'They were greatly amazed in themselves, for they did not understand concerning the loaves, but their heart was hardened' (VI, 52). 'Do ye not yet perceive nor understand? Have ye your heart hardened? When I broke the five loaves to the five thousands, how many baskets full of fragments took ye up?' (VIII, 17–19). Both voyages are directed towards Bethsaida (VI, 45, VIII, 22). Both are immediately followed by the acts of healing which complete the pattern of their respective cycles. In VI, 53–56 the description of healing is general, but in VIII, 22–26 the evangelist returns to his usual style and supplies a particular 'annexed' healing, the cure of the blind villager.

Here, perhaps, the reader used to our repetitive ways will

expect to see us claiming credit for a task performed. We said we would interpret VII, I–VIII, 26 as a complex or double cycle constructed on the model of III, 13–VI, 56, and designed to transfer the privileges of divine healing and divine sustenance from Jewry to the nations. Such was our proposal, and have not we fulfilled it? Yes, in a sense; but not without misgivings. Our new complex or double cycle is so called because it consists of a 'block' cycle (VII) together with the 'annexe' cycle belonging to it (VIII, I–26). Previous 'annexe' cycles have been modelled on the 'block' cycles to which they are annexed, and it seemed reason that they should be. For the annexe cycle got its name from the healing in which it concluded, because that healing was found to be the pair and counterpart of the last healing in the precedent 'block' cycle; the healing of the hand, for example, was pair and counterpart to the healing of the feet. It seemed unnatural to us that the matching of the 'block' and 'annexe' healings should be an isolated phenomenon, that they should beckon to one another over several paragraphs indifferent to their amity. It seemed more likely that the whole cycle leading up to the 'annexe' healing should model itself upon the whole cycle leading up to the 'block' healing. We were relieved to discover that such was the case.

What, then, is it that causes our present disquiet? It is that we have interpreted an annexe cycle as having nothing to do with the cycle it is annexed to, apart from the indubitable correspondence between the terminal healings. The opening of the eyes matches the opening of the ears, of that there can be no doubt; but we have derived the short cycle leading up to the opening of the eyes not from the short cycle leading up to the opening of the ears, but from an altogether earlier text, the second or 'annexe' part of a previous double cycle.

Well, but have not we made out our case? Surely we are not going to go back upon it? No, indeed, that is not what embarrasses us. It is that we are going to have it both ways, and we fear that we shall not be believed. The workings of the inspired imagination are endlessly complex, and especially of an imagination which draws inspiration from the suggestions offered by its own previous creations. The complexity of such a process is endless, but the description of it does not look plausible. Nevertheless we will persevere.

Very well, then; St Mark writes VIII, 1–26 on the model of VI, 30–56, as we have shown, and *also* on the model of VII. Naturally we are not pretending to describe what St Mark saw himself to be doing. Perhaps he did not know that he was using either model. He knew that he was inspired, carried on in a rhythm which he must complete, but did he know what factors, even in his own previous work, determined the rhythm in which he must move? We are not psychologizing St Mark, we are describing the phenomena in the text. We will simply write the two models in parallel columns, and the single antitype in one column below.

VI, 30–44. Feeding of five thousands.	VII, 1–16. Pharisaic questioners repulsed.
VI, 45–52. Voyage at sea; the disciples do not understand about the loaves.	VII, 17–23. The disciples do not understand, ask, and are rebuked.
VI, 53–56. Many healings.	VII, 24–37. Exorcism and opening of ears.

VIII, 1–13. Feeding of four thousands, and repulse of Pharisaic questioners.

VIII, 14–21. Voyage at sea; the disciples do not understand about the loaves and are rebuked.

VIII, 22–26. Opening of eyes.

St Mark begins, as it were—*as it were*, oh, blessèd phrase!—by putting down antitypes to the first lines of his two models one after the other in quite a staccato way. After feeding the four thousands in antitype to the feeding of the five, Christ sails to another part of the shore, lands, and dismisses Pharisaic questioners in antitype to the dismissal he gave them over the clean-and-unclean question. Only the dismissal is now much more rapid and unceremonious. They ask for a sign from heaven, and they are told that they will not get it.

So far the two models no more blend in their common antitype than oil with water. One merely floats on top of the other. But in the next paragraph the blending of the two is subtle and complete. The point of contact is the disciples' incomprehension. In VI, 52 they failed to understand the walking on the water, because they had not understood about the multiplication of the loaves. Having failed to recognize in Jesus the act of Providence sustaining man in dearth, they were unprepared to find in him the act of Providence which delivers man in danger. In the antitype their failure is even more elementary: they cannot reason from the sufficiency of seven loaves and Christ's blessing for the sustenance of four thousand men, to the sufficiency of one loaf and Christ's blessing for the sustenance of a dozen men. 'They had only one loaf with them in the boat . . . and they reasoned with one another saying, We have no bread' (VIII, 14–16).

So much for the influence of the first model (VI) on the antitype (VIII). The influence of the second model (VII) is seen in the curious doubling of the occasion for the disciples' display of their incomprehension in VIII. The simple occasion is surely sufficient; they have witnessed a second miracle of bread, and yet they worry at finding themselves with only one loaf on board. But St Mark complicates the occasion. The disciples' anxiety ignores not only the miracle they have lately seen, but also Christ's present warning. For he is bidding them beware of the leaven (that is, the bad and infectious old spirit) of the Pharisees, and the leaven of Herod. The leaven of the Pharisees must be interpreted by what the Pharisees have just done. Ignoring the abundant signs of Christ's divine mission, they require a sign from heaven. The leaven of Herod, to judge from VI, 14–29, is somewhat different. Herod can recognize the signs given him, in a certain fashion; but he has not the integrity to act upon them. The general effect of the warning against Pharisaic and Herodian leaven is a demand for lively faith in response to visible signs of divine action. But the disciples, ignoring or misunderstanding the warning, show the infection of the same leaven. They have not taken the miracle of the loaves to heart; they complain that they have no bread.

The disciples, then, have shown themselves not much better than the sign-seeking Pharisees; that is their disgrace. But so it had been in St Mark's second model, VII, 18. The Pharisees there attacked Christ's handling of clean and unclean. Christ's answer in effect retorted their accusation. Uncleanness is from within; the Pharisaic prevarication about Corban is an example of it. The Pharisees, of course, rejected his doctrine, but even his disciples could not understand it. 'Are you too so without comprehension?' was his rebuke to them. In VIII the point made in VII is assumed: the Pharisees are unclean and infectious. The disciples must guard against their 'leaven'. They are all too like the Pharisees. The Pharisees are more in our minds here than Herod, for the Pharisees have only just been left behind; and it is the mention of them that puts VIII in parallel with VII. But the somewhat surprising mention of Herod too carries our thoughts away to the other model, VI, where the miracle of loaves and crossing of the sea stands on an immediate background of Herod and his half-believing mind (VI, 14–29).

The occasion, let us conclude, of the disciples' incomprehension in VIII is curiously complicated, and the most intelligible thing we can say about it is that it blends together St Mark's two models. If he had not been under the double influence of VI and VII, he would, perhaps, have expressed himself more simply. So much for the occasion of the disciples' incomprehension. The rebuke it earns claims our attention next. It is a manifest blending of the two models, VI, 52 and VII, 18. The reader need do no more than compare the three texts.

VI, 52. They were greatly astonished in themselves, for they did not understand concerning the loaves, but their heart was hardened.

VII, 18. Are ye too so without understanding? Do ye not perceive that nothing entering a man from without can defile him?

VIII, 17–19. Why reason ye that ye have no loaves? Do ye not yet perceive nor understand? Have ye your heart hardened? Having eyes, see ye not, and having ears, hear ye not, and remember ye not? When I broke the five loaves for the five thousands . . . and when the seven for the four . . .

The last paragraph of the antitype is the healing of the blind. The paragraph calls for no discussion; it is plain that it owes everything to the healing of the deaf in the second model, and nothing to the general description of healing ministry in the first.

Shall we now return to our delayed self-congratulation and claim to have dealt with the double cycle VII, 1–VIII, 26 according to plan? Perhaps we might, if we could only make up our minds whether we have reached the end of the double cycle or not. For a new feature in the cyclic pattern arises somewhere between this cycle and the next, and it may be a matter of convenience only whether we regard it as a new sort of epilogue to the old cycle, or a new sort of prologue to the new. We will treat it here as an epilogue. For that will at least give us the opportunity of showing out of what soil it arises, and how strong its connexions are with what precedes it.

The feature we have to consider may be given the general description of 'the truth' or 'the teaching', and the particular example in which it makes its first appearance is the body of discourses which took place near Caesarea Philippi (VIII, 27–IX, 1). It may be viewed as the inevitable outcome of a theme which is strongly represented in VII, 1–VIII, 26, the theme of ears, tongue, and eyes, of hearkening, of vision and of confession. The disciples of Christ (let alone any other sort of people), can neither hear, see, nor discourse aright. Christ's divine work eludes them as a whole and perplexes or astonishes them in its parts. But meanwhile Christ's healing power is being directly brought to bear upon the sorts of defect from which his disciples suffer: he rectifies the tongue, he opens the ears and eyes. Surely the effect of such power must become evident in some hearing, vision, and utterance of the truth, in spite of human folly.

St Mark is using a triad of sensitive and communicative powers, ears, tongue and eyes, the special instruments of the mind. Christ completes the healing of all three when he heals the blind villager's eyes (VIII, 22–26), for he has already healed tongue and ears in the Decapolitan (VII, 31–37). No sooner is the threefold healing complete than St Peter sees, hears and confesses. Nothing but Christ's healing act upon the villager's eyes intervenes between the disciples' incomprehension and Peter's confession. Before the healing act they have neither perception nor understanding, their hearts are hardened, their eyes without vision, and their ears without hearing. Christ opens the villager's eyes, and St Peter confesses Christ.

The villager and the apostle are, then, symbolically equivalent: the physical healing of the one stands for the spiritual enlightenment of the other. Now the most striking feature of the villager's cure is that it is achieved in two stages. At the application of spittle and a first laying on of hands, the patient sees men, if he can be said to see men who sees figures like trees walking. By a second laying on of hands he obtains perfect sight. Peter's enlightenment also has two stages. He sees something, certainly, at the first—he sees God's Anointed, the Scion from the root of Jesse, when he says, 'Thou art the Christ'. But he does not see the truth of the Son of Man. That is a second stage of learning, and Christ has to impart it, not without a dramatic rebuke. We may add that Peter and his companions, like the blind man, are enjoined to silence.

We have said that St Peter's confession comes as a dramatic reversal of the disciples' condition before the healing of the blind, when they had no use of ears, eyes, or heart. That lamentable unperceptiveness was virtually described as a failure to put away the leaven of the Pharisees or of Herod (VIII, 15). St Peter's confession is so presented as to make it an abjuration of Herodian leaven—a fortiori, therefore, of the Pharisaic kind; for while Herod is half-hearted in responding to divine signs, the Pharisees do not respond to them at all. The very name of 'Philip's Caesarea' recalls the story of Herod and John Baptist, for there and there

alone we heard of the tetrarch Philip (VI, 17), and to remember
him is to remember the brother who took his wife. On the road
to Philip's Caesarea Christ asks his disciples who he is said to be,
and they repeat the opinions of the crowd from the beginning
of the same narrative about Herod and John (VI, 14–15, VIII,
27–28). After recording the popular opinions in VI the evangelist
went on to say that the superficial Herod was content with one
of them. Not so St Peter; he abjures Herodian leaven when he
rejects the popular fancies and declares, Thou art the Christ.
Nevertheless he had not learnt all the lessons that the story of
John and Herod could teach; he had not reasoned from the fate
of the forerunner to the fate of his successor; he did not understand that the Son of Man must suffer many things, be rejected
and killed, and rise again; rise not as John had done, metaphori-
cally in the person of another (VI, 14), but actually and in
his own.

In a sense Christ's unveiling of the truth begins at Caesarea
Philippi. Christ has taught hitherto, but in parables; has answered
scribal criticism, but has not defined scriptural truth; has promised
his disciples the secret of the kingdom, but has not expressed
it to them without a figure. Henceforth the teaching whether
public, private or controversial takes on a new character of
openness. It is false to say that the new revelation is for the
disciples only at Caesarea Philippi. There is, indeed, something
reserved for the disciples, but there is an accompanying proclamation to the world. The disciples alone received the prophecy
of passion and resurrection, but the multitude was called in to
share with them the lesson of self-renunciation and the bearing
of the cross. Uninitiated ears heard how the Son of Man in glory
would disown the disowners of Jesus, and how among the men
standing there, some would see the kingdom of God present in
power before they tasted death (VIII, 34–IX, 1). The world had
never heard such things from Christ before. The public preaching
advances with the advance of the private instruction, though
always some paces behind. One thing which has altered is the
order in which public and private instruction are placed. Hitherto

private instruction has been a comment on public teaching (III, 20–IV, 9 and IV, 10–32, VII, 1–16 and VII, 17–23, VIII, 11–13 and VIII, 14–21). Now public teaching becomes the subsequent extension of private instruction (VIII, 27–33 and VIII, 34–IX, I, IX, 30–50 and X, 1–31).

CHAPTER V

LAST TWO DOUBLE CYCLES

If an analytical or 'dry' treatment of the Gospel always seems profane, it seems so most where divine mysteries shine brightest in the text; and here we are in face of the Transfiguration itself. But there is little the author can do except to sympathize with his reader's disquiet, and remind him of the limited scope of the present enterprise. We are in no way concerned to say here what the Transfiguration was, or even what St Mark saw in it. All we attempt is to show the place it occupies in the rhythmic development of St Mark's thought. We are to consider it not as the Transfiguration, but as the first element in a Marcan cycle (IX, 2–X, 31).

We have just been examining a double cycle (VII–IX, 1) from which the feature of the apostolic calling was absent. We did our best to account for its absence. We suggested that the theme had been in a manner worked out; for all the apostles had been called in III, and all sent out on mission in VI; their initiation was therefore complete. The double cycle which lacked the usual scenes of calling did not feel the lack, for it built upon the callings the apostles had already received. They had already been instituted, already sent on mission; what the new cycle added was simply the true scope of their field, as including Gentiles as well as Jews.

But if the scene of apostolic calling is a used-up theme, how is it that it reappears in the Transfiguration? For here are Peter, James, and John summoned up the mountain, as the whole Twelve were summoned before (III, 13–19), and vouchsafed peculiar privileges. We answer that two themes are contained in the apostolic institution of III, 13–19. One of them has been worked out, as we said, but the other has lain dormant, and awakes in the Transfiguration. The two themes are those of the Twelve and of the Three.

We think of III, 13–19 as the institution of the Twelve, but it is no less the institution of the Three. For in giving the list of the Twelve the evangelist removes Andrew from Simon's side where he has hitherto belonged (1, 16, 29) and places him below James and John. Moreover, he marks off Simon, James and John from all the others by the special surnames given to them by Christ. The same divine authority which had called Abram 'Abraham' and Jacob 'Israel' named Simon 'Peter' and the Sons of Zebedee 'Boané-R'ges'.

What is the meaning of the Three? The meaning of the Twelve is the wholeness of Israel; the meaning is in the number. Is there a similar significance in the mere number of three men? Far too many alternative significances, perhaps, but 'witness' is one of them. The law had said, 'At the mouth of two or three witnesses shall every word be established' (Deut. XIX, 15). Two is the minimum; three is sufficiency. The use of *two* witnesses had received a special application in Jewish practice. It was customary to send two emissaries or 'apostles' to be joint witnesses to the intention of their sender, and St Mark makes a full use of this idea. The apostolic institution of III also appoints the Three Witnesses, but the apostolic sending of VI commissions the apostles two by two; and when Jesus afterwards sends disciples to fetch the ass in his name, or to arrange a supper room, he sends two. Two witnesses, then, to authenticate a commission; and three to establish a point of fact. It is fair to judge of the function of the Three from the first thing that is done with them. It is to be Christ's chosen witnesses at the raising of Jairus's child, when all else are excluded. They are the special witnesses to the resurrection of the dead.

According to the epistle to the Galatians, St Paul once found it necessary to refer the articles of his gospel-preaching to the judgement of older apostles (Gal. II, 1–10). We might expect him to go to the Twelve, or to so many of them as could be found. No, he is emphatic that 'those held in special estimation', 'those reckoned to be pillars', were his court of appeal; and they were James, Peter and John. It was not the same James as St Mark names among the Three; it could not be, for Herod Agrippa had killed him. James the Lord's Brother takes his place, and the alteration is not greatly felt; the Three are still in being. St Paul consulted them not as an authority under which he acted—he is anxious to repudiate the suggestion. As what, then, if not as official witnesses to the content of the saving truth? We may speculate in vain about the meaning of the name 'pillars'. 'Pillars' of what? 'Pillars of the house of God' or 'Pillars of the truth' (cf. I Tim. III, 15); the three props of witness by which the Word of God is 'established' or 'made to stand'?

To return to St Mark; the theme of the Three Witnesses is in abeyance while the theme of the twelvefold mission holds the field; the twelve are sent out two by two; there is no special function for the three. But when the truth breaks forth and is revealed, when revelation itself becomes the theme, then the Three Witnesses step forward to play their part.

When it places the three in a scene of apostolic calling, the Gospel returns to the scene of calling in which they previously appeared, that is to say, the mountain (III, 13–19). The mountains of III and IX are not physically identical, but symbolically they are equivalent, for both are Sinai. In III Christ had made an exodus, and his exodus, like that of Israel under Moses, led to the mountain; and on the mountain he constituted the Twelve his new Israel, the patriarchs of a new and spiritual twelvefold people. Sinai was the mountain of covenant; it was also the mountain of revelation. As the covenant aspect of the mountain appears in III, so the revelation aspect appears in IX. The Three, having ascended, see Moses and Elijah, and the divine glory shining in Christ. Moses saw the glory on Sinai, and so, in his own day, did Elijah; they have returned to see it again. The Three alone go up to witness to the mysteries; all the Twelve went up to enter into the covenant.

By placing a Marcan paragraph in a certain class we do not reduce it to the level of that class. The Transfiguration is the calling of the three apostolic witnesses to the full exercise of their function, and as such it takes its place in the series of apostolic scenes. But that is not to say that their witnessing of the mystery is more important than the mystery they witness. The many-sidedness of the Transfiguration is the despair of its expositors, and we shall make no attempt to deal with it here. The Transfiguration reveals many things, but above all it reveals Revelation, for it enthrones Christ as the supreme mediator of divine truth, and sole teacher of the world. Moses and Elias, Law and Prophecy, are not to be enshrined beside him. They pass away, and he remains; he has the testimony of the Father's voice: 'This is my only Son; to him hearken.' The vision amounts to this, Jesus is the truth. Now witness is, characteristically, witness to truth. The function of the Three as witnesses is manifested in the scene which enthrones Jesus as the truth. Because he is *the* truth, therefore they are *the* witnesses.

Let us agree that our new cycle has its scene of apostolic calling, a scene standing in the series of such scenes. What else has it got? Calling and healing were the elements of the first four cycles. The cycle we are examining follows the elementary pattern and moves directly from calling to healing. Christ and the three descend the mountain, and there is the epileptic boy waiting for them at the foot (IX, 14–29). We have sufficiently discussed the miracle elsewhere. It is a 'block' miracle, not an 'annexe', but here the block has dwindled to one. Its model is to be sought in the previous block, that is, in VII, 24–37.

Calling and healing: is that all? No, we have still to reckon with a second example of the new feature which appeared as a kind of epilogue to the last cycle, and which we named 'the truth, or the teaching'. It consisted there of two bodies of discourse, one private and one public, and both taking place at Caesarea Philippi (VIII, 27–33, VIII, 34–IX, 1). We have now to consider a much enlarged antitype to it. The division between private and public teaching is now emphasized by a difference of scene. The private is at Capernaum (IX, 30–50), the public beyond Jordan (X, 1–31).

We will take the private teaching first, and show how it answers to the private teaching given at Caesarea Philippi. 'And Jesus and his disciples went forth into the villages of Caesarea Philippi. And in the way he asked his disciples, Who do men say that I am? . . . And he charged them to speak to no man about him, and began to teach them that the Son of Man must suffer many things, and be rejected by the elders and high priests and scribes, and be killed, and rise again after three days.' Compare the beginning of the antitype: 'And thence they went forth and began to pass through Galilee. And he would have no man know it, for he was teaching his disciples that the Son of Man is delivered into the hands of men who will kill him, and when he is killed, he will rise again after three days. . . . And they came to Capernaum, and being in the house, he asked them, What were you discussing in the way?'

The model contains two discussions. (a) The first is introduced by Christ himself, who puts a question to his disciples on the way. The question is, Who am I? and it results in the revelation of the suffering of the Son of Man (VIII, 27–31). (b) The second arises through the intervention of Peter, and results in a denunciation of man-mindedness, or the demand for glory without abasement (32–33).

The antitype similarly contains two discussions. (a) The first is introduced by Christ himself, who puts a question to his disciples: What had they been debating on the way? It appears that while Christ had been repeating to them the doctrine of the sufferings of the Son of Man, they had been debating 'Who is greatest?' His reply has the effect of extending the paradoxical character of a suffering Messiahship from the person of the king to the persons of his representatives. He is rejected and killed; it is intolerable that they should argue about precedence. Nothing accredits or ennobles them except their Master's name in which they come. To receive his emissary, though it be but a child, is to receive him; to receive him is to receive the Eternal King himself (IX, 30–37). (b) The second discussion in the antitype is introduced by a burst of arrogant zeal, like the second discussion in the model. There the zeal was Peter's, here it is John's. The zeal of Peter defends the honour of Messiah against himself; the zeal of John defends the honour of Messiah's commission against a man whom he holds to have usurped it. 'We found one casting out demons in thy Name, and we stopped him, because he is not one of our company.' John, like Peter, soon discovers that he is *plus royaliste que le roi.* Christ's answer sets carefulness not to offend existing faith above any defence of privilege. Nothing justifies the endangering of eternal life (IX, 38–50).

The discourses at Capernaum are given what seems a casual setting—the company are travelling quietly through Galilee, and here they are, resting by the way in Peter's house. But Peter's house at Capernaum is also the first Christian Church, and when Christ takes his seat there and summons his disciples, he is addressing them from what might be called the only Christian *cathedra* then existing in the world. Such is the scene of the private teaching, and the setting of the public teaching which follows it is no less impressive, though of course equally natural. 'Thence he arose and went into the region of Judaea, and over the Jordan. The crowds collected round him again, and as his manner was, he began again to teach them.' The repeated 'again' and the phrase 'as his manner was', give some emphasis to the point that the private teaching is over, and the public teaching is resumed. And where resumed? Across Jordan, in the only part of the Israelite land on which Moses had set foot. Here Moses had passed away and left Jesus (the Son of Nun) to achieve his work; here Moses had delivered the Deuteronomy.

We follow St Mark's guidance into the Deuteronomic land with a Deuteronomic oracle already ringing in our ears. We heard it on the mountain, the witness of the heavenly Voice to a Beloved Son, 'To him hearken'. For Moses in Deuteronomy promised the people a prophet like unto himself. 'To him', he said, 'hearken' (XVIII, 15). The first such prophet had been Jesus the Son of Nun, who brought the people over Jordan. Moses had to pass away, and Jesus succeed, before they could cross into Canaan. In the Transfiguration Moses visibly witnesses to Jesus the Son of God, to whom man must hearken, and then once more passes away, that Jesus alone may finish the saving work and give the people rest.

Moses is not the only ancient saint appearing in the Transfiguration; Elijah accompanies him, and he also passes away, leaving Jesus there alone. Elijah had this in common with Moses: he too was snatched out of the world, that his work might be accomplished in another. And it was in much the same region, beyond Jordan and opposite to Jericho, that Elijah went up in fire, and Elisha received his mantle and his spirit (II Kings II).

How appropriate it is, then, that the next public teaching, the next legal teaching after the Transfiguration should be given beyond Jordan. The subject of the teaching is no less appropriate. John Baptist has perished as a second Elijah to make room for his fulfiller, Christ; the identification of Baptist and second Elijah is made explicit at the descent from the mount (IX, 9–13). And for what had John perished? For the sanctity of marriage. Jesus shows himself the fulfiller of John's work by prohibiting not merely such gross irregularities as John had rebuked in Herod, but all remarriage after divorce without exception (X, 2–12).

The prophet John had merely enforced Moses, but Christ left Moses and the prophets clean behind. Christ's marriage law was the best known and the most formal of his corrections to the law of Moses. According to Tertullian and the Montanists, it was the hall-mark of Christ's dispensation; and if a better dispensation still, that of the Paraclete, was destined to follow, it must be characterized by a further severity in the same province and prohibit remarriage even after the death of one's spouse. Montanism was a heresy, but it is evidence for the position occupied by the prohibition of divorce in the mind of the Church. Another evidence for it is the text before us. St Mark, desiring to show Jesus as the new and greater Moses, begins with his prohibition of divorce. In the very place where Moses gave the law of dissolution (Deut. XXIV, 1–4) Jesus overrules him.

After writing of what Christ did for marriage and especially for the protection of wives, the evangelist very naturally goes on to tell us what he did for children; how he took them in his arms and blessed them, how he rebuked those who would not have him troubled with them. But in so doing St Mark picks up a theme which occupied the very centre of the private teaching in Peter's house at Capernaum. The child at Capernaum was embraced by Christ, the Transjordanian children are both embraced and blessed. Of the Capernaum child it is said that Christ is received in such a one, if he is received in Christ's name; and when John begins to boast of having *forbidden* an unlicensed practitioner of Christian exorcism, Christ extends the principle of receiving little ones in Christ's name to cover the case of the unlicensed exorcist. But the pure case of *forbidding* little ones arises in Transjordan when the disciples turn the children away. 'Forbid them not,' Christ replies, 'for the Divine Kingship belongs to such', they are royal princes. 'Amen, I say to you, he who will not accept the Kingdom of God under the guise of a child shall never enter it.' The tenth chapter is to be interpreted by the ninth: to 'accept the kingdom of God in the guise of a child' is to accept a child as presenting Messiah's person, and therefore the person of the Divine Majesty. The ninth chapter has already taught us that those who will not so accept the little ones, had better have been dropped at sea with millstones round their necks; it is only by making every personal sacrifice that men can *enter into the Kingdom of God* and not fall into the gehenna of fire.

It seems right that the public teaching should extend the private teaching from the disciples to the crowds, and should be based upon what had been privately given to the disciples. Such is the relation between public and private in the discourses at Caesarea Philippi. But when we come to compare the public teaching of X with the private teaching of IX, the one does not simply develop from the other. A new factor intervenes, the presentation of Christ as the Lawgiver, the author of a better Deuteronomy. And this factor supplies the first paragraph of the public teaching beyond Jordan (X, 1–12). But St Mark has not forgotten that the public teaching should draw from the private teaching which precedes it; and the second paragraph of the public teaching does so (X, 13–16). The evangelist then proceeds to a third paragraph which does equal justice to both factors and

fuses them in one. This is the paragraph of the rich man (x, 17–31).
It is a striking illustration of the private teaching, and it is at the
same time as Deuteronomic as it could well be.

To take its relation to the private teaching first. The latter part
of the private teaching says two things. First, that we cannot
hope for divine reward unless we accept little ones in Christ's
name (ix, 41–42), and, second, that we should cast away hand,
foot or eye to assure entrance into 'life', or 'the Kingdom of
God' (43–49). Of these two doctrines the first is illustrated by
Christ's comment on his blessing of the children, as we have just
seen. The second is illustrated by the story of the rich man. When
the rich man is called upon to rid himself of his 'only hindrance'
(x, 21) that he may follow Christ, we begin to understand what
may be meant by the casting away of hand, foot, or eye. The
parable of hand, foot, and eye is concerned with 'entrance into
life', for which 'entrance into the Kingdom of God' is used as
an equivalent. Christ has been speaking of entrance into the
Kingdom of God (x, 15) when the rich man runs up and asks
how he may 'inherit eternal life'. Christ answers him, and begins
presently to speak of the rich man's difficulty in terms of
'entering the Kingdom of God' (23–25), returning finally to the
language of 'eternal life' (30). So much for the way in which
the paragraph of the rich man develops the private teaching.

The Deuteronomic character of the paragraph could scarcely
be stronger than it is. It is not *a* Deuteronomic scene, like the
discussion of divorce, it is *the* Deuteronomic scene, for it com-
prehends the whole lesson of Deuteronomy. The Moses of
Deuteronomy, after a narrative recapitulation, proceeds to give
Israel the heart of the matter in the fifth and sixth chapters.
'Hear, O Israel . . . the Lord our God made a covenant with
us . . . saying . . . *Honour thy father and thy mother . . . thou shalt
do no murder, neither shalt thou commit adultery, neither shalt thou
steal, neither shalt thou bear false witness . . . neither shalt thou
covet. . . . Ye shall walk in the way your God hath commanded
you, that ye may live. . . . Hear, O Israel: the Lord Our God is One
Lord, and thou shalt love the Lord thy God with all thy heart. . . .*

And when the Lord thy God shall bring thee into the land . . .
to give thee great and goodly cities which thou buildest not and
houses full of all good things which thou fillest not . . . *and thou eat
and be full, then beware lest thou forget the Lord thy God.'*

Compare the Marcan paragraph. 'And as Jesus went forth
into the way' (we know already and are presently to know better
what this way is; it is the way of obedience, the way to Jerusalem,
the way through death into life, *the way the Lord our God has
commanded, that we may live*), 'one ran to him and knelt to him
and asked him, Good Rabbi, what must I do to inherit *eternal
life*? Jesus said to him, Why callest thou me good? None is good
but *One, God.*' (The Lord our God is one Lord.) 'Thou knowest
his commandments: *Thou shalt do no murder, thou shalt not commit
adultery, thou shalt not steal, thou shalt not bear false witness, thou
shalt not defraud; honour thy father and thy mother.* He said to him:
Rabbi, all these things have I observed from my childhood.
Jesus looked on him and loved him and said to him: One thing
is lacking to thee; go sell all thou hast and give to the poor, and
thou shalt have treasure in heaven; and come, follow me' in
this *way* of mine through death into life. 'But the man's coun-
tenance fell at the saying and he departed grieved, for he had
great possessions', the supreme cause, as Moses had seen, why a
man should forget the Lord his God. And the remaining chapters
of his Deuteronomy are full of the rich man's duty towards the
poor.

We need not follow the paragraph of the rich man as it swings
from the negative into the positive, from the rich man's refusal
to the apostles' willing sacrifice. We will only observe that it
ends with an echo of the first word of the private teaching at
Capernaum: 'There are many first which shall be last, and last
first' (x, 31, cf. IX, 35). The refrain has a ring of finality, and fitly
brings the cycle to a close (IX, 2–X, 31).

We have guided our study of the Marcan cycles throughout by
the rhythm of the healing miracles. There is only one more such
miracle remaining, the cure of blind Bartimeus (x, 46–52). What
are we to say of the cycle which contains it? It is reasonable to

117

ask whether the form which we have seen to be common to the last two cycles will apply again. It consisted of four elements: (*a*) apostolic calling, (*b*) healing miracle, (*c*) private teaching, (*d*) public teaching. Of these four elements, (*a*), (*b*), and (*d*) apply comfortably to the text which extends in front of us; it is (*c*) which at first sight gives trouble.

(*a*) It is surely 'apostolic calling' when Jesus calls the Twelve about him and tells them what the journey is in which he has engaged them: they are following him to Jerusalem and to death (X, 32–34). And the theme may be thought to run on, when the Sons of Zebedee so far misunderstand their calling as to ask for privileges in glory, and are promised no privilege but martyrdom (35–45).

(*b*) Bartimeus is healed of his blindness; a healing of blindness being what the pattern of healings demands in this place (X, 46–52).

(*c*) Triumphal entry, cleansing of temple, and attached incidents (XI, 1–XII, 12). However this section of the Gospel ought to be described, it is not a 'private teaching'.

(*d*) Public teaching in the temple-courts, in which the themes of the public teaching beyond Jordan are gone over again: the Deuteronomic doctrines of marriage, of loving God with all the heart, and of not over-prizing wealth (XII, 13–XIII, 2).

Before we turn to the detail of the cycle we may observe its unity. The theme is 'Jerusalem', and it describes Christ's journey to the city (X, 32) by way of Jericho (X, 46) Bethphage and Bethany (XI, 1), his arrival, and the whole of his free public action there. It closes with his withdrawal from town and temple, prophesying its overthrow as he goes (XIII, 2).

The first paragraph of the cycle concentrates on one of the oldest elements in the scene of apostolic calling, the following of Jesus. Simon and his brother, the two sons of Zebedee, and Levi had all been called to follow, and had done so. But it had not at first appeared whither Jesus would lead them. It becomes clear now. 'They were in the way going up to Jerusalem, and Jesus was leading them on. And they were bewildered, and those that followed were afraid. And Jesus took the Twelve and began to tell them what was to befall him: Behold, we go up to Jerusalem, and the Son of Man shall be betrayed. . . .'

The paragraph is, then, a dramatic exposition of the call of the Twelve, their call to follow; and merely as such, it takes its place in the series of apostolic callings. But St Mark also gives it a special relation to the last of such scenes, the Transfiguration. For the Transfiguration was concerned with the calling of the Three Witnesses, Peter, James and John, and the new call-story is a short paragraph inserted between two longer narratives, the former concerned with the calling of Peter, and the latter with the calling of James and John.

The story of the Rich Man may be described as the story of a failed Levi, a man who would not leave his cash-desk to follow Christ, and so it acts by contrast as a sort of prelude to the scenes of apostolic calling. The man will not follow Christ on the way to Jerusalem; the apostles do, though with fear and trembling, and their Master teaches them to count the cost. But the contrast between the rich man and the apostles does not wait for the scene of calling (x, 32–34) to bring it out; it is already there when *Peter* begins to say to Jesus, 'Lo, we have left all to follow thee' (x, 28). The generosity of Christ holds no rebuke for this somewhat premature protestation. He assures Peter and his like of their rewards in the next life and in this 'with persecutions', and adds that many first shall be last, and last first.

The 'persecutions' begin to loom up immediately in the call scene (x, 32–34); the warning about 'first and last' comes to bear directly after it. For *James* and *John* ask to be first, and are told that Christ can promise them nothing but the 'persecutions', to drink of his cup and be baptized with his baptism. James and John, like Peter, pass unrebuked, perhaps because their readiness to suffer is sincere, perhaps because rebuke turns aside from their ambition to strike the far more ignoble jealousy of their fellow-disciples. In Christ's correction of the ten, we are aware of fresh Deuteronomic echoes: princes in Israel are not to be like the princes of the gentiles; their heart must not be uplifted above their brethren (Deut. XVII, 20, cf. I Kings XII, 7, he must serve who would rule).

The scene of the Transfiguration is recalled, then, by the persons of the Three Witnesses, all asking about their share in that glory which they had seen on the Mount. The request of James and John seems to revive the very imagery of the Transfiguration. Jesus had been revealed in glory with Moses and Elijah, but Moses and Elijah had faded away, leaving (it might seem) empty places to his right and to his left. The vision contains just the suggestions required to give shape to James's and John's request: 'Grant us to sit one at thy right hand and one at thy left in thy glory.'

So much for apostolic calling. As to healing, it is unnecessary to dwell upon the incident of blind Bartimeus, for nothing could be a plainer pair to the exorcism of the deaf mute (IX, 14–29), or plainer antitype to the cure of the blind villager (VIII, 22–26). We may proceed, therefore, to our next section, the section which perplexed us (XI, 1–XII, 12).

Our perplexity was this. According to the model provided by the two previous cycles, the healing miracle of this cycle should be followed by a private teaching. The healing miracle of the cycle is the cure of Bartimeus, and it is followed by the triumphal entry; a scene which is so far from being a private teaching that it is a dramatic publication of the gospel mystery. Our perplexity can be resolved by a simple act of reflection about Bartimeus, and his relation to his model, the blind villager.

The healing of the sensitive and communicative powers, of ears, tongue, and eyes, is twice gone through in this Gospel. The healing of the blind villager is the climax of the first series; and the healing of blind Bartimeus is the climax of the second. The healing of the villager, as we remember, acted as a trigger, and discharged the disciples' confession of their Lord. They who had been hitherto hard of heart, without perception or understanding, with no use of the tongue, ears or eyes had at length proclaimed through Peter's lips the messiahship of Jesus. If the first series of healings had such an effect, what effect will the second series have? Not the same, surely; there must be some further effect, some real advance. It cannot be another secret proclamation of the disciples' faith; it must be a public proclamation this time, and it must come from outside the favoured circle. If the confession resulting from the first series of healings was secret, so, after all, were the healings themselves: both the deaf mute Decapolitan and the blind villager near Bethsaida were secretly cured. But the healings of the second series, the exorcism of the deaf mute boy and the cure of Bartimeus, both take place in a blaze of publicity, and it seems only proper that the confession which follows upon them should be equally public.

In the case of the blind villager we saw St Mark to be in a certain difficulty with his symbolism. He wants to make us feel that the healing of the bodily eyes is equivalent to spiritual illumination, and the simplest way of doing it would be to make the same person who receives power to see with his eyes, receive power also to see with his heart, and confess Christ. But he is precluded from saying this. For the secret confession of Christ is the theme, and that means his confession within the circle of the apostles; and none of the apostles had been cured by Christ of physical blindness. The evangelist is constrained therefore to acquiesce in a division of roles: the villager is cured, but does not confess; St Peter confesses but is not cured. And he has to do his best to make us feel the equivalence between the villager and St Peter by a correspondence between the stages of physical recovery in the one, and of spiritual illumination in the other.

But when he comes to Bartimeus, he is free of such embarrassments. The confession of Christ is now to be public, so why should not the man who 'sees' physically be the man who 'sees' spiritually? Bartimeus confesses the Son of David, and Bartimeus receives his sight. Blind Bartimeus 'sees' with the 'sight' which is a special gift of the blind, divination. Hearing that Jesus the *Nazarene* is passing by, he interprets *Nazar* as *Nesser*, the *Branch* from the stock of Jesse, of whom Isaiah had prophesied (Is. XI, 1). So he begins to cry and say, 'Son of David'. (The other possible divination on Nazarene has been made by the madman in 1, Nazir, Nazirite, Holy One of God.)

Blind Bartimeus has 'seen': Christ makes him see indeed, and he uses his new-won sight to 'follow Jesus in the way'. Jesus no more leaves Bartimeus to illuminate his neighbours than he left Peter to illuminate his fellow-disciples. No sooner had Peter confessed, than Jesus began to teach them the truth about the Son of Man. With Bartimeus healed and following him, Jesus sends for the ass and heads the triumph which proclaims the Kingdom of David. Having entered the city, he continues the enacted presentation of his Davidic power; he sweeps away the licensed market of offerings, overruling the priests in their own temple. Being confronted by the High Priests, he holds his own against them in debate and denounces them in parables.

The anomalous section which we have been studying (XI–XII, 12) turns out not to be anomalous at all. We supposed it to be anomalous because we assumed that the requirement for a 'private teaching' was still in force. But it was only in force until something else superseded it. It was in force while the secret gift of vision (VIII, 22–26) still made its influence felt, and it ceased to be in force when the public gift of vision (X, 46–52) was bestowed.

The 'private teaching' then is replaced by enacted proclamation, but there is no reason why its companion, the public teaching, should be in any way affected. It seems just as proper that enacted proclamation should be supported by teaching, as that private teaching should be extended to the public. And so we come to the last of the four parts into which we divided our cycle, public teaching in the temple courts. Not only does St Mark record such a teaching (XII, 13–XIII, 2): he models it with remarkable closeness on the public teaching in the cycle preceding (X, 1–31).

The link by which we pass from the dramatic events of XI, 1–XII, 12 to the quieter scenes of teaching and debate which follow is provided by the incident of the tribute-money. In his denunciatory parable against the High Priests, Christ has described them as the farmers who will not pay the rent. The lord's son comes demanding his father's dues, and they conspire to murder him. The High Priests find no reply; but conceiving that a

Messianic zealot for the rendering of God's dues to God may easily be put in the wrong about the rendering of Caesar's dues to Caesar, they send some Pharisees and Herodians to try Christ with the tribute question. In spite of the dangerous political issues involved, the question is put with exaggerated politeness, and in the style of academic discussion. So it opens the way to the proposing of other scribal problems; and at this point St Mark begins going over the ground of the last 'public teaching'.

Pharisees and Herodians having been already answered, Sadducean doctors try their hand. They propose their own riddle about marriage according to Deuteronomy (xxv, 5). We have already had the Pharisaic question on this subject in x, 1–12; now we hear the Sadducean equivalent. The Pharisaic question was a genuine question about the discipline of marriage; the Sadducean question is simply a catch-question for Pharisees or other believers in resurrection. Christ proceeds with both questions in the same order. First he solves the difficulty for his own position arising out of the text of Deuteronomy ('It was for the hardness of your heart that Moses gave you this commandment'—'When they rise from the dead they neither marry nor are given in marriage, but are as angels in heaven'). Then he gives his own opinion independent support by citing a text from the First Law (from Genesis–Numbers, not from Deuteronomy). In the one case it is, 'But from the beginning of creation male and female created he them', etc. And in the other, 'But that the dead rise, have ye not read in the Book of Moses at the Bush, how God said to him, I am the God of Abraham', etc. The two discussions could scarcely be more closely parallel.

The next piece of the model is the short paragraph devoted to the blessing of the children. But this is not a point of scriptural discussion, so that it hardly suits the scribal debates in the temple. Moreover St Mark has handled the theme twice, once beyond Jordan and once previously in the house at Capernaum; and it is his custom to handle a theme twice, but not three times or more, unless of course it is one of the standing elements of his structure (calling and healing, for example). So it is scarcely surprising that in the re-use of x he should pass direct from the marriage-question to the rich man.

The paragraph of the rich man is a long paragraph, if indeed it ought to be reckoned as one rather than two. It deals explicitly or implicitly with three issues, and each of the three receives distinct and explicit treatment in the antitype. The first is, How is a man to be saved in keeping the commandments? That, after all, is what the rich man intended to discuss with Christ. The second is, What is the relation between keeping the commandments of him who is good alone, and surrendering all for the sake of following Christ? The God who is good alone, and the Christ whom it is life to follow, are set side by side, and left unrelated. Can there be two absolutes? The third issue is wealth and poverty. For convenience, then, we may call the three topics: the command-ments, God and Christ, wealth and poverty.

The question of the good scribe (XII, 28–34) is almost a double of the rich man's question; St Luke, as we know, was caught by the resemblance, and still further emphasized it (Luke x, 25–28, XVIII, 18–23). Both discussions take place on the same scriptural ground (Deut. v–VI). The scribe's question is, Which of the commandments is first of all? Which, that is to say, deter-mines the sense of the others? Christ's reply is principally com-posed of words from Deut. VI, 'Hear, O Israel, the Lord our God is One Lord, and thou shalt love the Lord thy God with all thy heart and with all thy soul, with all thy mind and with all thy might'. He adds these words only from Leviticus XIX, 18: 'And thou shalt love thy neighbour as thyself.' The scribe, in approving Christ's answer, expands the Deuteronomic part of it, laying emphasis on the unity of God. 'Thou hast well and truly said, Rabbi, that he is One, and that there is no other but he. And to love him with all one's heart, one's understanding and one's might, and to love one's neighbour as one's self, is more than all burnt-offerings and sacrifices.'

The scribe's reply divides the Deuteronomic matter into two parts: the creed, and the whole duty of man. The creed is that

God is One, and there is none beside him; the duty of man is to love his God and his neighbour. Such an account of true religion is approved by Christ, just as the rich man's profession was previously approved by him. Christ looked on the rich man, and loved him; to the scribe he says, 'Thou art not far from the Kingdom of God'—that Kingdom which it had been the rich man's aspiration to inherit. 'Not far', as though there were a further step to be taken, a further test to be undergone. So there was in the case of the rich enquirer: his test was contained in the summons, 'Sell all and follow me'. It fell, that is, on the side of 'the whole duty of man'. In XII the matter is pursued on the credal side. The scribal faith in one God and Lord is sound so far as it goes; how much farther should it go? It should advance to the extension or distribution of the one lordship by the enthronement of Messiah with God. The scribes say that Messiah is (essentially) David's heir, but David himself is against them. He assigns Messiah a royalty which is higher than his own, for he calls him 'my lord'; and he defines the lordship of Messiah as a partaking in the Lordship of God, by his enthronement in the throne of the one Kingdom of God. It is in Messiah that the Lordship must be obeyed and the Kingdom received on earth. They who do not know this may not be far from the Kingdom of God, but they do not know where to lay their hands upon it.

It is easy for the modern reader to miss the absolute centrality of Mark XII, 28-37 in the evangelist's account of Christ's doctrine. The words of Deuteronomy about the oneness of God are the creed of Israel. The new faith accepts them, but it does not take the oneness in an exclusive or negative sense; it glosses it by the doctrine of the extension of the lordship, and finds scriptural support for the gloss.

We may usefully compare St Paul with St Mark. Christian knowledge, he writes (in I Cor. VIII, 3-6), instructs us in the spirit of Deuteronomy that God is One, and that no other pretenders to godhead are anything in the world; and such knowledge is fulfilled in loving the one God and one Lord with all our heart.

'If a man thinks to have obtained any knowledge, he knows not yet in such fashion as he must, but if any man *loveth* God, he is known to him. . . . We know that an idol is nothing in the world, and there is no God save one. For though there be that are called gods whether in heaven or on earth, as there are gods many and lords many, yet for us there is one God the Father from whom are all things, and we for him, and one Lord Jesus Christ, through whom are all things, and we through him. . . .'

St Paul's words are an example of the way in which the Deuteronomic creed is glossed in Christendom. Mark XII, 28–37 is another example. The scribe asserts with Christ that God is one, but Christ alone asserts the association of Messiah in the one lordship of the all-ruling throne. He implies that the Scribes deny it; the Sanhedrin is presently to condemn it as blasphemy (XIV, 62). 'I am Messiah', said Jesus in response to the High Priest's challenge, and added of his own will, 'Ye shall see the Son of Man sitting at the right hand of omnipotence, and coming with the clouds of heaven'. The High Priest rent his robe. 'Ye have heard', he said, 'the blasphemy.'

We found three topics in the paragraph of the rich man: salvation by the commandments, God and Christ, wealth and poverty. We have shown what Mark XII does with the first two of them; there remains the third.

The evangelist works round to the topic of wealth and poverty by continuing the criticism of the scribes. They who abase Messiah exalt themselves, they love robes, salutations, and chief seats; the poverty of widows supports their magnificence, and their long prayers in public do but cloak their pride. After such a preparation we are ready for the episode of the widow's mite (XII, 41–44). In the paragraph of the rich man, the disciples wanted to know who could be saved if the rich cannot, having presumably in mind a piety furnished with the means of charity and set above the temptations of meanness. Such a piety is now dramatically presented in the rich men throwing their handfuls into the Temple treasure. Who is more surely accepted than they?

The widow, says Christ, who offers her two mites. God values the giver's intention, not the gift. Large gifts do more, no doubt, to sustain the temple; but the temple is not destined to be sustained. Splendid as the buildings may be, not one stone shall remain upon another. With these words Jesus leaves the temple for the last time, and St Mark's cycle closes.

It is the last cycle to contain a healing miracle of the ordinary kind, and we may wonder how to proceed with the rest of the Gospel. For the cycles have hitherto revolved about the healing miracles, and it seems strange to plot out a cycle without one. Nevertheless the cyclic form has become so vigorous and well-established that it would be surprising if it suddenly broke off within sight of the end. The whole rhythm of the evangelist's thought is not likely to change, merely because he has no more healings to record. In fact we shall find it necessary to allow two more cycles, XIII, 3–XIV, 31, and XIV, 32–XVI, 8.

These two cycles cover the dated part of St Mark's Gospel. The first date he gives us is XIV, 1, and if we are guided by St Mark's usage elsewhere, we shall take it to date the scene preceding it (XIII, 3–37), as well as the scene following it. 'Now it was passover and unleavened bread after two days.' St Mark twice elsewhere uses 'It was' with a date, and on both occasions he is telling us where the narrative has brought us to already, and not simply announcing the date of what comes next. They brought Jesus to Golgotha and crucified him, parting his garments among them, and casting lots for their shares; 'now it was the third hour, when they crucified him' (XV, 25). Similarly at XV, 42. Here St Mark is in the midst of narrating the events of Sabbath-eve. 'And when it began to be late,' he says, 'since it *was* Preparation, i.e. Sabbath-eve, Joseph of Arimathea' made haste to obtain the removal of Christ's body from the cross. By analogy, then, we should conclude that the evangelist is dating the discourse on the Mount of Olives when he follows it with the words, 'Now it was passover and unleavened bread after two days'.

What does 'after two days' mean? It ought in logic to mean

'On the third day' (by inclusive reckoning). But to judge, once more, by analogy, St Mark is not speaking either logically or correctly; he is using 'after two days' as an equivalent for 'on the second day', that is, 'next day'. For he habitually writes 'after three days' in speaking of Christ's resurrection. A great deal has been made of this, as representing a rival tradition to 'the third day', but St Mark shows no consciousness of the discrepancy, and when he comes to the history of the resurrection in XVI he places it unambiguously on the third day. By far the simplest supposition is that he used 'after three days' in the sense of 'on the third day', and so 'after two days' should mean 'on the second day', of course by inclusive reckoning. So when he says, 'It was passover after two days' he is talking about the day before the lamb-slaying. And this gives the most satisfactory sense, for it makes XIII, 3–XVI, 8 continuous. On the day before the paschal lamb-slaying Jesus discoursed with his four disciples on the Mount of Olives, and was anointed at supper the same evening. Next day was the day of the lamb-slaying (XIV, 12), and Jesus arranged for his passover, and in the evening ate it. That night he was arrested in Gethsemane, and suffered next day. The day following was Sabbath (XVI, 1), and the morning after, the women visited the sepulchre and found that Jesus was already risen. So much for the continuity of time in the last pair of Marcan cycles.

And now for the analysis of the former cycle of the two. We will interpret it by its immediate predecessor, and divide it into the following parts: an 'apostolic' scene (XIII, 3–37), an antitype to the healing (XIV, 1–11), and an antitype to Christ's action in the temple (XIV, 12–31).

The apocalypse on Olivet conforms to the general type of those scenes which set before us the calling of the apostles. Like the scene of the institution of the Twelve or that of the Transfiguration, it is on a mountain. A named group of four apostles is concerned in it; we are reminded of the three witnesses to the Transfiguration. The Transfiguration was a visionary apocalypse, this is a spoken one, and so the style and the length of the two texts is very different. The Transfiguration supplies no sort of model for the prophecy; and in any case the Transfiguration is two cycles back. The directly preceding apostolic scene is the ascent to Jerusalem, with its continuation, James and John's request (x, 32–45). Here we have something more like a model. The two brothers had something to ask of Jesus. On Olivet the other pair of brothers is added to them, and all four have something to ask. Both questions are concerned with the day of glory; but where the two asked for thrones, the four are content to ask for knowledge: 'Tell us, when shall these things be?' Very different sorts of requests, certainly; but the two answers are not unalike. The two ask for thrones, but 'to sit at my right hand and my left is not mine to give'. The four ask to know the time, but 'of that day and that hour none knoweth, not the angels in heaven nor the Son, but the Father alone'. The two gain something, however: 'The cup that I drink you shall drink, the baptism I am baptized with you shall be baptized with also.' And the four gain something—the knowledge of manifold opportunities to re-enact in their own persons the passion of Christ: 'Ye shall be brought before sanhedrins and scourged in synagogues, and summoned before governors and kings for my sake.' Needless to say, the story of James and John's request does not contain the text for the long prophecy of XIII, not, that is, for its prophetic substance. Where that text is to be found, we shall consider in another chapter.

We have now to consider the second feature of the cycle, an antitype to the healing story, that is, to the story of Blind Bartimeus. The healing miracles are ended; the antitype is not going to reflect the healing aspect of the Bartimeus incident. But the incident had other aspects, and in particular it was the public greeting of Jesus as Son of David; it was, indeed, from that aspect of the incident that the sequel unfolded; for Christ accepted the royal greeting, sent for the ass, and headed the triumph. A royal greeting has its counterpart and consequence in a royal anointing. The woman in the feast at Bethany pours her perfume on the head of Christ. It is no diminution of its

royal significance when Jesus declares the anointing to be for
his burial, for it is precisely the paradox of Christ's royalty that he
is enthroned through being entombed. The paradox will soon
be turned the other way. She who anoints for glory anoints for
burial, but they who come to anoint for burial will encounter
the herald of Christ's glory.

The relation between Bartimeus's greeting and the woman's
anointing is intelligible of itself, but it is illustrated and confirmed
by the most obvious of its scriptural types. When Bartimeus
hails Jesus as Son of David, he compares him first of all with
Solomon. And Solomon was established in his kingdom by two
signs. First, he rode in triumph on the King's mule; second, he
was anointed in the suburbs outside Jerusalem without the
knowledge of his rivals and enemies (I Kings 1). Both of these
signs are fulfilled in Christ. St Mark distributes them, one in
one cycle, the other at the corresponding point in the next.

Not quite at the corresponding point. The story of Bartimeus
matches the story of the anointing; the story of the ass matches
not the story of the anointing, but the story of the supper
chamber; the two narratives are carefully written in the same
form. In both of them Christ sends two disciples with supernatural foresight of what they will find; they go, and discover it
to be even so; and those with whom they have to do show them
spontaneous and surprising goodwill. Whether it is an ass or a
supper room that they require, it is enough that the Rabbi has
need of it. This carefully written pair of incidents stand on an
interesting scriptural background, which we will proceed to
identify.

If we are thinking of the two signs of the Son of David's
kingship, the mule and the secret anointing, we shall be readily
reminded of the signs divinely given when the kingdom was first
instituted in Israel. Samuel anointed Saul king; he did it secretly,
and at a feast. And he gave a sign to authenticate his action: the
finding of the asses. And forthwith he added a second sign. Let
us compare St Mark's two stories of providential encounter with
the first two signs given by Samuel to Saul:

I Sam. x, 2. When thou art departed from me today, thou shalt find two men by Rachel's sepulchre in the border of Benjamin at Zelzah, and they will say unto thee, The asses which thou wentest to seek are found. . . .

Go into the village over against you, and straightway on your entry ye shall find a colt tied on which no man yet sat; loose it and bring it. And if any man ask you why you do so, say, The Lord has need of it, and is returning it hither presently. . . .

Then shalt thou go on further from thence, and shalt come to the oak at Tabor, and there shall meet thee three men going up to God at Bethel, one carrying three kids and another carrying three loaves of bread and another carrying a skin of wine. And they will salute thee and give thee two loaves of bread, which thou shalt receive at their hand.

Go into the city, and there shall meet you a man carrying a jar of water. Follow him, and wheresoever he turns in, say to the master of the house, The Rabbi saith, Where is my guest chamber where I may eat the passover with my disciples? And he shall show you a large upper room furnished ready.

There is more in the comparison between Samuel's second sign and St Mark's than meets the eye at once. It is not simply that men carrying articles of food or drink are given in each case as signs. The men carrying their victims, their bread and their wine in Samuel's prophecy are taking them to the house of God, to keep festival. They make Saul partaker of their holy things in unconscious recognition of what is owing to the Lord's Anointed. So the householder to whom the two disciples are providentially led is felt by the Christian reader to be paying an unconscious tribute to Christ, when he so readily admits him to his hospitality. Nor is the occasion secular; it is a holy feast before God in Jerusalem, where Christ the true victim will set forth a mystery of bread and wine.

In comparing the finding of the chamber with the finding of the ass, we have already set foot upon the third and last part of our cycle, the antitype to Christ's action in the Temple. For the finding of the ass and the triumphal entry are the beginning of the story of Christ in the Temple, just as the finding of the supper chamber and the 'preparation of the passover are the beginning of the story of Christ at the supper. Whatever the reader may think about the influence of the history of Saul or of Solomon on these two narratives, he will scarcely deny that they match one another in a striking manner. Whatever else the evangelist is or is not telling us, he is telling us that Christ made two entries into Jerusalem, both prepared for with providential foresight and marked by miraculous circumstances of the same kind. Scenes of entry derive their character from that to which they lead. Christ's two visitations of Jerusalem, the visitation of the Temple, and the visitation of the supper room, are being set in comparison with one another, not withstanding the fact that his presence in the Temple continued for days, perhaps weeks, whereas his presence in the supper chamber was limited to a few hours.

The device of comparing the two visits by assimilating their introductory parts is all the more valuable, because there is no question of the evangelist's assimilating the main bodies of the two narratives. He cannot bring the account of what took place at the supper into detailed analogy with what took place in the Temple, for the narrative of the supper was sacred tradition, it already had a set form and was incorporated in the catechism of the neophytes. We can be certain of that from what St Paul says in I Cor. XI.

But the history of the supper does not need to be decked with any borrowed colours; merely by being what it is, it provides the true antitype to Christ's actions in the Temple. For Christ came to the Temple to worship and to teach. Finding the worship of God hindered by corruptions, he assailed them, and hearing his teaching interrupted by critics, he silenced them. He turned at length from the Temple, because the priesthood rejected him and sought his life; he denounced its overthrow, and predicted the scattering of its stones. The old temple gives way; the new abides; and what is the new but Jesus Christ himself in sacramental fellowship with his disciples? Here is the worship, the teaching, and the availing sacrifice.

Jesus Christ is the true temple. St Mark uses the false witnesses in the High Priest's house to remind us of this basic piece of Christian symbolism. 'We have heard him say, I will destroy this temple made with hands, and in three days build another not made with hands.' This is both false witness, and tragic irony. The witness is false, because Jesus had not threatened the temple, either with the crowbars of a gang or with the power of a spell. It is dramatic irony, because the existence of their temple is bound up with the body of Christ. If they kill that body, Christ will raise it in three days as a temple made without hands, and the temple of Herod will give place to it, and ultimately fall.

The contrast is not between a temple which is overthrown, and a temple which abides; both temples are overthrown, for the one falls in the fall of the other; but the one rises the third day, and the other does not. Nor is it a contrast between a temple of murderers and a temple of saints, for in the supper-chamber it is said, One of you shall betray me. When the spiritual house falls, its stones also are scattered, not one of them shall remain upon another; not even that Stone whom Christ himself had named. Protest as he may, the word applies to him, 'I will smite the shepherd, and the sheep will be scattered'. But the stones of the old temple will lie, and not be gathered; the shepherd, being risen again, will draw his flock after him into Galilee. The prediction about the scattering of the sheep holds the same place as the prediction about the scattering of the stones: Christ says the one thing as he comes forth from the temple, and the other as he comes forth from the supper room. And both goings forth lead to the same place—the Mount of Olives.

The last Marcan cycle is the passion history, from Gethsemane to the empty tomb. It would be fantastic to suppose that St Mark had shaped this part of his book on models supplied by earlier parts; we are not proposing to dissent from the commonly held opinion, that the passion-narrative was one block of tradition, and already set in its main lines before St Mark wrote it down. The truth will be the other way about—not that St Mark shaped the passion narrative on the cycles of the ministry, but that he shaped the cycles of the ministry with a view to the passion narrative. We have, indeed, supposed from the start that the sequence of healings is a sequence of anticipations, and that Christ's death and resurrection is what they anticipate. And, to take another standing element of the cyclic form, apostolic calling: it has become clearer and clearer since the Transfiguration, that the calling of the apostles is to follow Christ into his passion, and that they will fail to do so now, though they will hereafter.

We need not seek in the Passion any other elements but these two, calling and healing. Now in the last cycle there was no healing, but the story of the anointing at Bethany did duty for one. And so, if the passion narrative consists of calling and healing only, we should look for its immediate model (to use the word without prejudice), in XIII, 3–XIV, 9 only, from the four disciples on the Mount of Olives to that anointing at Bethany, which Jesus said was for his burial.

Now without question the passion narrative begins with a second scene on the Mount of Olives, for Gethsemane was there; and ends with a second anointing, or attempted anointing, at the hands of women, when they endeavoured to complete the Lord's burial. The scene in Gethsemane has the formal character of an apostolic scene. Christ calls the three witnessing apostles, Peter, James and John, into privileged communion with a divine mystery, when he makes them the companions of his prayer and agony; and our thoughts run back to the Transfiguration.

The two anointings are obviously parallel. The earlier one we were led to describe as a substitute healing, and in a sense the same description fits the later one too. For the healing with which the last cycle is concerned is the resurrection, and the story of the women at the tomb is not a story of the resurrection. The resurrection had no direct witnesses, no one saw Christ's return to life as the parents and the there apostles saw the revival of

Jairus's child. The women at the tomb simply discover that they have come too late to honour the Lord's sepulchre; so the woman at the feast discovered that she was beforehand to honour it; they, like she, are carried clean outside their calculations.

So far we have established a parallel between the beginning and end of the passion history, and the beginning and end of what we are calling its model. The three in Gethsemane match the four on the Mount of Olives, and one scene of anointing matches the other. But what is the model for the whole body of the passion-history which lies between Gethsemane and the Empty Tomb? We must reply, the model is all that intervenes between the mention of the four on Olivet, and the anointing at Bethany. And what is that? It is the apocalyptic discourse. And how can the apocalyptic discourse, which prophesies the last things, be a type of the passion? Let us consider the question.

At first sight it appears that the apocalyptic discourse deals with things which cannot be the type of the passion, because they come after it. We may say if we will that the Exodus from Egypt was a type of the passion, or we may say that the passion itself is a type of the Church's sufferings under the tyranny of Antichrist hereafter. But to make the tyranny of Antichrist a type of the passion is to turn things upside down.

The objection must, of course, be admitted in the form in which it is stated. The usual sense of the word 'type' implies that its antitype follows it in time, and the passion does not follow but precede the tyranny of Antichrist. But we must observe that the apocalyptic discourse is not a record of the tyranny of Antichrist, as the passion history is a record of the tyranny of Caiaphas and Pilate. What the apocalytic discourse sets forth is the prophetical images of Antichrist's coming tyranny. What we have to ask is, whether these prophetical images can stand in a relation to the actual events of the passion, for which 'type' is a possible description? They very well can, and an analogy may help to show how they can.

Let us suppose the case of some visionaries who conceive a world utopia, projected on principles of rose-tinted idealism, and worked out in all the impressive architecture of universal and local government. Let us further suppose that they form themselves into a voluntary society, which they declare to be the first unit or cell of their world-wide structure. All that is needed, they say, is for other men by degrees to see the light and form more and more such cells, until one fine day the plan is found to be complete and utopia to be operative. Now such people begin with their utopian dream of universal order, and shape their little society in accordance with it. They begin with the end of the world and work back into the present. And if we, the onlookers, wish to understand them, we must do the same. If we want to understand what the society is about, and why its officers and committees bear the names they do, we must begin from the futuristic dream, and apply it to the present reality. I do not know whether the reader will agree to our calling the utopian image the 'type' of the actual society in such a case, but I am sure that he will recognize what would be meant by such a use of the word.

In the same sense it will be said that the image of Antichrist's tyranny is the type of the passion. For in the history of our faith the image of Antichrist came first, and the passion of Christ came afterwards. Long before Israel had heard of a suffering Messiah it had been accepted that Israel would go through great sufferings, a sort of national martyrdom, before the glorious days of Messiah came. The prophecy of Daniel is largely devoted to such a theme, and it is the prophecy of Daniel which gives its decisive shape to Christ's prediction on the Mount of Olives.

When Christ began to speak of the sufferings of the Son of Man, he appeared to be talking not of what Caiaphas or Pilate did, for they had not yet done it, but about the figures of prophecy. He was saying that the Messiah would be first in the sufferings, as he would be first in the deliverance of Israel. This was a new and a scandalous doctrine. It might seem to mean that when Antichrist came Christ would suffer, and afterwards rise to lead the Israelite victory. But this was not what Christ either said or meant. When Antichrist came, Israel would suffer and Christ would not; Christ's part would be to bring deliverance simply, as men had always supposed. But at a quite different and previous time Christ would have suffered, and risen, and ascended. Christ would have his own passion, and his own antichrist, and his own deliverance; the antichrist, and passion, and deliverance of Israel, for which men had always looked, would be hereafter.

From the modern Christian's point of view, it is natural to speak of the sufferings of the Church under any antichrist who may arise, as a second Calvary, a repetition of the sufferings of the divine Head in his members. And so we easily forget that there ever was a time when it was more natural to speak the other way about, and to describe Calvary as a summing-up in the Head of that martyrdom under Antichrist which was destined to befall the members. To say that it was once natural to speak thus, is the same thing as to say that the images foreshadowing the tyranny of Antichrist were once the natural types of Christ's passion. And so there is nothing that ought to surprise us in the fact that the cycle of the Gospel which immediately foreshadows the passion finds its heart and substance in the prediction of the days of Antichrist.

We must now observe what measures the evangelist employs to apply the image of Antichrist's tyranny to Christ's passion. To take a purely formal point. Immediately after the end of the apocalyptic discourse St Mark tells us that we have reached the day before the paschal lamb-slaying. Then he goes on to tell us how Christ was consecrated to his own death at supper that evening by the woman's anointing of him and by his own interpretation of her act; and by way of giving substance to Christ's saying about his burial, St Mark goes on to tell us how Judas arranged Christ's betrayal with the priests, presumably about the time of the anointing, or anyhow the same evening. For the evangelist opens his account of the next day directly afterwards. His continuous and dated passion story runs from the Wednesday evening, when Judas betrayed, until after daybreak on the Sunday, when Christ was found to be risen. The suggestion is made to us that Christ rose with the sun, or as soon as it could be called the third day from his passion. If that is so, then the period from Judas's selling of Christ until the moment of Christ's resurrection will be part of Wednesday, and the whole of Thursday, Friday, and Saturday. Or, if you like to use a Judaic reckoning from sundown to sundown, call it the whole of Thursday, Friday and Saturday, and half of Sunday. On either reckoning it is half a week. St Mark knows nothing of a Holy Week; what he describes for us is a half-week of the passion.

Now half a week is the conventional reckoning of the days of Antichrist. Daniel ix gives a forecast of history in 'weeks' of years, as though that were a standard measure of time; so that it appears to be a special dispensation of the divine mercy, when not a whole 'week', but a half 'week' only, is assigned to the oppression by Antichrist. And the whole prophecy of Daniel ends with a picture of a mighty angel swearing that the oppression shall be for a time, (a couple of) times, and a half, but no more. And when Christ says in the Marcan apocalypse 'For the elects' sake whom he has chosen, the Lord has shortened the days' of the last oppression, he is referring to Daniel, and means the same thing. He means that the 'week' of oppression is halved.

To men so accustomed as the ancient Jews were to number-symbolism, one obvious way of setting forth the passion as a pre-enactment of the days of Antichrist was to describe it as a half-week of the tyranny of evil. To do this there was no need to manipulate history. There were so many alternative points in the story which you could chose as the beginning of the passion. If you counted from the moment when Judas stepped forward out of the shadows and hands were laid on Christ, you would have a period of two and a half days, and perhaps that would be the most natural reckoning. But if you chose to go back to the beginning of Judas's plotting in the dark, there were your three and a half days, and no one could grudge you them.

The comparison of the half week *of years* with a half week *of days* is implicit in Daniel's language already. If you call $3\frac{1}{2}$ years *half a week* of years, you are comparing them with half a week of days. That the passion is reckoned in days, and the great tribulation in years, would merely help to say what the primitive Christian wanted to say in any case: that the future sufferings of the whole Church are drawn together, summed up, or epitomized in the single passion of Christ. The eleventh chapter of St John's apocalyse illustrates the use of the same proportion. The profanation of the temple continues for three and a half years, at the end of which period the Two Witnesses are killed, and lie unburied for three and a half days. Their bodies lie on the street of the city in which their Lord was crucified, until they, like him, receive their resurrection, and like him ascend. It is tempting to say that St John must have felt that the 'three and a half days' applied somehow to the passion of Christ, as well as to the martyrdom of his witnesses; but perhaps that would be to force the point.

It is noteworthy that the apocalyptic discourse and the passion history both end abruptly; neither goes farther than is necessary to establish the termination of the half-week. The apocalyptic half-week ends with the appearance of the Son of Man on clouds, come to harvest his elect, and the half-week of the passion ends with the empty tomb. If we ask why the evangelist did not record the appearances to the apostles and the sending forth of the great mission, seeing that he must have believed in these things, we may just as well ask why he did not record Christ's predictions of the establishment of the kingdom, the judgement of quick and dead, and the happy-making vision of God; for he must have believed in these things too, and it is unlikely that Christ had been silent about them. The apocalyptic prediction breaks off at the same point as the Gospel does, that is, with the end of the half-week.

The Gospel does not simply leave us to infer that the whole weight of the apocalyptic discourse falls upon the passion. The apocalypse is carried into the passion by means of the exhortation with which XIII concludes. After prophesying the advent of the Son of Man, our Lord proceeds to enjoin watchfulness by the parable of the fig. The exhortation appears at first sight to be concerned with watching for the end of all things, but as it proceeds it presses with such urgency upon the listening disciples that it must concern their present state. In some sense the days of Antichrist must be upon them. The last words of the exhortation appear to draw a parallel between the disciples faced with the imminence of Christ's passion, and the Christians whom St Mark addresses, with persecution rising, and Antichrist at the door: 'What I say to you (disciples) I say to all (Christians), watch.' I say it to you, for (St Mark immediately proceeds), 'It was then the day before the feast of the passover and the unleavened bread; and the chief priests and the scribes sought how they might take him by treachery and kill him'.

As we read on into the Passion, we see the details of the exhortation to watchfulness in XIII, 32–37 applied to the events of the passion itself. The application begins where we should expect it to begin; that is, when St Mark begins to pass back over the ground of the Apocalyptic discourse in a new cycle. We have seen that he begins to do so in the story of Gethsemane. 'About that day and that hour', says the discourse, 'none knoweth, not the angels in heaven, nor the Son, but the Father alone.' And here in Gethsemane is the Son praying to the Father, that if it might be, the hour might pass him over[1]; as the dreadful midnight passed over Israel and smote Egypt in the first passover of all. It was not to be, and he was presently declaring to his sleepy followers, 'the hour has come'.

'Observe, watch, and pray,' says the apocalyptic exhortation, 'for ye know not when the moment is.' While the Son waited for the hour in Gethsemane, he set his disciples to watch and pray with him; but they could not. The hour came suddenly, and found them sleeping (XIII, 33, 36). 'Watch, then, for ye know not when the master of the house cometh, late, or at midnight, or at cockcrow, or early.' When it was *late*, they sat at their last supper (XIV, 17), and heard a last warning of the coming betrayal (XIV, 18–21). But when it was *midnight*, the paschal midnight, the hour of the destroyer against which Christ prayed, then the armed men were upon them, and they were not ready; they aimed useless blows, they ran in shameful flight.

[1] St. Mark's verb is that of LXX in Exod. XII, 13, 23, 27.

When it was *cockcrow* condemnation fell on Christ and accusation on his following, but Peter was not ready; the cock could not crow the day up fast enough to keep pace with his denials. And therefore when it was *early*, and Christ stood before Pilate, he stood there alone. 'Early' was not an hour for Christ's disciples then. Yet an early hour remained for some of them to face. Very early on the first day of the week came the women to the sepulchre, to meet the tokens of the resurrection and receive the angel's message. But they were not ready; they went out and ran from the tomb, taken with an ecstasy of terror, and said nothing to anyone, such was their fear.

On Wednesday evening betrayal, the desolating abomination, was set up in the true and spiritual temple of Christ's company. On Thursday at midnight the eleven saw it standing where it ought not, within the very garden of Christ's prayer. 'When ye see the abomination stand where he ought not,' Christ had said, 'then let them that are in Judaea flee to the mountains . . . and let not him that is in the field turn back to fetch his coat.' When the disciples saw the abomination, they were in the field, and they fled fast enough. And one of them, a young man, feeling the hands of the enemy upon his coat, left it to them, and fled without it. Christ counselled flight from the abomination in the last days. We can hardly think he counselled his disciples to desert him in the garden or that they did well to flee. Nevertheless their flight was predestined. The providence of God overrules the desertion of the disciples as it overruled the apostasy of Judas. Peter was not destined to stand firm, for all his protestations, for Christ must suffer alone. Christ dies now in himself; at a later day he will suffer in his apostles. For the present it is not theirs to die. The young man puts off his *sindon* and escapes alive. Christ is destined, at this season, to wear the *sindon* alone. The Arimathaean wraps him in it; it is his shroud.

CHAPTER VI

THE PREFIGURATIVE SENSE

Before we go farther, let us recall the journey we have so far made. We have described a pattern of healing miracles, thirteen if we count the literal healings only, fourteen if we reckon in the healing of the world, Christ's own resurrection. We have shown how the pattern evolves by a formal principle of its own. And we have shown that the evolution of the healing pattern is no erratic streak in the fabric of St Mark's book. It is part and parcel of a similar development in the whole of his material. As the group of healings recurs cyclically, a whole associated complex of other themes recurs with it. We have examined the cyclic rhythm of St Mark's story with some care, not so much to prove a thesis, as to enter (if we can) into the movement of the evangelist's mind. If we have in any degree thought his thoughts after him, then our trouble has not been in vain.

But the study we have made, whether successful or unsuccessful, is incomplete. What we have studied is a steady cyclic development, so arranged that each cycle evolves out of its recent predecessors, and out of its last predecessor especially; a steady advance from beginning to end. That is an important part of the truth about the shape of the Gospel, but it is not the whole truth about it. It ignores the fact that the Gospel is strongly broken in the middle, and that the end of the first piece matches the end of the second piece. Here, then, we have a correspondence other than the correspondence of each cycle with its direct predecessors: the correspondence of the latter part of the Gospel with the former part.

The fact to which we now refer is a fact with which we are already acquainted. The healing pattern is broken after the raising of Jairus's child, and the raising of the child, being a resurrection, anticipates Christ's resurrection and the end of the whole Gospel. In the raising of the child, miracle reaches a peak. It falls afterwards, and does not reach such a height again until the Lord himself rises. The two peaks challenge comparison with one another, and the Gospel appears as a composition in two principal movements, each rising to a climax, one in the fifth chapter and the other in the sixteenth.

The mere quality of the sign in Jairus's house would produce the effect we have described, even if nothing further were done to emphasize it. But in fact, as we have seen, the break after that sign is strongly marked by an actual break in the series of healings. The formula in general is, that a cycle containing a group of healings is followed by a cycle containing a single healing; this is the 'block, annexe, block, annexe' rhythm which we have found so illuminating. Now the healing of Jairus's child is the last of a block, and in the cycle following it there is no annexe, no healing of any particular person at all. We have done our best to explain why there cannot be an annexed healing here, and to describe what St Mark does in compensation for the absence of one. But no explanations and no compensations remove the effect of the fact. The series of healings is broken.

The suggestion made by such an arrangement is that the sign of Jairus's child is an end, even though it is not *the* end. Being a resurrection, it rhymes, as it were, with the end. As though St Mark's Gospel were a poem in two stanzas, the end of the first rhyming with the end of the second. Let me represent what I mean by fabricating an old-fashioned rhymed 'argument' of the Gospel:

> Baptized of John, the Gospel he proclaimed,
> Cast demons out, restored the halt and maimed,
>   Defied the scribes, and raised the ruler's child.
> Men's hearts with truth he cleared, their eyes with
>   sight;
> Betrayed, against the world upheld his right;
>   And dying, of his booty death beguiled.

This 'argument' misrepresents the facts in having the two parts equal; the two parts of the Gospel are unequal. According to the analysis which we completed in the last chapter, there are ten cycles in all, arranged in pairs (block and annexe, block and annexe . . .). So there are five double cycles. Two of them are in the first part, and three in the second. If, on the other hand, we reckon by healings rather than by cycles, the proportion is reversed. There are eight healings in the first part, and six in the second (counting in the resurrection of Christ).

It will be worth while to pay some attention to the number of healings, since St Mark belonged to a people and to an age much affected by the symbolism of numbers. It does not seem likely that St Mark's numerical patterns will prove to be very abstruse; the reader need not be afraid that he is going to be called on to consider cabalistical puzzles. Deep numerical complication is one thing, and simple numerical symbolism is another. What we have to observe is in fact straightforward enough.

We have already suggested, and shall later confirm, that St Mark's thirteen persons healed represent the longer of the two reckonings of the Israelite tribes. Thirteen was to the Jewish mind a ragged number, and for that very reason no one ever added up the tribes and brought the answer out as thirteen. Either one talked of twelve tribes in all, of which one was double, or else one talked of Levi and the twelve (lay) tribes. Fourteen, on the other hand, was a good number, being a double seven; and it is reasonable to suppose that St Mark felt some kind of mental comfort when he saw that the addition of Christ risen from the dead to the other persons healed gave a total number of fourteen, with Christ himself as the fourteenth. It gave a sort of roundness to the whole.

Fourteen is not only a good number in itself; it is a specially good number round which to shape a Gospel composed in two movements. For fourteen is a couple of sevens, and the Jewish passion for arranging things in sets of sevens can scarcely be exaggerated. It seems inevitable that St Mark should count two sets of seven persons healed, the one ending with Jairus's child and the other with Christ himself. But St Mark does not do it. Jairus's child is not the seventh, but the eighth person healed.

It is not that St Mark loses interest in the symbolism of numbers, but that he feels the pull of a numerical symbolism even stronger than that of arrangement by sevens. The healing of Jairus's child is a resurrection, and resurrection cannot be a seventh. For Christ himself had risen not on the sabbath of the week, but on the Sunday. Sunday, reckoned to the new week, is the first day; reckoned with the old, it is the eighth. St Mark could not make resurrection the first miracle he records, without undermining his whole system and overthrowing the climax. It remains that the Jairus story should stand eighth.

John xx illustrates the principle that resurrection is reckoned by the eighth day as well as by the first. Christ's first appearance in the upper room is dated on the first of the week by St John, his second appearance there on the eighth day afterwards. St Luke follows the same plan in his dating of the Transfiguration; for he views it as a prefiguration of resurrection-glory. On an undated day Christ makes the first prophecy of his resurrection, and 'about eight days afterwards' prefigures his glorified state on the mountain. (Anyone who doubts that St Luke conceived the Transfiguration to be a foretaste of the resurrection should compare ix, 29 with xxiv, 4. 'And in his praying his . . . robe came to be white and dazzling, and lo, two men . . .'—'And in their wondering thereat, it came to be, and lo, two men in dazzling raiment . . .') It is conceivable that the mere number eight suggested the resurrection to St Peter. 'The ark . . . wherein few, viz. *eight*, lives were brought to safety through water which, now the type is fulfilled, saves you—baptism, no mere putting away of fleshly defilement, but request to God for good conscience *obtained through Jesus Christ's resurrection*' (I Peter iii, 20–21). It is hard to understand why the number of persons should be so pointedly particularized unless it carries a symbolical value, and what other value can it carry?

Christ rose on the third day from his passion, and the eighth of the passion week. And St Mark sets the raising of Jairus's child before us as both a third and an eighth. It is the eighth healing absolutely, and it is the third healing of its group. Legion, the impure woman, and Jairus's daughter are a group of three. And St Mark seems to underline the *thirdness* of Jairus's daughter, by telling us how Christ brought his *three* witness-apostles to be present at her resuscitation. He probably felt that there was a special congruity between the number of the three witnesses, and that which above all else they were witnesses to, Christ's resurrection, because it was the act of the *third* day. We might write it off as fortuitous, that the three witnesses should be present at the third healing in a group of three, had not St Mark already introduced the fourth person healed among a group of four as carried on the shoulders of four bearers (II, 3).

We conclude, then, that motives of Christian symbolism pulled the resurrection of Jairus's child into the position of an eighth-and-third. These motives operated upon St Mark as he wrote, and he yielded to them, without troubling about the effect they would have on the numerical arrangement of the latter part of his Gospel. And so the first part (I–VI) has all the satisfying completeness of a Christian octave, while the latter part is left to shift for itself, with five ordinary healings and Christ's own resurrection to be arranged into such a pattern as they can.

How the latter part of the Gospel is arranged, is a question we will leave for the present. The point which we want to take up here is the rounded completeness of the octave of signs in I–VI. These chapters by themselves compose a carefully finished Gospel in miniature.

It tells us how, after John Baptist had been arrested, Jesus began to preach and to heal. He taught first of all in the synagogues, but opposition grew, and led to a crisis—the Jewish spiritual power conspired with the state for his destruction (III, 6). Jesus's following was therefore virtually withdrawn from the synagogue, and he instituted the Twelve to formalize its distinct existence. Sharp exchanges with *Jerusalem* leaders (III, 22–30) prefaced a withdrawal of Jesus with his disciples alone, to whom he gave his secret teaching (IV, 10 ff.). They ran together into a 'storm' of danger, in which Jesus showed his divine calm, but his disciples panicked (IV, 35–41). And so he reached the shore on which mighty acts of salvation began. It was the Gentile shore: hitherto Jesus had confined himself to the Jewish side, but his redeeming work could not be performed without his passing into the hands of the Gentiles; and there he achieved the great exorcism of the world which was fulfilled in his death. But he was back in Jewish hands—in the tomb of the worthy sanhedrist Joseph, in the house of the ruler of synagogue, Jairus—when resurrection was accomplished (v). Nevertheless, his own country-men rejected Jesus, and he sent out his disciples on mission far and wide (VI, 1–13). The ruling power took notice of the publi-cation of Christ's name, and of the miracles it wrought. They were forced to see that by killing him whom God had sent they had multiplied the effects of his mission (VI, 14–29). He had given his people supernatural bread and withdrawn from their sight, he had returned to his disciples across the waves of their distress, not as the apparition of a dead man, but in his own real person and being (VI, 30–52).

The reader will have seen by what device the little Gospel (I–VI) can be read as a complete Gospel. It is by jumping from the literal to the prefigurative sense somewhere about the crisis described in III, 1–7. Up to that point, we are simply reading about the Galilean ministry, but then we begin to read the Galilean ministry as a foreshadowing of events at Jerusalem. The crisis in the synagogue is the crisis in the temple. The secret teaching given to the disciples in the boat is the secret teaching given to them on the Mount of Olives. The 'storm' in which the disciples panic is the arrest in Gethsemane. The exorcism on the Gentile shore is the death of Christ at the hands of the Gentiles. The resurrection in Jairus's house is the resurrection from the Arimathean's tomb. The 'countrymen' who reject Jesus are not the Nazarenes but the Jews. The apostles are sent on mission not into Galilee but into the world. It is not John but Jesus whose death and resurrection have added strength to his cause. The story of the feeding of the five thousand and the return over the waters prefigures the return from the dead of him who had instituted the eucharist.

From III to VI, therefore, the sense runs double. There is, of course, a literal sense, and it would be a very serious error to suppose that St Mark held it in light esteem. But there is also a prefigurative sense, hardly less continuous than the literal, and it brings us as far as the end of the Gospel, or even a little farther; for St Mark's Gospel as we now have it does not contain any account of certain things prefigured in VI—the return of Christ to his disciples, and the sending forth of the world-wide mission.

The double sense runs to the end of VI. What happens to it then? Does it break off there? By no means. But the prefigurative sense has already reached and indeed over-reached the end of the Gospel; where is it to go after that? Well, there is the history of the apostolic Church; there is everything up to the end of the world. Why stop before the end of the world? That is the only fixed end, after all; every other ending is arbitrary. So let the prefigurative sense run on to the end of the world. It sounds a long journey to us, it would not sound a long journey to St Mark. Forty years had scarcely elapsed between the resurrection and the time of his writing, and I see no reason to suppose that he gave human history more than a dozen years further to run.

Let us take up the prefigurative sense where we left it at the end of VI and pursue it onwards. We may take the next double cycle as a unity (VII, 1–IX, 1). We have already seen in a previous chapter that the main theme of that double cycle is the admission of the Gentiles. If so, the prefigurative sense of VII is absolutely continuous with the prefigurative sense of VI: VI showed us the launching of the great mission. The next vitally important step after that is the admission of the Gentiles. Can Peter go into the house of Cornelius, and eat with men uncircumcized? To minds pondering such a problem, it became gradually clear that the teaching of Jesus, directed in its literal sense against Pharisaic scruples, had in a spiritual and prefiguring sense made all meats clean (VI, 53–VII, 23). Peter was taught in a vision not to fear the fellowship of uncircumcized men, under the figure of a divine command to eat the flesh of unclean beasts. The Syrophoenician woman had been a 'dog', but she had obtained crumbs from the children's table. The historical sense of the Gospel incident records Christ's willingness to step outside the normal bounds of his personal mission, in favour of a Gentile with some feeling for the sanctities which dwell with the people of God. The prefigurative sense includes Gentiles in the normal scope of the Church's fellowship (VII, 24–30). And so, of the twelve loaves given to God's Israel, seven are for the Gentiles; so abundant are the 'crumbs' which fall to them from the table of Israel-after-the-flesh. Such is the prefigurative sense of the second miracle of bread; the literal sense is a miracle in relief of hunger performed on the Gentile shore of the Galilean lake (VIII, 1–10). The extension of privilege to the Gentiles corresponds with the final rejection of Pharisaic Jewry; the Pharisees demand a sign, but Christ and his Church turn from them and depart to the Gentile side (VIII, 11–13).

It is noteworthy that in this part of St Mark's story the gospel is being carried into the non-Jewish or mixed territories surrounding Jewish Galilee. Hitherto we have read of only one excursion to the Decapolitan shore, in the prefigurement of Christ's passion at the hands of the Gentiles. His departure to the Greek world is not really fulfilled until after his resurrection, when the gospel begins to be given to the Gentiles. In VII Jesus departs for the borders of Tyre and Sidon, and only returns to the Sea of Galilee to pass it and push on again into Decapolis (VII, 31). He touches the Jewish shore only to reject the Pharisees and re-embark (VIII, 11–22). He goes up into Philip's tetrarchy (VIII, 27) and on his return passes through Galilee unobserved; his goal is Peraea (IX, 30, X, 1). The literal sense of these geographical indications is clear enough. Having evangelized the heart of Jewish Galilee, Jesus sought out the scattered communities in neighbouring lands, for he has taken Palestinian Israel for his province. The prefigurative sense is hardly less clear. After the resurrection Christ goes to the nations.

In our previous analysis we reckoned the discourses of Caesarea Philippi to the double cycle preceding them, the cycle we have been discussing (VII, 1–VIII, 26). We have still to consider the prefigurative sense of these discourses. They begin with St Peter's confession of Jesus as Messiah. Now the first and most obvious prefigurative sense attaching to St Peter's confession of the Messiah is the prefigurative sense implied in any confession of Messiah. To say 'You are the Anointed' is to say 'You are destined to rule the world in the Name of God and of Israel'. It is to prefigure either the Millennium or the World to Come.

What relation has this dazzle of glory to the events prefigured in VII, 1–VIII, 26? We are told that the disciples could not understand concerning the loaves; but the healing of the blind man in VIII, 22–26 stands for such an increase of vision that St Peter sees, and confesses Christ. What is the truth concerning the loaves? Is it not that Jesus feeds the world with supernatural bread, that he brings Gentiles and Jews to the table of a new twelvefold Israel embracing both? And is not he who does this Messiah, and when he has thus drawn mankind together must not he become manifest in glory, and take the kingdom? The Marcan apocalypse (XIII) appears to confirm the sequence which makes the evangelization of the nations the prelude to the kingdom. The disciples who ask about the kingdom are there told 'The end is not yet . . . The gospel must first be preached to all the nations'.

Peter's confession of Messiah takes us to the end of the world in a single leap; Christ's comment upon it begins to insert intermediate stages, of which St Peter at first refuses to hear. Before the day of glory, Christ must be rejected by Israel, and die and rise again. The Christian reader knows what St Peter did not know then, that Christ was speaking of things which were to come to pass almost immediately, and that an interval would still elapse between the rising again and the end of the age. But when Christ began to call upon his followers to renounce themselves and take their crosses, to lose their lives so as to gain them, of what time was he speaking? We may believe that greater heroism on the part of the apostles might have involved them in sharing Christ's passion, in the sense of being crucified beside him. But we also know that he was predestined to die alone and that he did not consider them capable of such heroism then. The more important sense of his exhortation, therefore, and the sense most relevant to St Mark's readers, is that which bears upon a time of serious persecution for the Church after Christ's resurrection; and from St Mark's point of view, that would be the time of the Neronian persecution and onwards. Then it was, after all, that St Peter himself had shown what it meant to confess Christ. He had confessed him at Caesarea Philippi and denounced the doctrine of the cross in the same breath. Under the shadow of the cross at Jerusalem he had not confessed but denied Christ, and wept for his infirmity. It was tolerable, even glorious, to recall these things, because St Peter had lately confessed Christ at Rome, at the price of his own crucifixion.

Christ's sayings at Caesarea Philippi clear up and define the prophecy implied in Peter's confession of him. To call him Messiah is to predict a complex of events, his death and resurrection, the subsequent martyrdom of many of his followers, and his coming in power to judge and to reign. Christ gives definition to the last and decisive element of the messianic expectation no less than to the preliminaries of it. 'Whosoever shall disown me and my words in this apostate and offending generation, him shall the Son of Man disown, *when he comes in the glory of the Father with the Holy Angels.*' This is the first open prediction of the end of the world which the Gospel contains. Though St Peter will have suffered before the day comes, some of his companions will still be living. 'Amen I say unto you,' Christ continues, 'there are some of those standing here that shall not taste of death till they see the kingdom of God present in power.'

At Caesarea Philippi the prefigurative sense strikes against the end of the world and rebounds. After the evangelization of the Gentiles Messiah will come to reign, but not until a serious persecution has taken place, in which St Peter and others will give their lives. And before that again—very soon, indeed—the whole drama of martyrdom and deliverance will have been enacted in the person of Messiah himself. Caesarea Philippi is a turning-point. The prophetic sense, swinging free, has touched

the end of the world, and can go no farther. Henceforward the
direction of divine revelation alters. The last things, indeed, are
kept before our eyes, but the arrow does not point towards
them; it points back from them towards the pre-enactment of
them in the death and resurrection of Christ. The Church cannot
be martyred and glorified until Christ has been martyred and
glorified. Salvation must be fulfilled in him before it can be
extended to mankind.

The experience of swinging into the end of the world and
rebounding can be already felt in the discourses at Caesarea
Philippi. It is dramatized in the Transfiguration. The three
apostles who are privileged to ascend the mountain have a
visionary enjoyment of Messianic glory; they touch that con-
summation to which Law and prophecy had borne witness. It is
good for them, says St Peter, to be there. But they cannot catch
or hold the glory in any tabernacles; it slips away from them and
fades, and they descend the mountain. On their way down they
are taught the reiterated lesson that Messiah must first die and
rise; that no smoothing of his path by any Elijah can spare him
the hard necessity.

The Transfiguration is a perfect example of the tension between Messiah's future glory and his present passion. Prefiguratively it sets him in the throne, but immediately it sets him in the
cathedra of Israel, to teach in word, and by dying to confirm, that
which Law and Prophecy have foreshadowed. The exorcism
beneath the mountain which Christ comes down from glory to
perform is an enacted parable of his coming passion. In face of
scribal hostility and unbelief, and of weakness in disciples who
cannot pray, Christ masters the devil, but only through a falling
dead and rising up again.

From Caesarea and the Transfiguration onwards we are
shown how the mystery of the last day is pre-enacted in Christ's
death and resurrection. But we are shown something else at the
same time. For Christ's death and resurrection are also the fulfilment of the prefigurations contained in the 'little Gospel,' with
which St Mark begins (I-VI). The end of the whole Gospel is set

between a past which prefigures it, and a future which it pre-figures: between the 'little Gospel' behind, and the end of the world before. We have been attending to the prefiguration of the end; we will now attend for a while to the fulfilment of the little Gospel.

For this purpose we will recur to an earlier point in the present chapter, at which we were discussing the formal architecture of the Gospel in numerical terms. We made two different numerical reckonings. We said that the Gospel contained five double cycles, and fourteen healing signs. And we said that the 'little Gospel' (I–VI) consisted of two double cycles, and embraced eight healing signs. We will look at the analysis in terms of double cycles first. Of five double cycles in all, two are devoted to the little Gospel (I–VI), and one to the continuation of the prefigurative sense from the resurrection to the end of the world (VII–IX, I). And so two are left for the fulfilment of the little Gospel in Christ's passion and resurrection (IX, 2–XVI, 8). The whole arrangement of double cycles is thus symmetrical (2 + I + 2); and the same number of double cycles is devoted to the fulfilment of the little Gospel as were devoted to the little Gospel itself (2).

Now let us look at the distribution of the fourteen healing signs. We were puzzled about this for the following reason. There is every evidence that St Mark was happy to be able to count his little Gospel as an octave of healings, so that the resur-rection of Jairus's child appeared as an eighth. It seemed sym-bolically right, for the resurrection belongs to the eighth day. But in making the resurrection of the child an eighth, St Mark did not leave himself enough healings over to make the resur-surection of Christ an eighth; and the resurrection of Christ has a better right, surely, to be an eighth than has any mere pre-figuration of it.

Such was the difficulty. What is the solution? It is, perhaps, not so much a solution as a weakening of the difficulty. If St Mark's Gospel had consisted of two simple and comparable parts, the little Gospel (I–VI) and its fulfilment (VII–XVI), we should then feel that the second part ought to be a 'week' of healings like the first part, and to end in an eighth. But as it is, VII–XVI has no such unity; it does not challenge comparison with I–VI in so simple a way. It falls into two parts, VII–VIII, a continuation of I–VI, and IX–XVI, a fulfilment of I–VI. Each of these two parts contains three healings, and we do not feel any shock or surprise. Indeed, if we wished to reform St Mark so as to make Christ's resurrection an eighth sign, we should hardly know where to begin counting from.

The whole Gospel, then, may be analysed as follows:
(*a*) Little Gospel: two double cycles and eight healings (I–VI).
(*b*) Continuation of little Gospel: one double cycle and three healings (VII–VIII).
(*c*) Fulfilment of little Gospel: two double cycles and three healings (IX–XVI).

We will now set aside every part of the analysis we have made except one. The only fact we wish to retain for further examination is this: the little Gospel (I–VI) contains two double cycles, and the fulfilment of the little Gospel (IX–XVI) goes over the ground again likewise in two double cycles. That means that in writing his last two double cycles St Mark had his first two double cycles for a model, and it is our next business to show what use he made of it.

As I announce such a programme I am overcome once more by that confusion of face which falls upon me when I am forced to admit that I am going to add a further complication to my account of St Mark's imaginative process. I see the smile of incredulity rising on some of my reader's lips, and the frown of impatience on the foreheads of others. 'What!' I shall be told, 'have we not already had a story so elaborate as to tax our powers of belief, about the composition of the last two double cycles of the Gospel? According to that story each cycle was composed on the model of its predecessor. And are we now to hear that the evangelist was also and at the same time composing each of those cycles on another model, a model provided by the appropriate part of I–VI?'

What can I say to persuade my readers to read on, nevertheless? I can only say that the proof of the story is in the telling. You cannot decide about the probability or improbability of what I am going to write until you have read it. You do not know how the evangelist's (alleged) use of this other model will work out. Perhaps his use of it is much slighter than his use of the models already discussed by us in our last chapter. Or perhaps he does not use both models equally all the time, but alternates the use of them, so that some parts of his new writing have their model in the cycle directly before them, and other parts back in the 'little Gospel' of I–VI. Then any one part of the new material may have only one model; and that may strike us as more credible than the balanced use of a double model throughout.

We will now explain how we propose to go about the business of comparing I–VI with IX–XVI. We will take up I–VI in an orderly manner, piece by piece, and see what corresponds to each piece of it in the appropriate piece of IX–XVI. Into how many pieces shall we divide the two blocks of chapters we have to compare? We have said that they both consist of two double cycles. We will begin by breaking these down into four simple cycles. And we will break our simple cycles into two parts each, remembering that their basic elements are calling and healing. And so we shall have eight pieces in all.

We will take our start throughout from the model and not from the antitype. The antitype is, after all, longer and more complicated. Several new themes and new forms have worked themselves into the Marcan cycle since the point reached by the end of the 'little Gospel'. To look for the model of all this material in the 'little Gospel' would be to look for more than we can hope to find. But if we start the other way round we shall not err. We will take up what the model really does contain, and see what antitype, if any, is provided for it by IX–XVI.

We begin, then, by taking the first cycle of the Gospel and dividing it into calling (I, 1–20) and healing (I, 21–II, 12), and consider the calling first. Christ calls four apostles, and his calling of them is the extension of his own vocation. He himself has just been called by the heavenly voice in his baptism at John's hands; and since then he has resisted the temptations of Satan in the wilderness. He calls the four men to partake of the power of these mysteries, but the mysteries remain hidden from them. They do not hear the heavenly voice proclaim the only Son of God, they do not understand the significance of John the Forerunner and Baptist, they have no experience of the Satanic temptation Christ resisted in the desert.

In the antitype these hidden things are all revealed. Christ calls the three witness-apostles, that is, the first four apostles with the exception of Andrew, into the mount of Transfiguration. There they see the transcendent purity of Christ, a purity which makes him the living exemplification of the power of baptismal water. His garments shine whiter than any fuller on earth can make them. The phrase has often been put down to St Mark's clumsy naïveté, but the evangelist is neither naïve nor clumsy. He says exactly what he means. These are the garments which went down with him to Jordan, these are the garments washed so clean that the unclean woman by touching them was purified; and her purification, a Jew would readily feel, was a manifestation of the power of 'water'. While the mystery of water is thus revealed in Christ, Moses and Elijah stand with him, for lustration belonged to the old dispensation also, and John Baptist himself had said, 'I baptize with water'. But Moses and Elijah pass wholly away at the manifestation of Spirit, when the divine breath once more descending from the skies is vocal in the proclamation of the Only Son. The voice at the Baptism was for Christ alone: 'Thou art my Only Son, in thee I am content.' The voice in the Mountain is for the apostles, and through them ultimately for the world: 'This is my Only Son, to him hearken.'

As they descend the mountain Christ reveals at length to his disciples the meaning of the Baptist's person. How can it be, the three apostles ask, that Messiah must die and rise if, as the scribes allege out of the last words of Malachi, Elijah first comes and puts all things to rights? For then Messiah will not be rejected or killed; he will be welcomed by a penitent people. Jesus replies in truly Jewish vein, setting text against text, and then giving the reconciliation of the two. There is certainly the text according to which Elijah first comes and works for general reformation. But there is also the text which says of the Son of Man that he must suffer many things and be set at naught (Is. LII–LIII). A third text will provide us with a reconciliation between the two. 'Elijah has come, and they have done to him all that they wished to have done in the text about him.' The text is that which describes Elijah's vision of the divine glory in the mountain, a vision directly evoked by the Transfiguration, for there Elijah is on the summit, conversing with the divine glory once more. In that text Elijah says, 'The people of Israel hunt after my life to take it away' (I Kings XIX, 10, 14). Their purpose was prevented; God took up Elijah in the chariot of fire and reserved him for the latter days. In the latter days he returned, and Israel saw their ancient purpose fulfilled: John Baptist was betrayed and put to death. Elijah's reformation having thus been thwarted, Messiah comes to be set at naught, to die and rise again. John Baptist prepares the way of Messiah not by smoothing the path to glory, but by paving the path to execution with his own blood.

The hidden mystery of Christ's baptism was revealed on the mountain top and the hidden mystery of the Baptist's passion was revealed in the descent; the mystery of Satan tempting Christ had been revealed before they went up. Satan had tempted Christ in the wilderness; what that temptation was is not revealed. (It would be a mistake to attribute to St Mark or his audience an acquaintance with the temptation story in its Matthaean form.) St Peter discovered how Satan could tempt Christ when he found himself to be the mouthpiece of Satan and denounced the doctrine of the passion. 'Away from me, Satan,' Christ said to him, 'for thou art not godly-minded but man-minded.' To judge from St Mark's Gospel alone, the substance of the Satanic temptation is simply the horror of the passion. It is with this that Christ wrestles again when he prays in Gethsemane, and calls on his disciples to pray with him 'Lest they enter into temptation'.

'The Spirit', that is, their godly-mindedness, 'is willing,' he says, 'but the flesh', their man-mindedness, 'is weak'.

Let us now take up the second piece of our model, the four healing miracles in I, 21–II, 12. These four are the first 'block' of miracles in St Mark's design and the corresponding thing in IX is the last of the 'blocks', which does not deserve the name of 'block', because it has dwindled to a single miracle, the so-called epileptic boy (IX, 14–29). We have nothing fresh to say here about the condensation of the earlier 'block' themes in this one but many-sided healing. The epileptic boy is followed by paragraphs which have no analogy in the cycles of the 'little Gospel'— a private teaching (IX, 30–50) and a public teaching (X, 1–31). And so we reach the end of the first cycles (I–II, 12; IX, 2–X, 31).

We take the next cycle of the model (II, 13–III, 12) and divide it into two parts, all that hangs together with Christ's call of Levi and eating in Levi's house (II, 13–22), and all that hangs together with Christ's breach of Sabbath-rule by healing the withered hand in synagogue (II, 23–III, 12). To take the call of Levi first. The call story belonging to the corresponding cycle in the antitype is the disciples following Jesus in the road to Jerusalem (X, 32–34) after the rich man had refused to take the road with him. The correspondence here is slight and purely general. Levi the tax-gatherer may have been a minor clerk in that discreditable service, but he was a man whose business was money, and he was in fact rich enough to entertain a considerable party in his house. That was wealth, no doubt, by fishermen's standards. And so we may, if we will, pair Levi and the man in X as the rich man who followed, and the rich man who would not follow. Levi followed, though he was disreputable, a publican and law-breaker. The other rich man did not follow, though he was highly respectable, and could claim to have kept the commandments from his youth up. The contrast between him and Levi may be held to add point to Christ's saying in Levi's house, 'I came not to call the righteous, but sinners'.

The second part of the second cycle of the model (II, 23–III, 12) is of much more serious concern to us, and has a much greater influence on the antitype. For it contains the history of that crisis in the synagogue at Capernaum which is so plain a pre-figuring of the crisis in the Temple at Jerusalem. The Pharisees went out and took counsel with the Herodians how to compass Christ's death (III, 6). We cannot read this without seeing in it a warning and sign of the actual death of Christ, effected by a combination of the spiritual power with the secular government. And if the model seems such as to be likely to exercise a real influence on the antitype, the antitype at this particular point appears to be in need of contributions from the model. For when we were analysing the story of the crisis in the Temple (XI, 12–XII, 12) we found no detailed or sufficient model for it in the cycles of narrative directly preceding it, nothing that cast any light, for example, on the mysterious sign of the barren fig-tree, or the cleansing of the Temple. We treated these things provi-sionally as a new development; but that is only another way of saying that the way is open for referring them to a model, if that model can be found.

The theme of II, 23–III, 12 is the (apparent) violation of the Sabbath, as illustrated by two events: Christ's disciples plucking corn with his permission, and Christ healing the withered hand in synagogue, both on the Sabbath day. The paragraphs of the corn-plucking and the healing are united in the closest possible way by Christ's citation of the example of David. For while the citation is introduced in comment on the plucking, it receives a more serious and direct application in the healing. Jesus defends his disciples for taking corn which is supposed to be *tabu* to them by the law of Sabbath. He makes it free to them, quoting the example of David, who made free to his companions bread which was undoubtedly *tabu* to them by the law of the sanctuary. 'Have ye never read what David did, when he had need and was hungry, he and his companions? How he entered into the house of God when Abiathar was High Priest and ate the shewbread, which it was not lawful to eat save for the priests, and gave also to his companions? And he said unto them: The Sabbath was made for man, and not man for the Sabbath; so that the Son of

Man is lord also of Sabbath. And he entered into the synagogue.'

David goes into the house of God, Jesus into the synagogue. What outrage upon pious convention is the new David going to commit in the house of prayer, to show that, in spite of the local Abiathars, he is lord of Sabbath also? 'There was a man there who had his hand withered, and they watched him, to see if he would heal him on the Sabbath day.' He did, and the offence of it was so great that 'the Pharisees went out and straightway with the Herodians took counsel against him how they might destroy him'.

In considering St Mark's use of David's example, we must interpret it as St Mark makes it look, and not as it looks in the text of I Samuel XXI. According to the ancient text, David obtains shewbread of the priests by fair request. He does not himself ask for shewbread, but simply for bread; the priests answer by offering shewbread, because they have no other bread ready. St Mark's words give a somewhat different impression. 'David went into the temple of God and ate the shewbread.' When such a statement is used to uphold the sovereignty of Messiah's decision, it suggests that David's action was of his own motion, and that Abiathar's part was limited to acquiescence.

The synagogue is not the temple, Jesus has not yet come publicly forth in the character of a new David, and the local synagogal elders (the 'Pharisees' of St Mark's story) are not the successors of Abiathar. But the time was to come when the type of David's action would be more perfectly fulfilled in Christ. He would be hailed as Son of David, he would enter the temple of God in royal triumph, and he would infringe the privileges of the High Priest himself by throwing out the market which he licensed and from which he profited.

In II–III the type of David's entry to the temple is connected, as we have seen, with the healing of the withered hand. The corresponding miracle in the antitype is the healing of blind Bartimeus. The whole structure of the healing pattern requires that Bartimeus's affliction should be blindness, and no sort of 'withering'. His direct contribution to the fulfilment of the type is limited to his hailing Christ as Son of David; the first act of the Davidic drama is Christ's assumption of the Davidic role. He himself completes it by sending for the ass, and riding into Jerusalem amid a shower of benedictions on the Davidic Kingdom.

When David went into the house of God, says the evangelist in his second chapter, he was hungry. It was because he was looking for food that he violated the sacred table. And in the morning when the new David came to disturb the temple, he too was hungry. But his hunger had a purely symbolical relation to what he looked for in the temple, the fruits of righteousness. What is one in the type splits and becomes two in the antitype. In the type God's Anointed is hungry, looks for bread in the temple, and eats shewbread. In the antitype God's Anointed is hungry and searches the fig-tree; he looks for righteousness and searches the temple. Finding no fruit on the fig-tree, he curses it. Finding no prayer in the traffic of offerings, he casts it out. Next day the disciples call attention to the withering of the fig, and the High Priests to the clearing of the market. Christ denounces the High Priests as the wicked vinedressers, the tenants who withhold fruit from their landlord, mishandle his servants and plot the death of his son. In the parable of the vinedressers hunger for fruit and hunger for righteousness, two things which have hitherto stood side by side, coalesce at last. The temple priesthood is the barren fig-tree, the vineyard of the Lord of Hosts is the sanctuary of Zion (Is. v, 7, Mic. VII, 1–2).

The symbolic equivalence of temple and fig-tree has been long recognized, and we have nothing here to add to the common account of it, except the indication of its origin. The single fact of David's hunger in the type becomes the double fact of unsatisfied hunger and of indignant disappointment in the antitype.

And now as to 'withering'. In III, 1–6 Christ goes into the synagogue and overrules the scribes by the miraculous healing of a withered hand. In XI he enters the temple, and overrules the priests by an act not itself miraculous, but doubled in the miraculous withering of a tree. The word for 'wither' in the two narratives is the same. Condemnation has become sterner. In the Galilean synagogue Christ gives the Pharisees the sign of life, asking them about his healing of the deadened hand, 'Is it lawful to make dead on the Sabbath or to make alive?' They condemn themselves by siding with death. In the temple at Jerusalem Christ himself makes the condemnation, and places the priest-hood under the sign of death by withering the fig-tree. The contrast could hardly be more exact, unless Christ were to wither a human limb at Jerusalem, as he had healed a withered limb at Capernaum; and no Christian, perhaps, will expect to find that in the Gospel.

Further light seems to fall on the unwithering and the withering from the strongest type for these episodes which the Old Testament contains. When we say 'the strongest type' we mean this. It is always possible to ask the following question about any incident in the Gospel: 'What is the most obvious Old Testament type for this incident?' Such a question can be answered purely objectively, and without considering what evidence there is that the Gospel-writer had the type-passage in mind as he wrote. For example, the strongest type for the multiplications of bread in Mark VI and VIII is unquestionably Elisha's miracle recorded in II Kings IV, 42–44. That is the strongest type; yet it may still be an open question whether other types less close in form may not have meant more to St Mark, for example, the miracles of manna and quails in Exodus and Numbers. In spite of such queries, we may lay it down as a sound canon of interpretation, that the 'strongest type' has a first claim on the interpreter's attention.

What, then, is the 'strongest type' for the withered hand? Undoubtedly it is the story of the prophet from Judah, and his denunciation of Jeroboam in his apostate sanctuary at Bethel. Jeroboam stretched out his hand against the prophet and it 'dried' or 'withered': the word used by the LXX translators is the word used by St Mark. Presently at the prophet's inter-cession the king's hand was restored. The withering of the king's hand was a companion sign to something else: the bursting of the altar, and the outpouring of the offering (I Kings XIII, 1–5). It is obvious that this story makes the withering and unwithering of the hand appropriate signs for divine rejection of a corrupt sanctuary, whether it be the synagogue of Mark III or the temple of Mark XI.

It is as though St Mark divided the Old Testament sign. The milder part of it, the restoration of the withered hand, suffices against scribal perversity in Galilee. The more grievous part, the attack on the sacrificial offerings and the withering, is reserved for priestly corruption in Jerusalem. It is remarkable that both in I Kings XIII, 4–5 and in Mark XI, 12–21 the withering is doubled with a sign against the offerings. Christ does not only wither the tree, he turns out the market for sacrificial victims. The signs given at Bethel were signs of the ultimate overthrow of the sanctuary and the destruction of its priesthood. The signs given by Christ have the same significance, as is shown by XII, 9–12, XIII, 1–2. The temple and the priesthood are virtually removed by Christ's acts of power, the rock consecrated by David and Solomon must make room for a better sanctuary; and therefore in commenting on the apparently trivial withering of the fig, Christ speaks to his disciples about the removal of the mountain.

The working out of the double sign of fig-tree and temple carries us to the end of the parable of the vinedressers (XII, 1–12), for it is only in that parable that the equivalence between yielding fruit and administering temple worship becomes explicit. After the parable, the High Priests, outfaced in their own temple, hand over their cause to a conspiracy of Pharisees and Herodians (XII, 12–13). We remember how the outfacing of the scribes in their own synagogue led likewise to a conspiracy of Pharisees with Herodians (III, 6). Jesus made a solemn exodus from synagogue and town in consequence, and in the same way Jesus now withdraws from the Temple and the city (XIII, 1–3). Not, however, until his debate with the scribes has been carried through to a finish (XII, 13 to end). The model for the debate is not to be found in III, but in X, as we showed in the last chapter.

We can now take the next piece of our model, the apostolic calling which opens the third cycle. Jesus, having made his exodus from the synagogue (III, 7–12) ascended the mountain, summoned to him whom he would, and instituted the Twelve

(III, 13–19). Jesus, having made his exodus from the Temple, ascended the mountain, viz. Olivet (XIII, 1–3). But what happened upon it bore no sort of resemblance to the institution of the Apostolate. It was the questioning of Jesus by the Four, and the apocalyptic discourse he gave them by way of reply.

We might be disposed to dismiss the subject, and to conclude that the apocalyptic discourse was not seriously influenced by anything in the 'little Gospel'. If we formed such a conclusion, we should fall into a serious error. The scene on the mountain in III, 13–19 contributes nothing to the apocalyptic discourse, but the sequel to the scene on the mountain contributes a great deal to it. Christ instituted the Twelve for a double purpose—to enjoy the privileges of disciples as such, by accompanying him; and to be sent on mission. The sending on mission does not begin until VI, 7, the accompanying begins immediately. The disciples are privileged to hear their Rabbi's disputes with the learned (III, 20–30), his casual dicta (III, 31–35) and his public preaching (IV, 1–9), and when they are alone with him, they ask him for explanations and are rewarded with much doctrine (IV, 10–34). The whole stretch of discourse from the disputes with the learned to the private explanations, the whole, that is, of III, 20–IV, 34, has a common character, for it is all 'parables' or 'riddles', and their solutions. St Mark himself had a strong feeling of the unity of these parabolic discourses, for when he wrote an antitype to them in VII, 1–23 he pulled them together into a single episode, the dispute about hand-washing. We have given the evidence for this statement in a previous chapter (p. 97). In XIII the unification of the material is still more drastic: all the Lord's 'parables' become a single discourse, addressed to his disciples in answer to a single question. They do not, as in III, 20, descend from the mountain and go about with Jesus picking up his words, before they begin to question him. They remain on the mountain, and question him about something he has already said to themselves.

The discourse in XIII has many ultimate sources or types, above all in the prophecy of Daniel, and it would be absurd to suggest that it could be educed from III, 20–IV, 34 by any sort of magic. It is rather that the evangelist started with the Lord's predictive utterances in mind, shaped as they were in Danielic figures; and passing over the parabolic discourses in III, 20–IV, 34 took from them such points as could be applied to the matter of Christ's predictions. What is remarkable is that he took what he took in the order in which it came.

In III, 22–26 Christ is accused by the scribes, as Micaiah was accused by Zedekiah (I Kings XXII, 24), of being a false prophet possessed by an evil spirit. He replies by a 'parable': a kingship divided against itself cannot stand, no more can a household. If Satan be divided against himself, he is at an end. The point is, that Satan is not at an end yet, so he is not fighting himself, he is fighting the Spirit of God. But when Christ comes to predict the last things, the point he has to make is different. His disciples will live to see ungodly power rising against itself, nation against nation *and kingship against kingship*. They might well think that this is the *end*, but it is not; it is only the beginning-pains of the world's travail. And this warning he prefaces with another: a warning against false Christs or prophets (XIII, 5–8).

In III, 28–30 Christ tells his enemies, scribes from the Jerusalem synagogues, or perhaps from the Sanhedrin itself, that in resisting and blaspheming him they are blaspheming the Holy Ghost. In XIII, 9–11 he tells his disciples that they will be brought before sanhedrins, synagogues and secular tribunals, and that the testimony they give there will not be their own utterance, but that of the Holy Ghost. The title 'The Holy Ghost', with the definite article, belongs to these two texts alone in the Gospel and one other (XII, 36). All three are concerned with the speaking of the Spirit through human lips; but it is only in the two texts we are comparing that the inspired utterance is a testimony against the opponents of the Gospel.

In III, 31–35 Christ's mother and brethren are seeking, with however innocent an intent, to call him away from his work, and he dissociates himself from them. 'Who are my mother and my brethren?' he says. 'Whosoever will do the will of God . . .' In

XIII, 12–13 a more fatal division of the Christian from his family is predicted. 'Brother shall betray brother to death, and father child, and children shall rise against parents and do them to death, and ye shall be hated of all for my name's sake.'

In IV, 1–20 the parable of the sower teaches the lesson of endurance. So little of the seed takes firm root or makes lasting growth. In particular there are those who 'When oppression or hunting-out arises on account of the word, break down directly'. In XIII, 13–20 we read that he who endures to the end shall be saved, and then we learn of the great oppression of Antichrist, 'oppression such as was not since God's creation of the world until now, nor shall there be the like', in which 'no flesh could have been saved, had the Lord not cut those days short for the sake of his chosen elect'. We shall search St Mark in vain for an example of the word 'oppression' outside the pair of texts we have here.

The parable of the growing harvest in IV, 26–29 shows us the God-given increase from blade to ear, and from ear to full corn in the ear. Then the landowner sends out the sickle, because harvesting (*therismos*) has come. In XIII, 24–27 we read how, after the great oppression, the Son of Man will come, and send out his angels to gather (the Greek word is used for harvesting) his elect from the four winds. Christ immediately adds: From the fig-tree learn her parable. When her twig becomes tender and puts out leaves, you know that harvest-season (*theros*) is at hand.

In IV, 35–41, parables and interpretations being ended, Christ and his disciples sail across the lake. A storm arises and they wake him from his sleep to save them. He rebukes them: quiet confidence would have sufficed. Nevertheless there will be a time to wake and to watch and it is of that time that Christ speaks in XIII, 32–37. Because the day of the Son of Man is unpredictable, his disciples will have to be on their guard, to wake and pray; to watch like the porter watching for his absent master, lest coming suddenly he catch them sleeping. We have seen in a previous chapter how these sentences of the apocalyptic discourse prefigure Gethsemane; and in Gethsemane the scene on the lake is exactly reversed. The Master wakes and prays, the disciples sleep, and the hour takes them, but not him, unprepared.

I hope it has become clear in the course of our comparison, in what sense the topics of the parable-discourses are taken up in the apocalyptic discourse. They are taken up in quite a general form: 'Christs false and true', 'kingdom against kingdom', 'the testimony of the Holy Ghost against the adversaries', 'family divisions due to the Gospel', 'endurance of oppression', 'growth the sign of coming harvest', 'sleeping and watching'. These topics have one set of applications to the present, and another set of applications to the future. Because both sets of applications can be made, it is possible to compose an apocalyptic discourse by running over the topics of the parabolic discourses with the pattern of Christ's prophetic doctrine in one's head.

The next piece of the model which we have to take up is the healing miracles of v, Legion, the impure woman, and Jairus's child. These three form a 'block' of miracles, and ought, as we may feel, to be answered by similar miraculous action in the antitype. But there are no more healing miracles now, except the Lord's own resurrection, and the place of the healing miracle in xiv is taken, as we showed above, by the story of the woman who anoints Christ (xiv, 3–9). Here, then, we have all the antitype there is to the healings of v, and we must make the best of it.

There does indeed appear to be some sort of echo of the woman who touched Christ (v, 25–34) in the woman who anointed Christ. Both women have the boldness to touch Christ's sacred person without asking leave, the one with her hand, the other with her unguent. Both women are defended or encouraged by Christ in respect of what they have done. The woman in v is impure, and the direct antitype of the leper in i. The woman in xiv is not impure, but Christ's defiance of impurity is suggested by the context—he was at that very time supping in the house of Simon the leper.

If anyone thinks the comparison between v and xiv far-fetched, he would do well to hear St Luke, for he tells a story in which the types of the two passages are actually fused. A woman anoints Christ at table, and the woman is unclean; Christ's critics assume that had he known what manner of woman she was, he would have shrunk from her touch. Christ answers them, and dismisses the woman with the very words addressed to the impure woman in Mark v: 'Thy faith hath saved thee: go in peace' (Luke vii, 36–50).

The story of the impure woman in v is intertwined with the story of Jairus's daughter. The narrative of xiv, 3–9 answers to the story of the impure woman only, so far as its main action goes. But the saying of Christ with which it concludes may be held to echo the story of Jairus's child. After being touched by the impure woman in v Christ entered the house of funeral to raise the dead. The touch of the woman's perfume in xiv is said by Christ to be a preparation for his own burial, the burial out of which will spring the resurrection of the dead.

We are now left with one cycle in the model (vi, 7–56) and one in the antitype, the passion itself. Nothing in the passion is written as it is in order to square with the contents of vi; it is the other way about. In vi St Mark has heaped together paragraphs which contain images of the saving events. The prefigurative sense of these paragraphs cannot be understood as a single sequence; they require to be placed in three sequences standing parallel with one another.

(a) Jesus, who has raised Jairus's child and been rejected by his own countrymen, sends out the apostolic mission.

(b) John Baptist, who has been betrayed and then brought to his death by unscrupulous influence, is said to be risen from the dead in that wonder-working Name of Jesus which is the power of the apostolic mission.

(c) Jesus, who has made a supernatural feast for his people by eucharistic blessing and withdrawn from them, appears to them like an apparition from the dead on the waters of the lake. But he convinces them that he is no apparition, but his own very self.

Of these three sequences (c) provides the image of the Supper and of Christ's withdrawal after it to pray in the mountain (Olivet). On Olivet he takes his disciples with him, but they cannot follow him into that ultimate withdrawal which removes him from human sight.

At this point of the passion history we may turn from (c) to (b), and find in the story of the Baptist's death a type of the political villainy which brought the passion about. Christ, like the Baptist, is killed for speaking the truth. Herodias's setting on her daughter to ask for the Baptist's head is like the priests' setting on of the people to ask for Christ's death and Barabbas's release. Pilate, like Herod, is weak, and allows himself to be bound by the custom of the feast.

We may invoke (a) and the memory of Jairus's child to supply an actual raising of the dead, but no such arising is described in xv–xvi, any more than the subsequent sending forth of the apostolic mission with which (a) concludes. What is described in xvi is the confrontation of the women with Christ's angel; and that scene is closely matched with the scene on the lake (c), when the disciples are confronted with Christ himself. The one is by position the last particularized scene of the little Gospel (there is nothing but the general description of healings after it, vi, 53–56). And the other is the last scene of the whole Gospel. In vi the disciples saw Christ as an apparition and 'cried out, for they all saw him and were distraught'. He told them not to fear, and joined himself to them, but still their minds were not quietened. 'They were inwardly beside themselves, for they had not understood about the loaves, but their heart was hardened.' Compare the even more extreme case of the women's distress according to xvi. Seeing the angel, they were terrified. He told them to lay aside their terror; that Christ was rejoining his disciples, being risen and alive. But their minds were not quietened. They went out and fled from the tomb, trembling and beside themselves, and said nothing to anyone, such was their fear.

We have now completed our task, and shown how far the four cycles which begin from the Transfiguration express and fulfil the four cycles which begin from the Baptism. There is one loose end left for us to take up, and then we can conclude the chapter.

We said above (p. 152) that from the Transfiguration onwards the Gospel runs between the shadow of the future and the shadow of the past. St Mark is showing us how the decisive events fulfil the prefigurations of them, and themselves prefigure the end of the world. And we said that the image of the end of the world, once called up at Caesarea Philippi, continues to haunt the narrative, reminding us that the Last Things are being pre-enacted in the history of Christ. Since we made these observations we have been intent on showing how the end of the Gospel fulfils its prefigurements; we have said nothing about the way it prefigures a last fulfilment. We will devote a few lines to the matter now.

Is it true that the Last Things are kept before us in IX–XVI? We will say no more of the Transfiguration, but pass on to observe how in the discourses at Capernaum (IX, 30–50) Christ returns again to the matter of the Last Judgement, which he had introduced into the discourses at Caesarea Philippi (VIII, 35–38). The preservation of hand, foot or eye, he says, would be a bad exchange for the plunging of the whole person into Gehenna (IX, 43–48). The blessing of the children in the next chapter is connected with entry or non-entry into the kingdom of heaven (X, 15), and so is the rich man's request. What he desires is to inherit life (X, 17), but alas, he cannot pass the needle's eye into the kingdom (25). Whereas those who have made the true apostolic renunciation shall have life everlasting in the world to come (30). James's and John's request (X, 35–45) is concerned with places in the state of glory.

The entry to Jerusalem draws our attention upon the present (X, 46–XII, 12), but out of that present a new series of prefigurations ranges forward into the future. In XII, 1–12 Christ prophesies in the parable of the vinedressers that the priests will contrive his death. This amounts to a prediction of his arrest by the High Priest's men, and his condemnation by the Sanhedrists. They were not, in fact, going to be able to effect their purpose, without putting Jesus in the wrong with Caesar's procurator; and a prefiguration of this is seen in the parable of the vinedressers and its sequel. For the priests, finding themselves unable to make any answer to the parable, withdraw and send Pharisees and Herodians to put Jesus in the wrong with Caesar over the question of the tribute. St Luke appreciated the point that this plot was a sort of stage-rehearsal for the prosecution of Jesus before Pilate, and added to the account of the accusation of Jesus before Pilate the charge 'He forbids the giving of tribute to Caesar' (XXIII, 2). He also adds to the account of the tribute-question in the temple, the statement that it was designed to provide a ground 'for delivering him up to the rule and authority of the Governor' (XX, 20). Jesus baffles the attempt of the Pharisees and Herodians to entrap him, but his condemnation and execution by the Roman power on an unreal charge of treason are nevertheless prefigured by the incident. The next act after Christ's passion at the hands of the Romans will be his resurrection, and this is prefigured in the next paragraph, in which Christ vindicates against Sadducean questioners the power of God to raise the dead (XII, 18–27). After the resurrection comes the enthronement of Messiah at God's right hand, until his enemies shall have been put under his feet; and this mystery is directly set before the listening people by Christ in a psalm-quotation, when he follows up his answer to the good scribe by revealing the deficiencies of scribal doctrine (XII, 35–37). His enemies will be put under his feet, and in due time the temple will fall; Christ predicts to his disciples as they go out, that not a stone of it shall remain upon another (XIII, 1–2). Upon this saying the apocalyptic discourse is hung, in which things preceding, accompanying, and succeeding the fall of the temple are foretold, and we touch the end of the world once more.

What we have said may suffice to justify the statement that the End, once revealed at Caesarea Philippi, is kept before our minds up to the brink of the passion. How the image of the last things, elaborated in the apocalyptic discourse, is brought down to earth and applied to the passion itself, we found occasion to explain in the previous chapter, and will say no more about it here.

CHAPTER VII

THE ENDING

How St Mark meant his Gospel to end is a famous question much discussed by the learned. We have already prejudged the answer, and no one who has read the preceding chapters can fail to see it: our analysis of the Gospel implies that the words 'They were afraid' (XVI, 8) are its proper conclusion. Nevertheless it seems right to discuss the question by itself and in a formal way, even though what we have to do will be little more than to draw together what we have already either suggested or said. And so what follows here will be more like an overgrown note than a full chapter.

There is no need for us to dwell on the commonplaces of the subject. We all know that the ending of St Mark printed in our Bibles (XVI, 9–20) has no sound authority, and is manifestly composed in a style other than St Mark's. We know that the alternative short ending which some of the manuscripts exhibit has even less evidence for it, and is even more flagrantly non-Marcan in phrase. The best Egyptian manuscripts agree with the learned opinion of Eusebius in stopping at XVI, 8. Eusebius simply tells us that nearly all the oldest and best manuscripts ended there, and it is likely that Eusebius's statement rests on the authority of the first of Christian textual scholars, Origen.

These things being so the burden of proof lies on anyone who asserts that St Mark wrote more; for if we hold that he did, we shall have to admit that what he wrote has perished without trace. And it perished very soon: not only before the earliest manuscripts known to Eusebius (or Origen) were written, but before the composition of St Matthew or St Luke. For it is the common agreement of scholars that, for all we can discern, the two synoptic evangelists had the same short text of St Mark before them which our best Egyptian MSS. put before us. If there was a longer text, it must have vanished within about ten years of being written.

The force of these considerations is said to be greatly weakened by the danger in which ancient books stood of losing their last page or column. As a generalization that is no doubt sound enough; but it is difficult to apply to the particular case. Was there ever a time when the only existing copy of St Mark was rotting on a shelf unused? Was it not from the first in use for the purpose for which it was surely designed—for Church reading and common edification? And if so, would the last page have been allowed to wear out or drop off without being copied? Or was there a day when the reader turned to the congregation in confusion, and said, 'I am sorry, brethren, but the mice have eaten this morning's lesson'? Even so, could not the missing leaf have been written again from memory? The ancients used few books and readily memorized what they used.

Even so, it would be foolish to say that the last lines St Mark wrote cannot have been lost within a decade of his writing them. They may have been; but the chances are that they were not, and we should need strong grounds of reason to conclude that they were.

Strong grounds are alleged, of course. They boil down to a supposed psychological impossibility. No believing Christian of St Mark's time, it is said, could have wanted to end his book abruptly with the flight of the women from the sepulchre; and no one with even such a command of Greek as St Mark shows could have wished to end a book with the particle *gar*.

The second, or grammatical, point has been effectively dealt with by Dr R. H. Lightfoot in the first chapter of his book, *Locality and Doctrine in the Gospels*. He shows over a wide range of Greek writing that sentences, and even paragraphs, ending in *gar* are nothing out of the ordinary. 'They said nothing to anyone, they panicked so' may give some sort of equivalent for the Greek construction; the little word which really acts as the conjunction comes last. But the suggested English misrepresents the Greek in another way: it is odd, whereas the Greek is perfectly normal. *Ephobunto gar* is certainly an abrupt ending for a paragraph. But then no one denies that St Mark ends abruptly. The question is whether he may not have meant to.

The most relevant example of a *gar* ending is Genesis XLV, 3. Joseph is manifesting himself to his brethren as though alive from the dead; nothing is more likely to be in St Mark's mind as he writes XVI, even though the new and greater Joseph manifests himself through his angel and not yet in person. 'Joseph said unto his brethren, I am Joseph. Does my father yet live? And his brethren could make him no answer, they were confounded so' (*etarachthesan gar*). The parallel speaks for itself.

So much for the grammatical point. We turn to the wider psychological objection: no early Christian writer, it is said, could have wished to conclude with the scene at the tomb.

Psychological generalizations are a poor substitute for personal acquaintance. Those who conclude that so-and-so cannot act in such-and-such a way, on the grounds of psychological generalization only, and without taking the precaution of getting to know so-and-so, commonly miscalculate. When we come to know the man, we can *understand* his acting as he does; we can even see, perhaps, that his action conforms to the psychological generalizations which, viewed from a distance, it appeared to violate. If we had no opportunity of knowing St Mark, we should have to do the best we could with generalizations about the primitive Christian mind. But we are not in that unhappy position. His book is in our hands, and we can try to understand him.

The argument for accepting XVI, 8 as the end of the Gospel amounts to this: the scene at the empty tomb is a final chord which draws together, echoes and concludes the preceding music. I discussed the poetical effectiveness of St Mark's conclusion in *The Glass of Vision*, Lecture viii, so I will proceed more scholastically here. I will show that XVI, 1–8 is a strong complex refrain, answering to all the ends of previous sections in the Gospel to which we might expect it to answer.

For the purposes of this demonstration a slightly more careful analysis of VIII, 27–XVI, 8 will be required than the analysis which has served us hitherto. We have been content to analyse in terms of what we have called 'cycles'. We have now to show that in these last chapters the cycles tend to fall into halves, and the halves to organize themselves as cycles on their own account.

In saying this we are not introducing a sudden novelty but merely turning our attention to a fact with which we have had to reckon already. We had to admit that a new feature in St Mark's cyclic rhythm appeared in the discourses at Caesarea Philippi. These crucially important discourses interposed themselves between one cycle and the next, in a way which made us doubt whether it were better to credit them to the cycle before or the cycle after them. We decided on the whole to take them with the cycle before, but we knew that it was very much a matter of convenience. It would have been a trifling decision, if the Caesarean discourses had had no successors. But in fact a similarly ambiguous feature appeared between the two next cycles, and so on to the end of the Gospel.

What we shall now do is to detach the new-type feature from both the cycle before and the cycle after, and to put it by itself. Since it is no part of the old cyclic form, and because it tends to assume the style and extent of a cycle itself, we will call it 'paracycle'. And so we may divide VIII, 27–XVI, 8 into paracycles and cycles, as follows:

P.	C.
VIII, 27 – IX, 1	IX, 2 – IX, 29
IX, 30 – X, 31	X, 32 – X, 52
XI, 1 – XIII, 2	XIII, 3 – XIV, 11
XIV, 12 – XIV, 31	XIV, 32 – XVI, 8

There is nothing new in the table we have just written. The evidence for the divisions we have just made is to be found in ch. v, pp. 108–141. All we have done is to isolate under the name of 'paracycle' the feature which we tried there to call 'the teaching' or 'the truth', and then got into difficulties, because the later examples of it hardly fitted the description.

What we will now show is the way in which the paracycle declares its independence of the cycle and puts on cyclic form. The first thing that happens is that the paracycle develops a set exordium of its own. For the second paracycle begins with a solemn repetition of the passion prophecy embedded in the beginning of the first paracycle (IX, 31 = VIII, 31). So strong does this form of exordium become, that it transfers itself from the paracycle and imposes itself on the beginning of the next cycle. The cycle keeps its own exordium, but embodies the paracyclic exordium in it: apostolic calling and passion prophecy are combined, when Jesus leads the Twelve forward in fear and trembling along the road to Jerusalem, and gathers them about him to hear the passion prophecy once more (X, 32–34).

Thus the cycle begins to be assimilated to the paracycle and the two begin to feel as though they stood on the same footing. The impression is strengthened when the borrowing is reversed, and the paracycle takes over the characteristically cyclic exordium, that of apostolic calling or sending. The remaining two paracycles begin with a carefully matched pair of scenes, in each of which Christ sends two disciples to throw themselves on the goodwill of strangers: to borrow the ass from some (XI, 1–6), and to beg the use of the supper-chamber from others (XIV, 12–16). As we read these narratives our minds recur to the cyclic exordium in VI, 7–13, where Christ sent out his disciples in twos, to throw themselves on the world, and see what reception they would get.

So much for the beginnings; let us turn to endings. There is nothing like a set ending of any kind to the first two paracycles, but the endings of the last two match in quite a striking way with the endings of the cycles which directly follow them. The third paracycle ends with Christ leaving the Temple. As he is at the Treasury, he commends the poor widow who lavishes 'all her living' on the Temple offerings, and then he prophesies the fall of the Temple (XII, 41–XIII, 2). The following cycle ends with Christ supping at Bethany. This is the table-fellowship of disciples, the place of the new temple, Christ's body; and here Christ commends the woman who lavishes on his body her treasured perfume. He proceeds to prophesy the death of his body, and Judas goes away to contrive it (XIV, 1–11).

Now to take the other pair of endings. The last paracycle ends with the discourse in which Jesus prophesies, 'After I am risen, I will go before you into Galilee', and the last cycle ends in the appearance of an angel with the very same prophecy on his lips (XIV, 26–31, XVI, 1–8).

These facts do not show, of course, that St Mark thought out an elaborate scheme of cycles and paracycles, but simply that the rhythm in which he moved was doubling itself in the last part of his Gospel. We are now in a position to advance the formal argument we proposed above. How many endings of previous sections in the Gospel should we expect, on formal grounds, to find echoed in the ending of the whole? We may reply: (a) the ending of the last paracycle, according to the analysis given in the present chapter; (b) the ending of the last preceding cycle, according to the analysis given in ch. V; and (c) the ending of the 'little Gospel', according to the analysis given in ch. VI.

(a) XVI, 1–8 = XIV, 26–31. The angel at the tomb restates Christ's prophecy, that being risen he would go before his disciples into Galilee. By adding the words 'as he said unto you' the angel actually refers us to the text of XIV, 28. But there is more in the parallel than this. In XIV, 27–28 the prophecy 'I will go before you into Galilee' is the continuation of another prophecy: 'You will all break down, for it is written, I will smite the shepherd and the sheep will be scattered.' Since the Biblical shepherd 'goes before' his flock, the sense is quite continuous when Jesus proceeds to say: 'But after I am risen, I will go before you into Galilee', thereby gathering you again, and leading you back to your fold. The angel at the tomb recalls the second part of Christ's prophecy, but the women in their frailty enact the first. They do not deliver the message about the gathering of the flock, but themselves run from the sepulchre like frightened sheep. They do, in fact, just what the disciples did at Gethsemane, when, in direct fulfilment of Christ's prediction, they turned and ran.

When Christ prophesied that all his disciples would break down, Peter protested, and tried to make an exception in his own favour, but Christ would not allow it. Then the other disciples came in with similar protestations (XIV, 29–31). The special part played by Peter in that dialogue adds point to the direction of the angel's message, 'Tell his disciples *and Peter*, He goes before you into Galilee (there shall ye see him) as he said to you'.

(*b*) It is not necessary to say much here about the match between the end of the Gospel and the end of the previous cycle, that is to say, between the woman's anointing of Christ at Bethany and the women's attempt to anoint him in his sepulchre. For these two scenes, like the pair we have just discussed, are directly joined together by a prophecy of Christ. He himself says that the woman who anoints him at supper does so by anticipation of his burial. The women who come to the tomb do so to make good a burial ceremony which has had to be postponed. They forget two things: first, that Christ has had his burial anointing already, according to his own word at Bethany; second, that according to his oft-repeated prophecy, he must rise again the third day.

(*c*) The endings of the 'little Gospel' and the 'great Gospel' have been compared in the last chapter. We will here add the remark that the apparition of the angel at the tomb is the only apparition that St Mark's Gospel records, apart from the apparition of Moses and Elijah in the Transfiguration. The whole character of the Transfiguration, however, is different; Moses and Elijah are not simply apparitions in their own right, so to speak, but adjuncts to the glorifying of Jesus before his disciples' eyes. The closest type for the apparition of the angel is not the Transfiguration, but the *apparent* apparition of a phantom to the disciples on the waters of the lake (VI, 49), even though it turned out to be no phantom but Jesus himself.

We have now simply to ask ourselves whether St Mark wrote so firm a threefold refrain as XVI, 1–8, not to finish his Gospel off, but to spoil the effect afterwards with an appendix of additional scenes? And if the mice in the bishop's house at Rome ate the appendix, what highly discriminating mice they must have been!

But even when we have decided that St Mark finished his Gospel in a satisfying way at XVI, 8, we may still ask why he chose to employ his skill on finishing it just there rather than at some later point. He may have been skilful about the termination he has contrived, but if he had wished, he might have been equally skilful about another, for example, a sending forth of the apostolic mission from Galilee, as in Matthew XXVIII. Why should not he record at least one appearance of the risen Christ?

The answer we have to give to this question is not a simple one. There can be no final answer. St Mark chose to do what he chose to do, or to speak more Christianly, was inspired to do what he was inspired to do. His inspired choice might have been different, for the inspired choices of the other evangelists were in fact different. All we can do is to advance a number of considerations which help us to see that the choice he was inspired to make was a possible choice, and consistent with other choices he made in the composition of his book.

First of all, then, an evangelist has to make a choice about the representation of the supernatural. St Mark, of course, has no hesitations about describing what we call the miraculous. But is not the risen being of Christ on a completely different level of supernaturality from the miracles he performed in the days of his flesh, or from the wonders which descended from heaven to touch his fleshly existence with gleams of glory? Are not all these things mere tokens, pointing beyond themselves to something inexpressible? Christ risen from the dead is the Son of Man enthroned at the right hand of power; St Mark gives a slight indication of that when he describes the angel at the tomb who speaks for Christ as 'a youth seated at the right hand side in a white robe'. Is it wise for the evangelist to attempt the description of two completely different levels of the supernatural side by side in one book—the tokens of the World to Come in this world, and the living heart of the World to Come itself?

In saying this we are not suggesting that St Mark held the belief that the self-manifestation of the risen Christ to his disciples was overwhelming or terrifying. It was all mercy, like the speaking of God with Elijah in a small voice of calm. Mercy is condescension; 'Who is like the Lord our God, who though he be so high yet humbleth himself?' But how to express the dimension of that descent, the depth of that mercy, the earthquake and the fire in the still small voice?

We may the better appreciate the nature and the consistency of St Mark's representation of the true supernatural if we compare his treatment of the Lord's resurrection with his treatment of the Lord's death. The death was a natural event, in a sense in which the resurrection was not; we all know the recipe for death, we do not know a recipe for resurrection. But the death of the Lord was more than a natural event; it was the casting out of Satan, the purification of fleshly uncleanness, the ending of an old dispensation. How does St Mark express the supernatural efficacy of the Lord's death? He expresses it by a portent. The going forth of the Lord's spirit was accompanied with a loud cry at which the veil of the temple split from the top to the bottom. That is all. It means plainly enough that when Christ's spirit leaves his temple (that is, his body) the divine presence leaves the Holy of Holies to go forth into all the world. Jewish privilege ends, and the Roman centurion standing by is there and then inspired to confess the Son of God. Christ was a Jew by reason of his fleshly temple, and the presence in the Holy of Holies made God the God of the Jews. The two limitations end together at Christ's death.

The veil is rent, the spirit has gone forth, but the body remains in human hands and is sealed in a sepulchre. But spirit returns to redeem flesh; the power which rent the veil removes the stone; nothing can limit the sovereign freedom of God's will. As the victorious death is revealed by the opening of the sanctuary, so the victorious resurrection is revealed by the opening of the sepulchre. The passage of God is not seen; but He gives physical tokens of his passage. The open tomb is the portent of the resurrection; the angel is little more than a voice, a personified exposition of the portent. Such is St Mark's handling of the supreme mystery; and if he felt that a description of the Lord's return was not part of such a treatment of the matter, it is surely possible to understand him.

Another reason can be adduced from the Gospel for St Mark's

not wishing to add an account of the Lord's return. And that is, that if he had, he would not have felt that it brought the story to any sort of an end. His management of the prefigurative sense in the middle part of the Gospel seems to show that there was for him no end, short of the end of the world. He could not carry the Gospel history on to the end of the world; what he could do was to show the prefiguration of the end in the body of the Gospel, and so to conclude the Gospel itself as to make contact with that prefiguration. The words of the angel, 'He goeth before you into Galilee' (XVI, 7), flash us back to the sequel of resurrection in Galilee (VI), when, after the miracle of raising the dead, Jesus sends the apostolic mission forth, appearing to his disciples as an apparition, and yet not an apparition, but in his very being. Even that is not an end; we follow the sequence of prefiguration forward through the admission of the Gentiles to the age of persecutions and the threshold of Advent.

We commonly make St Matthew and St Luke vote together against St Mark about the proper conclusion to a Gospel; but that is an arbitrary representation of the facts, based on the ignoring of St Luke's second volume. St Matthew, certainly, decided to round off and finish St Mark with two rather slightly drawn scenes of Christ returning; I prefer St Mark's poetry, but I allow that St Matthew better meets the need of Christian people for plain instruction. St Luke's attitude was completely different from St Matthew's. He adopted the Marcan programme of running the story on, not however in prefiguration, but in actual history. (He was limited, of course, by the historical form; he could not carry history beyond the present; he could not take it to the end of the world.) Such being his programme, he very naturally omitted from his own Gospel most of the most strongly prefigurative scenes of St Mark's (VI, 45–VIII, 26). Was not he going to give a straight historical account of the same matters in his narratives of the resurrection appearances and of the extension of the Gospel to the Gentiles? To show the influence of the Marcan prefigurations on the Lucan histories would take us too far from our present subject, and we will leave it for another occasion.

CHAPTER VIII

THE HISTORICAL SENSE

The principal importance of St Mark's Gospel lies in its historical content, and a main object of any study in the pattern and movement of the evangelist's imagination must be to assess more accurately the bearing of his historical testimony. All historical writing exhibits a pattern of some kind, and all historical writing involves the use of the imagination. If we are going to make an independent use of any historian's work, and not simply consign ourselves to his guidance blindfold, we have to appreciate the laws of his imagination, and the assumptions he makes about the pattern of events.

We may usefully distinguish two sorts of pattern in St Mark's history, a pattern of events and a pattern of exposition. The pattern of exposition belongs simply to the telling of the story and is no part of the events narrated. A good example is the numerical patterning of the healing miracles. By the evangelist's own admission, Christ healed many more persons beside the thirteen whose histories he chooses to record in detail. It is not true in any objective sense that Bartimeus was the thirteenth person healed by Christ or Jairus's child the eighth. If we wish to find an historical reality to which the numerical pattern belongs it must be found in the mind and teaching of Christ, or failing that, in the mind and teaching of the apostolic Church. The numerical reckoning of the healings is the symbol of the doctrine that Christ's healing work was in principle the healing of all Israel. Now it may be a fact that Christ so viewed his healing work, and said things that showed it. Or it may not be so, in which case it is the apostles looking back on Galilean days after the Resurrection who were moved so to view the healing work of Christ. Whatever historical reality corresponded to the expository pattern was either in Christ's mind or in his apostles'. But it was not there in the form the pattern gives it. Neither Christ nor St. Peter supposed that only thirteen persons had been healed, or that among all the healings performed, thirteen had been marked with an asterisk of peculiar memorability. What they believed was something about the significance of all the healings in general.

By contrast, what we call the pattern of event is supposed by an historian to lie in the events themselves, as well as in his story about them. It is his business to draw it out, and make it visible, to exaggerate it, to stylise it, to make diagrams of it. There will be more or less artificiality in his representation of the pattern of event, but unless he believes the pattern to be really in the events in some sense, he is no true historian. A writer who is concerned to exhibit the influence of ideas on political action must believe that such an influence really operates and that the lines it takes are such as he indicates; and so with the writer whose formula is the interplay of economic forces or the development of civil institutions. None of these men supposes that he is simply playing a game of which he has invented the rules, and in which the facts of history are used as counters.

The pattern of event as St Mark understands it may be put in one word, prefiguration. The present was prefigured in the past, the future is prefigured in the present. It is needless to give examples of prefiguration as St Mark understands it, for we have been discussing nothing else for several chapters. Every cycle of his narrative prefigures the next, and the 'little Gospel' prefigures the great Gospel. Christ's ministry prefigures the apostolic mission, his passion and resurrection prefigure the end of the world.

We ask ourselves how it is possible that St Mark should process his story with such elaborate artificiality, and the question merely shows that we are outsiders and onlookers and have not understood him. Prefiguration is his form of historical thinking. You might as well ask how a scientist can be so elaborately artificial as to pattern all events in sequences of natural causality, or how a biographer can be so perverse as to interpret everything by the interplay of circumstance, character and purpose.

Prefiguration is an historical form, and not something else. It does not impose on events a pattern borrowed from somewhere outside the realm of events; it simply imposes on one stratum of events the pattern of a succeeding stratum. Nor is it a rigid or unadaptable form. On the contrary, it is far less rigid and doctrinaire than many formulae which have been used by would-be scientific historians. There is no inflexible scheme which must be everywhere imposed. The pattern is always changing, because the events to be prefigured are always different. The effect of writing history prefiguratively is, as it were, to spread and fuse the character of successive events; the earlier stratum is infected with the nature of the later by prefiguring it, and the later is infected with the nature of the earlier by fulfilling it. Yet if such writing is done well, the distinct characters of the successive phases are not blurred or lost. In prefiguring the Jerusalem ministry, the Galilean ministry retains its own vivid identity.

Prefiguration is an historical form, but it is unlikely that any historian would use it apart from theological belief. It belongs to history viewed as divine revelation. What God has begun to reveal he will reveal more perfectly; 'there is nothing hidden but that it may be manifested'. What one cycle of events has sketched, the next will fill in. What has been achieved imperfectly in John Baptist will be achieved perfectly in Christ. What Christ has enacted in principle and substance will be re-enacted and spread abroad in the destiny of the Church. Each phase is a divine word of which the next phase is the inspired exposition.

There is a perfect concord between St Mark's doctrine and his literary practice. He feels in his bones the power of one historical phase to beget the next because, as he writes, he experiences the power of one cycle of narrative to beget its own exposition or development in the next cycle. What the Spirit of his inspiration does with his thoughts is but the tracing over of what Creative Power did with the events about which he thinks. Historical reality grows by the same dynamism as that by which his Gospel grows. Everything becomes the seed of its own subsequent exposition or manifestation.

Modern historical writers, believing Christians among the rest, are in difficulties about the unique place of Christ in the historical series, because it is at seeming variance with their historical practice. History is for them a continuous chain fastened behind to the hidden origins of our race and stretching invisibly on before. No link in it is more than a single link, restricted to its place, and placed by relation to other links. A person, an event, may be of great importance, yet it seems that nothing can have any significance for what preceded it in time, and that the significance it has for time following is bound to be a diminishing factor; it must gradually taper away and be crowded out by other and later influences.

This is not the place to break the idols of the historical imagination against the standards of philosophic truth. All we wish to remark is that the men of the New Testament were untroubled by our difficulties, whether our difficulties are or are not of our own making. They saw the history behind them as of finite length, and Gospel history could obtain unique importance in relation to previous history by being the retrospective epitome of its pith and substance. All that men had been or done had prefigured Christ, and all they had prefigured, Christ did and was. But in being and doing that, Christ also made the prospective epitome of all that men were still to be or do; he was the text, they were to be the manifold expositions of it.

Any historian, Christian or otherwise, may apply his historical scheme or method with such doctrinaire violence as to override the facts and destroy the historical value of his work. The question is not whether he has used a method or scheme; of course he has. The question is whether he has used it in such a way as to force the facts, or, if he has, how far the forcing has gone. In many fields of historical enquiry it is fairly easy to form an opinion on such a point. We may obtain independent access to the evidence which our historian is interpreting, and check his interpretation by our own; or we may compare his work with that of other historians, working independently of him. In the case of St Mark we have no real power to do anything of the sort. He is our evidence for the Gospel tradition, we have no exterior evidence by which to check him. And the other evangelists, so far from operating

independently of him, build upon him as their corner-stone. There
are scholars who feel confident that they can construct a parallel
non-Marcan tradition called Q, and even establish an historical
order in the sequence of its material. They can then check Mark
and Q by one another. They are fortunate in their faith. I wish
I could share it. Since I do not, I am left with one criterion only.
Does St Mark tell a story which, as a story, makes sense?

The question cannot be avoided, but it is a question full of
ambiguities and pitfalls; who is to be trusted with it? Not we,
surely. What does the question anyhow mean? Does the story
make sense—but on what assumptions? On the assumption that
nothing supernatural ever occurs? On the assumption that
Christ's range of topics and code of conduct never strayed outside
what one would expect of a self-taught Galilean Rabbi moving on
the fringe of orthodox Pharisaic circles? The former is the assumption of rationalists, the latter is the assumption of friendly Jews.
Problems of an ultimate kind arise here into which it would be
madness to plunge. All that we can do is to give notice that our
judgement of what is a sensible story will be a Christian judgement;
we can only hope, not a bigoted or antiquated one; in any case
it will be ours.

We desire to view the Marcan history as a history, that is, as a
connected narrative. Now there are scholars who think that they
know this to be a foolish enquiry, because they think they know
that tradition came to St Mark in such a form that he had no connected story to go upon. But when I look at this supposed knowledge, I find that it depends on a way of analysing St Mark himself
which I hold to be fundamentally erroneous. I say, then, that we
have no such knowledge. Suppose, for the sake of argument,
that we are able to guess in what form, and in units of what size,
traditions about Jesus were commonly recited in the Christian
assemblies before St Mark wrote; and suppose that the form of
the typical Marcan paragraph was influenced by the form of such
recitations. We should still have no reason at all to assume that
St Mark's information was limited to what such recitations im-
parted to him. Say he was writing in Rome between A.D. 65 and 69.

Had he then never met an apostle? Is it certain, after all, that he was not the John Mark of *Acts*, the man from Jerusalem, the companion of Barnabas, Peter and Paul? Was there a special social *tabu* in St Peter's entourage against ever talking about the sequence of events which led from Christ's baptism to his passion? If one mentioned it, did the apostle turn slightly green and suggest with embarrassment that one's proper course was to listen to third- and fourth-hand recitations given in Church piecemeal by local elders? That an apostle could scarcely misuse his superior knowledge to interfere with the growth of a genuine Christian folk-tradition?

Those who allow that the evangelist had any tradition about the general run of events sometimes suppose that he had it in the form of a short and bare summary, taught as a repetition and learnt by heart. And they make the supposition the starting-point of yet another endeavour to analyse the Gospel into sources. It is taken to consist of two sorts of material, the traditional anecdotes as recited by the elders, and the narrative summary. Cut out the traditional anecdotes, and the summary remains. For the evangelist is held to have used it as a frame for the anecdotes, fitting them in as he would or could. No such opinion appears to us to be admissible, for the more we examine St Mark, the more his sentences are seen to flow away into the continuous process of his thought, and to bear the stamp of having been composed for the place in which they stand. Any line of the supposed summary is found to presuppose the anecdotes which on this hypothesis have been fitted in above it.

There is nothing for it but to take the Gospel as it stands, and see whether it tells a sensible story or not. The study of St Mark's imaginative rhythm does not stand in the way of such an endeavour; on the contrary, it is indispensable to it. It is by grasping the rhythm of his mind that we must grasp what he saw as the rhythm of events; and then we can proceed to ask whether that rhythm admits of what we call historical interpretation.

For us to interpret St Mark historically will mean to translate the pattern of prefiguration into another pattern—whatever we

take to be the historical pattern of cause and effect. In order to do
that successfully we must understand prefiguration to start with,
or we shall be misled. For example, in III, 6 St Mark tells us that
the Pharisees went out and consulted with Herod's people against
Christ's life, after he had healed the withered hand in synagogue.
What is the relevance of such a remark? As a mere factual statement, it says that some angry Pharisaic elders talked to some
supporters or officials of the Tetrarch, and said to them, 'Can't
we get rid of this man?' Likely enough; but would an historian
trouble to record it, unless he wished to suggest that the mind of
the government began to be poisoned against Jesus, and that this
had some effect on events? So shall we infer that when Jesus began
to frequent the neighbouring countries (from Mark VII onwards)
he was keeping out of Herod's way? But St Mark says nothing of
the kind. The approach of the angry Pharisees to the Herodians
has no sequel. Three chapters later the Tetrarch apparently takes
notice of Jesus for the first time, and then only to make a remark
about his being a sort of John back from the dead. The general
analogy of events in the Gospel suggests that Christ's journeys
into surrounding countries from VII onwards were for the extension of the gospel (and why not?); and when St Mark once tells us
that Jesus passed through Galilee as quietly as possible, he says
expressly that it was because he was teaching his disciples the
religion of the passion, and presumably did not wish to be interrupted; not that he was avoiding the police.

Why then did St Mark record the plotting of the Pharisees
with the Herodians, and place it in a position of emphasis? The
prefigurative scheme gives us a sufficient answer. The event is
important, not because of its political consequences, but because it
foreshadows what would happen at Jerusalem. The Pharisees
consulting with the Herodians, however abortively, prefigure the
priests compassing Christ's death by bringing the secular power
into the case.

If we desire to experiment with the historical interpretation of
St Mark's rhythm, the rhythm we shall naturally take is that of
the steadily succeeding cycles. For that is how history moves,

in our opinion—one stage leads on to the next. Not, indeed, by prefiguring it; but it leads on to it nevertheless. We will therefore simply write our historical interpretation of St Mark's story in five double cycles, in accordance with his own rhythmic movement.

I (a). The baptism of Jesus at the hands of John is seen by the evangelist as a transcendent mystery. It is not clear whether he is claiming to tell us what it was to Jesus at the time, or what Christian faith perceives it to have been in its essence. In any case it was, historically, a simple event: among the many who came to John's baptism, Jesus also came. He withdrew afterwards into solitary places, and endured spiritual struggles for something over a month.

Some time after this John's mission was ended by his arrest, and Jesus appeared in Galilee proclaiming the imminence of the Kingdom of God and the necessity of repentance and faith. He appeared on the shores of the Lake near Capernaum, and called upon four fishermen to become his companions. With them in attendance upon him he made a day's mission in Capernaum; he gave the sermon at Sabbath synagogue, and established himself in Simon's house. There was general amazement and some enthusiasm. He exorcized the possessed and touched the sick. He would stay no more than a day. Early next morning he went straight on from a place of solitary prayer outside the town to some other centre of population, and thus he proceeded to carry the gospel through the Galilean villages, preaching in the synagogues. Crowds began to collect, attracted chiefly by his cures, and he could not shake them off, even by keeping out of town. In healing the sick, he was observed also to pronounce the forgiveness of their sins, and the Pharisees were scandalized.

(b). Scandal increased when the number of Christ's adherents and constant companions grew. For it was found to include men like Levi-bar-Alphai, Jews careless of their religious duty, and held by the Pharisaic brotherhoods to be untouchable. But Christ's brotherhood, his table-fellowship, actually embraced such men, and he made their inclusion a point of principle. The criticisms of the orthodox were stiffened by evidence of freedom in Christ's own observance of the Law. He defended his disciples for neglecting the weekly fasts, and himself for healing on Sabbath. He made the purpose and nature of his divine mission, rather than pious custom, his rule in such matters. Affairs reached a crisis in the synagogue at Capernaum. The elders would have procured the hostile intervention of the Tetrarch against Jesus if they could. Jesus withdrew from the synagogue and taught in the open outside the town. The multitudes who attended him continued to increase, and to come from wider afield.

2 (a). Christ's abandonment of the synagogal pulpit at Capernaum gave emphasis to the distinct identity of his following; and he gave it formal shape himself by conferring on twelve men a definite standing as his chosen companions and representatives. Three of them were distinguished by special surnames and by a privileged nearness to Jesus on certain occasions. The Twelve listened to his debates with the learned, his casual sayings, and his public teaching, and then questioned him in private about the things they had heard him say. Thus it was that they learned from their master. He spoke to the Twelve about the privilege of such discipleship, and spoke of the whole body of his faithful hearers as being his true family. He taught about the action of God in present events, but always in riddles or parables, and interpreted them to his disciples in further sayings of the same kind. His healing and exorcizing meanwhile continued, and he visited the farther shore of the Galilean Lake.

(b). The time came when Jesus began to employ the Twelve. He sent them on healing and preaching missions. Their message was simply that with which Jesus himself had entered Galilee at first—repentance in view of the coming Kingdom. As they went in twos, the mission could be in six places at once. From the point of view of a political observer, the movement took on a far more considerable character. The public speculated about it and the Tetrarch took note of it, and compared it with the previous movement centred in John Baptist. Those whom the mission touched followed the missionaries when they attempted to retreat with Jesus into the uncultivated lands, and difficulty arose about the provisioning of the crowd. Such was the occasion of the miracles by which Jesus relieved their hunger.

3 (a). As though the mission-field of Jewish Galilee had now been covered, Jesus began to tour the Jewish villages scattered through Phoenicia, Decapolis, and Philip's Tetrarchy. His disregard of Pharisaic rules concerning cleanness had already been illustrated by his fellowship with law-breaking Jews. It received more radical expression in his contact with mixed populations. He himself taught that cleanness and uncleanness came from within the heart, and not from outward contact. On one occasion at least he went outside the normal scope of his personal mission for the benefit of a Gentile who showed some sense of what the divine gifts to Israel were.

(b). The mission of Christ being a mission to Israel must take him south as well as north, and must find its culmination in Jerusalem. When Jesus was at the extreme northern limit of the Promised Land, he drew from his disciples a confession of their faith in him as God's Messiah, and went on to explain to them that this meant a visitation of Jerusalem, but a visitation which would lead to his rejection by the priestly power, and his death. But after death, resurrection.

4 (a). Jesus prepared for the southward expedition by a with-drawal into Mount Hermon with his three chosen companions, a retreat implicitly compared by the evangelist with that which Jesus had made in the wilderness before he began his Galilean mission. But whereas he had been then alone, his three witnesses now had some sight of the divine mysteries into which he was taken up. Turning south, he passed through Galilee without attracting public notice, and crossed North Judaea (that is, Samaria) into Peraea. There he resumed his public teaching, pronouncing with a more formal authority on the definition of Law and the conditions of salvation. Meanwhile he had been instructing his disciples in the religion of the Passion, applying the principle of redemptive sacrifice to practical matters small and great.

(b). Jesus took the second and final step of the southward journey when he left Peraea on the road through Jericho to Jerusalem. He told his disciples that the road to Jerusalem was the road to death and resurrection. They followed him in a confused state of mind, trembling at death and catching at glory. He arrived in the city some time before Passover. He entered with a crowd of pilgrims. The cry broke out 'Son of David!' and Jesus, who had previously discountenanced such tributes, accepted this, and sent for a beast that he might ride in triumph. He used his popular prestige to order the traders out of the Temple court, and the high priestly power dared not take action against him. He taught in the Temple with popular acclaim and silenced scribal objectors.

5 (a). Jesus left the Temple courts for the last time on the day before the Paschal sacrifice, and as though impelled by a perception of the secret movement of events, entrusted four of his disciples with his last predictions and warnings about the future of God's Israel. He commanded them, then and always, to watch. And indeed the imminence of Passover had at length decided the priests to act, in fear of popular disturbance. Not venturing to use the temple police for a public arrest, they entered into correspondence with the traitor Judas. He undertook to conduct the High Priest's men to a place where they could take Jesus without fear of effective resistance by Galilean partisans. Passover came, and Jesus ate the feast with his disciples at a house in the city, and consecrated his coming death in bread and wine.

(b). His enemies took Jesus at his prayers on Passover night, and so his passion began. The Sanhedrists gathered in the High Priest's house about cockcrow and heard witnesses who professed to accuse Jesus of threatening to destroy the Temple, but the evidence was not good enough to proceed upon. Obtaining from Christ's own lips a confession of his claims, they both satisfied their own minds that he was a blasphemous pretender worthy of death, and realized that they had a political charge which could be presented in the governor's court. After deliberation they resolved on this course, and brought Jesus before Pilate as soon as the hour permitted. Since Jesus could not and would not deny that he was in some sense King of the Jews, and since Pilate would not and could not enter into fine theological distinctions, there was no more to be said, and Jesus said no more.

We will break off here for a moment, because the story of the passion bristles with points of historical dispute which require a more detailed interpretation. To plunge into them would be to distract ourselves from our present concern. We are trying to show that St Mark's five double cycles can be historically interpreted without any violence; that they yield a sensible story. We have not attempted to summarize everything St Mark tells us, but to concentrate on that aspect of each successive cycle which reveals the forward movement of events. There is nothing new in the interpretation we have made: it is all implicit in the analyses of the foregoing chapters. We have done no more than collect together the historical fruits of those analyses.

We say that the result is a sensible story, but not, of course, for those to whom no story makes sense in which the Christ of St Mark's and our faith intervenes. There are even special canons of evidence applied by some people to the Gospel and to no other record, as for instance, that no man must be admitted ever to foresee that the course of action in which he is involved will lead to his death in a certain way; or, having seen this, ever to persist in such a course of action. But I do not suppose that my readers will accept such surprising canons of evidence.

It is in the passion narrative that St Mark's historical value is most exposed to detailed criticism, because there alone he gives us a continuous system of causes and effects, and there alone he advances into the public and political arena. Christ's journeys, sermons and miracles are affairs of private life, which have no place in the fabric of political history. From the political point of view, they merely illustrate the religious life of the people and the opportunities it lent to political agitation. But Christ's conflict with the Sanhedrin and condemnation by Pilate are part of the public history of Pilate's procuratorship. Strictly political questions are involved, such as the nature of the policy attributed to public persons and the nature of the legal or constitutional procedure involved in it.

The opinion which I wish to defend is that St Mark's narrative is free from inconsistencies or absurdities, and that it is single and continuous. At the same time I admit that he was not interested in legal and political niceties. His story is not always politically correct, because it is that of an amateur in political matters. But he admits of interpretation. That is the most we can expect. Obviously St Mark is not going to handle the relations between Sanhedrin and Procurator with the nicety of Tacitus describing the relations of the Senate with the Emperor.

What I have to say in the remainder of this chapter is very largely apologetic. I am not considering the story on its merits but untying knots which the learned have—often, I think, unnecessarily—found in it, and which have become the commonplaces of study. Many of them have been dealt with by others, but the student is still so generally confronted with them that I think it well to gather them here. My purpose will not be to demonstrate St Mark's story against any other story, but simply to show that, as a story, it is free from the difficulties which have been found in it.

It is said first of all that St Mark's account of the High Priests' plot is unintelligible as it stands. What he says is this: 'It was Passover and Unleavened Bread next day, and the High Priests and scribes began to look for a way to seize him by guile and kill him. "For", said they, "not at the feast, or there will be an uproar of the people"' (xiv, 1–2). The objection urged is that there is a contradiction between the short quotation of what the priests are saying and the course of action presently attributed to them. For the quotation records a resolve to get hold of Jesus before the feast began, whereas what the priests did with Judas's help was to arrest him on the most sacred night of the feast.

But if St Mark had meant what his critics make him mean, he should have written: 'They began to seek a way to seize him *with the utmost expedition* and kill him: "For," said they, "not at the feast,"' etc. But what he does say is, 'They began to seek a way to seize him *by guile*', etc. Early arrest is not discussed, but 'guileful', i.e. private and sudden, arrest is. It is in terms of the implied contrast that 'Not at the feast' must be understood. 'Guilefully, and not at the feast' is a different thing from 'Immediately, and not at the feast'. The priests exercised ordinary and continuous police in the Temple courts alone. Public order in Judaea was the affair of the Procurator and the cohort. So that if the priests talked of 'making an arrest' simply, they would be understood to mean, to make an arrest in the temple. This being so, no difficulty attaches to the sentiment: 'It would never do to make an arrest at the feast. We shall have to arrest him by stealth and secure his execution.'

In xiv, 10–11 St Mark records how Judas came forward and promised to do what the High Priests wanted. A needless mystery has been made about the role of Judas. In fact there is no mystery at all. The High Priests were not furnished with a corps of intelligent detectives. They wanted someone to guide their men, so that they could seize Jesus without fear of a crowd collecting to rescue him. 'A crowd' for these purposes might mean anything over twenty men with daggers and sticks. The Galileans were reputed to be tough and there were plenty of them about at feast-times. If the High Priest's servant and his raiding party simply followed Jesus from the Temple towards the pilgrim camp round Bethany, they would be unlikely to make neat work of it. Someone who knew his way about was required; Judas would do very well, but there is no reason to think of him as irreplaceable. The High Priests did not sit spinning their thumbs and wondering if a traitor would perhaps come forward. If they had not found Judas they would have made other enquiries. St Luke sums up with perfect exactitude the part played by Judas: 'He served as guide to those who arrested Jesus' (Acts i, 16).

There might be a mystery about Judas's motives, if, but for his treason, Christ would have been let alone. But Christ was to be taken one way or another, and to-morrow if not to-day, and Judas put himself on the safe side. He received a fee, which aggravates the loathsomeness of his part, but the suggestion of cupidity as a motive does not appear before St John, and we are here concerned with St Mark's story only. It is sufficient to see in Judas the man who made a job of being a coward. St Peter premeditated heroism and succumbed to danger. Judas premeditated the policy of safety.

We may be told that St Mark does not impute motives of any kind to Judas. Very true, and therefore it is relevant to point out that he does not need to, because the most commonplace of all motives suffices; motive is not a problem. We are not anxious to put forward a theory about Judas's motives, but simply to satisfy those who find St Mark's story unintelligible and say it is necessary to invent a whole novel to explain it. For myself I understand Judas by looking into my own heart. I hope I would behave better, but I see what the temptations would be.

The next problem we will take is concerned with the words of Jesus in Gethsemane when Judas came upon him. 'Sleep on now and take your rest. It is enough. The hour is come. Lo, the Son of Man is betrayed into the hands of the lawless. Arise, let us go. My betrayer is at hand.' It is very fairly objected that the speech as so written is unintelligible without the insertion of stage-directions. (E.g. 'At this point torches and sword-blades flash through the olive trees'.) And the insertion of stage directions is not a permissible method of exegesis. Apart from such tricks, we cannot make out what course of action is being recommended to the disciples. They are to sleep on, and they are to rise and depart. Nor can we understand the reasons given for these opposite commands. Are they to sleep on, because the attempt to watch has been long enough sustained ('It is enough')? Or because it is useless to resist predestination, and the Son of Man's hour has come to be betrayed? And why are they to rise and depart? In the hope of escape, or to confront their fate with dignity?

From these confusions and ambiguities the conclusion has been drawn that St. Mark ran together contradictory accounts of what Christ said at this critical moment, and then, perhaps, threw in a dogmatic clause of his own invention for good measure.

Which is as much as to say that the evangelist was well content to write nonsense and in writing it to aggravate it. Surely a heavy accusation.

I reply that there are two difficulties in the text: an unnecessary translation, and the mystery of predestination. First, as to the translation: 'Sleep on now' is an unnecessary translation. It takes two Greek words as meaning 'Sleep henceforward'. But the first word need not be an imperative, and the second can mean 'then' in a merely logical sense. The right translation can be found by comparing what Christ has said just above. 'Thou art sleeping, Simon! Thou couldest not watch a single hour! Watch you and pray, that you enter not into temptation.' The new saying stands in parallel: 'You are sleeping, then, and taking your ease! Enough of that! The hour has come; see, the Son of Man is being traded to the Gentiles. Rise, let us go; see, my betrayer is at hand.'

We must not write 'the Son of Man *is betrayed*' because that is ambiguous and liable to suggest that the action is completed, so that nothing can be done about it. All the Greek means is that the action is on foot, or being attempted. 'See, they are betraying the Son of Man into the hands of the lawless; arise, let us depart; see, my betrayer is at hand' is just as good sense as 'The flames are cutting us off. Quick, let us get out! Look, the fire has reached the bottom of the stairs!'

There remains the difficulty of predestination. Christ prayed, with submission to the Father's will, that 'the hour might pass him over', as it passed over the Israelites in the first passover night. But now he seems to be saying that it has not passed him over, but come; and that the Son of Man is being betrayed. But is this a necessary interpretation? The hour has come, in the form of attempted betrayal; but if he escapes it, it *will* have 'passed him over'. The difficulty of predestination is, of course, implicit in the Gethsemane prayer itself. Christ had foretold his betrayal and death several times before he ever prayed in Gethsemane. But to deny him recourse to prayer because of predestination is to turn a faith in Providence into a soulless fatalism. The problem of predestination and human action is universally difficult, and it must be solved by theological reflection, not by sawing St Mark up into separate sources. For when you have sawn him up, the difficulty of predestination will be just as great as it was before.

We will now move on to the examination of Jesus before the Sanhedrin. It is one of the most widely accepted of critical positions that St Mark describes two meetings of the Sanhedrin between Thursday midnight and Friday dawn: first a trial, narrated at length, and assigned to the depths of the night; then a conference in the first light of morning, of which nothing is stated except its result—that Jesus was taken before Pilate. It is then suggested that the story of the two meetings is highly improbable (as indeed it is); and the hypothesis is advanced that St Mark has blunderingly juxtaposed two accounts of the same event. The old and authentic account pretended to no knowledge of proceedings transacted behind closed doors, and was content to say that they took place. A later account supplied picturesque details. It was not strong enough, however, to oust the primitive tradition. St Mark, acquainted with both and not skilful enough to combine them, was driven to find a place for the longer story in the depths of the night, confronting us with the improbable tale of a full Sanhedrin leaving their beds in the small hours to conduct a trial in form.

I reply that there is no double narrative in St Mark, nor does he collect a Sanhedrin in the depths of the night. These are illusions, due to the misreading of the text. The so-called second meeting is not a further session of the Sanhedrin, but simply the beginning of the trial before Pilate. 'And as soon as it was morning the high priests with the elders and scribes and the whole assembly' (they were all in it, they were all guilty), 'having considered their course of action, put Jesus in bonds and handed him over to Pilate. And Pilate examined him. . . .' No one would ever have mistaken this for a separate narrative of the Sanhedrists in conference if it were not cut off from the main story of their proceedings by the episode of St Peter's denial. But there is no mystery about the position of the episode. It could not well stand in any other.

The position of St Peter's denial may be considered either from an historical or from a symbolical aspect. To take the requirements of history first. What St Mark has to tell us is that as soon as the High Priest had succeeded in putting Jesus in the wrong, he began to be maltreated. The discredit of the master spread to the disciple. St Peter was in the High Priest's court, the servants began to taunt him, and he denied Christ. That is the proper historical sequence; St Peter's denial stands where it ought to stand. It would be far worse placed if, after the account of Christ's condemnation and mishandling, the evangelist passed direct to the Sanhedrists' final deliberation and resolve to present Jesus before Pilate, and then introduced St Peter's denial. In that case he would cut the denial off from its roots in the condemnation and maltreatment of Jesus, and cut the presentation before Pilate off from its roots in the Sanhedrists' deliberation and resolve.

Now to consider the requirements of symbolism. Christ is the type of all martyrs, because he first confesses Christ. He is the first to come under the scope of his own prophecy: 'They shall betray you to Sanhedrins . . . and before governors . . . shall you be set on on account of me, for testimony to them' (XIII, 9). Christ is the example of confession, and Peter (at that time) of denial. The confession and denial must be juxtaposed as closely as possible.

So St Mark describes a continuous session of the Sanhedrists, with a digression on St Peter's denial. He does not time it, except by saying that cocks were crowing at the time when, Jesus having confessed, Peter denied. How long had the Sanhedrists been sitting by then? Long enough to hear and to dismiss some inconclusive evidence of Christ's seditious preaching. How long would that be? We can scarcely guess. St Mark says that 'many' came forward with this inconclusive evidence. 'Many' should be taken here as meaning no more than 'a number', as when St Luke says that 'many' had tried their hands at writing Gospels before him. The witnesses ought to be understood to be Sanhedrists, who had heard Christ preaching in the Temple. Did it take the Sanhedrists an hour to discover that they had not amongst them sufficient evidence on which to prove a charge of incitement to attack the Temple?

Suppose that the arrest in Gethsemane was made about midnight. How long the High Priest's men took chasing the apostles, returning to the city, knocking up the High Priest and waiting about, St Mark naturally does not trouble to tell us. The High Priest collected his colleagues as early as possible, say by the first streaks of light. The cocks are still crowing when St Peter denies; and the Sanhedrists are ready to present Jesus to Pilate at the beginning of business hours.

St Mark may be exaggerating when he says that the whole high-priestly clan was present and the elders and the scribes. But that is what he says, and he may well have supposed that the High Priest had sent round to their lodgings for them. What is more certain is that he has exaggerated the formality of the proceedings in suggesting a trial with the passing of a sentence of death. But he has only suggested these things; his language is vague and non-technical. He was not interested in constitutional niceties. What he wishes to tell us is that the Jewish governing power in effect decreed the death of Jesus, and so they did, even though formally speaking they went no farther than deciding whether they would proceed against him by way of temple police,[1] or take him to Pilate on a political charge.

More real difficulty attaches to the episode of Barabbas. To begin with, there is St Mark's statement that Pilate used to release to the people at the feast a prisoner for whom they interceded. It may be taken for granted, surely, that the evangelist's knowledge of this alleged custom is limited to the part it plays in the Barabbas story. Pilate had so acted in the past as to arouse the expectation that he would listen to popular intercession on behalf of a

---

[1] Supposing that the Sanhedrin could pass any sentences which required no more than the Governor's permission for their execution, offences in or against the Temple would surely come under the Sanhedrin's competence if anything did. Hence, perhaps, the attempt to find evidence for Christ's having preached in the Temple against the Temple. Compare the case of St Stephen, stoned by the Sanhedrin on a charge in which alleged attacks on the Temple were prominent, Acts VI, 12–14.

political prisoner at the Passover of that year. That he had done so twice before is all the story requires; and we are not to know that he ever did so again. It is hard to see how historians can be in the position to refute anything that St Mark need be taken to affirm.

We are told of Barabbas that he was in irons with the revolutionaries who had shed blood in the revolutionary fighting. A difficulty is made of this: St Mark's words are said to presuppose an episode to which he nowhere refers. He is suspected of copying in an odd scrap of tradition without digesting it or suitably re-phrasing it. There is no need to suppose anything of the kind. In the days when St Mark wrote, his readers would readily assume that 'revolutionary activity' had always been chronic in Palestine under the Procurators. They would feel no surprise in being casually informed that Pilate's prison contained a sort of people called the rebels or revolutionaries, guilty of shedding blood in the revolutionary fighting.

A more serious difficulty is one of time. Are we to understand St Mark as saying that Pilate left the case he was judging in the air, while he listened to the popular intercession? Or that he attempted to grant to the people a man who had not been sentenced and who might deserve his freedom on his own merits? St Mark does not actually say these things. He is, once more, completely vague about the forms of law, and does not record the passing of sentence at all. The Barabbas paragraph ends with the words: 'He released to them Barabbas, and consigned Jesus, after a scourging, to crucifixion.' If the consigning to crucifixion is the sentence, and not merely the order to proceed with execution of sentence, we shall have to say that Pilate gave sentence *after* the scourging. But, in spite of St John, we cannot have that. The scourging was part of the penalty to which the prisoner was sentenced.

We conclude that St Mark records no sentence; but we, interpreting him, are at liberty to say that sentence was given immediately and as a matter of course; Christ pleaded guilty and Pilate had no ground to withhold it. But, says St Mark, Pilate saw that the crime was technical rather than real, and Christ was the victim of Jewish malice. He saw, in fact, what so many later Roman judges saw, when Christians were delated by Jews, and pleaded guilty. So he hoped to escape the execution of a sentence he had been unable to withhold. It was the first Roman business-hour within the compass of the feast, and here, very naturally, were the people craving their feast-time boon, and Pilate offered them Jesus. They would not have him, however, and the execution had to go forward.

The Barabbas-story is not absurd. We may suspect it for being too much like drama and too little like life, or too convenient to the Christian apologist in fastening guilt on the Jewish people. It would take us out of our way to discuss objections of that kind. All we are at present concerned to show is that St Mark's story is straightforward, consistent, and capable of reasonable inter-pretation.

A further crop of difficulties has been raised on the supposition that various things could not have been done at feast-time, whether by the Sanhedrists out of respect for the Law, or by the Romans out of respect for Jewish sentiment, or by those who made purchases for the burial of Christ, because the shops were shut. The questions which arise on such ground do not affect the unity and consistency of St Mark's story, or its intelligibility to his first readers. What they do affect is the degree of interpreta-tion his story may require if it is to be reduced to historical accuracy. Has he reported inessentials broadly, or has he even (as some think it necessary to suppose) dated the Jewish paschal sacrifice of that year on Thursday by error for Friday? Even if I had to accept the fact of such a misdating, it would not destroy St Mark's historical credit with me. He was concerned for the substance of events, he might err a day in chronology. But I do not feel forced to accept the fact. The questions involved are too complex for discussion here, but I may refer the reader to the very weighty article of Dr J. Jeremias defending the Marcan chronology of the Supper, in the January–April issue of the *Journal of Theological Studies* for 1949, and to his *Abendmahlworte Jesu* for a fuller treatment.

CHAPTER IX

ST MARK, ST PAUL AND ST JOHN

The demonstration that St Mark's story is a reasonable story leaves us unsatisfied. We should like to apply some external check. And we have all at some time entertained the dream of finding impartial, or anyhow, non-Christian, evidence of some kind by which to check it. But the obvious truth is that the Christians were the only people sufficiently interested to memorize or record the Christian facts while there was still living witness to them. By the time the world began to explore into the origins of a troublesome sect, there was nothing to go upon but what the sectarians said. If men did not wish to talk like Christians about Christian origins, they must rationalize, satirize or denigrate the Christians' story. It is conceivable that a research into the procuratorial archives might have revealed an entry stating the name, crime, and penalty of Jesus, and a date. It would scarcely have revealed more, and no one, so far as we know, ever troubled to make it.

If there is no non-Christian evidence by which to check St Mark, is there not at least independent evidence? Well, there is St Paul, an altogether older witness, a companion and contemporary of St Peter. His witness is indirect for the most part, and amounts, roughly, to the following:

The Lord Jesus, though by nature existing in the form of God (Phil. II, 6) was born of a woman (Gal. IV, 4). His standing in the world was that of a Jew with Davidic blood (Rom. I, 3), but his position was so humble that the prophet had described it as servile (Phil. II, 7). He proclaimed what he employed others to proclaim—the gospel (I Cor. IX, 14); that is, the good tidings proclaimed by St Paul himself with whatever degree of further definition the actual occurrence of the saving events had added. Anyhow, the Lord Jesus predicted his second advent in some detail, for he said among other things that the faithful who died in this age should have no disadvantage as compared with those who survived at the last trump (I Thess. IV, 15, cf. Mark VIII, 35–IX, 1).

The Lord employed others under him to spread the gospel, commanding them to live on the charity of those to whom they preached (I Cor. IX, 14, cf. Mark VI, 8–12). Twelve of his associates formed a distinct body at the time of his death and resurrection, and it is natural to suppose that Peter, to whom the Lord first appeared alive again, was the leader of it (I Cor. XV, 5). And, as we have said above, St Paul appears to recognize the group of three witness-apostles, whose institution St Mark attributes to Christ (Gal. II, 9, *supra* p. 109 f.).

The Lord's earthly mission was to the Jews, not to the Gentiles (Rom. XV, 8), and he lived subject to the Law (Gal. IV, 4). It was his death that first broke the legal yoke. That does not mean that he was content in all things with current orthodoxy. He was himself a teacher, and gave his own decisions. He ruled, for example, that there should be no such putting away of wives as allowed their remarriage with others. Spouses who became separated might not alter their condition except by reuniting (I Cor. VII, 10, Mark X, 2–12).

Was the Lord Jesus a healer and wonder-worker? St Paul does not say so, but he freely attributes such powers to the inheritors of Christ's Spirit, and it is scarcely credible that he believed otherwise of Christ.

The ministry of Christ was brought to an end by organized Jewry (I Thess. II, 15) and he was betrayed into the hands of his enemies. On the night of his betrayal, after saying the grace before meat, and in breaking the bread of thanksgiving as the custom was, he said 'This is my body which is for you; do this in remembrance of me'. So also with the cup, in the grace over wine, saying, 'This cup is the new covenant in my blood; do this as oft as ye do it in remembrance of me' (I Cor. XI).

Though it was the Jews who were the real authors of his death, he was executed by the Roman power in the Roman fashion, that is, by crucifixion (Phil. II, 8). Having died, he was buried; but the grave did not retain him, and he rose on the third day (I Cor.

xv, 4). It was presumably the first of the week, for the Christians keep that day (I Cor. XVI, 2). He lives, transmuted into the substance of glory (I Cor. xv, 42–49). He appeared to Peter first, then to the Twelve, then to many others, St Paul himself being the last (I Cor. xv, 5–8).

Such is St Paul's testimony. If it appears meagre to us, that is largely because we separate out of the body of St Paul's teaching those things alone which bear the mark of historical reference. All that St Paul writes he writes as an exposition and application of the gospel of Christ, and he has for the most part no occasion to distinguish what belonged to the form of the teaching on Christ's lips, from what the Spirit afterwards made plain. It would have astonished him greatly to learn that his modern readers would attribute none of his teachings to Christ in the flesh, beyond what he expressly assigns to him. For example, St Paul preaches Jesus as the New Adam, and makes many developments on the theme. That Jesus had preached himself as the New Adam, or, to put it in Palestinian phrase, as the Son of Man, he does not tell us, and has no occasion to do so.

There is hardly a line in St Paul's testimony which St Mark does not confirm. The wording of the supper story is somewhat different, but substantial agreement remains. The detail of the persons to whom the risen Christ appeared is passed over by St Mark; as we have seen, he sets that part of the story outside his province. Otherwise St Mark everywhere upholds St Paul.

There is indeed one serious point of disagreement which has been alleged, but not rightly. St Mark records that Christ's sepulchre was found empty; St Paul has been held implicitly to deny it. For he puts his own vision of the risen Christ on the same footing as the appearances to Peter and the Twelve. But surely, it is argued, the vision on the Damascus road shone on St Paul from heaven and was spiritual in nature. It was not an encounter with the body of flesh and blood which had lain in the tomb. But if so, neither, presumably, were the meetings of Peter or the Twelve with their risen Master. And if Christ did not manifest himself in the flesh and blood which had lain in the tomb, surely the vanishing of his body from the tomb is an irrelevance, and we have no business to attribute to St Paul a belief in it.

The argument as we have put it rests on the detail of St Luke's accounts of the vision on the Damascus road, and it begs a good many questions. St Luke did not share St Paul's (apparent) belief that the vision on the Damascus road was of the same kind as the appearances to Peter and the Twelve, and he does his very best to make that clear. The appearances to Peter and the Twelve were bodily enough, according to him; but then Christ once for all ascended, and no subsequent appearances are bodily at all, until the second advent. Now it is surely most arbitrary to assume that St Luke's theology tends wholly in the direction of physicalizing the appearances to Peter and the Twelve, and not at all in the direction of dephysicalizing the appearance on the Damascus road.

It is better to let St Luke alone and keep to St Paul himself. In the text we have cited from I Corinthians xv St Paul says that Christ 'made himself seen' to him: in Galatians 1, 16 he says, 'When it pleased God to unveil his Son in me'. It is easy for the modern reader to take the Galatians text as an admission that what St Paul 'saw' was in his own mind; but no student of the New Testament and of the literature contemporary with it can take such a suggestion seriously. What a visionary saw was never said to be 'in himself', least of all when the object of vision was a living person 'appearing' to him. The phrase in Galatians makes, in fact, no direct reference to the vision of the risen Christ. St Paul is giving a summary account of his whole conversion: it was a process by which God had unveiled the divine Sonship of Jesus in his mind. In this process the vision on the road played its part, but so, perhaps, did the martyrdom of St Stephen and the words of Ananias. None of these things were 'in' the apostle's mind; the discovery they brought about was.

When we attribute to the apostle a 'spiritual' doctrine of the resurrection, we can quote his own words in our support; but when we suppose that it excludes the resurrection of the physical body, we fall into an absurd anachronism. Neither St Paul nor the common philosophy of his time had a doctrine of spirit as sheer

act of consciousness and nothing else. Spirit was for them a
refined sort of substance or body. We should not call it 'material',
perhaps, since that word is commonly used to distinguish body of
the cruder sort. But the difference between material body and
spiritual body might be conceived as a difference of degree; the
one might be refined into the other, just as, according to ancient
physics, water was refined into air and air into fire. Our body, says
St Paul, is 'sown' (i.e. buried) an animal body, but raised up a
spiritual body, that is, the resurrection is accompanied by a trans-
mutation; what inherits the kingdom of God is no longer flesh
and blood.

Using a less philosophical and more Jewish form of speech, the
apostle could speak of the glory that shall be ours as a garment,
wherewith our mortality shall be clothed, so that it is swallowed
up in immortal being. In the same way the 'naked' seed is clothed
with the plant, and disappears in it. Even so God 'clothes' the grass
of the field. A strange way to speak of organic growth, but certainly no argument for supposing that the plant can do without
the seed, or man's future glorious being without the body 'sown'
in the grave. The case was not altered, even if the Jewish mind
went so far as to think of the garment of glory as pre-existent,
and laid up for us in a heavenly wardrobe. It still needed our body
to 'clothe', in order that it might become ours. In much the same
way the New Jerusalem was said to pre-exist in heaven, and to be
destined to descend; but it still needed an earthly site to clothe, if
it was to belong to the saints. Borrowing the language of the New
Jerusalem, or rather of the new temple which was to be the heart
of it, St Paul talked of our immortal glory as a house laid up for us
in heaven, not made with hands, and destined to occupy the place
of our fleshly tabernacle, when it falls in ruins. No such language
must be taken to exclude what every Jew in the main line of
orthodoxy believed, real bodily continuity, true resurrection.

St Paul, like other men of Pharisaic education, attributed a
conscious though attenuated state to the souls of the righteous
awaiting the resurrection of their bodies. In that intermediate
condition he taught that the Christian soul was already with the

Lord, and that the advantage of being with him was so great as to outweigh the misery of disembodiedness. For disembodied it still was, and still in need of resurrection; so nothing St Paul says about its condition casts any light on his thought about the Lord's risen state.

To finish the discussion we may retort the original argument on those who advance it. St Paul lists his own vision of the risen Christ with those of St Peter and the Twelve; granted. But he says it was the last. He, Saul the Benjamite, is the Benjamin of the apostolic family, born long after the other apostolic patriarchs, and as a disastrous birth ('abortion') which killed the womb (Gen. xxxv, 16–19). There are no more 'sons' to be expected; St Paul's vision of the risen Christ is the last. Last of what? Not, surely, of mere visions vouchsafed by way of 'angel' or 'apparition'. Such remain always possible. It was the last bodily appearance of Christ on earth. His body was spiritualized, transmuted into the substance of glory; but it was the 'true body, born of Mary', and not an *idolon* of it, such as God has shown to the saints and ecstatics since. St Paul holds something akin to St Luke's ascension doctrine, but either he does not date the ascension by the Lord's leave-taking vision at Bethany as St Luke does, or else he thinks of a special but unrepeatable descent afterwards, for the calling of the Benjamin among apostles.

So, then, when St Paul says that Christ was buried, and the third day rose, he means what St Mark means, and all his spiritualizing refinements are the reflections of an educated Pharisee on what happens to the body when it rises. He does not, of course, refer to the visit of the women or to any other event which proved the Lord's sepulchre to be empty, but then he has no occasion to do so. Neither he nor St Mark supposed the empty tomb to be the principal evidence of the resurrection. St Mark's disinclination to describe the appearances of the risen Christ is not to be attributed to his poor opinion of their evidential value, but to his poor opinion of the resources of narrative description. It was the business of the credal statement to affirm the fact of the appearances, for they were the foundation of faith; it was not the business of a story-teller to describe them, for he would make poor work of it.

St Mark and St Paul bear one another out, and this is a very important fact so far as it goes. But St. Paul does nothing to support the outline of the Marcan story. From St Paul alone you might, for example, suppose that Christ's mission was in Judaea throughout with Jerusalem as its centre. If we want support for the lines of the Marcan story we must turn to the other evangelists. Some may say that we may turn to the summaries of Christ's life given by certain speeches in the Acts of the Apostles, of which perhaps the fullest is in the sermon of St Peter to Cornelius's household. But I think it is absurd to suppose that St Luke's apostolic sermons are unaffected by the Gospel he has himself written before he composes them. They may provide evidence that it was quite usual to refer to the outline of Christ's life in a missionary sermon; they are not evidence what that outline would be like outside the range of St Mark's influence. To appeal to the speeches in Acts is to appeal to St Luke the evangelist; and his account of the Lord's life can be more usefully studied in the former of the two treatises he addressed to the excellent Theophilus. If we study it there we find it to be a Marcan account.

The testimony of St Matthew and St Luke amounts to this, that neither of them was acquainted with a general pattern of Christ's ministry which he was inclined to set against the Marcan pattern. St Matthew supplies an infancy narrative and rearranges the Marcan history to a certain extent, but it seems pretty evident that his motive in rearranging is rather the systematic presentation of Christ's teaching than a different conception of his life. Indeed, the general effect of St Matthew's additions and alterations is to blur the movement of the history altogether. The case of St Luke is somewhat different. He allows the Marcan narrative to make itself felt, and does not swamp it with additional teaching material as St Matthew does; he restricts his additional teaching material to a few places, principally to one place; he makes an enormous development of a single Marcan feature, the 'Deuteronomic' teaching which Christ gave on his way to Jerusalem (Mark x, 1-31, Luke x, 25-xviii, 30). He makes clear at the beginning of this section, and at several points along the route, that the southward journey is the setting, and so his reader does not get lost (IX, 51, XIII, 22, XVII, 11, XVIII, 31).

The late Dr Streeter put forward a theory which still has adherents, to the effect that St Luke had already composed a Gospel out of other materials before he found St Mark. Then he inserted St Mark into his existing work in great blocks. This theory is, in my opinion, incapable of reasonable defence, but those who do hold it will concede that the first draft of St Luke was historically amorphous and contained no scheme of events comparable with St Mark's. They will also concede that when St Luke inserted St Mark into it, the effect was that the Marcan story took control. There was no serious rival account of the whole run of events which St Luke was prepared to oppose to the Marcan account, and so the 'Proto-Luke hypothesis' leaves us where we were: the Marcan history enjoyed unique prestige and there was nothing to set against it.

There is an hypothesis more widely accepted than the Proto-Luke hypothesis, and designated by the letter Q. Those who believe this hypothesis think that there was an actual written book in existence other than St Mark, and that St Matthew and St Luke made independent use of it. Reconstructing Q is a valuable academic exercise, but there can be few scholars who would be prepared to build a history of Christ's life, or any general order of events, on any one proposed order or reconstruction of it. Q is, in fact, very like the electron in developed physical theory. You think the appearances demand that you should postulate it, and you can describe it quite well in terms of the phenomena to which it gives rise, and you may carry a vague imaginative model of it in your head. But when you try to define its existence in itself by where, when, and what, you fall into contradictions. Such being the state of the Q hypothesis, it is vain to set the Q story in comparison with St Mark's story.

We have, in fact, no rival story until we come to St John. Here indeed is a story on the face of it so different from the Marcan, that we feel confident in affirming that we have met a tradition which has an historical outline of its own and rejects the outline of St Mark. This is not really so. The distinctive outline of St John is not historical but symbolical, and it can be shown (a) that St John is careful to respect the Marcan outline, even though he writes all round it rather than inside it, and (b) that his own apparently least Marcan features are drawn from no independent tradition, but from a curiously systematic adaptation of St Mark's matter to a new scheme.

It is admittedly plain that St John's history is no simple development from St Mark's. It is the product of an interaction between the Marcan scheme and a totally different scheme. We have first to show what this different scheme is, and whence it comes; and then to show how it is made to accommodate the Marcan outline.

The Johannine scheme is the scheme of the Jewish feasts. St John, or a predecessor if you think so, had already employed it in the Revelation. Divine action was to be seen as a progression through the Jewish calendar, fulfilling the mysteries of the old religion in order, and so bringing it to an end. The feasts of the Apocalypse are celebrated in the temple of Heaven, those of the Gospel in its earthly double, the temple of Herod. The series of feasts in the two books is the same. The first ascent into heaven in the Apocalypse takes place in IV and reveals a celestial Passover, the adoration of the slaughtered and redeeming Lamb. The first ascent to Jerusalem in the Gospel is in II, and brings us to Passover likewise. The whole series of feasts kept by Christ in Jerusalem is Passover (II), New Year (V), Tabernacles (VII), Dedication (X) and Passover again (XII ff.). The series of festal liturgies in the heavenly Temple of the Apocalypse is identical, as I hope I have shown in a published study of the book. (A Rebirth of Images, chs. IV–VI.)

All the feasts attended by Christ at Jerusalem are unambiguously named by St John, except New Year (V). In V, I we have a choice of readings: 'It was the feast-time of the Jews' or 'It was feast-time of the Jews'. If the definite article is read, Tabernacles must be meant. But probably it ought not to be read; and then it is natural to understand the Evangelist as referring to the next feast-time after the events he has just described. For 'After these things', he says, 'it was feast-time with the Jews, and Jesus went up to Jerusalem'. 'These things', i.e. the events of IV, have been described as the aftermath of Passover (IV, 45; cf. II, 23) with hints of Pentecost (IV, 27–38). The next feast of importance would be New Year, and the themes of V strongly suggest that day.

The ceremony of New Year was the proclamation of the new era by trumpet-blowing. Now the Mishnah (Rosh-ha-Shana, I, 7, 9) shows us that the day was not fixed by the calendar, but by personal testimonies to the appearance of the New Year light (the new moon). Two witnesses were required; would a father and a son (the Mishnah asks) count as two? According to St John, the Baptist was a witness, a pilot-light of Advent, but weightier is the witness of the Father and the Son (V, 31–40). New Year's day was itself sabbatical, and it introduced the seventh, or sabbatical, month. Here, therefore, Jesus begins to heal on sabbath (V, 9–20). The trumpet proclaiming the sabbath of the year reminded Israel of the jubilee trumpet, which proclaimed the sabbath of sabbaths of years, the year of general release. The cripple at the pool awaits the appointed moment of deliverance, but he finds it in Christ (V, 2–9). The trumpet of new year anticipated also the trump of judgement (Rosh-ha-Shana, I, 2) or of resurrection. St John represents the voice of the Son of God as the signal which both wakes the dead and effects the judgement (V, 21–30).

If John V is concerned with New Year, Christ keeps a complete calendar of feasts in Jerusalem from Passover to Passover. But if so, what is the use of saying that St John respects the Marcan outline? For whatever St Mark does or does not tell us, he certainly does not present the picture of a constant alternation of scene between Galilee and Jerusalem, governed by the occurrence of the Jewish feasts. According to him, Jesus is first in the north, then in the south, and the period in the north is surely meant to be of considerable duration.

The answer is as follows. St John inserts a gap of a year in Christ's pilgrimages to Jerusalem, and during this year Christ fulfils the Galilean ministry described by St Mark. And when Christ comes south at the end of the year, he never goes north again. Let us take these two points in order.

St John tells us about the miracle of Bethzatha and the discourse Jesus made upon it, and shows these events to be connected with New Year. He tells us that the miracle led the Jews to seek Christ's life, but he does not tell us whether the threat caused him to withdraw from Jerusalem before Tabernacles, he simply breaks his narrative off at the end of Christ's discourse. Then he begins to tell us about Jesus in Galilee at the next Passover-time, that is, six months later. He records no ascent to Jerusalem for the Passover, and tells us instead that Jesus moved in Galilee, and would not move in Judaea, because of the Jewish threat to his life recorded in v (VII, 1). The restriction to Galilee continued until Tabernacles came round again. This time Jesus did not go up in good time for the feast, as his brethren would have had him do, but arrived halfway through the octave of Tabernacles (VII, 2–14). Thus he resumed feast attendance where he had broken off, but a year had intervened.

That year is the year of the Galilean ministry according to St Mark; St John shows this to be his meaning in two ways, by his handling of the episode itself, and by his references to the Baptist. The episode (i.e. John VI) contains the only preaching of Christ to the Galileans which the Fourth Gospel records. We are told that Christ preached to them from the cathedra of the synagogue at Capernaum with full formality, and we are told what came of it— he was rejected by the Galileans; only his disciples stood by him (VI, 59–71).

According to St Mark the Galilean ministry began when the Baptist had been committed to prison. Then it was that Jesus came into the country preaching, and taught in the synagogue at Capernaum as one having authority (Mark I, 14, 22, III, 1–6). Now according to St John, the Baptist is still at liberty during the continuous story which fills III–IV. His arrest is presumed for the first time in Christ's visit to Jersualem for New Year (v, 35. 'He was the lamp kindled and shining'). Christ's return to Galilee in VI, I is therefore his first entry to that region after John's arrest, and corresponds accordingly with Mark I, 14.

St John assigns a year to the Galilean ministry, although he only describes one episode in it. St Mark assigns the Galilean ministry no period, but for all he does say, a year gives reasonable enough room. His account of the Galilean ministry contains an implied date towards the middle, and a symbolical date at the end. The implied date is given by the mention of green grass in the narrative of the feeding of the five thousand (VI) and in the previous mention of growing corn (II). Everything from the call of Levi until the feeding of five thousand, that is to say, the second double cycle of St Mark's narrative, requires a date round about Passover. St John agrees: he describes the feeding of five thousand only, and he places it towards Passover.

The Galilean Ministry according to St Mark ends with the Transfiguration. For then it is that Jesus reveals his passion and commits himself to it by turning south. The Transfiguration has no literal date, but it has what we call a strong symbolical date: it makes a strong suggestion of Tabernacles. The feast is more properly described as Booth-Making, which is what its Greek name means. It celebrates the sojourn in the wilderness as a blessed time, when Israel dwelt in booths or tents under the light and shadow of the presence of God, the Glory in which he had pitched his tabernacle amongst them. The Mount of Transfiguration appears as a new Sinai where glory is manifested; and Peter proposes the making of three booths for Jesus and the two prophets, because it is good to abide there. St Mark says, moreover, that the Transfiguration was 'after six days' from the episode at Caesarea Philippi. When he says 'after six days' he is presumably employing his usual idiom and means 'on the sixth day' by inclusive reckoning. Now Tabernacles is on the sixth day, so reckoned, from Atonement, and the scene at Caesarea expresses the very spirit of Atonement Day: the repulsing of Satan and the proclamation of the means to obtain mercy at the judgement. And so St Mark's 'six

days' strengthen the Tabernacles symbolism of the Transfiguration by linking it with an Atonement Day scene.

Now to return to St John. He also dates the end of the Galilean
ministry by Tabernacles, and then it is that Jesus commits himself to
his passion, to a migration into Judaea where men seek his life. But
according to St John Tabernacles is not kept symbolically on
Mount Hermon, but literally on Mount Zion. Such a substitution
of Zion for Hermon is in accordance with St John's dominant
scheme of festal pilgrimages. Jesus remains in Jerusalem long
enough to keep 'little Tabernacles', that is, Dedication; then he
goes where St Mark takes him after 'Tabernacles' on Mount
Hermon—into Peraea (John x, 40–xi, 16). After leaving
Peraea, Jesus divides his time between Bethany and Jerusalem
according to St Mark. So he does according to St John, except
that a brief withdrawal into the Judaean country is added
(xi, 54–57).

To conclude: St John squares his narrative in v–xxi with what
appears to be the Marcan chronology. From the time of the
Baptist's arrest Jesus devotes an unbroken year to Galilee, comes
south at Tabernacles time, visits Peraea, and dies next Passover at
Jerusalem, six months after his turning south.

For completeness, let us glance at the chronology of John i–v.
The Gospel begins with Christ's visit to Judaea for his Baptism,
which is, of course, how St Mark's Gospel begins. St Mark then
leaves an indefinite period in which nothing happens, and in
which John Baptist continues to minister. Whenever it is that the
Baptist is arrested, then it is that Jesus enters Galilee with the gospel.
St John fixes this indefinite period at about six months. For Jesus
returns to Galilee after his baptism by John, stays 'not many days'
and ascends to Passover at Jerusalem. Thence he returns by easy
stages, staying in the Judaean country and in Samaria on the way.
Then he goes back to Jerusalem for New Year, and speaks
of the Baptist as newly removed from the scene. From the
baptism (some little while before Passover) until the comment
on the Baptist's arrest (New Year) will be six months or a little
more.

Let us write out a table of the Johannine method of using the Marcan outline, with a third column of chronological notes:

St Mark	St John	
Jesus in Judaea for his baptism.	Jesus in Judaea for his baptism.	
Continuation of the Baptist's mission.	Jesus goes to Passover and returns by stages.	1st month, year 1.
The Baptist arrested.	Jesus at New Year Feast.	7th month, year 1.
Galilean mission.	Galilean mission.	
'Tabernacles' on Mt Hermon.	Tabernacles and Dedication on Zion.	7th–9th months, year 2.
Peraean mission.	Peraean mission.	
Bethany and Jerusalem.	Bethany and Jerusalem.	1st month, year 3.

The conclusion to be drawn from the facts is this. St John desired to write a symbolical Gospel as unlike St Mark's as well could be, turning upon a series of events at the major feasts in Jerusalem. Nevertheless he has so written it as to respect the Marcan outline. It would be natural to infer that he knew of no other; that for him the Marcan outline was history, and history was the Marcan outline.

We have now completed the first part of our task, and can turn to the second: we are to show that the apparently least Marcan thing in St John, the series of episodes in Jerusalem at the successive feasts, rests on a Marcan basis. The fact is simply this: St Mark tells us of one visit to Jerusalem only, and at Passover time. St John stretches out the material of this single visit over all the visits he records. The drama of Christ's relations with the priestly and scribal power at Jerusalem which covers a few weeks or even days in St Mark is stretched over two years by St John, with, of course, a number of intervals or intermissions. A partial and somewhat misleading recognition of the fact takes shape in the common statement that St John has transferred the cleansing of the Temple from the end of the ministry to the beginning. The phenomenon is not so isolated as the remark suggests. St John's Jerusalem ministry follows St Mark's piece by piece; in St Mark it consists of one visit, in St John it is distributed through four.

There is one important exception to the rule that St John takes the Marcan material in order, and that is the Triumphal Entry. It is the first scene of the Marcan Jerusalem ministry, but it cannot be placed in the first visit to Jerusalem according to St John, because it is manifestly the direct prelude to the passion. It is the Triumphal Entry, not the Cleansing of the Temple, which is taken out of order by St John, and settled on a piece of Marcan ground where it does not belong. But St Mark himself seems to have prepared a piece of ground for its new location. For he wrote the entry for the supper (XIV, 12–16) as the Christian antitype to the entry into the Temple, because the supper-room is the true temple. All St John needs to do is make the entry to the supper the triumphal entry. With his Marcan model thus corrected, he can proceed to work straight through it.

Before we show St John at work, let us consider what he is doing and what it means. Why should he wish to spread the history of what Christ did at one feast through four? Was he so zealous for the observance of the Jewish calendar? Quite the reverse. Of the yearly Jewish feasts the primitive Christians kept Passover alone; they kept it yearly, and they commemorated it every Sunday. For Passover was the only feast at which Christ had offered the sacrifice of the New Covenant, that is himself. But his sacrifice was the fullness of sacrifice, and therefore (such was the mind of St John) Christ's great Passover at Jerusalem was virtually all the other feasts also, from Passover to Passover all round the year. In keeping Passover the Christians keep every feast. St John's 'stretching' of the Marcan Jerusalem ministry is a symbolical device and does not imply a different belief about what really happened from St Mark's. On the contrary, St John's way of working from St Mark implies that he believed St Mark's Jerusalem story to be simply true. Now let us see how St John worked.

(a) Mark XI, 12–18 describes a single visit to Jerusalem from Bethany, in the course of which Jesus cleansed the Temple and incurred the hostility of the ruling power. This visit reappears in the form of the Passover visit of John II, 13–22, upon which is hung the discourse with Nicodemus (II, 23–III, 21).

(b) The next day's visit to Jerusalem in St Mark extends from the discourse about the withered fig-tree at least as far as the end of the parable of the vinedressers (XI, 20–XII 12). The next episode, the tribute-money, need not belong to the same day, though of course it may. Since St John is out to divide for his own purposes, he draws the line (it would seem) at XII, 12, and founds John V upon what precedes it.

According to St Mark, Jesus said that the withering of the fig-tree showed the power of faith to lift a mountain and cast it into the sea. According to St John, they find by the gate of the city a multitude of sick, blind, lame, and *withered* people, and in particular a man in despair of ever being cast into the 'sea' of healing at the saving moment. Christ shows that there are no obstacles to divine power by making him well at his word. St John has, it would seem, travelled back along a line of genuine Marcan association from the withered tree of Mark XI to the withered hand of Mark III, and to the more impressive pair of the withered hand, the withered or paralysed man in Mark II. It is this man who is most obviously taken as a model in John V, and used to prove that the mountain can be cast (or does not even need to be cast) into the sea.

To return to St Mark's story. Christ proceeds to enter the Temple where he is confronted by indignant priests and scribes demanding an account of his actions. In answering them, he cites the example of John Baptist, and pronounces the coming judgement of God on the wicked vinedressers. Jesus is come as an only Son in his Father's name and is not received. The topics of Christ's discourse in John V are the same. He has proceeded from the city gate to the Temple when 'the Jews' confront him. He speaks to them as the Son, the perfect emissary of his Father, who is not received precisely because he comes in his Father's name. He discusses the mission of the Baptist and proclaims the coming of judgement.

(c) Mark XII, 13–44. The priests are intent to kill Jesus, and yet they have retreated without effecting anything. There follows a period of indefinite duration, in which Christ is said to be publicly teaching in the Temple—for example, in the Treasury. Men are set to entrap him in his talk, so as to make possible an arrest—such is the implication of the story of the tribute-money, and it is drawn out quite unmistakably in St Luke's version of the story, which St John of course knew well (Luke xx, 19–20). But Christ confutes his questioners, and at length denounces the Rabbis. St Matthew's expansion of the denunciation is especially impressive; with his Gospel also St John was acquainted. According to St Matthew, Jesus denounced the Rabbis as *blind guides*. Finally, according to St Mark and St Matthew, Jesus withdrew from the Temple.

In John vii, 24–x, 39 the situation is the same. It is a subject of public amazement that 'he whom they seek to kill' teaches openly, and they can do nothing to him. Here for the first time Jesus is said formally to teach in the Temple; for example, in the Treasury. The Sanhedrists send men to effect his arrest, but as long as he holds his own in debate, they can do nothing; and they return defeated to their masters. Jesus, retiring before a threat of immediate violence, heals the man born blind. His healing becomes a revelation of the pastoral perversity of the blind guides. They claim to see, yet cannot, and they excommunicate the man who has really received his sight.

Mark xiii, the Apocalyptic discourse, has no antitype in St John. It is no part of the drama of Christ's relations with the Jewish power; St John (in our opinion) had already written a long spiritual exposition of it in his own Apocalypse, and in any case he was not going to turn aside from his Gospel story to do it justice.

Mark xiv, 1–11 is the episode of the anointing at Bethany. It is obvious that St John writes the whole Lazarus story (xi, 1–xii, 11) into the frame of the anointing. For he begins from it, and then works round to it again. The first thing he tells us about Lazarus is that he was the brother of Mary and Martha, Mary being the woman who anointed the Lord with myrrh (xi, 2). We work round through the raising of Lazarus to the place where she actually does so, with Lazarus sitting by. Through the Lazarus episode the meaning of the anointing is fully brought out. 'Let her be', says Christ in St Mark's narrative; 'She is beforehand to perfume my body to the burial', and St John gives an equivalent form of words. The burial of Christ in St Mark is foreshewn by the woman's action only; in St John it is foreshewn by the burial of Lazarus. Needless to say, St John's story presupposes his knowledge that Christ had actually raised the dead, for example, the widow's son on his way to burial. It also presupposes many other things into which it is no business of ours here to enquire.

Mark XIV, 12–16, the entry to the supper, becomes the triumphal entry in St John, as we explained above. But although St John makes of it the triumphal entry and dates it back to Palm Sunday, it is nevertheless followed directly by the Supper. No narrative, but only a hiatus, divides the Supper from the entry and the episode dependent upon it (the Greeks).

We may leave our comparison off here. The supper and passion in St John are of course the equivalents of the supper and passion in St Mark.

Our first evidence for Christ is St Paul. Some of the things he tells us are intelligible by themselves, others become so as soon as we open St Mark. St Paul gives us facts, but he does not give us a story. St Mark gives us a story, for which he may have had excellent authorities, and which allows of reasonable interpretation. The other evangelists hold it in high regard, and show no knowledge of any rival history. They do, of course, show knowledge of many additional anecdotes, and much additional teaching. But there is only one history, and it is St Mark's.

CHAPTER X

SECRECY

Surprising views have been held by modern scholars about the silences imposed by Jesus on the witnesses to his works and the hearers of his claims. St Mark, it has been supposed, knew that Christ's contemporaries in the days of his flesh observed him neither to make messianic claims nor to do messianic works; but the hardy evangelist was not deterred by such awkward facts from painting a highly coloured messianic picture. All he felt it necessary to do was to state that Christ would not allow his works or his claims to be talked about in his earthly lifetime, and if anyone objected that the truth must have leaked out nevertheless, the evangelist still had an answer. A special visitation of spiritual blindness prevented even Christ's friends (let alone his enemies) from seeing what he was and what he meant.

Unhappily for such a view, St Mark only remembers to apply the silencer about once in three times; he brings about many situations in which a conspiracy of silence is out of the question; and, most disconcerting of all, when he does report the injunction to silence, as often as not he adds that it had no effect, or served to stimulate publicity. And so the extreme view we have stated above has few adherents now, but there is no conviction either that the problem of 'messianic secrecy' has been cleared up. And I suspect that a number of students think that St Mark is not to be called to the bar of exact reason in this matter, but that he proceeded impressionistically. He felt that a pinch of the flavour of concealment would give the right taste to the whole dish, and scattered injunctions to silence from a random editorial pepper-pot; not overdoing it, however, for fear of wearying the reader's palate.

One of the advantages which we may modestly claim for the analysis of the gospel which this book contains is that it makes good sense of the topic of secrecy, and shows the evangelist to have been both subtle and consistent in his management of it.

The general lines of the solution are supplied by what we have already written on the subject of prefiguration. What is prefigured is never open, for if it were it would not need to be fulfilled or actualized. The fulfilment of the prefigured is the revelation of the hidden. A prefiguration hides seed in the ground, which will shoot up and manifest itself in the fulfilment.

It follows that the rhythm of veiling and unveiling will go with the rhythm of prefiguration and fulfilment. Now in St Mark's Gospel that rhythm is subtle and manifold. It is true so far as it goes that Christ's ministry prefigures the Church after his resurrection. If this were the only prefiguration and the only fulfilment, then we could reasonably expect to find a single and uniform veil of secrecy spread over the face of Christ's ministry, not to be withdrawn until his resurrection. But the rhythm of prefiguration and fulfilment is far more complicated than that. Some prefigurations in the ministry await the Resurrection for their fulfilment, for example, the raising of Jairus's child. But others find their fulfilment in the next cycle of the ministry itself, and with their fulfilment comes their unveiling.

Let us make a provisional distinction. There is secrecy in St Mark's Gospel about three sorts of testimony to Christ: the testimony of his works, the testimony of demons, and the testimony of men. We begin with the testimony of the works.

It is plain that St Mark did not think that miracles of every sort were distinctively messianic because they were miraculous. Such an opinion was scarcely open to him. He had not, to start with, the notion of 'miracle' at all, if by that word we mean an event outside the working of inflexible 'laws' of nature. It would be curious to hear St Mark explaining his views about 'natural laws'. Perhaps he would say that they were rules customarily obeyed by a number of angels who push the stars round the sky and otherwise operate the cosmic system. An angel may deviate in obedience to a divine command or of his own judgement; and then, besides the angels there are rebellious spirits in the world which do not keep God's laws, or the laws of nature, any more than they are constrained to do. What wicked spirits do has a natural cause, just as much as the things that the good angels do. The angel is the cause in one case, and the demon in the other. Yet what the demon does is not in accordance with the customary rules of nature, and what the angel does is in accordance with them. Then besides the angels who operate the cosmic system, there are angels who execute special commissions which have nothing to do with the set laws of nature, but may either supplement or override them.

In such a picture of the world there is no simple division of events into 'natural' and 'miraculous', and no one would conclude from the occurrence of any single event outside the customary order of nature, that Almighty God was uniquely present in it. But if a man arose who was constantly able to effect designs outside the common order of events, the question would arise, whether he had the special assistance of angels or of demons. If he was devout and his preternatural acts were good, it would be right to conclude that he was a saint, and that his prophecies and spiritual teachings had the divine approval. And it might be that there were certain notable works specified in Holy Writ which God would not accord to any man except the Messiah.

St Mark plainly did not regard exorcisms and healings by touch, word or prayer as messianic in themselves. Exorcism was widely practised, and was no doubt also widely effective—for the moment. (The trouble about the demons of mental disorder is not that they refuse to be exorcized, but that they return next day or next week.) And several rabbis and devout persons had the reputation of healing by touch or by prayer. St Mark does not record any attempt to conceal the fact that Christ performed exorcisms or restored health to the sick. The mere fact of his exorcizing was no danger to any secrecy Christ might wish to maintain about his person. The threat lay, according to the evangelist, in what the demons said about Christ when he cast them out. Christ silenced the demons; he did not conceal his exorcisms.

What acts of healing, then, does the evangelist regard as specially messianic, and as concealed by Christ for that reason?

The act of 'cleansing', that is, the removal of disease which carried a ritual taint, such as leprosy; the act of healing the deaf and dumb or of opening the eyes of the blind; and the act of raising the dead. Raising the dead is plainly in a class by itself. As to the rest, medical learning, perhaps, would not pick them out as specially remarkable. Deafness, aphasia and blindness can be psychologically caused, and if so, healed by words of power without invoking miracle. As to leprosy, a large number of quite different skin diseases were lumped under the name, and unless some sort of visible sores were responsive to spiritual healing, the King of England would not for so many centuries have maintained the reputation of curing 'scrofula' by his touch. The only other case of touching for 'uncleanness' which the Gospel records beside that of the leper, is the case of the woman who touched the Lord's garment. Her ailment, I suppose, might well have been hysterically conditioned.

But St Mark's mind did not run on medical lines. He was thinking of theology, not physiology. The cure of leprosy and hæmatorrhoea showed Christ to be the more-than-Levitical healer, able to cleanse the flesh from every defilement; and the cure of leprosy in particular had been given a special position in scripture as an evidence of God-given power (Exod. IV, 7, Num. XII, 10–15, II Kings V, 7–8). The Law declared that it is God who makes to hear, speak, and see (Exod. IV, 11), and prophecy gave such cures as messianic signs (Is. XXXV, 5–6).

In the case of all such specially significant sorts of healing St Mark proceeds in an identical manner. He records two and no more instances of each sort, and in every such pair the first healing is accompanied by the injunction to silence, and the second is performed with open publicity. The leper is bound to silence about his cleansing, the impure woman wishes to steal her cure but is exposed before the crowd by Christ himself. The deaf stammerer's cure in VII is covered by an injunction to silence, the deaf mute demoniac in IX is healed with full publicity. What is true of the two deaf persons is true of the two blind men who are their pairs or 'annexes'. The case is not quite the same with the resurrection of the dead, for while it is true that Jairus's child is raised under strict secrecy, it is not true that Christ himself publicly rises. Nevertheless, his resurrection is published by divine command; the whole world must hear of it before the end can come.

The placing of the veilings and revealings is very careful, and corresponds to the arrangement of the Gospel in double cycles, as the following table will show:

First double cycle	Cleansing hidden (the leper)
Second double cycle	Cleansing opened (the woman) and Resurrection hidden (Jairus's child)
Third double cycle	Healing of senses hidden (deaf stammerer, and blind)
Fourth double cycle	Healing of senses opened (deaf mute, and blind)
Fifth double cycle	Resurrection opened (Resurrection of Christ).

The first half of the pattern covers the healing miracles of the 'little Gospel'. The 'little Gospel' has only two double cycles, and the rest of the book three. And so the hiding of resurrection has to be squeezed into the same double cycle as the opening of cleansing, whereas the opening of resurrection can have a double cycle to itself.

One could scarcely exaggerate the beauty and balance of this pattern, or its harmony with St Mark's general design. For in his general system of prefiguration and fulfilment, the second double cycle fulfils the first and the fourth the third, whereas the fifth fulfils the second more closely than it does the fourth. So in the pattern of hiding and opening, the second double cycle opens the first and the fourth the third, but the fifth opens the second.

Then again, to take another beauty. St Mark uses a fundamental division of healing works into purifications and restorations, while resurrection stands in a class by itself. Purification, as though standing for the power of water, comes first; restoration, as though standing for the power of Spirit, comes second.

And so in every block of healing miracles purification comes before restoration. We now observe that the same order is maintained in the pattern of hiding and opening. It is purification which is hidden and opened in the first part of the Gospel, and restoration in the second. And resurrection is by itself as the crown of the whole, and the refrain, as it were, which joins the two parts of the pattern into unity.

Of the mysteries hidden, none but resurrection is hidden for long. The seed of resurrection matures a long while in the ground, the seed of cleansing, hearing and sight shoots into the light quickly. And it is in accordance with this contrast that Christ's injunction to secrecy in the case of resurrection is effective, whereas in the cases of cleansing and hearing it is not; the seed begins to shoot as soon as it is buried. The leper, charged to keep silence, so spread abroad and published the matter that Jesus could no more come openly into the town, but was without in uncultivated country; and there the crowd flocked to him from every side. And it is said of the witnesses to the Effatha miracle, that the more Christ charged them to tell no man, the more exceedingly they published it, and were beyond measure astonished, saying, He hath done all things well; he maketh both the deaf to hear and the dumb to speak. In the case of the 'annexe' to the Effatha miracle, the healing of the blind villager, St Mark does not repeat the statement that the command to silence led to publication. For, as we have seen above (p. 105), the evangelist was now concerned to describe a more specific effect. The result of the healing of the blind was not a general praise of Christ for doing all things well, but the particular confession of him as Messiah by St Peter on behalf of the Twelve.

One of the most important effects of the pattern of hiding and opening is to provide the reader with an opportunity and stimulus to reason from analogy. We see cleansing hidden and opened, restoration of sensitive powers hidden and opened, before our eyes. Meanwhile we see resurrection hidden. We know that it must break open too, and so a force of dramatic expectation is built up in our minds. Delay only strengthens it, until it is at length released with mighty power when resurrection bursts from the open sepulchre of Christ, and sweeps over the world.

The place occupied by resurrection in the pattern of the hidden and the opened may have something to do with the fact, that no miracles except healing miracles are ever said to be concealed by Christ. Healing miracles have the closest affinity with resurrection, and resurrection is the supreme secret, and also the supreme proclamation. To take an example, the two miracles at sea might have been made the subject of secrecy, for none but the Twelve need be present on either occasion, and the evangelist certainly feels both to be messianic signs of great power. But they have no place in the pattern of the hidden and the revealed, for they do not fit into the system of the healing and resurrection of the human person.

Let us turn now to a different range of injunctions to silence. The witnesses to Christ's mighty works are silenced, because they would publish an aspect of his power which has its due time of manifestation presently, but not yet. The demons and the disciples are silenced because they are in the secret of Christ's messianic dignity; they know, in a fashion, who he is. They know, but must not proclaim what they know, partly because they are indiscreet confessors, and partly because they are unworthy confessors of Christ. He alone is worthy to confess what he is, and he alone knows the time, and manner, and degree of his self-manifestation.

The first thing that we will try to show is that the place occupied by the testimony of demons in the first part of the Gospel is occupied by the testimony of disciples in the second part. We may take our start from the voice at the Baptism in examining the testimony of the demons, and from the voice at the Transfiguration in considering the testimony of the disciples. We are already familiar with the relation between the two voices. We know that the 'little Gospel' takes its beginning from the one, and that the fulfilment of the 'little Gospel' takes its beginning from the other. And the testimony of the disciples is to be seen as a fulfilment of the testimony of the demons. That is to say, it is something more like true testimony, yet it is still imperfect, still in a certain degree demonic.

It is probably right to suppose that St Mark conceived the world of spirits as overhearing the voice at the Baptism, 'Thou art my only Son'. Therefore Satan plied Jesus with temptations forty days, and therefore the angels ministered to him. Such was certainly the interpretation of St Matthew and St Luke. 'If thou art the Son of God' (as the voice from heaven has just testified) 'command these stones to be made bread', or 'cast thyself down hence', says the Tempter in their narratives. According to St Mark, the first spirit to proclaim Christ is the demon in the synagogue at Capernaum (I, 24). As we have seen in another connexion, he bans Jesus in the name of all his brethren: 'Away from *us*, Jesus the Nazarene, thou art come to destroy *us*.' Then he adds in his own name 'I know who thou art, Holy One of God'. We have said that 'Holy One of God' is to be understood as a divination from 'Nazarene', through 'Nazir', nazirite, or consecrated man. But the divination by no means excludes or dispenses with the influence of the baptismal voice. The mere title of 'Nazirite' would make Jesus one of many consecrated persons; the perception that the Nazarene is that Holy One whose holiness ruins the whole kingdom of spiritual impurity presupposes a knowledge of the voice from heaven, and of the victory over Satan in the wilderness.

The demon's confession of Christ is silenced by Christ. 'Be muzzled and come out' is his command. The reason of the silencing is not given. The reader may feel that no explanation is required; everything that demons say of their own motion is ill-omened and tends towards mischief. But presently, in the account of the many healings at Peter's door, we read, 'And he would not let the demons speak, because they knew him'. The next mention of exorcisms is at III, 11, in the story of Christ's 'exodus' after the Pharisees in synagogue had rejected the sign of the withered hand. 'And the unclean spirits, when they saw him, fell before him and cried, Thou art the Son of God. And he charged them with many rebukes not to make him known.' Here at length the theme of demonic testimony has worked itself right out; what the demons proclaim is the full truth which they had overheard at the Baptism: 'Thou art my Only Son, in thee I am content.'

228

The confession of the demons in III, 11 provides the doxology which brings St Mark's first double cycle to an end. It is a strange doxology, certainly, for it is suppressed by Christ; but it is fitting to its place. For the first double cycle is the period of suppressed demonic testimony. From III, 11 onwards we hear no more of it. The Legion addresses Christ as Son of God Most High; the place is desert, so that the question of publicity does not arise, and the demons are not enjoined to silence. Nothing more is said in the Gospel about demonic testimony, let alone the suppression of it.

As the topic of the special knowledge of the demons occupies the first double cycle, so the topic of the disciples' special knowledge occupies the fourth. As the origin of the demonic knowledge is associated with the voice at the Baptism, so the origin of the disciples' knowledge is associated with the voice at the Transfiguration. There is, of course, a difference. Demons by virtue of their membership in the unseen world simply overhear the heavenly voice. It is the nature of demons to be aware of spiritual reality, and to draw no profit from their knowledge. St James in his epistle quotes them as examples of unprofitable faith—'They believe, and shudder'. No words can better express the attitude of the demons to Christ in St Mark's Gospel. The evangelist illustrates the nature of human faith by contrast with demonic. The disciples do not simply overhear a heavenly voice. They do not overhear at all, for the voice in the Transfiguration is addressed to them: 'This is my Only Son, hear ye him.' They hear only what is addressed to them by God. And before God addresses them so, He has so wrought upon them as to restore the life and use of their ears, their eyes, their tongue and their heart. These things are symbolized by the healings of sensitive powers in the third double cycle (VII–VIII), and more directly expressed by the struggles of the disciples to understand the mysteries performed in their presence, and by Christ's reproaches and exhortations to them. St Peter's faith must actually break out in confession, before the vision and the heavenly voice are vouchsafed.

What the heavenly voice confirms is not merely St Peter's confession, but Christ's comment upon it: If the Only Son is to be heard as the sole teacher of Israel to whom Moses and Elijah witness, he is to be hearkened to in what he has just said and will presently repeat: 'The Son of Man must suffer.' This is the secret which is shared between Christ and his disciples in the fourth double cycle—the suffering messiah. It is their discourse together all the way to Jerusalem.

There is of course nothing here to compare with the repeated outbursts of demonic testimony and their repeated suppressions. The disciples are lovers of Christ, not enemies, and having been once enjoined to silence, they observe it. They are with him in the veiling of the mystery from those without. But in another way the evangelist draws a positive comparison between the testimony of the demons and the confession of the disciples. When Peter confesses, Christ silences him and his companions with a 'rebuke' or 'admonition'. The phrase grates harshly on our ears, for it recalls the peremptory silencing of the demons, for which the same word was used (I, 25, III, 12). Surely there is nothing demonic about Peter's confession? Yes, but there is, for he confesses messiah in the spirit in which Satan would have Christ confess his own messiahship. This becomes clear when Christ speaks of the sufferings of the Son of Man, and Peter dares to 'rebuke' or 'admonish' Christ. 'Get thee behind me, *Satan*.' The equation between demonic and Petrine confession appears to be absolute. But the next words qualify it: 'for thou art not godly-minded but man-minded'. Peter is speaking, indeed, on Satan's side, but not with satanic malice. He is just all too human.

The silencing of Peter and his fellow-disciples 'until the Son of Man shall have arisen from the dead' is not simply a political precaution. It is not simply that they will blurt out the truth unseasonably. It is that all testimony to Christ has a tinge of the satanic, if the witness is not prepared to witness with his life. St Peter came as far as thinking he could witness with his life on the road to Gethsemane, but in the High Priest's courtyard he found that he could not.

We ought not to draw a hard-and-fast line between the political and the spiritual aspects of Christ's injunction to silence.

The disciples are not silenced for separate reasons, because they are unworthy witnesses, and because they are indiscreet witnesses. If they were already worthy witnesses, if they already possessed the Spirit whom Christ would earn for them by his own sacrificial confession, they would share his mind, and speak in season. They would not be indiscreet.

Within the pages of the Gospel, Christ is left as the sole true witness to Christ, and our final task here is to examine the economy of secrecy and revelation which he himself uses through the several stages of the history, not merely in silencing the testimony of others, but in giving public testimony to himself.

There are two principal periods of Christ's testimony to himself, the sequels to the two periods we have just been comparing. The insufficiency of demonic testimony is replaced by the sufficiency of Christ's own word; and so is the insufficiency of the disciples' testimony. Peter is forbidden to confess Christ, but unless, in the sequel, Christ confesses Christ, there will be no passion of the Son of Man. Such is the sequence of events in the climax of the gospel, and the 'little Gospel' prefigures that sequence. Between the testimony of the demons (I–III, 12) and the events which prefigure the passion (V–VI) there intervenes a testimony of Christ to himself.

But if Christ testifies to himself so early in the Gospel, how can it fail that his passion should be brought on prematurely? Did he walk abroad unharmed in the character of a self-confessed messiah through the greater part of his ministry? No; for at that early stage he confessed himself in 'parables' or 'riddles' only: in sayings which his disciples did not fully penetrate, and which uncovered to the world no more than a vague awareness of high spiritual claims.

When Christ returned to the public confession of himself in the climax of the Gospel, that is, from XI onwards, he began again with 'parables', but the parables were far more open, more plainly messianic; though he avoided any explicit claim amounting to the statement 'I am the Christ, the Son of the Blessed', he said things which aroused in the minds of his enemies the question, 'Art thou the Christ, the Son of the Blessed?' The High Priest put it to him after his arrest. Then he replied without a parable, 'I am; and ye shall see the Son of Man seated on the right hand of Divine Power, and coming with the clouds of heaven'.

So much for the general lines of the pattern; let us now study the degrees of secrecy, the depths of parable, in more detail.

Part of Christ's economy of secrecy, and indeed the first part, is his silencing of the demons; and before we can examine his own management of parable, we must meet a difficulty arising out of the demons' witness. In spite of Christ's injunctions to silence, so many demons would seem to have blurted out so much truth, that there is nothing left for Christ to conceal. The answer must be, that most of what madmen say is folly, or to put it from the point of view of the doctrine of possession, demons are the greatest of liars and mischief-makers. Thus it would require an already instructed faith, or a true gift for the discernment of spirits, to pick out among the exclamations of the demoniacs an unwilling and direct testimony of demons to the presence of divine power. 'Thou art the Christ' is the sort of thing a lunatic in first-century Palestine might well say to his exorcist; and if the exorcist rebuked him for saying it, the witnesses to the exorcism would have no obvious grounds for concluding that the title was either claimed or merited. No doubt St Mark wishes to suggest to us that the volume and unanimity of demonic testimony was such that only the spiritually blind could fail to see the sign. But it is also essential to his meaning, that the sign should be the sort of thing to which a blind eye is easily turned.

When Christ begins to speak about himself, he does not speak to men who have already learnt his secret from the demons. He speaks in 'parables' or riddles; but he does not baffle his hearers, or merely put them off; he tells them always a plain spiritual truth, with something in reserve behind it. The scribes protest that the forgiving of sins is a power reserved to himself by God, but Christ both forgives and heals the paralytic, that they may know their error: the son of Adam has been given the power on earth to forgive sins (II, 10). Part of what Christ says is perfectly clear, being the direct refutation of what the Pharisees say. What they say is reserved to God has been given to the progeny of Adam. But a riddle remains behind: in what son of Adam is such a power actual, since, for example, the Levitical priesthood lays no claim to it? Jesus exercises it. By what title, or under what covenant?

Presently we hear Christ dispense his disciples from Sabbath-rule. He defends his action by the admitted maxim that Sabbath was made for Adam and not Adam for Sabbath; drawing from it the new maxim, that the son of Adam is therefore master of Sabbath. Again, one part of what Christ asserts is perfectly clear. But again the obscurity remains. In what family or person among Adam's seed is such authority vested? In Jesus, evidently; but under what covenant or in virtue of what right? In the case of the Sabbath dispute Christ makes the first use of a method which finds its classic expressions later in the Gospel—he sets one 'parable' alongside another, without explaining the connexion; but the discerning mind should be able to perceive it. Beside the maxim drawn from 'Moses' (creation of Man and creation of Sabbath) he sets an example from 'the prophets': David 'loosed' the law of the sanctuary, as Jesus 'looses' the law of the Sabbath, when the relief of hunger was in question. If the David-saying is taken by itself, it need mean no more than that ritual restriction allows exception, but when taken in connexion with the saying about mastery over Sabbath, it suggests that such mastery is vested in the Lord's Anointed (II, 25–28).

If the two riddles about the Son of Man are not explicit claims, still less so is the saying about the bridegroom, which comes between them (II, 19–20). Is the 'presence of the bridegroom' which disallows fasting, or the subsequent 'removal of the bride-groom' which allows it, a mere figure for spiritual joy present or absent? Or is the bridegroom to be understood personally? And if personally, then with what force? Are we to think of a rabbi with peculiar gifts of the Holy Ghost as 'the bridegroom' among his friends, or must we think of *the* Bridegroom of the daughter of Israel?

The saying about the bridegroom, and the two sayings about the Son of Man, are within the first double cycle, after the principal passage about the suppression of demonic testimony (I, 25 and I, 34), but before the last mention of it, the strange demonic doxology which concludes the double cycle (III, 11–12). After the demonic doxology, and well within the next double cycle, the question of Christ's claims is raised in a new way, and for the first time the question is explicitly discussed, wherein Christ's peculiar spiritual power lies. Hitherto his critics have simply objected to his acts, and he has answered with defences which suggest but do not define unique authority. His critics have not hitherto admitted that he has even the semblance of such authority. But now they do admit it—they raise for the first time, in however hostile a sense, the question of the person of Jesus, when they say,' He hath Beelzebul; by the prince of demons he casts out demons' (III, 22).

These critics must appear to the reader of St Mark to be putting two and two together: they draw an inference from two premises which both stand in the text. We have just read that Christ's enthusiasm for his mission, and neglect of his food, lead people to say that he is overstepping the bounds of sanity; and a little farther back we have read the passage which we call the demonic doxology, in which the demons grovel before Christ as soon as they see him, and proclaim him Son of God. The scribes put the two together, and make Christ's 'ecstasy' the explanation of his exorcism: when the demons yield to him, they yield to their master, for he is himself possessed by the prince of demons.

Since our thesis is that the topic of suppressed demonic testimony is succeeded and replaced by the topic of Christ's 'riddling' testimony to himself, it is of interest that there should be so direct a connexion between the last text about suppressed demonic testimony, and the passage in which Christ speaks of his own spiritual powers openly for the first time. It is as though the subject of demonic testimony were being dragged into the light and discussed, and that once it had been discussed it lost interest and dropped out of the Gospel. There is perhaps some truth in such an interpretation, but we must observe that the discussion of demonic testimony is at the most indirect. Neither the scribes nor Christ deign to discuss the significance of what the demons say. What is discussed is the broad effect, the attitude of complete abasement of the demons before Christ, as though they knew their master. Such a wholesale surrender of the hosts of Satan is something more than the mere fact of an exorcism here or an exorcism there; and it is this wholesale surrender which the scribes undertake to explain in their malicious speech.

Jesus made his answer to them 'in parables'. How can Satan cast out Satan? A house or kingdom divided against itself cannot stand. If Satan is thus bent on self-destruction, his end has come. But it is more reasonable to look at it another way. If the strong man's house is being plundered, someone who has the power has bound him first. So it is better not to speak of the exorcist as working by the power of the prince of demons, for blasphemy of God's Name is, as every Jew knows, among all sins the irremissible sin. And where is the inviolable Name so evidently present, as when the Holy Spirit is visibly at work? (Christ's argument presupposes two things: that his exorcisms are made in the Name of God, and that the power which operates through the use of the Name is the Holy Ghost. This does not mean, of course, that in exorcizing he pronounced the ineffable Name JHVH aloud, or he would have been accused of blasphemy himself.)

Christ's discourse produces the greatest possible weight of suggestion with the minimum of direct statement. He first tells his critics that they themselves are acknowledging by what they say that Satan's kingdom is falling, and so, presumably, that the kingdom of God has come. He then goes on to suggest his own description of the degree and manner in which the kingdom of God has taken control. Satan is bound. The 'binding of Satan' was a recognized feature of the messianic reign, as we may see from a popular pre-Christian book, the Testament of Levi. St John's Revelation is quite Jewish and quite traditional, when it makes the binding of Satan correspond with the beginning of the Days of Messiah, and the destruction of Satan with the beginning of the World to Come. When Jesus says that no one can spoil the strong man's house without binding the strong man first, he suggests that he himself who 'spoils the house' (that is, makes havoc of the demons) has bound the master, Beelzebul. If so, is not he the Messiah? Last of all, by throwing in the saying about blasphemy, Christ suggests that to blaspheme his action is direct blasphemy of God.

Has this speech of Christ's revealed the true nature of the testimony afforded by his rout of the demons? It has revealed it, and yet not revealed it, for it has put it in 'parables'. The sense of the parables is there, to be taken by discerning ears, but equally the meaning of the demonic rout is there, to be taken by discerning eyes. Parables, like miracles, can be misconstrued or ignored; hearing ears are as rare as seeing eyes. Parable may be a verbal comment on miracle, but equally miracle may be an acted comment on parable. After the end of the parabolic discourse of which the Beelzebul parables are the beginning, Christ lands on the Gerasene coast and turns his sayings about Satan into act. His word visibly binds the strong man 'whom none could any longer bind', and in consequence a whole host of demons, a 'legion', is visibly put to the rout.

Between the Beelzebul controversy in III and the messianic salutation of Bartimeus in X there is no advance in the degree of Christ's public self-confession. We need take notice of two texts only—the public part of the discourses at Caesarea Philippi, and the dialogue with the rich man. At Caesarea Jesus says to the multitude, and not to his disciples only, 'He who disowns me and my words in this apostate and offending generation, him shall the Son of Man disown when he comes in the glory of his Father with the Holy Angels'. The disciples know that the Son of Man who will disown is identical with the Jesus who is disowned, but the crowd are under no necessity to suppose it. All they are told is that the cause of Jesus is the cause of God, and that men will be judged by their loyalty or disloyalty to it. This is not necessarily to make Jesus more than a prophet of God. Could not the same be said of any prophet? Perhaps a mere prophet would more naturally say, 'He who disowns my words' rather than 'He who disowns me and my words'. Even so, the claim to be more than a prophet is only the slightest hint.

The dialogue with the rich man makes exactly the same point without either increase or diminution of emphasis. If the man wishes to be sure of 'life', that is, of a favourable verdict in the day of judgement, he should renounce everything and follow Jesus. It follows that the cause which Jesus represents is the cause of God. If so, the question is raised, who or what Jesus is, but it is not answered.

Christ's public self-disclosure marks time in VIII–X, but meanwhile his self-disclosure to his disciples advances. This is the part of the Gospel which we discussed above, the part in which Christ shares with the disciples the secret of the suffering messiah. This was the secret which we compared with the secret about demonic testimony in the beginning of the Gospel.

The next advance in Christ's self-disclosure is marked by the episode of Bartimeus. The blind beggar divines 'Jesus Son of David' from 'Jesus Nazarene' by hearing NZR as NSSR, the Branch (from Jesse), the Scion of David's line. The flattering of begging soothsayers was no more evident truth in Palestine than it is in England now; the bystanders were no more obliged to believe Bartimeus when he called Jesus the Son of David, than we are obliged to believe a gypsy who addresses a commoner as 'my lord' or 'your grace'. The significant thing was not what Bartimeus said, but that Jesus acknowledged what he said. It was the people standing by, not Jesus, who wished to silence him. Yet the acknowledgement of Jesus was implicit only. He healed Bartimeus, he said nothing about the form of his greeting. If Jesus had sent for the ass there and then, and the triumphal procession had there and then begun, his acknowledgement of Bartimeus' salutation might have seemed unmistakable. But it was not until most of the journey from Jerusalem to Jericho had been covered that the ass was fetched. The people's memories retained the cry of Bartimeus, and they began to hail the entry of Jesus as the coming of the Davidic kingdom. The silence of Jesus was eloquent when compared with his previous rebukes to the demons and to Peter.

From this point onwards Christ's secrecy about his own person takes on a different character. He still 'speaks in parables' and avoids any direct claims. But the veil of parables is so thin that it requires no special discernment to penetrate it. In that sense Jesus reveals his claims before the High Priest obliges him to admit them in so many words; by letting his meaning be visible to the priests in the temple-courts he was, in a sense, the author of his own death. For this was the truth he had come to proclaim; he could not preach the Kingdom of God without preaching the Kingship of God's Anointed. He was willing to die for the truth, but he was not a suicide and he would not so proclaim the truth as to place himself under any penal statute. He threw the responsibility on the priests; they made a treacherous and violent arrest, they extorted his confession.

Christ fences with the priests when, after he has cleansed the temple, they confront him and demand his authority for his acts. His answer consists of two parts, a counter-question and a parable. The counter-question is, 'Was John's baptism from heaven or from men?' The fact that the priests found it inconvenient to answer Christ's question, and so forfeited any direct answer to their own question, does nothing to obscure Christ's real meaning. He is obviously claiming for his own acts the authority which covered John's baptism, the authority, that is, of God. The second part of the answer is the parable of the vinedressers. Because the vinedressers plot and execute the murder of the landlord's only son, they will be destroyed. The parable fits the saying about John. John came with the authority of God, and was killed, and now Jesus has come. The landlord had previously sent his servants, who were mishandled and at length killed; last he sent his only son. The evangelist says that the priests saw that the part of the vinedressers was being fitted upon themselves. They can hardly have failed to see that the part of the son belonged to Jesus. But still they had no word out of his mouth on which they could ground a political charge.

In the same chapter, Jesus discusses the scribal doctrine of the messiahship and finds fault with it, because it limits the office of Messiah to a mere revival of David's kingdom. Jesus says not a word which suggests that the Messiah is himself; yet after his answer to the priests, and his unprotesting acceptance of Davidic salutations, we can hardly suppose that he was without hearers who drew the inference. Secrecy is at the breaking-point, and in the High Priest's house it bursts. 'I am; and ye shall see the Son of Man sitting at the right hand of power divine, and coming with the clouds of heaven'.

A new stage of self-revelation begins with the healing of Bartimeus. We suggested at an earlier point in our discussion, that this stage of Christ's self-revelation stood related in much the same way to the disciples' suppressed knowledge of Christ in VIII–X, as the dark parables of II–III stood related to the suppressed knowledge of the demons in I. We were able to show a direct relation between the topic of demonic testimony and the dark parables, anyhow in the case of the most important of them, the Beelzebul parables. Is there the same sort of direct relation between the disciples' confession of Christ and Christ's more open proclamation of himself after the incident of Bartimeus? St Mark makes the confession of Christ in the latter part of his Gospel spring out of the healing of the sensitive powers. There are two double cycles of such healing, in each of which ears, tongue, and eyes are healed. In the former of the two double cycles they are healed secretly, and the effect is St Peter's secret confession of Christ, and Christ's secret supplementation of it. In the latter of the two double cycles the sensitive powers are healed openly, and the effect of it is Bartimeus's open invocation of Christ, and Christ's open exploitation of it. Such is the formal relation between the disciples' silenced testimony and the beginning of Christ's more open testimony to himself.

We have given some account now of the stages of secrecy according to St Mark, or, shall we say, the degrees of revelation. We have still to examine the theology of secrecy and revelation which his fourth chapter contains. It is to be found in the answers which Christ gave to his disciples in the boat, when, after the giving of the parable of the sower to the people, they asked him 'concerning the parables'. The plural number is important: they did not ask him about the parable of the sower only, but about other parables as well. What other parables? Other parables, perhaps, which Jesus had given to the people from the boat, for it seems that the sower is no more than a specimen. 'He taught them in parables many things, and said to them in the course of his teaching, Hearken; behold, a sower went forth to sow.' But of these other parables from the boat, St Mark's reader knows nothing, nor, perhaps, does St Mark; we are obliged to form our conjecture of their character from previous parables which St Mark has actually recorded for us. It is of these previous recorded parables that he is thinking when he tells us that the disciples asked Jesus about 'the parables'. For the evangelist's aim is a practical one. He is anxious to report Christ's own comment on such a use of parables as we have heard him make. He has no interest in telling us how Christ explained something of which neither the evangelist nor we have any notion.

In particular it would seem that he is thinking of the Beelzebul parables. For these are the only sayings of Christ previous to the teaching from the boat which the evangelist calls parables. 'He called them to him and began to say to them in parables, How can Satan cast out Satan?' Moreover, we have seen in the course of our analysis of St Mark's cyclic structure, that both in VII and in XIII he treats what he has written in III, 23–IV, 34 as a unity, a single sequence of parabolic teaching extending from the beginning of the Beelzebul parables to the end of the private discourse with the disciples in the boat. Nothing intervenes between the Beelzebul parables and the parable of the sower except Christ's reply about his mother and brethren, and this is undoubtedly a 'parable' or 'riddle' in St Mark's sense of the term. 'Who are my mother and my brethren? Behold my mother and my brethren! For whoso will do the will of God, the same is my brother or sister or mother.'

The parable of the sower is not a characteristic parable, nor is it a parable which could well stand first in the Gospel. For it is a parable about hearing such doctrine as depends for its effect on a responsive ear, and especially, perhaps, parabolic doctrine. The evangelist will not record a parable about hearing before he has given us any parables which set before us the sort of thing we ought to hear. In particular, the sower is not characteristic of the difficulty of parables; it is a simple parabolic exhortation to us to receptiveness and responsiveness, in order that the word, parabolic or otherwise, may have its fruit in us.

If we pay attention to the logical order of St Mark's matter, and neglect the divisions into scenes and episodes, we shall best appreciate how methodical and how reasonable the sequence is. After a good number of sayings in parabolic form, having their culmination in the Beelzebul parables, St Mark adds a parable on profitable hearing, as a comment on so much parabolic discourse; and then, by way of further comment, and to make the matter still more plain, he adds Christ's answers to his disciples, when they asked him about his parabolic teaching.

Christ's immediate answer to his disciples is complex. They want to know about his parables in general; but they have been stimulated to ask by one parable in particular, the parable which teaches men to listen to parables. Christ gives first a general, then a particular answer. (a) The general purpose of my parables is to instruct those alone to whom God has given discernment, such as you. (b) How can you have failed to understand this parable (about listening)? In that case, how are you going to understand the parables in general? (or, any parables?). Here, anyhow, is the interpretation of this one . . . The parables in general hide and reveal, says Christ; but the parable about listening is not typical of such as hide and reveal. On the contrary, of all parables it should be most readily understood. If it is not known, how is any parable to be known? Such appears to be the plain sense.

But a large body of interpreters will not have it so. They complain that Christ's answer as reported by St Mark is contradictory. The first part of it (a) is inappropriate to the parable of the sower, for that parable does not hide-and-reveal, it simply reveals. And the second part (b) is at odds with the first part, because it assumes that the parable of the sower is perfectly intelligible, and reproaches the disciples for failure to understand it. These difficulties fade away when we perceive the continuity of St Mark's writing, and realize that in (a) Christ is speaking of his parables in general, and in (b) of the Sower.

The parables which hide and reveal, says Christ, are those concerned with 'the mystery of the kingdom of God', that is to say, 'the secret of the advent of the Divine Majesty'. It is of this theme that Christ says, 'The whole matter comes riddlingly to those without', that is, not only is it propounded to them in riddles or parables, but it remains a riddle to them. Now the parable of the sower is not specially concerned with the secret of the advent of Divine Majesty, whereas the Beelzebul parables are, and so are several parables preceding them; for example, the two hard sayings about the Son of Man's authority, or the saying about the presence of the bridegroom.

It is a commonplace to object against the statement that parables conceal the truth from those without. It is said that the saying represents a reflection on the parables of Christ made by a generation which had forgotten what they originally meant, and was digging theological allegories out of them by forced interpretation. Whereas Christ's own use of parables is to be judged by the common rabbinic use. The rabbi used a parable not to baffle, but simply to illuminate his hearers; not to make the plain obscure, but to make the difficult plain.

There are two answers to this objection. We have already virtually stated the first answer. The parabolic story, like the Sower, is almost in the nature of a pulpit illustration, and such stories are not riddles challenging the discernment of the hearer. Christ's parabolic stories, like those of the rabbis, have an expository aim. In St Matthew's and St Luke's Gospels there are many such parabolic stories, but St Mark reports few of them. Jewish spiritual teachers also used another sort of parable, which was not an illustrative story, but a pregnant saying, a figurative aphorism, a riddle. St Mark's Gospel contains many such sayings; their predominance is characteristic of his Gospel. And it is of such sayings that Christ is speaking. Riddles and parabolic stories were covered by a single name, 'parable'. It is natural that the magic of language should prevail and that what has a single name should be treated as of one nature. The parabolic story plays a subordinate part to the riddle in St Mark's Gospel, and so riddle gives to 'parable' its standard meaning. A 'parable' is a 'riddle'; and so a parabolic story is seen as a weak case of a riddle—it is an easy riddle. The story of the sower is, in fact, propounded as an easy riddle. Christ does not say, 'Whereunto is he like who speaks the word of God, and whereunto are they like that hear him? It is as when a sower . . .' He simply says: 'Hearken: behold, a sower went forth to sow . . .'

The second answer to the objection is this. A parable about the Kingdom of God is made mysterious by its subject-matter, whatever may be true of its form. The secret of the advent of Divine Majesty may be compared with the most ordinary and straightforward things, but we shall still not understand the parable without divine assistance. We cannot understand the analogy of a mysterious thing to a plain thing without some grasp of the mysterious thing. The common man might no doubt interpret a rabbinic parable about virtue and its reward; but could he interpret a parable which taught him a new and supernatural doctrine about the advent of Divine Majesty?

Let us turn back and look at an example. 'They that are well have no need of a physican, but they that are sick. I have not come to invite the righteous but the sinful.' What sort of a 'physician' is Jesus to the publicans at whose table he sits? To what does he 'invite' them by accepting their invitation? Whence and whither is he said to have 'come'? Perhaps the reader thinks that the answers to these questions are exceedingly obvious. Jesus *cures* the publicans of their vices; he *invites* them to serve the will of God; he *came* out of a carpenter's shop into the field of his mission. To me it does not seem at all obvious that these are the right answers, or, indeed, that they are 'answers' at all. Is it an 'answer' to Christ's parable, to translate his living poetry into our dead prose? I will in any case believe what Christ says to me through St Mark, and acknowledge that any answer must be false which does not bear upon 'the secret of the advent of Divine Majesty'. The parables could not be more illuminating than they are, but the rays they shed fall into the abyss of Godhead.

After giving his disciples his general statement about the use of parables, and his particular rebuke for not understanding that of the sower (IV, 11–13), Christ proceeds to a detailed exposition of that parable (14–20). Then he returns to the general question of hidden mystery and its revelation. A man buys a lamp and stows it away under his bushel-measure or under his bed. That is not what he buys it for, but for the hour when it is set on the stand and gives light to the house. Nothing is hidden away but that it may be some time manifested, nor concealed but to be revealed. Therefore Christ's teaching, however mysterious, is to be listened to with all the ears a man has; according to the measure of our attention, the heavenly seed will be measured to us. He who holds shall receive more; he who holds not shall lose what he holds. Or again: the seed is planted, and we go about our daily business, and it grows and develops and bears the fruit which is the heavenly harvest. It grows of its own power, not by man's; the process is mysterious to us. Because the growth is divine, the harvest is out of all proportion to the sowing. Mustard seed is the least of seeds, but a large shrub comes of it (IV, 21–32).

Such is the theology of secrecy. On the face of it, it is concerned with mysterious teaching, but it is no less concerned with mysterious act; the two are inseparable. For Christ's 'parables' in II–III do not stand on their own feet, they are all given as comment on his strange acts. The mystery of the Kingdom of God is presented in the parables of the kingdom divided, the strong man bound, and the blasphemy of the Holy Ghost. The parables would mean nothing apart from the antecedent actions, and their effect is to concentrate our attention upon the actions: on the spoiling of Satan's household, and on the power of God's Name to bind him. The parables of the Kingdom are not the description of something absent, but a means for apprehending something present in power. They are not verbal substitutes for the substance of the Kingdom, but intellectual instruments by which it may be seized.

The theology of secrecy is itself expressed in parables; 'let him hear that has ears to hear'. It may seem an impertinence to express in cold prose the truth conveyed. When the disciples asked the meaning of the parables, and in particular that of the sower, Christ did not state in cold prose what that parable had meant, but gave them a string of fresh parables developing the details of it. The interpretation of the sower is rejected by modern expositors as artificial allegory and ecclesiastical moralization. It would be interesting to hear how they think the true Christ who stands behind St Mark's story would have answered his disciples. Surely the parable of the sower was to him the substance of statement on the matter it set forth. It was not a popular substitute for preconceived theoretical prose. The truth that Christ's mind was entertaining was precisely this, that the scattering of the word is as the sowing of the seed. One could not say to him, 'But what is your point? Is it that much seed is sown, and little takes root? Or that the little that takes root nevertheless so increases as to reward the husbandman? Or that the fortunes of the seed are very various? Or that the growth comes from the seed, and the recipient soil merely conditions it?' The parable was not made on any of these points. It was a concrete symbol expressing what it expressed. And when Christ was asked for an interpretation, he first gave the general clue (the sower sows the word) and then went over the story, drawing out of it fresh divinations of spiritual truth. What else would you expect him to do?

Of the figures used in IV that which bears most directly on the purpose of secrecy is the burial of the seed. The lamp need not be stowed under the bushel in order to shine, but the seed must be buried in order to bear. We are supposed to see that it is fitting that the word should be similarly buried, if the Kingdom of God is to be its fruit. In burying our seed, says St Paul, we bury not that body that shall be, but bare grain. We may sink ready-grown and flowering geraniums in our beds, pots and all, but that is not horticulture. The gardener plants not the body that shall be, but a seed or a slip, that God may clothe it in its growing. Christ does not encourage the spreading of ready-made formulae divided from living act, whether in the form of rumour or of doctrine. He plants living seeds of act, and adds parables which feed their natural force; and so he leaves them to grow. He restrains the publication of new degrees of supernatural act, but if they nevertheless burst forth, then it is of their own power and has not been forced; it is as when the seedling moves the stone and pushes into the light. The greatest act of all, the saving passion, must in the nature of the case receive its comment beforehand, afterwards would be too late. But only chosen ears receive it, and until the act has happened the comment is not, and cannot be, fully understood. Messiahship is not taught even to the initiate as a thing by itself, but as that which death and resurrection will express. Messiahship means ultimately a coming in judgement and glory, but these things are not understood, except in so far as passion and resurrection prefigure them.

Such is the doctrine of St Mark. But did Christ reveal himself with the degree and sort of reserve St Mark describes? Well, what do you think? I find in myself no power to conceive Christ's mission otherwise. I do not mean that every line of St Mark's representation is literal transcription of what Christ said. St Mark tells his story in his own manner, and a natural way of expressing some things to Roman Christians towards A.D. 70 would have been an unnatural way of expressing them to Galileans in 29 or 30.

CHAPTER XI

SON OF MAN BEFORE ST. MARK

Great complexities of interpretation have gathered round the title 'Son of Man'. Our concern is only with the part it plays in St Mark's Gospel, but unhappily the Marcan question is not wholly separable from the more general question. We will begin by stating briefly the position which we shall maintain.

1. In the first centuries before and after Christ the five Books of Moses were held to contain the substance of all doctrine; the prophetical and other inspired writings were treated as a commentary on the Law. Any article of faith which was to be taken seriously as such must find a basis in the Law. Now the Messiah appears at first sight to belong not to the Law but to the histories and prophecies; the Messiah is a returning Son of David. No worthy basis for the Kingdom can, in fact, be found in the Law, other than the universal Kingdom of Adam. If the kingdom of the Son of David cannot be viewed as a revival or fulfilment of Adam's kingdom, then it cannot be really found in the Law at all.

2. The prophecy of Daniel VII takes the step of treating the coming world empire of Israel as a fulfilment of Adam's kingdom, and applies to the new Adam the description Son of Man. Daniel does not distinguish the figure of the Davidic king from the body of saints who hold the empire. The writer of the Similitudes of Enoch makes the distinction, restricting the description 'Son of Man' to the New David.

3. St Mark, or Christ as reported by him, is more concerned than any mere Jew to find the Kingdom in the Torah. The evangelist is not independent of the developments of thought and language represented by Daniel and Enoch, but, like a true Israelite, he uses such writings to interpret the Law, and sees his own way through Genesis by their guidance. He builds up a consistent doctrine of the Son of Man, in which Genesis and Daniel are present from the start and become visible as the exposition proceeds.

4. The question whether Christ taught the Marcan doctrine himself cannot be settled by direct proofs. The doctrine can, however, be shown to lie at the root of St Paul's Gospel-preaching, than which we have no earlier testimony to the content of our faith. St Paul does not explicitly give the doctrine on the authority of Christ, but he supposes 'the Gospel' to derive from Christ.

The importance of Adam's kingship to a high Christology may be seen against the contrast afforded by the low Christology of the Books of Jubilees and of the Twelve Testaments. These writings accept as axiomatic the everlasting privileges assured to the two houses of Aaron and of David, the two anointed heads of Israel, the priestly and the royal. The privileges of Aaron find their full expression within the Torah, in Leviticus and Numbers. Those of David belong to the Prophets, but they can be traced back to their root in the promises made to Judah by his father Jacob. 'The sceptre shall not depart from Judah nor the ruler's staff from between his feet' (Gen. XLIX, 10). Judah is the king among the Twelve Patriarchs. But equally Levi is the priest (Deut. XXXIII 8–11). When we see Levi and Judah side by side in Genesis, we have uncovered roots of priesthood and royalty in the Torah, and indeed in the first of its five books. But which of the two patriarchs is the greater? The Law tells overwhelmingly in favour of Levi. For Moses found occasion to legislate fully concerning the priesthood, and himself instituted it; he clothed Aaron with every circumstance of hieratic glory. Whereas the Mosaic law of kingship (Deut. XVII, 14–20) is no more than permissive: the Israelites may have a king if they will, but he must be kept humble, and subjected to the Law of which the priesthood is the guardian. The authors of Jubilees and the Twelve Testaments had strong reasons in their own working faith for setting Levi above Judah, but we must concede that 'Moses' bears them out.

There is nothing accidental about the balance between Priesthood and Kingdom in the Torah. For the Torah took its final shape in a period during which the Davidic kingdom was in abeyance, and the national existence was bound up with the High Priestly office; and it was in this period that the whole of the

Biblical material about the institution of Aaron was composed. When Israel regained independence under the Maccabees, the attitude represented by the Torah was so established that the question of the restoration of Davidic monarchy was scarcely even raised. The High Priest ruled as an independent prince; lip-service was paid to the Davidic prophecies by the doctrine that when God had fully established the kingdom and the glory through the instrumentality of the Aaronic priesthood, he would bring forward the promised Son of David to take over purely secular functions. Such is the doctrine held by the Book of Jubilees and the Twelve Testaments. It is the doctrine of men either satisfied with the existing High Priestly regime, or looking for no more than a reformation of it. Hyrcanus or Jannaeus might be a disappointment; but one might hope better things of their successors.

The corruption and fall of the Maccabean house turned interest in the direction of the Davidic Promises. The high priesthood, it now appeared, could not be left to look after itself. It was not only corrupt, it was subservient to an ungodly kingdom, which instituted and removed high priests at will, and for causes which had nothing to do with the honour either of God or of the priesthood. The essential thing was to have a godly kingdom; then everything, including the priesthood, might be reformed. And no kingdom could be effective except a world empire. It was not a question of changing the form of a puppet government; so long as the kingdom of the world was in heathen hands, there was no security for the good cause. The kingdom of the world must become the kingdom of God and of his Anointed.

The pious Israelite would now scan the Torah with altered eyes. What foundation could be found in it for a sufficient doctrine of the kingdom? There stood the figures of Levi and Judah, in themselves no more glorious the one than the other. If one traced their lines downwards within the limits of the Torah, one came to Aaron the Levite and Amminadab the Judaite; and what was Amminadab to set against Aaron? To reverse the balance, one must go on as far as David; but then one was far outside the limits of the Mosaic books. But suppose one traced the line upwards instead of downwards; suppose one went back from Levi and Judah through Abraham, Noah and Enoch to Adam himself. Adam was given a kingdom but no priesthood; it was said to him at his creation, 'Subdue the earth and have dominion'. The divine promise of dominion is connected with creation itself, the foundation on which both the Torah and the World are built. When in the sequel promises of kingdom are made to Judah and of priesthood to Levi, it is plain that Judah inherits the glory of Adam, and Levi does not. When the Son of David comes into his kingdom, he will reign not simply as the Son of David, but as the Son of Adam or of Man, and in all the glory which Adam forfeited by his fall.

The position which we have just outlined is the position of the Enochian Similitudes, a stratum of the great Book of Enoch which dates probably from the middle years of the first century B.C. The author combines in one figure the Son of Man and the Davidic King. There is no sort of doubt possible about the Davidic character of this figure, and it is astonishing that writers of repute have been able to treat it as an open question. For the whole basis of the Enochian Similitudes is scriptural; and the author's use of Davidic prophecies is most marked. He is especially fond of Isaiah XI, 1–9 (the shoot out of the stock of Jesse on whom rests sevenfold the Spirit of the Lord) and of certain Davidic Psalms, for example, II and LXXII. At the same time the Adamic character of the promised king is no less marked. Enoch himself who sees the visions is the seventh, and perfect, descendant of Adam, the son who recovers the original righteousness and the original immortality of our first father; it is revealed to him that he is himself the Son of Man who will return in the last days to establish the kingdom of David, of Adam, and of God.

The Enochian position is a solid position, a position in which to rest, for it takes up what are, after all, the most developed Messianic prophecies, those connected with the house of David; and it grounds them firmly on the very foundation of the whole Torah. Without this foundation, the Davidic Messiah is a mere accident, external to the substance of the Jewish faith: no more than the name of a person who will *de facto* preside over the restored people of Israel. His standing as himself the heart and substance of the Kingdom cannot be justified in Judaic terms, unless he is a second Adam.

It is the Similitudes of Enoch which present us first with an unambiguous fusion of the Davidic and Adamic promises. But for the Adamic part, for the figure and title of the Son of Man, the Enochian writer found an earlier model in the prophecy of Daniel. If the Similitudes belong to the time of Maccabean decline, Daniel belongs to the moment of prostration before the success of the Maccabean uprising. The Aaronic priesthood had failed, the Maccabeans had not yet renewed it; the scene was dominated by a tyrannous royal power which nothing, it would seem, could displace, unless God should restore the divine kingdom which fell in Adam, a world empire of the man in the image of God. This empire is seen by the seer as an empire of Israel; the Babylonians, Medes, Persians, Greeks, have in turn held the kingdom, and now the Israelites are for ever to hold it. He does not go so far as to consider the person of the prince in whom the imperial power will be summed up. Needless to say, he does not suppose that the power will be republican. King and kingdom alternate easily in his mind; the kingdom of the Babylonians is the kingdom of Nebuchadnezzar, the kingdom of the saints will doubtless be the kingdom of the Lord's Anointed, and almost without consciousness of a change in the sense, 'Daniel' might have transferred to the prince everything that he said of the saints. If we ask why he did not, the proper answer will be that he preferred to speak of real and visible persons. Nebuchadnezzar and Antiochus were historical characters, and so were 'the Saints of the Most High', the faithful Israelites then struggling against tyranny. What he was inspired to say was that these people, now abased, would be presently enthroned; that they could not be enthroned except in the person of a prince was true, doubtless, but it was not the point.

When Daniel was composed, the greater part of the Old Testament, and especially the Pentateuch, was already almost as authoritative as it was ever destined to become. No new prophecy could be accepted beside what was written. This did not mean that no one any longer prayed for, or received, clear inspiration, but that the means of seeking it had altered. Earlier prophets had divined from portents and voices. Divinations were still made, but they were now made from the holy letters of the ancient scriptures. The Old Testament originals of Daniel's visions, oracles and edifying tales are seldom difficult to detect. That is not to say that he ever transcribes; the old material takes new shapes, and enters into new combinations, in his inspired imagination.

Daniel himself, the hero of the book, is presented to us as a new Joseph. What Joseph was at the court of Pharaoh, Daniel becomes at the court of Nebuchadnezzar. He too is a captive who keeps himself pure from heathen defilements, and is rewarded by promotion to be first minister of the Crown. And this he achieves through his skill to divine the King's dream. Daniel outdoes Joseph, for there is revealed to him not only the interpretation of the dream, but the dream itself, the royal dreamer having forgotten it.

The matter of the dream is a meditation upon the Biblical law against idolatry. 'Gods of silver or gods of gold thou shalt not make unto thee. An altar of earth shalt thou make unto me. . . . Or if thou make me an altar of stone, thou shalt not make it of hewn stones, for if thou lift up thy tool upon it, thou hast polluted it' (Exod. xx, 23–25). Gods of silver and gold are rejected because they are made with hands; natural stones, stones not cut out with hands, better express the place of God's presence. For they are parts of living nature. In Nebuchadnezzar's vision the idol of gold, silver, bronze and iron is smitten and destroyed by a stone not cut out with hands: a living stone which shows itself to be such by growing to a great mountain and filling the earth. There are several texts in Isaiah which prepare the way for this conception of the growing stone.[1] The idol represents heathen empire, the stone the empire of God's Israel. The one must at length fall before the other, as the idol of Dagon fell before the holy stones in the Ark. But the seer desires to particularize the history of the heathen

[1] Isaiah xxviii, 16 and ii, 2.

empires, and this he does by placing in the image the Four Metals, a list which is a Biblical no less than a gentile commonplace.[1] The succession of one empire to another, of Media to Babylon, Persia to Media and Greece to Persia, permits a lower and lower element to dominate. The weakness of all the empires is in their base on which they stand, a mixture of peoples. This becomes most evident in the Greek empire: the iron ruthlessness of Greek military power cannot bring about a union between itself and the 'miry clay' of disintegrating Asiatic nationality; the feet of the great image split into ten toes, many kingdoms and factions, and even they are composite and weak. So heathen power becomes vulnerable and collapses, struck on the feet by the living stone.

Undeterred by the moral of the vision, Nebuchadnezzar proceeds to epitomize his idolatrous empire in a mighty image of gold, which he compels all men to worship under pain of death. The Saints, represented by the 'Three Holy Children', are as resolute as they are powerless before him. The ultimate vindication and enthronement of the Saints over the whole world is prefigured in the miraculous deliverance of the three children from the furnace, in the king's recognition of their God, and in his promotion of them over the affairs of Babylon. The material of this episode is directly drawn from the preceding vision of the great image, helped out by the scriptural commonplace, that as gold is tried in the furnace, so are acceptable men in the fire of adversity. They, and not the golden image, are seen to be that genuine metal which is prized by the wise.

In the next episode Nebuchadnezzar dreams again, and sees empire this time as a great tree. The image is drawn direct from Ezekiel XXXI, helped out by Ezekiel XVII, 24 and, it may be, by Isaiah VI, 13. Nebuchadnezzar the great tree is cut down, but sprouts again when he comes to understand that his kingdom is the kingdom of God entrusted to him (Jer. XXVII, 5–8). And this prefigures the destruction of self-deifying heathendom, and the renewal of empire in a stock which administers its dominion as the dominion of God. The figure of the great tree cut

---

[1] I Chron. XXII, 16, XXIX, 2, 7; II Chron. II, 7.

down is overlaid with another, the figure of the king brutified. When Israel revolted from the kingdom of God and from Moses his servant, they set up their own devices. 'They made a calf in Horeb, and worshipped a molten image. Thus they changed their Glory for the likeness of an ox that eateth grass' (Ps. CVI, 19–20). Nebuchadnezzar denies the kingdom of God, and asserts his own; but he has no sooner made himself the God of the world than he is seen to have changed his glory for the fashion of an ox that feeds on grass. For this is the inwardness of all idolatry: it deifies the beast. So it befalls to Nebuchadnezzar, who deifies himself. The light of humanity, the divine similitude, shines in those eyes alone which look up to heaven, and acknowledge the dominion which is an everlasting dominion, and the kingdom enduring from generation to generation.

Nebuchadnezzar, after seven years' punishment, is allowed space of repentance. Belshazzar his son, not heeding so evident a warning, brings forth the vessels his father had taken from the Temple at Jerusalem (II Kings XXIV, 13, Jer. XXVII, 18, Dan. I, 2), and profanes them in an idolatrous banquet. He is answered by the portent of the writing on the wall (Is. VIII, 1–4), which allows no time for repentance, but is immediately fulfilled in the fall of Babylon. We observe that Belshazzar's sin is the exact complement of his father's: Nebuchadnezzar exalts the symbol of idolatry, the golden image; Belshazzar abases the only symbols of the true cult which are in his possession, the temple vessels, by feasting with them in honour of the gods of gold, silver, brass and iron, of wood and stone.

The narrative theme of Daniel is now almost completed. We have seen royal arrogance humiliated and repentant; and we have seen it unrepentant and overthrown. Only one thing remains to be told. Daniel must be consecrated as the Three Children have already been. He must dedicate his life a sacrifice to the honour of God's Name, and must be miraculously delivered. The story of the den of lions fulfils this function. Just as the story of the Three Children developed the commonplace about acceptable men proved in the furnace of adversity, so the story of the den develops

'My life is among lions'. All the essential features of the story find their text in Psalm LVII; the Psalm even includes a link between the trial of Daniel and that of the Three Children. 'My life is among lions, I lie among them that are set on fire.'

Being now made perfect, Daniel is ready for his great visions. He has formerly interpreted the dreams of kings, but now he dreams on his own account. Everything that he has hitherto learned is drawn together and more perfectly set forth by his own first dream, the dream recorded in ch. VII. This dream is the symbolical centre of the book. In it the theological meaning of the succession of empire is most deeply expressed. The visions and oracles which follow it make the details of the predicted history more precise, and give exact assurances to the afflicted saints. But it is the seventh chapter which sets forth 'the mystery of the kingdom of God'.

The part played by the Four Metals in Nebuchadnezzar's first dream is taken by the Four Winds in Daniel's. The four winds break loose on the great sea, and under their life-giving breath arise four monsters. Babylon had arisen and possessed the South, Media had seized the North. Persia had arisen from the East and swallowed both, Greece had advanced and overthrown her from the West. All the quarters have yielded their monsters; that is the end. The invasions from the great deep are finished; the next empire will be an invasion from the sky. In the same way, when all the four metals had had their day, it was the turn of the living stone.

The beasts from the four winds are the empires through which God has afflicted Israel from the day of exile onwards, as he had said by his prophet: 'According to their pasture, so were they filled and their heart was exalted, and they have forgotten me. Therefore am I unto them as a lion; as a leopard will I watch by the way; I will meet them as a bear that is robbed of her whelps and I will rend the caul of their heart. There will I devour them as a lion; the wild beast shall tear them. Thy destruction, O Israel, who shall help? Where now is thy king, that he may save thee in all thy cities? And thy judges, of whom thou saidst, Give me a king and princes? I have given them a king in my anger, and taken him away in my wrath' (Hos. XIII, 6–11).

The chapter of Hosea from which we have just transcribed was in Daniel's mind. He had used the directly preceding part of it in his first dream of Nebuchadnezzar. The Image of Four Metals expressed the fate of idolatry in these words: 'Thus was the iron, the clay, the brass, the silver, and the gold broken in pieces together, and became like chaff of the summer threshing floors; and the wind carried them away, and no place was found for them.' Compare the oracle against idolatry in Hosea XIII, 2–3. 'They have made them molten images of their silver, even idols according to their own understanding, all of them the work of the craftsmen. They say of them, Let the men that sacrifice kiss the calves. Therefore shall they be as the morning cloud and as the dew that passeth early away, as the chaff that is driven with the whirlwind out of the threshing-floor, and as the smoke out of the chimney.'

To return to the Hosea text which immediately occupies us. The second half of it shows that it is concerned with the succession of kingdoms. 'I have given thee a king in my anger, and removed him in my wrath.' The first half deals with the same matter, indeed, but under the familiar metaphor of shepherding. The Lord no longer rules his flock through, or as, a shepherd, that is to say, in human guise, but abandons it to the tender mercies of bestial forces: the lion, the leopard, the bear, and the wild beast. Daniel applies the list to the four idolatrous tyrannies which have ruled Israel since he lost his own king. The order has to be altered, and the Bear put second, so that it can stand for Media, the empire of the North: for the Bear is the Northern constellation *par excellence*. So we have the Lion for Babylon, the Bear for Media, the Leopard for Persia, and the Wild Beast for Greece. The general description 'Wild Beast' enables the seer to let his fancy fly, and depict a monster of no admitted species. The second beast, commanded to eat much flesh, carries three ribs between his teeth: three not four, because Media was never sole mistress of the world, she never seized the four quarters. The third beast, by contrast, has four wings and four heads, and (absolute) dominion is given to it. The fourth beast has *iron* teeth, as corresponding to the iron dominion which was fourth in Nebuchadnezzar's dream; the iron dominion constituted the feet of the great image, and this wild beast 'tramples the residue with his feet'. Feet divide into ten toes, and the monster has ten horns, interpreted in the sequel as the rival kingdoms into which the Greek empire divides.

The description of the first beast links not with Nebuchadnezzar's first dream, but with his second dream and with its fulfilment. Nebuchadnezzar is seen as a beast plucked of its eagle-wings (in his bestial state, the king's hair had grown like eagle's feathers; now it is cut again). He is raised to stand upright like a man, and a man's heart is put into him. This is to recall to our minds the truth that bestiality characterizes world empire only in so far as it is self-deifying and idolatrous. When Nebuchadnezzar learnt that *the heavens do rule*, he became a man and no beast, and the end of the vision in Daniel VII is going to show this very thing. The three beasts which follow the first are unmitigated in their bestiality, and especially the fourth; they show no recognition, that is, of the kingdom of heaven; and so their dominion is taken away, and replaced by that of the king from the sky. The Son of Man is from heaven, the beasts are from the abyss.

It is interesting also to note that the first Beast is treated not as a corporate representation of Babylonian empire, but as Nebuchadnezzar in person, in correspondence with Daniel's interpretation of the first vision: 'Thou, O King, art this head of gold.' The other beasts will naturally therefore be personally interpreted, and the fourth in particular appears as one kingship (Alexander's) which becomes ten *kings* (VII, 24); among them in due course the new horn arises and he is King Antiochus. And so an interpreter who goes on to interpret the beast's opposite, the Son of Man, as likewise a king, is scarcely open to blame; and to talk of the Enochian author, or indeed of the Christian evangelists, as simply 'misunderstanding' Daniel by such an interpretation, is absurd. They were not like stupid children taking the figure of John Bull for the figure of King George VI, as sometimes appears to be suggested.

King Nebuchadnezzar is brought to ultimate 'humanity', that is, to the recognition that the heavens do rule, by an intervention from heaven, the descent of 'a watcher and a holy one'. But empire is not effectively or permanently humanized by these means; his successors relapse, and the human image is not permanently enthroned or fixed in lasting dominion until it is sent down from heaven. The writer no more means that Israelite rule will fly down from the sky, than he means that Nebuchadnezzar or Alexander crawled up out of the sea. He does mean that it will be of direct divine institution, whereas Nebuchadnezzar's kingdom was established by divine permission, and mitigated by divine discipline.

The older Israelite tradition had scarcely distinguished between the direct effects of God's will, and what that will permits. The distinction is, indeed, full of theological dangers, however convenient it may be; and there is great virtue in the robuster faith which ignores it, as Hosea does when he makes the Lord himself fall upon Israel as a lion, a leopard, or a bear. But the mind of Daniel's age did make the distinction: there is something indirect about God's action by way of penal judgement. God is not in the lion, leopard or bear as he is in the true shepherd of the flock.

The mysterious relation between what God directly wills and what he permits and uses runs right back into the story of creation itself. There was, somehow, in the beginning something for God to overrule, the chaotic deep of sea. The creatures of God arose out of it by the evocation of his voice or the influx of his breath. 'The earth was in chaos and confusion, and darkness was on the face of the deep; and the breath of God fluttered on the face of the waters and God said, Let there be light.' So again when God proceeded to the creation of life; he evoked it first from what remained of the chaos of waters, the now tamed and confined tract of sea. In this way God formed the great sea-monsters, the age-old symbols of chaos itself. They were the children of the deep, and yet they played their part in the design of Providence. Not, however, a dominant part. For, after God had caused the earth likewise to bring forth its progeny, he proceeded to a different work. A new creative intention laid its command on neither sea nor land, but on God's own making power: it is not 'Let the waters bring forth' nor 'Let the earth bring forth', it is 'Let us make', and not only this, but 'Let us make in our own image, after our likeness'. Man is the offspring not of earth or of sea, but of heaven, and the dominion on earth is therefore his. 'Let them have dominion over the fish of the sea, and over the fowl of the air, and over the cattle, and over all the earth.'

Here Daniel finds the manifest model for his vision. The Semitic mind had always seen the creation of the world from chaos as a prototype of the continual overruling of death and disorder by powers of nature and life, and Israel had applied the pattern to sacred history. The Exodus from Egypt in particular became a new overthrow of chaos and the sea-monsters, a new creation of the world. The author of the later chapters of Isaiah saw the coming deliverance from exile and oppression as a second and greater Egyptian exodus, and therewith as a new creation (Isaiah LI, 9–11, 15–16, LXV, 17). Daniel follows Isaiah in thus throwing the new creation into the future. There is nothing startlingly novel about the general sense of Daniel's vision. The novelty is in the detail. For 'Daniel' had what 'Isaiah' had not; he had the 'priestly' account of creation in front of his eyes. He read it where we read it, in the opening scene of the Books of Moses. So he was able to apply the detail of that scene to the shape of the new creation. He was able to see the enthroning of Israel over the heathen as an establishment of the dominion of Adam over the beasts and over all the earth.

As when God first created, so in Daniel's vision the breath of God breaks forth upon the great deep, and does so in fourfold fullness. The four winds of heaven blow and the four monsters come up. Their detailed character is studied, as we have seen, from Hosea, from the previous episodes of Daniel's own book, and from what he took to be the facts of world history. When we come to the Son of Man, their supplanter, the text of Genesis comes back into force. He is in human not in bestial form, from heaven, not from the deep, and his wearing of the image and likeness of God is emphasized by his juxtaposition with the man-like figure of the Ancient of Days.

The solemn decree for man's creation and enthronement is given a new aspect in Daniel. What the seer is reading into Genesis is precisely this, that the creation and enthronement of Adam is by implication the subjection of the beasts, the removal of their dominion. Since the Creation story allows the beasts only one day before Adam is set over them, there is no need for Genesis to make much of the termination of their empire. But the beasts of Daniel's vision reign for 'seventy weeks of years' and the termination of their empire is a weighty matter. The divine decree is first of all their condemnation; the scene of its promulgation becomes the judgement upon the kings and the mighty, as Daniel might read it in Isaiah XXIV, 21–23, with the help of Isaiah XXVI, 16–XXVII, I.

Nevertheless the decree of Genesis I, 26 is not wholly effaced in the judgement scene of Daniel VII. It is to be observed that as Adam makes his appearance after the decree and in consequence of it, so does the Son of Man in Daniel, a point which does more justice to the Genesis pattern than to the facts Daniel is expressing by means of it. Adam did not exist until the dominion of the beasts was removed, but the Saints of the Most High were already there as the victims of the beasts, before they were glorified as their masters. When Daniel comes to the interpretation of his vision, he unobtrusively corrects the misleading feature of the picture. The kingdom is given to the suffering saints of the Most High. If we do not wish to admit that Daniel makes a correction, we may say that he interprets the Son of Man not of the saints as such, but of the saints as glorified. They become the Son of Man in being enthroned; or, Son of Man in the name of the dignity they put on. It is the dignity alone that comes down from heaven. It does not matter whether we say that Daniel corrects his vision, or subtilizes his interpretation. Whichever he does he is squaring a difficulty which arises out of his faithfulness to Genesis, in his placing of the heavenly decree before the advent of Adam.

It may be observed that the interpretation of the Son of Man's kingdom as the kingdom of the Saints has its prototype and justification in the heavenly decree of Genesis. The decree makes man in the singular, and then pluralizes his kingship. 'Let us make *Man*

in our image ... and let *them* have dominion ... ' The Son of Man
is likewise revealed as one, but the Saints are presently manifested
as the new mankind who exercise the dominion inherent in the
possession of God's likeness.

Another point in which Daniel appears to be somewhat artificially conforming to Genesis is the preservation of the lives of
the first three beasts 'for a season and a time'. The last and worst
beast is slain and burnt, to do justice to such prophecies as Isaiah
XXVII, 1 and XXX, 33. The rest survive. Why? It is easy to say that
the Gentile world is not to be annihilated but subjected to the
Israelite empire. No doubt. But the Grecian race is surely not to be
annihilated either. It is the dominion which is annihilated, together
with its head. The dominions of the first three beasts are not in any
case to survive, and their dynasties were extinguished long ago.
So what is preserved in their preservation? There is a confusion in
Daniel's symbolism here, with which we must do the best we can.
But we need not feel any difficulty about the origin of that confusion. The Genesis picture absolutely requires the survival of
beasts, that Man may have dominion 'over the fishes of the sea,
the fowls of the air, and the cattle'.

The text of Genesis explains a further puzzle in Daniel's vision.
Why is it that the monsters, being the progeny of the deep, are
not described as sea-monsters? There is plenty of authority in
Scripture for the figure of Leviathan. Why then does Daniel prefer
to take up the Hosea text with its beasts of the land? And why, in
addition, does he wing them like fowls? The four wings of the
third beast needlessly duplicate its four heads and mean the same
thing; the wings of the first beast are forced to do duty as a
symbol for the excessive growth of Nebuchadnezzar's hair in his
bestial state. Would the king's locks ever have been compared
to eagle's feathers, were it not in anticipation of the winged
representation of the beasts in VII? And would the point have
seemed worth taking up in VII, unless the seer had been determined to talk about wings by hook or by crook? Everything
is plain, when we see that Daniel was aiming at a synthetic effect.
The beasts are to sum up in themselves the characters of the fishes,

birds and beasts over whom Adam reigns. They are the progeny of the deep, like the fishes of Genesis 1, 20–22, they are beasts in form, and they are winged like fowls.

Another feature of the decree in Genesis 1 to which Daniel may be at least said to do justice is the plural 'Let *us* make'. Daniel actually begins from the plural. 'I beheld till *thrones* were set, and an Ancient of Days did sit. . . . Thousand thousands ministered unto him, and ten thousand times ten thousand stood before him. The court was set and the books were opened.' The picture presented is that of a decree of the court of heaven; compare the 'decree of the watchers' in IV, 17 which sentenced Nebuchadnezzar.

The real significance of the Son of Man emblem is seen in its relation to the kingdom of God. Because the Son of Man is in the image of God he reigns in God's name; his kingdom and the kingdom of God are one. In the days of Nebuchadnezzar it is right to say of the Most High alone, that his dominion is an everlasting dominion, and his kingdom from generation to generation and that he also rules in the kingdom of men, and gives it to whomsoever he will, according to the time; as he has given it for the while to Nebuchadnezzar. But the kingdom given to the Son of Man is the kingdom of God itself, for it is said of him, 'His kingdom is an everlasting dominion which shall not pass away, and his kingdom that which shall not be destroyed'. It is, indeed, immaterial whether it is called the Kingdom of the Son of Man, or the Kingdom of the Most High. In the interpretation, Daniel changes the ascription without seeming to observe it: 'And the kingdom and the dominion and the greatness shall be given to the people of the saints of the Most High: *his* kingdom is an everlasting kingdom, and all dominions shall serve him.'

The mere title or description 'Like a Son of Man' is not of itself either mysterious or interesting. 'Son of Man' means 'Man' with a slight emphasis on his specifically human character. It differs from 'man' much as 'human being' differs from 'man' in our own vocabulary. The term is implicitly comparative, and ennobles or degrades the person to whom it is applied, in accordance with the standard of comparison which is presupposed. 'Human being' is a title of dignity when the comparison is with unreasoning beasts, but a badge of humility when the comparison is with pure incorporeal spirits; and the same is true of 'Son of Man'. In Daniel VII the comparison is with the beasts, so that the description is one of dignity. It is an extra point which may just make itself felt, that the Hebrew for Son of Man is ben-Adam, so that the term is doubly appropriate: the Son of Man is both he who is the natural superior of the beasts and he who holds the title from his father Adam. And this may be felt by the writer, even though he is composing chapter VII not in Hebrew but in Aramaic. In the sequel he rings the changes on the phrase: VIII, 15, X, 18, 'As the appearance of a man', X, 16, 'As the similitude of the sons of men'. There is no reason to doubt that VII, 13 would run 'like a son of man' if it had been written in Hebrew.

When the phrase is revived in the Enochian Similitudes or in the Gospels, it draws its force from the Daniel context to which it points, not from any sense inherent in the syllables themselves. In Enoch the whole Danielic picture is redrawn; in the Gospels it is implied by the very strangeness of the term. A man who writes anything so barbarous as *ho hyios tu anthropu* in a Greek book is evidently speaking in inverted commas. But to say that the reference is Danielic is not to say that the later writer's vision terminates against Daniel's page as against a brick wall, or that he is unable to see back through Daniel into Genesis. As we shall see, St Mark works from Genesis primarily in his use of the phrase. The reference to Genesis would be kept in mind by the words of the eighth Psalm, quoted by St Paul and the author to the Hebrews to illustrate a doctrine of Christ as the New Adam.

> When I consider the heavens, the work of thy fingers,
>   The moon and the stars which thou hast ordained,
> What is man that thou art mindful of him
>   Or the son of man that thou visitest him?
> For thou hast made him but little lower than God
>   And crownest him with glory and honour.

> Thou madest him to have dominion over the works of thy
> hands,
> Thou hast put all things under his feet
> All sheep and oxen
> Yea, and the beasts of the wild
> The fowls of the air and the fish of the sea
> And whatsoever walketh through the paths of the seas.

The Psalm builds on just those features of Genesis 1 which
interest Daniel, and throws in the phrase 'Son of Man' on the way.
It is likely enough that Daniel had the Psalm in mind; whether he
had or no, there it stood in the synagogue hymn-book to keep the
clue to Daniel's riddle before the eyes of every pious Israelite.

To conclude: the meaning of the phrase son of man (without
inverted commas) is not in dispute. Place it in inverted commas,
and it means the bearer of an Adamic dominion yet to come, and
to be made effective over all the world. Who the bearer of the
dominion will be, is another question, and a question not settled
by the phrase as such. According to Daniel, it will be the people
of the Saints of the Most High. 'Enoch' and Mark say that it will
be, or is, the Son of David. They are simply pointing to the prince
in whom the kingdom of the Saints will be actualized, rather than
to the Saints who, through his kingdom, will enjoy the glory of
being an imperial people.

The detail with which we have examined Daniel's vision may
seem irrelevant to our purpose. And yet such an examination is a
salutary exercise. To understand Daniel is not to summarize his
ideas but to think his thoughts. His thought was essentially a
divination from virtually cannonized scriptures, and his elaborate
dovetailing of one text with another is perfectly characteristic of his
age. When he wrote, all the best intellects of a subtle people had
been concentrated for a couple of centuries on mastering the whole
body of traditional scriptures and making one text the comment on
another. It is not surprising if they were better at this sort of thing
than we are, nor if they made immediate associations where we lum-
ber after them by the aid of concordances and reference margins.

CHAPTER XII

SON OF MAN IN ST MARK

What sort of currency did the phrase Son of Man obtain round about the beginning of our era? It is not possible to say. There is in any case no evidence for any sect or coterie which preferred the title to 'Son of David' or 'Anointed King' as the ordinary designation of the Messiah, and it is unlikely that any such people ever existed. There were plenty of men who set their hopes on the coming of King Messiah, and held a high doctrine of his power and glory; and Enoch may be taken for evidence for this at least, that it was possible to make oneself understood in some quarters, if one grounded Messiah's kingdom in Adam's, and drew upon the language of Daniel vii for the purpose. One might then perhaps summarize one's doctrine in the form: the 'Son of Man' is God's Elect.

According to the Gospels, Christ was hailed by demons and men as Holy One, Son of God, Anointed, Son of David, all of them Messianic descriptions; and he was accused of claiming to be Anointed, Son of God, and King of the Jews or of Israel. No one ever called him Son of Man, but he himself taught a deeper doctrine of his person, and centred it upon this phrase. When he so taught, was he understood? The Gospels do not suggest that Christ's hearers had any difficulty with the mere sense of the phrase, or with allowing its applicability to the Messiah. What they could not understand was the sort of thing Christ said about the Son-of-Man Messiah.

John xii, 23–34 provides the sole instance of the people picking up Christ's phrase from his lips. It is therefore of peculiar interest. 'The hour has come for the Son of Man to be glorified', says Christ. 'And I, if I be lifted up from the earth, will draw all men unto me.' In so saying, says the evangelist, Christ signified the manner of death he was to die. The crowd replied: 'We have heard from the Law' (in the extended sense of *scripture*) 'that the *Anointed* remains' (on his earthly throne) 'for ever; how then

sayest thou, *The Son of Man* must be lifted' (from the earth)?
'Who is this Son of Man?' We observe that the crowd start from
the assumption that the phrase 'Son of Man' is normally applied
to the Anointed. But since it is a dogma that the Anointed, the
Son of Man, is enthroned on earth for ever, they take it that
Christ must be speaking of some other Son of Man than the
Anointed; for (*a*) he applies the phrase to himself, (*b*) he says
that he must be lifted from the earth.

The Law[1] on which the Jews rely will probably consist of
Daniel VII itself, supported by such texts as II Samuel VII, 12–16,
Psalms LXXII, 17; LXXXIX, 36–37; Jeremiah XXXIII, 14–21. The
supporting texts prove the eternal throne of the Anointed,
David's Son; Daniel VII, 14 says expressly that the dominion of
the Son of Man shall never be 'lifted' from Israel (*arthenai*). We
need not consider here what texts could be advanced on the
other side to prove the 'lifting' of the Son of Man. All we need
at present is to see that St John attributes to the Jews an equation
between Son of Man and Messiah, Daniel VII and II Samuel VII.

St John's text may not be good evidence that Jesus preached
himself openly as Son of Man to Jewish crowds, but it may be
evidence that had he done so, they could have understood him
as claiming to be a Messiah eternally enthroned over the earth.
St John is more likely to force the theological point of a Gospel
incident than to presume non-Judaic thinking in the Jews he
introduces. He may, indeed, have made his 'crowd' more learned
than a crowd would be, but the learning he credits them with
will surely be current opinion among learned Jews. Otherwise
his narrative loses any kind of point. It no longer represents the
conflict of the gospel and the Jews, either in historical or in any
other terms.

If, therefore, we are to believe St John, it was possible to talk
to Jews of the first century about the Messiah as Son of Man, and
to be understood. But neither he nor any other New Testament
writer makes it a title in common use. It is a *theologumenon* about

---

[1] These texts are 'Law' because they are an inspired comment on the 'Law'
itself, e.g. on Gen. I, 26–28, Num. XXIV, 17, Deut. XVII, 15.

the Messiah which no one introduces but Christ himself. The Jews in John XII merely answer Jesus in his own phrase. Otherwise the sole exception is Acts VII, 56. St Stephen in the ecstasy of his martyrdom cries out: 'Behold I see the heavens opened, and the Son of Man standing at the right hand of God.' But then, the whole intention of St Luke is to show that in his martyrdom St Stephen becomes a second Christ. He prays for his enemies, he commends his spirit almost in the words of Christ, and he is one with Christ in proclaiming to the Sanhedrin the vision of the Son of Man at the right hand of God (Luke XXII, 69).

In thus restricting 'Son of Man' to Christ's own use, the evangelists are very likely stylizing somewhat. The phrase is so consecrated by the lips of Christ that they will allow it to no one else. Nevertheless, they are stylizing something, and that something is presumably their sincere belief that, in a world which talked easily about the Messiah, Christ taught a particular doctrine, and centred it round this phrase 'Son of Man'. What was his doctrine? Was it simply the doctrine of 'Enoch', that the Son of David is the bearer of the kingdom of Adam? Or was it something new and shocking? We must turn to the evangelists for an answer.

What method shall we employ upon the evangelists? The lexicographical method has often been used, but it has not yielded solid results. The lexicographical method is the correct method to employ, when we are out to establish the meaning of a phrase in current use. What do we do? We compare all the contexts in which the phrase is found, and try to fix a meaning which will give a good sense in all of them. Or if one sense will not do (for many words and phrases are ambiguous) we try to find a group of associated senses, all of which can be naturally derived from a single root-sense. This method is perfectly correct for its own purpose, but that purpose is not ours. We are already provided with the mere sense, the lexicographical sense, of 'Son of Man'. So, according to St John, were the Jews. It means 'the coming bearer of Adamic rule', and it may be understood of an individual (the Messiah). What we want to know is not this lexicographical sense of 'Son of Man', but Christ's doctrine of the Son of Man. And the lexicographical method will not give us that.

If we wanted to understand the Einsteinian doctrine of Relativity, we should not take Einstein's treatise, pick out all the paragraphs in which the word 'Relativity' occurs, and try to fix a meaning for it such as to make sense of them all. We should read his treatise through from the beginning, and see what it had to tell us about Relativity; or if we could not get it, or were not capable of reading it, we should put ourselves into the hands of an expositor or disciple, and read him. We might read several expositors, but we should read them one at a time, not jumble them up; and even if we discovered that one of them had used the work of another (a type of relation not altogether happily described by Biblical critics under the term 'synoptic') we should still think it best to follow the thought of each right through. After that we might proceed to a comparison of our authorities, and so form our own final estimate of the master's thought. But that would come afterwards; we should first have to understand the story that some one or more of the disciples had to tell us.

I hope that my parable will speak for itself, and require no application. We have not got any writing from Christ's own hand; we have the evangelists. We take St Mark to have been used by his successors, and he may (though I do not think so) have used some predecessor's work himself. On either supposition or on both, our first and principal business with him is to see what he has to tell us. And we must, of course, let him tell us in his own way and in his own order. We shall have no right to expect success if we begin at the end or in the middle.

There is one difficulty which had better be cleared out of the way first. It has been suggested that in the Galilean Aramaic dialect (of which, by the way, not much is known) the phrase Bar-Nasha (Son of Man) may have been hopelessly ambiguous, so that those of Christ's sayings which embodied it may have been grossly misunderstood. Sometimes he may have been talking indeed about the Danielic figure, sometimes about Man as such, and sometimes, by a third-person periphrasis, of himself, as the French use *on* in place of 'I', or as one of us may say, 'Under such circumstances, what was a man (a girl) to do?'

The reconstruction of the popular Galilean dialect is a pure effort of disinterested scholarship, and one can only regret that the evidence available does not promise more assured results. But we do not have to wait for a conviction that our learned contemporaries have a sufficient mastery of the spoken Galilean language. We can make do with a more economical supposition, that the apostles were the masters of it. In that case, we may credit them with knowing when Christ was speaking of 'the Son of Man' (in inverted commas) and when he was not. Or are we to be told that this dialect was so rigid as to make it physically impossible for any speaker of it to refer with sufficient clarity to Daniel's phrase? Surely that cannot be meant; for the seventh chapter of Daniel was sometimes (we must allow) read in the Galilean synagogues, translated into the vernacular by the targumist, preached upon by the rabbi, and understood by the intelligent.

As for St Mark, he is writing for an audience which does not know the niceties of Galilean Aramaic, but which has some acquaintance with the Old Testament in Greek. And when he introduces into his text the strange barbarism *ho hyios tu anthropu* it will evoke memories of the Septuagint and of nothing else. 'Evidently', his hearers or readers will say, 'he is quoting the Old Testament', and they will strain their attention to observe why he does so, and to what he is referring. 'He must be hinting at some theological mystery, for otherwise he would content himself with a more ordinary expression.' And when the strange phrase recurs, not once only but many times, it must be supposed that the same point of theology is being elaborated. To use so marked and so foreign an expression with several quite disconnected applications in one short book, would be to write for the purpose of being misunderstood.

We do not need, therefore, to agonize at this point over the possible ambiguities of *Bar-Nasha* in Galilean Aramaic. St Mark is building up a theology of the Son of Man with the Greek Old Testament as his background and our first business is to see what he constructs for us. We may reserve until afterwards the question, whether the teaching he thus builds up can actually have been delivered in Aramaic by Christ, and centred on *Bar-Nasha* or some equivalent phrase.

St Mark introduces the phrase 'Son of Man' in the paragraph of the paralytic, in the second chapter. Christ forgave the man's sins before he healed him, and Pharisaic onlookers protested: 'He blasphemeth; who can forgive sins but God alone?' Christ replied that he might well say, 'Thy sins are forgiven thee' who could say 'Arise, take up thy bed and walk', and proceeded: 'That you may know that the Son of Man has power on earth to forgive sins, arise thou (this to the paralytic), take up thy bed, and go to thy house'.

There are several layers of meaning in Christ's saying. The surface-layer is a simple opposition to the words of the Pharisees. They say that God alone forgives sins. Now there is Talmudic evidence[1] for early Rabbinic sayings about the prerogative powers which God reserves to himself, and has not given to man; or which he lends to individual saints on exceptional occasions, as he lent to Elijah the key of rain and the key of resurrection, and to Elisha the key of the womb. (The commonplace about Elijah and the key of rain appears to be already presupposed in Apoc. XI, 6, where the Moses-and-Elijah figures of the Two Witnesses receive power to lock—*cleisai*, cf. *cleis*, 'key'—the sky that it should not rain; so much for Elijah: and power over water, to turn it to blood; so much for Moses.) Here, therefore, the Pharisees are objecting that the power of forgiving sins is reserved by God to himself, and not given to men; whereas, for example, the power of expiating ritual defilements has been given to Aaron and his descendants. Christ's answer is a direct contradiction. The Son of Man has been given authority on earth to forgive sins; that is, man has it, and not God alone. Anyone who had the least knowledge of the old Biblical speech could understand so

---

[1] Strack-Billerbeck, *Kommentar*, I, 737, cites texts revealing a lively discussion of the topic *c.* A.D. 290.

much, without going any deeper, or recalling any particular text.

But Christ's words do suggest a deeper meaning, or, let us say, a more precise meaning. God has entrusted man with the authority to remit sins, and Christ supports his own exercise of that authority by performing a miracle of healing. But he has other witness beside that of the miracle: he has the witness of scripture. 'The Son of Man hath authority upon earth' puts together the most important phrases of Daniel VII. 'There came as *a Son of Man* . . . and there was given him *authority* and all the nations *of the earth* after their families and all glory serving him; his *authority* is an everlasting *authority* that shall not be taken away, and his kingdom that shall not be destroyed.' Daniel is saying that the human race (in its true royalty, the throne of Israel) is given all authority on earth. But does this get us any further towards establishing the particular point, that such authority includes authority to forgive sins? We need to take into account two other features of Daniel VII. With one we are already familiar: the equation drawn between the authority of God and the authority of the Son of Man, or of the Saints, on this earth. The other is Daniel's own paraphrase of his vision which he makes in recapitulating it. Where the vision says, 'There came as a Son of Man . . . and authority was given to him', the recapitulation says, 'He (God) gave the *judgement* to the Saints of the Most High' (VII, 22). It may be that the true meaning of Daniel's Aramaic is not 'judgement was committed to the Saints', but 'judgement was given in favour of the Saints'. This may very well be, but the Enochian Similitudes, the Septuagint, St Paul and St John in the Apocalypse agree in the other view, and we may safely suppose that St Mark would be on their side. Putting Daniel's several statements together, we get the result: the divine authority over the earth, and especially the divine authority in judgement, is given to the Son of Man. Now if the divine authority of judgement does not consist in the remitting and retaining of sins, in what does it consist? The Pharisees say that God reserves this power; but Daniel says he confers it on the Son of Man.

The first layer of sense, then, is that man has the power to forgive sins, because here is Christ doing it, and confirming his act with a miracle. And the second layer of sense is that in so doing he has the support of Daniel's vision, for Daniel had it revealed to him that the divine authority of judgement upon earth is conferred upon the Son of Man. So far, so good; but the second layer of meaning is one in which it is impossible to rest, and if we have got so far as to open it up, we are almost bound to dig in search of a third layer. For we can scarcely help asking, what the relation is between Christ's authoritative act here and now upon the paralytic, and the authority conferred upon the Son of Man according to Daniel's vision. There are two principal ways in which this relation could be conceived.

1. What Daniel foresaw and what Christ does are identical. The conferring of all authority on the Son of Man means the enabling of Christ to forgive and to heal as he now does. This interpretation is at least straightforward, but it is scarcely credible. Daniel's text places the enthronement of the Son of Man after the total overthrow of heathen dominion, and Jews and Christians agreed in looking for a literal fulfilment of the prediction. When Christ speaks to the paralytic, the Son of Man has not yet been thus glorified.

2. The enthronement of the Son of Man will impose the public recognition of an authority already spiritually actual, the authority to forgive sins; and it is this authority that Christ exercises here and now. This is the alternative we must accept, and we may call it the third layer of meaning. Christ exercises that spiritual power which will be enthroned over the world in the Son of Man.

Even now our search is not at an end; in fact, it is at this point that the critical question arises. Why does Christ in particular claim to exercise the authority which will be one day enthroned in the Son of Man? It may be fair to suppose that the Pharisees who hear Christ speak get as far as asking themselves such a question. But they cannot see how to answer it. If they could, they would have read 'the secret of the kingdom of God' which lies at the heart of Christ's 'parable'. And, according to St Mark, they cannot read it.

Alternative answers to the question might be these:

A. The authority enthroned in the Son of Man is the authority of *man*, as his title implies. Then the true mankind, faithful Israel, already has the authority *de jure*. Christ acts simply as a faithful Israelite. But such a solution is scarcely possible. In the days of Israelite freedom, Israel had exercised many judicial functions, but no one had ever supposed that they belonged to any and every Israelite, but only to lawful princes, judges or elders. The higher the function, the fewer the holders. The supreme power of forgiving sins must above all be limited; by what right, then, does Christ claim it? He is not even a synagogue-elder. It would have been possible for Christ to have taught the novel doctrine of a plenary authority inherent in every true Israelite, but he would have needed to teach it expressly, and this he nowhere does.

B. If God will presently confirm man's authority to forgive sins by investing the representative man with a divine power of judgement, it is plain that such authority is latent in man. It may be exercised, therefore, upon special occasions by specially inspired men. A prophet may anticipate what Messiah will do, and the miracle shows Christ to be a prophet, a new Elijah. This is certainly not what the evangelist understands Christ to mean, but it may very well be what he would expect the Pharisees to take Christ as meaning.

C. Christ exercises upon occasion the power in which the Son of Man will be confirmed by his enthronement, because Christ is the Son of Man, though not yet enthroned or 'glorified'. This is what we may safely suppose the evangelist to understand by Christ's words. It constitutes the *fourth* layer of his meaning. It is the straightest of the senses the words allow, and for that reason the true sense. The true sense of a 'parable' should always be the straightest sense, for otherwise the speaker speaks to mislead. It is the mental blindness of the Pharisees which hides from them the truth; it is not given to them to know the secret of the kingdom of heaven.

St Matthew's treatment of the story of the paralytic is in part a useful commentary on St Mark, and in part a development of his own special views and concerns. After repeating the Marcan narrative without substantial alteration, St Matthew thus concludes it (IX, 8): The multitudes that beheld feared, and glorified the God who had given such *authority to men*. 'Men' has the definite article and therefore means not 'some men' but 'mankind'. Such is the comment of the crowd upon the words which St Matthew has recorded just before. 'The Son of Man has authority upon earth to forgive sins.' The gift of authority to the Son of Man is understood as a gift of authority to mankind. Well, certainly, for this is the basic idea in Daniel's vision and in St Mark's text, and it is all that the bystanders need to grasp of Christ's meaning. The question remains, through what organ or organs 'mankind' exercises such a power.

So far we may see St Matthew as the mere exponent of St Mark. But we may also observe that he has a particular interest in the extension of the power to forgive sins. He tells us that Christ entrusted the keys to St Peter, promising that what he bound or loosed on earth should be bound or loosed in heaven (XVI, 19), and that he afterwards showed how the whole body of the saints of the Most High in any place should share the power: any Christian may judge his brother as a court of first instance; if the judgement is challenged witnesses are called; if there is still disagreement, it goes to 'the congregation', in which, we are to presume, there sits a presiding elder, or bishop, who is the Peter in that place. The judgement of the Church is the judgement of heaven (XVIII, 15–20). We may infer from these texts how Matthew read Daniel. The Son of Man is related to the Saints of the Most High as the source of their authority. He is given 'authority', they are given 'judgement'; that is to say, he extends to them his own authority to judge. 'All *authority* is given to me in heaven and earth', is his last word; 'go *ye* therefore' (Matt. XXVIII, 18). Such will have been St Matthew's exposition of Daniel, and it would be surprising if St Mark should have thought differently; but he does not in fact pursue the point of the extension of the power to bind and loose, as St Matthew does.

The doctrine of the Son of Man has two bases, Daniel VII and Genesis I. The Marcan text about the forgiving of sins bears more directly on Daniel than upon Genesis, but its pair in the same chapter, the text about the Sabbath, reverses the stress. 'Sabbath arose for man's sake, not man for Sabbath's; therefore the Son of Man is lord also of Sabbath.' Man and Sabbath arose, or came to be, on the sixth and seventh days of Creation-week. It would be possible, by a sort of crazy logic, to argue that as all the works of the previous days were made for man, and he set over them, so all the works of all six days, including man, were made for Sabbath, for Sabbath comes last. But scripture will not allow this argument to stand. Sabbath is not one of the creation-works, but a resting of God from his works. He had finished and reviewed all the works he had made before Sabbath began. And he had explicitly given man dominion over all things on earth. Man is not for Sabbath. Whereas Sabbath is for man, for it is written, 'That thy servant may rest as well as thou' (Deut. v, 14). Lordship over Sabbath, then, belongs ideally, to mankind; but the free exercise of such lordship, like the exercise of authority to forgive sins, may be in abeyance. It may seem that Moses has put Israel under the Sabbath, without right of appeal. Nevertheless, the enthronement of the Son of Man must revive or actualize man's authority over Sabbath. If the Sabbath arose for man, not man for Sabbath, then the Son of Man is lord of Sabbath also.

It is plain that the mystery of the relation between Christ's authority and the Son of Man's authority is the same in the matter of Sabbath as it is in the matter of forgiving sins, and there is no need to explore the several layers of meaning in the second riddle, for we have done so sufficiently in connexion with the first. But we may observe that the Sabbath-text carries an important additional clue, for those who have eyes. The clue lies in the context. Christ is defending the action of his disciples in plucking corn on Sabbath, and he gives two authorities. The second is the argument from the creation, which we have been examining; the first is the precedent of David. Did not David make free to himself and his companions the shewbread, in spite of the law of the sanctuary? (May not Christ, then, in spite of the law of the Sabbath, make the standing corn free to his disciples?) It is perfectly characteristic of St Mark to put the two sayings down side by side and leave it to the reader to divine the relation between them. For according to him Christ sets forth the mystery of the kingdom of heaven 'in parables', leaving much to the discernment of his hearers. The learned Pharisee could scarcely fail to see that Christ was making the two points:

(a) If David could free the shewbread in spite of the law of the sanctuary, Jesus can free the standing corn, in spite of the law of Sabbath.

(b) The Son of Man being lord of Sabbath, Jesus can dispense from Sabbath-rule.

But the Pharisees might suppose that the points have no relation to one another; that Jesus claims (a) to follow the moral principle of David's action, (b) to assert a human right which the enthronement of the Son of Man will establish beyond question. But the true sense is obtained by taking the two points together. (a) Jesus shows himself to be a true Son of David, in doing the deeds of his father. (b) *The* Son of David is he who, enthroned as Son of Man, will exercise Adam's dominion over Sabbath; and though not yet enthroned, he exercises it already upon occasion. David was not, for that matter, himself enthroned when he took the shewbread; his position was as equivocal in the eyes of the world as Christ's own. He had been secretly anointed by Samuel, as Jesus had been mysteriously anointed from on high on the occasion of his baptism by John. He had not been made king by the people. Yet because of his natural royalty he suffered, like Jesus, under persecution and mistrust.

We have now looked at the pair of texts in Mark II which introduce the name of the Son of Man. The name does not recur until VIII, and its reappearance there opens a fresh development of the theme. It may be well, then, to take stock of what we have learnt so far. Jesus is the Anointed Son of David, in whose enthronement the Son of Man is enthroned; that is to say, in whose dominion the dominion of Adam is established. The enthronement has not visibly taken place yet, but Christ already exercises certain spiritual powers of the Son of Man. He does not proclaim these truths unmistakably, but in riddles or parables; and he is not, in fact, fully understood.

If we ask what Christ's doctrine is, we may say that it is the Enochian doctrine, with one highly significant addition: viz. that the Son of Man is already present half hidden in Israel before his enthronement, and already performing acts belonging to his dignity.

The Son-of-Man texts in II are the kernel of the mysterious doctrine in the first part of the Gospel, but they are far from being the whole of it, and it is worth just recalling, before we proceed, some of the other matter which is, as it were, focused in them. The miracle of the paralytic is made directly to reveal the *authority* of the Son of Man, *authority* being, according to Daniel VII, his distinguishing mark. But that miracle is the third of a series revealing *authority*. It is the authority of the Son of Man which teaches not as the scribes (I, 22) and directly proceeds to lay its commands on the demons (I, 27). It is the same authority which cleanses the leper (I, 41). The authority of the Son of Man, according to Daniel VII, is no other than the authority of the Most High, his everlasting Kingdom brought on earth. The Christ who gives signs of the already active authority of the Son of Man is he who also preaches that the kingdom of God is at the door (I, 15). The authority of the Son of Man is the restoration or fulfilment of Adam's dominion, and Christ's first act after his baptism is to undergo the several circumstances of Adam's lot, cast forth into the wilderness by the Spirit of God, tempted by Satan, set amongst the beasts, ministered to by angels. Our thoughts recur to Psalm VIII. '. . . Or what the Son of Man, that thou visitest him? Thou hast made him a little lower than the angels, to crown him with glory and honour. Thou hast put all things under his feet, all . . . the beasts of the wild . . .'

Finally, Christ is the only beloved Son of God, a title proper to the Messiah, but easily conceivable in Son-of-Man terms. 'Creation' and 'begetting' are scarcely distinguished by the Jews; Adam is in a peculiar sense the direct Son of God and he who fulfils what Adam merely betokened will be perfectly and uniquely so. St Luke provides all the comment we need. Having recorded the voice at the Baptism, 'Thou art my beloved Son', he directly proceeds: 'Jesus was then entering on his thirtieth year; the son, by legal reckoning, of Joseph, the son of . . . the son of . . . Adam, the Son of God.' Jesus is not the Son of God by mere descent from Adam, but by a new and higher origin; for Joseph was his parent by legal reckoning only. Nevertheless, the legal reckoning is of consequence; Christ's two divine paternities, one inherited and one direct, are forced into comparison by St Luke. To understand the meaning of this comparison is to understand why he who is Son of Man is Son of God. For he is both heir of Adam, and a higher Adam.

To summarize: the first part of the Gospel sets forth in riddles the nature and the authority of the Son of Man, and adds the first mystery of the Son of Man—his presence and supernatural activity on earth before his enthronement. The second mystery of the Son of Man is that of his passion and resurrection. The second mystery is reserved for the last part of the Gospel (VIII, 27 ff.). VIII like II contains a pair of Son-of-Man texts. 'Peter said to him, Thou art the Anointed. And he charged them to tell no one of him; and began to teach them that the Son of Man must suffer many things . . .' (29–31). 'He that disowns me and my words in this apostate and offending generation, him shall the Son of Man disown when he comes in the glory of his Father with the holy angels' (38). It is important to observe what these texts take for granted, and what they assert. The first text takes for granted the identity between the Anointed and the Son of Man, while asserting his destiny to suffer. The second takes for granted that the Son of Man is to come in glory as Daniel had predicted, and that he is the Son of God; what it asserts is that he will acknowledge or disown those who acknowledge or disown Jesus in this life.

Let us consider the assumptions first and the assertions afterwards. We might suppose that the assumptions would be mere re-statements, and new teaching would be restricted to the assertions. This is in a sense true; everything now assumed has been previously hinted; but hinted only. The identity between the Anointed Son of David and the Son of Man is hinted in II, 25–28, but in VIII, 29–31 it is assumed without any ambiguity. The Son of Man's glorious advent with divine authority on earth is hinted at by the hidden citation of Daniel VII, 13–14 in II, 10. It is openly assumed in VIII, 38. Divine Sonship is brought into implicit relation with the function of the New Adam in I, 11–13. In VIII, 38 the relation is plainly assumed.

To turn now to the assertions. The first is, that the Son of Man must suffer many things. The necessity lies in the divine purpose, and the divine purpose is revealed in scripture. 'It is written of the Son of Man that he should suffer many things and be despised', just as it is written of Elijah that he returns and restores (IX, 12). It has often been said, and rightly, that the emphasis on 'contempt' and 'rejection' in IX, 12 and VIII, 31 shows that the Suffering Servant of Isaiah LII–LIII *et al.* is in mind. But we over-simplify the matter if we say that the proof of the necessary sufferings is to be obtained by attaching the figure of the Suffering Servant to the figure of the Son of Man. The texts about the Servant are certainly being regarded as a priceless comment upon the Son of Man's suffering destiny. But he is destined to suffer because he is the Son of Man, and not only because he is the Servant of the Lord. The whole theme is introduced by the words 'The Son of Man must suffer', and, taken by themselves, they have the ring of necessary truth. Since Adam's time, man must suffer; the representative man, the new Adam, supremely so. It was said to Adam, 'Thou shalt die the death', and only after the death has been died can the new life be manifested.

We must understand the Christian doctrine as a reflection on Genesis, Daniel and Isaiah together. Genesis tells us how Adam is given universal dominion, and Daniel VII tells us how the Son of Man fulfils or restores it. But Daniel also tells us that the glory of the Son of Man is awarded to the suffering patience, the martyrdom, of the Saints of the Most High; some will have been slain, but they will arise for their reward (VII, 8, 21, 25, XII, 1–2). They who are to share the kingdom must be ready to die; but what of him who is the head and substance of the kingdom? Must not he die Adam's death if he is to inherit Adam's dominion? Daniel asserts both suffering and glory of the Saints but glory alone of the Son of Man. Isaiah supplies what Daniel omits: he declares that he who is lifted up and greatly glorified is he who was rejected and led to the slaughter.

The Son of Man must suffer, for is he not the Son of Man? Christ takes Man upon him where he finds him, not in immortality, but in corruption, not in paradise, but expelled and in the wilderness. Adam is tempted in paradise, and then driven forth; Christ is first driven forth, then tempted, for he begins where Adam is, not where Adam was (I, 12–15).[1] It is not enough that Christ should suffer Adam's temptation and vanquish it; he must suffer Adam's death besides, and vanquish that. 'The Son of Man must suffer many things, and be rejected . . . and killed, and after three days rise again.' The threat of Adam's death is the preface to his seduction by Satan (Gen. II, 17), and the prophecy of Christ's death is no sooner introduced by St Mark than Satanic temptation follows, uttered through the lips of St Peter. 'Get thee behind me, Satan', is the answer of the Son of Man. Adam in listening to Satan braved death, and incurred death. Satan tempts Christ with life; and he incurs death, not by listening to Satan, but by rejecting him. So at least it looks on the surface of things; but in truth it is still death that Satan offers under the guise of life, and life that the Son of Man chooses under the mask of death. 'For he that will save his life shall lose it, and he that loses his life for the gospel shall save it' (Mark VIII, 35).

The association of the Son of Man's name with death and resurrection, once established in VIII, 31, recurs many times in what follows (IX, 9; IX, 31; X, 33–34; X, 45; XIV, 21; XIV, 41). It is also hinted, but only hinted at in what precedes. The first mention of the title (II, 10) authenticates the authority of the Son

---

[1] The temptations of Israel were a token of this, for they befell in the desert, and were the condition of recovering the promised land. Israel was tempted forty years, and Christ tempted forty days (Mark I, 12–13); the comparison with Israel's temptations is greatly developed by St Matthew.

of Man by a miracle which is a typic death and resurrection. The paralytic is carried out like the dead, and lowered like the dead into a hole which has been dug for him. It was only so that he could come into the presence of the Son of Man, and receive both the forgiveness of his sins and the command to arise. The modern reader is apt to complain that the power to heal the body is poor evidence for authority to purify the conscience; and if the objection is put in that bald form, it must be allowed to be unanswerable. But St Mark and his first readers were not such literalists as we are. The process of the man's healing expresses the mystery of death and resurrection; and the incident, as we have shown, forms one of a series leading up to the death and resurrection of the Son of Man himself. It is in the Son of Man's death and resurrection that man obtains forgiveness and life, for it is in the Son of Man that man both dies and rises. Evidence for the power of the resurrection of the dead is the best and most appropriate evidence for the authority to remit sins: and the raising of the paralytic is evidence of resurrection from the dead; not yet clear and explicit, indeed, but made so by the subsequent development of healing symbolism in this Gospel.

What is hinted in the second chapter is boldly stated in the eighth; St Mark says it in so many words, when he adds to Christ's prophecy of death and resurrection the significant remark: 'And he spake the saying without reserve', *parrhesiai*. The *parrhesia*, the openness, is of course for the disciples alone. Christ collects a larger audience to hear his sermon on the bearing of the cross, and in addressing them, returns to the same sort and degree of riddled speech, or 'parable', as he had used in the second chapter. Daniel had promised a share in the glory of the Son of Man to men who would be faithful until death. Faithful to what? Faithful to the good cause, the cause of God. Jesus now declares that the good cause is himself and his word or gospel. So much is open enough; there is no riddle there. The riddle lies in the undefined relation between Jesus and the Son of Man. 'He that disowns me and my words in this generation, him will the Son of Man disown when he comes in the glory of his Father.'

Naturally enough, if Jesus is the Son of Man to be; but the conclusion that he is so, is not inescapable.

The first four texts about the Son of Man, two in the second chapter and two in the eighth, set forth the whole substance of the doctrine; and it will be unnecessary for us to comment in detail on the texts which follow them. In IX and X we hear only of the Son of Man's sufferings and resurrection; in XIII, 26 of his coming in glory, in XIV, 21 and 41 of his sufferings once more, and in XIV, 62 of his glory, as he proclaimed it himself to the High Priest. And that is the last word about the Son of Man. Although we will not comment on these texts in detail, we will make some general observations.

The pairing of Son of Man with Son of David or Anointed, begun in II, 25–26 and repeated in VIII, 29–31, still continues. The long theme of the Son of Man's sufferings in IX–X is brought to a conclusion in the words: 'The Son of Man came not to be ministered unto, but to minister, and to give his life a ransom for many.' The words have no sooner been spoken, than Christ is at Jericho, hailed by Bartimeus under the title 'Son of David', and in that title he enters Jerusalem. 'Blessed be the coming kingdom of David our father' is the cry of the attendant multitude. It is as David's Son that Christ exercises his brief spiritual reign over David's city in XI–XII, in defiance of his enemies.

As the episode draws to a close, Christ himself raises the question of his Davidic sonship. 'How say the scribes that Messiah is David's son? For David himself said by the Holy Ghost: The Lord said unto my Lord, sit thou on my right hand, until I make thine enemies the footstool of thy feet. David himself calls him Lord; how is he then his son?' That the evangelist understands Davidic sonship to be in every sense denied by this utterance, is incredible. A scriptural problem is being propounded, of the sort more fully set out in IX, 11–13. It is assumed that a solution can be found, not that there is no solution. The problem lies in an apparent opposition between scriptural texts. On the one hand there are the many texts which place the Messiahship in the family of David; on the other hand there is the Psalm text, which

makes Messiah David's lord, and therefore, it would seem, something more than his son. Christ does not give a solution, but the
attentive reader of St Mark should by now be in a position to
propound one.

St Mark's reader is expected to accept the interpretation of the
Psalm which the evangelist sets before him, and to ask himself
what, as so interpreted, the Psalm shows. Not, surely, that
Messiah has no Davidic blood, but that his title derives from
some other source than Davidic inheritance. If to be Messiah
were simply to be the Son of David, David would not call
Messiah 'Lord'. From whom, then, does Messiah inherit his
title, if not from David? It is easy for the Christian to reply 'from
God', but the answer does not fit the question. All true titles,
including David's, are from God. What is being sought for is the
divine covenant or deed of gift under which Messiah inherits. It
is not, apparently, the covenant God made with David, and we
have to search the scriptures in order to find another. The Scribes,
whose doctrine Jesus finds defective, are well aware that Messiah
is the adopted Son of God; their error is, that they believe him to
be adopted in David. We may well declare that he is not an adopted
Son at all, being Son by nature. But though St Mark's teaching
points in our direction, he does not use our formulation; and our
solution would be outside the terms in which his Gospel is stated.

We ought, then, to accept the problem in the form: If Messiah
does not inherit under the covenant God made with David,
under what covenant does he inherit? And the proper answer
surely is: 'Under the covenant God made with man, when he
put all things under his feet.' The answer is, indeed, suggested by
the conclusion of the quotation: 'Till I make thine enemies the
footstool of thy feet.' Who can hear this, and not remember
that other Psalm: 'The Son of Man . . . thou hast made him a
little lower than the angels, thou hast crowned him with glory and
honour; thou hast set all things under his feet.' Christ is David's
lord, because he inherits not David's kingdom only, but Adam's.
And this he does, our faith will add, because, like Adam himself,
but in a more perfect way, he is the immediate Son of God.

The solution we have given is borne out by the sequel. The question about David's Lord is the last public doctrinal saying except one attributed to Christ by the Evangelist. The last of all is the confession before the High Priest. This is also the last pairing of Anointed (Son of David) with Son of Man. Peter had confessed Jesus to be the Anointed, and Jesus had gone on to speak of the sufferings and glory of the Son of Man. The High Priest challenges Jesus to confess himself the Anointed, and Jesus having done so, goes on to speak of the glory of the Son of Man. We notice that the High Priest takes for granted what we have just said that any scribe would assume—Messiah's being the Son of God. 'Art thou the Anointed,' he says, 'the Son of the Blessed (God)?' We notice also that in his reply, Jesus incorporates 'sitting at the right hand of God' into the Glory of the Son of Man. 'I am; and ye shall see the Son of Man sitting at the right hand of Almighty Power, and coming with the clouds of heaven.' The clouds belong to Daniel's Son of Man, and we have read of them in the closest of St Mark's Daniel quotations (XIII, 26). But the session at the right hand belongs to David's lord in Psalm cx, and it has appeared nowhere in the Gospel except in the passage where that Psalm is cited. The evangelist is surely showing us, therefore, that he who, by sitting at God's right hand, becomes David's lord, is the Son of Man; and that he lords it over his father David by asserting not David's dominion merely, but man's. We have been seeing in other examples how St Mark takes for granted in a later text what he has hinted in an earlier. It is in accordance with such a practice that the answer of Christ to the High Priest should take for granted the solution required by the riddle he propounded in the Temple.

We will make one further observation: on the apocalyptic discourse in XIII. Rightly to understand this discourse, it is necessary to note what is taken for granted in it, and what is asserted. Jesus predicts the fall of the Temple, and is asked by four disciples 'when these things shall be, and what is the sign when all these things are going to be accomplished'. Jesus in his reply is chiefly concerned to warn his disciples against regarding false signs, and

to turn their minds upon their own conduct. He tells them what
to do in the several stages of an apocalyptic history which is itself
referred to rather than described. The first decisive event will be
the desolation of Antichrist (XIII, 14), for which the reader is in
so many words referred to the text of scripture, i.e. of Daniel:
'Let him that readeth discern.' The second decisive event will be
the coming of the Son of Man and the gathering of the elect
(26–27). This event is stated with the utmost possible brevity, by
way of allusion to well-known texts (Dan. VII, 13–14;
Deut. XXX, 4). Christ is not concerned to add anything to
the doctrine of the Last Day, but rather to say what signs of it
can and cannot be looked for, and in what posture the disciples
should expect it. And as we pass on from XIII to XIV, we are led
to see that the attitude proper in face of Antichrist and advent is
the same as that with which the passion and resurrection must be
faced; for the substance of the Last Things and the substance of
the Passion are one and the same.

What we have been endeavouring above all to show is that
'the Son of Man' was not, and never had been, the name for a
mysterious allegorical figure destined to fly down from the sky
in the last days. It was the figure of him in whom the destiny of
Man, implicit in his creation, was fulfilled. The destiny of man is
to actualize the divine image, and to rule over all things on earth
with divine authority. It is his destiny also to suffer and to die,
and only so to enter into his glory. Two things are peculiar to the
teaching of Christ: that he insisted on the sufferings of the Son of
Man; and that he took the Son of Man upon himself.

The doctrine of the Son of Man, as placed by St Mark in the
mouth of Christ, is and is not a democratic conception. It is
democratic in the sense that Christ achieves the glory of man,
and therefore all men have, or if they will may have, a share in
it. The kingdom is given to the Saints of the Most High, and all
may be saints that are men. But it is not a democratic conception
in the sense that it starts from multitude. Daniel indeed had
thought of Israel as achieving corporately the destiny of the Son
of Man; Israel, or the righteous remnant of Israel. And the

attempt has been made to derive Christ's doctrine directly from this source. The Son of Man is the righteous remnant, but that remnant dwindles until, when the disciples have fled from Gethsemane and Peter has denied in court, Christ is the righteous remnant himself alone. He is all the Israel there is. Such a way of thinking is a perfectly proper Christian reflection on the Isaianic doctrine of the righteous remnant. If salvation is through the remnant which merits it, then that remnant is Christ. But it is another thing to allege that the doctrine of the Son of Man in the Gospels is conceived in such terms; for it is not. Enoch is evidence that the Davidic king had come to be looked for, anyhow by some Israelites, as the bearer of the destiny of the Son of Man; the kingdom will embrace all the elect, but it will be founded on the person of a New David who is also a new Adam. And it is really unmistakable that the doctrine of the Gospels, and especially of St Mark, is this. Christ does not gather into himself the scattered and divided streams of Messianic inheritance; he is a new fountain-head of royalty.

St Mark's doctrine is consistent, according to his own canons of consistency. If we are willing to think his thoughts after him, we can understand him with clarity and assurance. But are his thoughts the thoughts of Christ? Did Jesus teach the doctrine of the Son of Man? St Mark says that Jesus chose to die for it. For, when challenged by the High Priest, he was not content to answer his question in the terms set, but made his own addition, and marked out for himself the ground on which he would erect his cross. Not only did he say 'I am', but added: 'And ye shall see the Son of Man seated at the right hand of the Almighty and coming with the clouds of heaven.' If St Mark did not mean this as historical testimony it is indeed strange. Even supposing (as some have not hesitated to suppose) that the evangelist lacked genuine evidence for what had taken place in the High Priest's court, historical seriousness must still govern the symbolical picture. It must symbolize this, that Jesus died for the doctrine of the Son of Man, whether that doctrine was named in the High Priest's court or not.

Can we accept St Mark's testimony? Did Jesus name himself the Son of Man? The question may be brought under two further questions. Did Jesus teach his Messiahship? Did Jesus prophesy his passion? If he taught his Messiahship, he meditated, surely, on the deepest grounds of it; and if he predicted his passion, he surely reconciled it with his Messianic destiny. Apart from the doctrine of the Son of Man, we have no indication of how he did either. The kingdom of Messiah is scarcely more than politics, unless it is seen as the dominion of Man; and only if the destiny of the Messiah is the destiny of Man, does it plainly embrace the necessity to suffer and to die. So viewed, Christology is no extra, but the very root of scripture. For the whole dispensation of God springs from his creation of man.

If there is one article of Christ's teaching which is historically evidenced, it is his teaching on the indissolubility of marriage (I Cor. VII, 10). It is just conceivable that Christ gave no reasons for his pronouncement, or that if he gave any, they were forgotten, and others afterwards supplied by the Church. It is conceivable, but it is destitute of all probability. Christ must have been challenged to give scriptural support for so striking and practical a novelty, and he presumably gave it. And his teaching would remain in his disciples' minds tied to the scriptural text with which he had bound it up. Then when the evangelists give us Christ's teaching and his scriptural proof in one, they are to be believed. From the beginning of creation 'Male and female made he them'. 'For this cause shall a man leave father and mother and cleave to his wife, and the twain shall be one flesh.' Christ derived his law of marriage from the creation of man, treating Moses's ordinance as a secondary thing, accommodated to man's corrupt state. Is it not likely, then, that he derived his doctrine of kingdom from the creation also, treating David's kingdom as a secondary and partial thing? If marriage is to be founded on Adam, why not kingship?

St Paul is our best authority for Christ's doctrine of marriage. He is also our best, and far our earliest, authority for the substance of the Christian faith. What was the truth proclaimed in the name of Christ as necessary to salvation? For the most part the Apostle assumes it, but for the Corinthians' benefit he re-states it. 'I declare to you, brethren, the gospel which I preached to you, which you received, by which you stand, through which you are saved . . . I delivered to you first the tradition delivered to me: that Messiah died for our sins according to the scriptures, and that he was buried, and that he rose the third day according to the scriptures, and that he appeared to Cephas, then to the Twelve.' Such was the formula, but it was not, and never had been, self-sufficient. 'He died for our sins according to the scrip-tures, he rose the third day according to the scriptures.' What scriptures? If this faith goes back to Christ himself, so must the specification of anyhow some scriptures. St Paul, after a para-graph of practical argument (xv, 12–19) proceeds to scriptural authority. 'Now is Christ risen from the dead, the firstfruits of them that sleep. For since by man is death, by man also is resur-rection of the dead. For as in Adam all die, so in the Messiah shall all be made alive.' Having thus laid a firm foundation in Adam, the Apostle proceeds to build upon it Psalm CX, 'Sit thou at my right hand till I make thy enemies the footstool of thy feet', and Psalm VIII, 'The Son of Man . . ., thou hast put all things under his feet'. St Paul then has a further argumentative discursion (xv, 29 ff.) and leads it round safely to the funda-mental scripture. 'If there is an animal body, there is a spiritual, as it is written: The first man Adam became an animal life.' It would take us out of our way to analyse the argument St Paul bases on this text (xv, 45–49).

It is common form to discount the testimony of St Paul to the central importance of Adamic Christology. 'This', it is said, 'is St Paul's idiosyncracy. The primitive preaching of Christ knew nothing of it.' And what evidence have we more primitive for the preaching of Christ? 'The sermons in the Acts of the Apostles.' But the First Epistle to the Corinthians was composed less than thirty years after the Resurrection, whereas the Acts of the Apostles were composed thirty years later than the First Epistle to the Corinthians, and the sermons it contains are evidence of one thing only—how St Luke thought it fitting that the gospel preaching should be opened before unevangelized Jews and their uncircumcized fellow-worshippers. The sermons add up to a single testimony and contain a single doctrine. St Luke has many excellences, but when it is a question of the primitive faith, I will not deliver myself blindfold to the guidance of St Luke. He shall not persuade me against a consensus of St Paul and St Mark.

I am willing, indeed, to believe St Luke as far as this: that the proclamation of the gospel did not commonly start from the deepest point of doctrine; that one started from the Son of David and the Prophet like unto Moses and the promised Seed of Abraham, rather than from the new Adam. The deepest things were not for the beginners. But that is no argument for the conclusion that the deepest things were not there from the beginning. To deny that Christ thought deeply is to adopt the hypothesis of an infidel. Let it be granted that Christ thought in the terms which his inheritance supplied. His inheritance supplied the scripture, and the scripture contained Adam; and Daniel and Enoch had cast upon the figure of Adam a Messianic light. How could Christ fail to see his destiny in Adamic terms? How else can he have understood himself to be the Saviour of Mankind? In so saying, we do not simply argue that it was fitting, and therefore it was so, *decuit, ergo factum est*, as though we had no evidence. Our evidence is that it was so, but lest the evidence should be discounted, we say, 'And how could it have been otherwise?' *Et factum est, et decuit.*

CHAPTER XIII

LOAVES AND THOUSANDS

On several occasions in the course of the previous chapters we have taken for granted the interpretation of the numbers of loaves and thousands in the two narratives of the feeding of multitudes. We have assumed, that is, that the first feeding symbolizes the eucharist of the Jews, and the second that of the Gentiles. But it is necessary to give the question more careful attention than it has yet received, and to clear up the details of the symbolism as thoroughly as we can.

There are always several ways of telling any story. The arrangement of the matter, the details recorded and the details omitted are at the discretion of the narrator. There was no need, certainly, that the tradition of the miraculous feasts provided by Christ should have fallen into the pattern it retains. Nor would it have done so if the Church had been unacquainted with the history of Elisha. Elisha multiplied bread (II Kings IV, 42–44). He multiplied it once and not again, but since the two miracles of bread in Mark VI and VIII have a common narrative pattern, a single archetype will cover them both. 'There came a man from Baal-shalishah, and brought the man of God bread of the firstfruits, twenty loaves of barley, and fresh ears of corn in the husk. And he' (i.e. Elisha) 'said, Give unto the people that they may eat. And his servant said, What, should I set this before two hundred men? But he said, Give the people that they may eat. For thus saith the Lord, They shall both eat and leave thereof. So he set it before them, and they did eat and leave thereof, according to the word of Elisha.'

This is the type of the Gospel narratives. It counts the loaves, it counts the men to be fed, and it makes a great point of it that there are leavings over from the feast. It does not count the leavings, as the Gospel does, but to do so is merely to elaborate upon the same idea. The prophet's servant is the type of Christ's disciples, both in his initial perplexity and in his subsequent service.

The setting of the Old Testament story is a time of general scarcity. The people with Elisha at Gilgal are glad of an extra meal at such a time, and they get it. The setting of the Gospel narratives is somewhat different. Here are thousands of men faint with hunger in desert places, no apparent means of feeding them, and the disciples in utter perplexity. We cannot but be reminded of the predicament of Moses in the wilderness. It is to be observed that whereas Christ appears in the role of Elisha, and the disciples in that of Elisha's servant, the disciples and not Christ take the part of Moses. 'Whence should I have flesh', Moses says, 'to give to all this people? . . . Shall all the fish of the sea be gathered together for them, to suffice them?' (Num. xi, 13, 22). A further Mosaic feature of the Gospel narratives is the substitution of fish for the corn in the husk which we find in the Elisha story. Moses sought flesh for the people, and asked how he could find either fish or slaughtered beasts to satisfy them. He was in fact given quails. Bread and fish, then, is a fair analogy to 'manna and quails'.

A third Mosaic point may be seen in the very fact of the doubling of the Gospel narrative (Mark vi and viii). There is an account of the miracles of Manna and Quails in Exodus xvi, and a second account of a miracle of Quails in Numbers xi, in connexion with which the continuous provision of manna is described over again. The modern scholar may be content to say the the miracle in Numbers is a duplicate account of the miracle in Exodus, derived by the Pentateuchal editor from a different literary source. That is not the sort of thing, however, that St Mark would have told himself. And if he got as far as wondering in what significant point the second miracle of Quails differed from the first, he is likely to have fastened on the point that the second demand for flesh-food arose out of the 'lusting' of the *mixed multitude*, the non-Israelite people who had followed the host up out of Egypt. And this might give the evangelist a hint for the symbolism of his new double narrative: a table for Israel, and a table for the gentiles.

Are there any considerable features in the Gospel narratives which are neither Mosaic nor Elisean? There are the eucharistic features. Moses did not multiply food at all, it dropped from heaven in full abundance. Elisha simply told his servant to serve the loaves, and we are to think of what happened by the analogy of the widow's cruse: there were always more loaves in the basket as long as they were required. But Christ multiplies the loaves by saying grace for them and breaking them. The number of whole loaves never becomes any greater than it was at first, but each loaf breaks into a number of substantial pieces which are together many times the mass of the unbroken loaf. Such is the form of the miracle, and by this form it is related not to Old Testament types, but to Jewish and Christian eucharistic custom. The master of the feast says the blessing for bread over a loaf, and breaks the loaf into crumbs, that everyone present may eat a crumb of 'the bread of the grace'. That is Jewish custom, but when it is done in the Christian way, every crumb becomes sufficient spiritual nutriment, sustaining the receiver to ever-lasting life. And this was prefigured in Christ's miracles, though after an earthly manner; every crumb became a portion sufficient to sustain the eater for his present need in the life of this present age.

There still remains a feature of the Marcan narratives which is related neither to Moses nor to Elisha, nor to eucharistic custom; and that is the numbers of loaves, fragments remaining, and feasters. Moses fed six hundred thousand men with an abundance of manna and quails; Elisha fed two hundred men with twenty loaves. And eucharistic custom, if it required anything in the matter of number, would regard a single loaf as most perfect. 'Because there is one loaf, we are one body', says St Paul (I Cor. x, 17). More loaves might have to be used on occasion, but that would be a symbolical imperfection. What then are we to make of five loaves dealt to five thousands with twelve creels (great baskets) of leavings over, and seven loaves dealt to four thou-sands with seven (ordinary) baskets of leavings over?

We cannot simply set aside the numbers as unimportant. For apart from the lesson they convey (whatever it may be) it is impossible to explain the second narrative. The difficulty is not that a feature of the same sort, a miraculous feeding of crowds, is repeated by the evangelist, for his Gospel is full of pairs. It is indeed his common custom to double everything, apart from those features which belong to the standing form of his cycles, and are repeated many more times than once. Thus we find two cleansings of the defiled, two commissionings of the twelve, two miracles at sea, two healings of the deaf mute and two of the blind, two embracings of little children, and so on. What is surprising about the two feedings of crowds is (*a*) the closeness of verbal parallel between them and (*b*) the apparent bathos in the second. The second narrative scarcely differs from the first except by abbreviation, and by the diminution of the miracle. It is less wonderful to feed four thousands with seven loaves than five thousands with five, especially if only seven baskets of leavings remain, instead of twelve creels full of them.

In view of these facts it is possible to understand, though never to approve, the so-called theory of 'doublets': that is to say that St Mark was taken in by variant narratives of the same event (only that they scarcely do vary) and put them both down in all innocence as distinct happenings. Unhappily, the theory explains nothing. For even supposing that the evangelist was taken in, he was not obliged to put his 'doublets' in an order of bathos rather than of climax. It is not his usual practice; the walking on the water is more striking, not less striking, than the stilling of the storm.

We shall prefer the hypothesis that St Mark knew his own business. What then should make him write the second narrative as a simplified double of the first? It must have been his intention to eliminate all distracting features and concentrate our attention on the one significant point of difference, the numbers: not five loaves for five thousands with twelve creels of leavings, but seven loaves for four thousands with seven baskets of leavings. There must be here a slightly more complicated example of that number symbolism which we have already found elsewhere in this Gospel.

The conclusion is supported by a dialogue between Christ and his disciples which closely follows the second miracle of bread.

With an emphasis that could scarcely be exceeded, the disciples are exhorted to use their ears, eyes, hearts and understandings to comprehend the significance of the twelve creels full taken up when the five loaves were dealt to five thousands, and the seven baskets full when the seven loaves had been dealt to four thousands. There is, of course, a satisfactory surface sense for the reader who goes no deeper. If they tell us nothing else, the numbers tell us that God makes abundant provision. But do they not tell us something besides? Is there not a riddle here? Is not the evangelist saying to us, 'Let him that readeth understand'? (XIII, 14).

The dialogue to which we have just referred has the effect of drawing all the numbers together from the two feedings and setting them before us in a single group, so that we can grasp the relations between them. Let us put them in a table, and consider them simply as a pattern of numbers.

loaves	thousands of recipients	leavings
5	5	12
7	4	7

The most obvious fact about these figures is that in each line there are two numbers the same and one different; and so our attention is attracted by the odd number in each line and we are led to ask why it does not conform to the others in its line. The first line makes the suggestion that it is appropriate for five loaves to be received by five thousands, and the second line makes the suggestion that it is appropriate for seven loaves to yield seven measures of leavings. But if so, why are there twelve measures of leavings rather than five from the five loaves? And again, why are there four thousands of recipients rather than seven for the seven loaves?

Let us look at the two anomalous numbers, the twelve and the four, and see if anything strikes us about them. Well, obviously twelve is the sum of the five loaves and the seven loaves taken together; $5 + 7 = 12$. And four is the next whole number under five; $5 - 1 = 4$. These are not very profound arithmetical mysteries, and if St Mark was capable of buying fish in the market, he cannot have been unacquainted with them. And what do these simple numerical relations suggest?

Let us first take $5 + 7 = 12$. What we have to understand is the meaning of the contrast between the 'irregular' line

     5 loaves   5 thousands   12 measures of leavings

and the 'regular' line

     5 loaves   5 thousands   5 measures of leavings.

Suppose we had the completely regular line. We should be expected to feel, should we not, that 5 loaves is a suitable number to be dealt to five thousands, and that similarly five measures of leavings is a suitable provision for the five thousands on some future occasion, or throughout some future period. But if in fact there are twelve measures of leavings, that should signify a future provision not only for the five thousands but for twelve thousands—that is to say, for the five thousands already fed, and for seven thousands beside.

So we come away from the first feast with the expectation that we are going to hear presently about the feeding of some other seven thousand, divine bounty having made provision for them. We come to the second narrative, and our expectations look as though they are going to be fulfilled. Not that the second multitude is actually fed from those twelve creels of leavings from the former feast. The disciples cannot be carrying such a weight of bread about with them in case of emergency, and if they did, it would require an additional miracle to keep it always fresh. Besides, if Christ did not break loaves for the second multitude, there would be no eucharist, but only a communion in bread reserved from the former eucharist.

So it is not seven of the twelve creels of fragments that are produced for the second multitude, but seven loaves, that is to say, what remains over from the ideal number, twelve, after five have been already used. Seven loaves are blessed and broken, and seven basketfuls of leavings are taken up. Quite right, we say; there were twelve measures of leavings from the feast of five thousands, to signify that there were still seven thousands to be fed. But now that the seven thousands have been fed, all the twelve thousands have eaten for whom divine bounty at first provided. So the leavings taken up are no more than are required for the future provision of the seven thousands; there are no more thousands to be provided for.

The whole pattern seems now to have worked itself out perfectly. Five loaves yield twelve remainders, and five thousands are fed; seven loaves yield seven remainders, and seven thousands are—— But what is this? Here is a final surprise saved up for us by the evangelist. The very last sentence of his second narrative informs us that they who ate were not seven but four thousands.

Well, you may say, there is nothing strange here after all. The second feast is merely resembling the first in making provision for more thousands than come. When twelve measures of leavings remained from the feast of the five thousands, it meant that there were still seven thousands to be fed. And if seven measures of leavings remain from the feast of the four thousands, it means that three thousands remain to be fed. And when the three thousands come and are fed, then the sum will be complete. $5 + 4 + 3$ thousands makes up the twelve thousands provided for in the original bounty, the twelve creels of leavings.

Yes, that is true enough; but if that is St Mark's meaning, why does he assign seven loaves to the four thousands rather than four? The pattern we have been suggesting is a three-line pattern; there would be three feasts, in one of which five, in another four, and in a third three thousands would be fed, and it should go like this:

loaves	thousands	leavings
5	5	12
4	4	7
3	3	3

Whereas in fact (a) there is no third feast, (b) the three loaves for the three thousands are already used up, having been placed on the table of the four thousands.

I cannot conceive what St Mark means, unless he means this: there are indeed three thousands still to be fed, but the Lord does not make a separate eucharist for them. They are to be conceived as late guests still destined to appear and to feed on the broken pieces of the second eucharist. Their three loaves have already been broken.

On the assumption (which we shall presently support) that the two breakings of bread represent the eucharist of Israel and of the Gentiles respectively, it is quite easy to see what the evangelist means. Christ dealt bread to the Jews in the Last Supper and in the confirmation of it which was his death and resurrection. The Holy Ghost in the apostolic Church by a new covenant dealt bread to the nations. There are still more of the nations to be evangelized—they all must be evangelized before the end can come. But the evangelizing of them will not involve any new eucharistic covenant. It will simply bring more guests to the table on which the seven loaves have been already set.

It is easy to object here that if the evangelization of the Gentiles is incomplete, so is that of the Jews. How few Israelites had been converted, when St Mark wrote! But he is not thinking of individuals, he is thinking of communities. The Jewish world has heard the gospel, and so it is possible to believe that all the elect of Israel have been gathered in. But there are whole cities and countries of the Gentiles still to be evangelized.

We may now take up the simple arithmetical fact we noticed above—that four is the next whole number lower than five. If five thousands have been fed already, and now four thousands are fed, our minds are easily inclined to continue counting downwards, and to see that three thousands must be fed next. Thus there are two separate pointers to the number 'three thousands', (a) the principle of the sequence 5, 4, (3) and (b) the fact that 3 is the number required to make 4 up to 7.

Is it likely, we may ask, that St Mark felt 5, 4 . . . to be a sequence with an intrinsic tendency to run on? What could be more likely, since his pattern of healings is arranged on the same principle? Do not the former halves of his double cycles contain blocks of healing miracles, the first of them 4, the second 3, the third 2 and the fourth 1?

So far we have proceeded by a consideration of the numbers alone. We have been conducting a study in allegorical arithmetic. It is time that we set about relating our conclusions to other elements of symbolism which the Gospel contains. We have taken it that the first feeding represents the eucharist of the Jews and the second the eucharist of the Gentiles. The most obvious evidence of this is evidence with which we are already familiar. The feedings stand in the latter halves of consecutive double cycles. The first half of the former of these double cycles culminates in the healing of Jairus's daughter, the first half of the latter of them contains the healing of the Syrophoenician's daughter. The feeding of the five thousand appears as a pendant to the healing of Jairus's daughter, and the feeding of the four thousand as a pendant to the healing of the Syrophoenician's daughter. The one girl is a Jewess, the other a Gentile.

The raising of Jairus's daughter has a detail in its conclusion which appears insignificant when we first read the story but awakens in our memory as we pass on to the sequel. After raising the little girl to life Jesus directs that she should be given something to eat. Now whatever St Mark did or did not expect of his original readers, at least he expected them to see their baptism in the healing miracles, and above all in the miracle of resuscitation. If they were able to see so much, they might also see something else. The Christian's initiation was not completed in baptism alone; he was no sooner baptized with water and spirit, than he was brought to the table of the Lord. Christ not only regenerates by baptism, he also feeds with the food of eternal life. Jesus not only raised the little girl from death, he directed that she should be fed.

There is no more than a hint of eucharist in the story of Jairus's child, but the hint is not allowed to pass, it is taken up and developed in the feeding of the five thousand. Here the eucharistic meaning is unmistakable, for does not Jesus say the thanksgiving, break the bread and have it distributed?

Jesus regenerates none whom he does not also feed. The Syrophoenician woman asks exorcism for her daughter. Exorcism signifies one aspect of baptism, the renunciation and expulsion of the devil. Jesus says that to grant exorcism to the girl would mean the giving her a share in the bread of the children of God. 'It is not meet', he says, 'to take the children's bread and cast it to the dogs.' Such bread, for example, as Jesus ordered the daughter of Jairus to be given. For the request of the Syrophoeness inevitably reminds us of the request of Jairus; each parent intercedes on behalf of a daughter lying distressed at home.

So far the dialogue with the Syrophoeness finds its natural background in the healing of Jairus's daughter. But the woman's answer to Jesus shifts the ground, and makes us think rather of the feeding of five thousand. The dogs, she says, may well be spared the crumbs that fall from the children's table; and we are put in mind of that miraculous feast, where the crumbs remaining were in such great quantity, more than the feasters would need. If twelve creels full are left by five thousands, there is surely an available surplus.

We read on, and the next page brings us to the feeding of the four thousand. It hangs upon the incident of the Syrophoeness in exactly the same way as the feeding of the five thousand hangs on the incident of Jairus. And it picks up that relation of Gentile 'crumbs' to Jewish 'loaves' upon which the dialogue with the Syrophoeness turns. St Mark's symbolism does not allow that the second multitude should be fed from crumbs only, and that no new loaves should be broken for them. But in several different ways he expresses the idea that the second feast is the leavings of the first. (*a*) Out of the ideal number of twelve loaves five have been used for the first feast. The leavings (seven) are used for the second. (*b*) The actual leavings of the first feast were twelve creels, whereas those of the second are seven baskets, and seven is the leavings of twelve after five have been set aside for the five thousands. So the provision laid up for the four thousand is as it were the leavings of the provision laid up for the five thousand. (*c*) The leavings of the first feast are measured in creels (*cophini*) and the leavings of the second in baskets (*spyrides*). As the loaf is larger than the crumb, so the creel is larger than the basket. It would be easy to write off the distinction between creels and baskets as a mere variety of phrase, were it not carefully retained in the summary which draws together the several elements of the riddle (VIII, 17–21).

The relation of the first feeding to Jairus and of the second to the Syrophoeness sufficiently establishes the Jewish character of the first multitude and the Gentile character of the second. If we could be quite sure of St Mark's geographical indications, we might be able to claim a further support for the point: the first feeding is perhaps to be taken as situated on the Jewish side of the Lake, and the second on the Gentile side. In VI Jesus and his disciples use the boat to escape the crowds, but find they have been followed. It is more natural to suppose that they have simply sailed along shore, rather than that they have crossed. If they had crossed, they would surely have shaken off the crowds effectively. After the feeding Jesus sends his disciples away in the boat 'towards the further shore, to Bethsaida'. Bethsaida stood on the northern part of the farther shore, i.e. the eastern or Gentile side. But they encountered difficult winds, and it does not seem that they made land at Bethsaida, but in 'Gennesaret', which is more likely to mean the middle part of the western or Jewish shore.

The feeding of the four thousands is given the vaguest possible setting. 'In those days there was once more a great crowd, and they had nothing to eat.' If it is right to presume that the setting remains unchanged from the last incident recorded, then we are on the Decapolitan shore of the lake, that is, the southern part of the east or Gentile side. After the feeding, they departed by boat into the region of Dalmanutha, which cannot be placed, but must have been on the Jewish side, for we are told that when they re-embarked from there they crossed to the farther side and reached Bethsaida. If the evangelist means that they crossed the lake to reach Dalmanutha, then the feeding of four thousand must have been on the Gentile shore, but it is not evident that he means this. So far as it goes, evidence is in favour of placing the two feedings on opposite shores of the lake; but it is not conclusive.

Let us now consider the basis of the numerical symbolism. Twelve loaves are distributed, five to the Jews and seven to the Gentiles. Twelve is the number of the tribes of Israel. And so the plain suggestion is, that there is a new and spiritual Israel of God, in which Israel-after-the-flesh receive five portions, and the Gentiles seven. St Paul, of course, can be quoted for the doctrine that the Church, both of Jews and Gentiles, is the true Israel of God. It is but a step from that to the symbolizing of the new Israel as a twelvefold people. And I trust that I have shown that the tribal names in St John's Apocalypse (VII and XXI) stand for the whole Church and not the Jewish portion of it only (*Rebirth of Images*, pp. 250–251).

The question remains, why St Mark should assign *five* portions to the Jews. One can give symbolical answers, as, for example, that the Jews are the people of the five-fold Mosaic Law, or common-sense answers, as that St Mark thought 5 : 4 was about the proportion of Jews to Gentiles in the Church of his day (only that it is rather hard to believe; surely the Gentiles were in the majority). Or again, one can give a purely arithmetical answer: St Mark wanted to do what we have seen that he did do, and treat the Jews converted *plus* the Gentiles converted *plus* the Gentiles still to be converted as a declining series of consecutive whole numbers adding up to twelve. Well then, $5 + 4 + 3 =$ twelve.

None of these answers is really satisfying. The common-sense answer turns out, after all, not to be common sense. The symbolical answer lacks support from the context of the feedings. And the arithmetical answer fails to carry conviction; it seems more likely that St Mark started with $\frac{5}{12}$ and then went on to appreciate some of its simpler mathematical beauties, than that he started with a bare arithmetical function in his head, and arrived at 5 as the figure required by the function.

The sort of thing we require is an Old Testament story in which someone takes and distributes five out of twelve loaves, leaving seven over, as though for a future occasion. And if we could show that St Mark refers to such a story elsewhere in his Gospel, and that there is good reason for thinking that he had it in mind when he composed the narrative of the five loaves of the five thousand, then we might rest tolerably satisfied with our answer.

What had St Mark in mind when he composed the feeding of the five thousand? Many things, no doubt, the manna and quails, for example, and Elisha's multiplication of bread. He should also have had in mind the passage in his own last previous cycle to which the passage he was now composing corresponded. That, as we saw, was the corn parables (IV, 1–34). The corn parables are the spiritualization of a more concrete theme which occupies the corresponding place a cycle farther back still. The corn parables tell us how Christ sows the corn which is the Word, but their model, the episode of the cornfield, shows Christ making corn free to his hungry disciples. The cornfield is a better basis for the feeding of five thousand than the corn parables, for it is concerned with the relief of actual hunger. And so it is reasonable to suppose that in composing the narrative about the five thousands St Mark looks right back through the corn parables to their archetype, the cornfield.

In the cornfield Christ compares his own action in allowing the corn to his disciples with the action of King David in taking shewbread for himself and his companions (I Sam. XXI). The citation of David's example seems quite a casual thing, but we have already seen in other connexions (p. 159, p. 276) what a hold it took on the evangelist's mind. Now every Jewish child knew that the loaves for the shewbread were twelve, and that they lay upon the holy table before God as a memorial of the Twelve Tribes of Israel. And here, surely, is the basis of the whole symbolism of the loaves and thousands. The whole and perfect number is twelve loaves for twelve thousands—a 'thousand' standing evidently for a tribe. Christ is a new David, dealing the Bread of God to the whole of Israel, making all the people holy, and removing the narrow privilege of the Levitical priesthood.

Now it is said of David in the passage of I Samuel to which St Mark refers, that he asked for—and St Mark will presume, received—*five* loaves only. Why would that be? Because, presumably, his company was five. The ancient loaf was not, of course, a pound loaf, but a cake of bread, one person's portion. Five loaves are for five men. Now David is the Jew, the Judaean hero *par excellence*. So David's company means the Jews. And when the ancient scripture makes David's company receive five loaves only, leaving seven behind, it is hinting at a later and better dispensation, when all the twelve loaves will be distributed, five to the Jews, and the remaining seven to the Gentiles, uniting both peoples in a single new twelve-fold Israel, a single sacramental fellowship; a church in which the Jews have five portions, and the Gentiles seven.

We have now got to the bottom of the symbolism of loaves and thousands; it is unnecessary to proceed further. But there is a subsidiary detail still worthy of attention in that dialogue of Christ and his disciples which puts the several parts of the numerical pattern so carefully together. 'And they forgot to take any loaves, and had no more than one loaf with them in the boat . . . And they questioned one with another, saying, We have no bread. Jesus perceived it and said to them, 'Why question ye about your having no bread? . . . Remember ye not, when I broke the five loaves for the five thousands . . .' What is the point here of the curious detail, that they had just *one* loaf? Would not the point be clearer if the evangelist merely said that they had forgotten to bring bread? But then, perhaps, the analogy of the disciples' predicament to the cases of the five thousand and four thousand quoted by Christ would not hold good. Christ had not called manna from the skies, he had multiplied bread. If there is even one loaf on board, and Christ to bless it, his disciples have no ground for anxiety. If five loaves served for five thousands, how much more will one loaf serve for twelve men.

'One loaf among twelve.' Here surely we have the Last Supper prefigured. The symbolism of the shewbread is borrowed from the story of King David and made as Christian and as eucharistic as it allows of being made. But there is an imperfection in it which every Christian must feel. For while a Christian mind will acknowledge that what Christ distributes in the supper is the substance of God's Israel, and therefore in a manner twelve-fold, yet it is a more immediate thought to us, that Christ distributes the substance of Israel because he distributes himself, his body; and Christ is one. Because there is one loaf, therefore we many are one body. So St Mark makes haste to supplement the symbolism of the twelve loaves with the sacramental reality of the one, which alone is needful.

CHAPTER XIV

THE APOSTLES

St Mark's system of symbolism is neither very abstruse nor very varied. He uses it, indeed, with much subtlety and flexibility, but the system of symbols themselves is clear and limited. The bony structure of it, so to speak, is provided by the figure of the tribal Israel. It is given a three-fold expression. There are first the twelve apostles called by Christ, together with Levi, a thirteenth but not an apostle. Then in the second place there are the thirteen persons healed by Christ, one for Levi and one for each of the Twelve. Thirdly, there are the twelve thousands who are at length to be fed by Christ with the twelve loaves. All Israel is called by Christ, healed by Christ, and fed by Christ. Calling and healing both suggest baptism, which is the sacrament of the individual, and so the tribal number is reckoned in individuals called and healed. But feeding is eucharist, which is essentially a sacrament of fellowship, of multitude; so the tribal number is reckoned in thousands fed.

What we will now endeavour to do is to show how the three tribal numbers, the called, the healed, and the fed, are related to one another and grow out of one another in St Mark's living thought. And first of all we will take up the question of the relation between the twelve-fold and the thirteen-fold counting of the tribes of Israel.

Israel, or Jacob, had twelve sons and no more. But on his death-bed, and before he made his oracles of (sometimes rather equivocal) blessing on his twelve sons, he blessed the two sons of Joseph, Ephraim and Manasseh, adopting them as his own children on a footing of equality with any of the others (Gen. XLVIII). So Joseph became two tribes, Ephraim and Manasseh. And so it proved in historical fact. There was no such thing as a tribal unit or a tribal territory called 'Joseph'. There were just Ephraim and Manasseh. One might still speak poetically of 'the house of Joseph', but if one did, the sense was uncertain; one might be understood to include Benjamin.

In fact there were thirteen tribes. But it was not considered proper to say so. No Biblical writer ever makes a simple list of the thirteen names, or says in so many words that the tribes were thirteen. There are two methods of evasion. The more obvious is to use the twelve original names, and to subdivide Joseph. 'Joseph', one said, 'that is, (*a*) Ephraim . . . (*b*) Manasseh . . .'. The other method is introduced in the Book of Numbers and several times repeated there. According to this method one let the name of Joseph go and counted the actual tribes, but without Levi. Levi is taken out of the list that he may be offered to the Lord. He is on a completely different plane. So now we have 'Levi and the twelve tribes'. This idea receives perfect expression in the arrangement of the camp in the wilderness according to 'Numbers'. The Levites camp about the tabernacle in the midst, the rest around them in a hollow square, three tribes to the north, three to the east, and so on (Num. II).

Let us now compare what St Mark does. He keeps to Biblical usage in never making a list of thirteen names, and never actually counting on a basis of thirteen. There is a list of apostolic names; it contains twelve, and we are told in so · many words that Jesus instituted twelve. Then again the loaves and thousands are handled by actual counting, and the basis taken is twelve. On the other hand the persons healed are nowhere counted by the evangelist or set together in any list. No Biblical convention is violated by there being actually thirteen of them.

Nevertheless we may fairly ask, why should St Mark introduce the refinement of having an uncounted thirteen alongside his counted twelves? Surely his symbolical scheme would have been simpler and more manageable if he had been content to narrate twelve healings only. What could he have lost, to outweigh the gain in simplicity and plainness?

We are already acquainted with the answer to the question we have just asked. Twelve is a self-contained number, it has the character of completeness. But it was St Mark's purpose to suggest that the series of healing narratives is fundamentally incomplete. The Gospel healings are nothing in themselves. They merely prefigure the great healing which is the resurrection of the Lord. That is the fourteenth healing.

Thirteen is an untidy number, to the Jewish mind. It requires either to be reduced to twelve, as was done in the Old Testament tribal lists, or to be increased to fourteen, for fourteen is almost as good a number as twelve, being a double seven. St Mark handles the thirteen in both ways. He begins by deriving the thirteen healings from the official twelve tribal persons by one of the two Old Testament methods of reckoning indicated above. Then, having got his thirteen healings, he crowns them with a fourteenth, the Lord's resurrection.

To begin with, how does St Mark get the thirteen healed out of the Twelve called? He uses the second Old Testament method, that is to say, he reckons Levi as additional to the Twelve called, and quietly pairs a person healed with each of the Twelve, and one with Levi too.

It was fortunate for St Mark that Christ called a man named Levi into the number of his disciples, without actually making him one of the Twelve. It was fortunate, but it was not very surprising. A few names did very hard service in plebeian Galilee. Johns, Simons, Judahs, Josephs, Jacobs and Levis abounded. According to St Mark's second chapter, the disciples of Jesus who went about with him were already numerous before he instituted the Twelve from amongst them by his own personal choice. It was as likely as not that the group of those who had been called to be companions but were not called to be apostles should include a man named Levi; and in fact it did. St Mark is acquainted with his father's name as well as his own. This Levi was the son of Alphaeus, and he was a publican—let us say, a customs clerk—by trade.

Provided by happy chance with the person and name of Levi, St Mark has no difficulty in managing the twelve and the thirteen. His first concern is to get into our heads the general equivalence between callings and healings. So, after recording the historical fact that Jesus began his public ministry by calling two pairs of brothers, he proceeds to use the freedom of an historian and to

select out of the many healings Jesus performed two pairs of cures
for detailed narration. Moreover, he underlines the relation of
the two pairs of persons healed to the two pairs of brothers called,
by narrating in the first pair of healings the cure of a family relation of one of the first pair of brothers called. As soon as we have
read enough healing stories to be aware that there is a pair of
them—as soon, that is, as we have reached the second—we discover in the person healed the mother-in-law of Simon Peter.

So far we have four persons called, and four healed. No sooner
is the fourth healed than Christ calls a fifth man, Levi; he calls
him in a way which cannot fail to remind us of the calling of the
four—from beside the sea, and from the midst of his business.
This time the attentive reader may naturally expect that the
single call will be followed by a single healing. Nor is he dis-
appointed; Levi having been called, the man with the withered
hand is healed. So five have been called, and five have been healed.

The principle that there is a healing for every calling having
been now sufficiently established, St Mark can proceed to the call
and institution of the whole Twelve. Among the Twelve the four
first called are found, but Levi is not found. So there are eight
fresh apostolic names. As we have by now got hold of the principle of one healing for every calling, we know that the Gospel will
contain eight more persons healed, and of course it does. Such is
St Mark's simple way of reconciling the thirteen healed with the
twelve called. Levi is called and then discounted, but the healing
which matches his call, the healing of the withered hand, is in no
way discounted. So there are twelve apostles (and Levi), but
there are just thirteen persons healed.

The twelve-fold number of the apostles is obtained by discounting Levi; the twelve-fold number of the loaves and thousands is
also connected with the discounting of Levi, as we now proceed
to show. We saw in the preceding chapter that the numerical
symbolism of the loaves and thousands derives from the act of
David when he took the priestly shewbread for himself and his
lay companions. According to the Law, all the twelve loaves are
the perquisite of the Levitical priests, even though they stand for

the twelve tribes of Israel. What David begins and Christ completes is the distribution of the priestly bread to the laity. There is no question of the distribution of it *to* the priests; it is taken *from* the priests, and given to the laymen. Therefore the twelve thousands who are in the end to receive the twelve loaves must be seen as the lay tribes—the longer tribal list, with Levi taken out of it.

If the symbolism of the twelve loaves springs from the text about David and the shewbread, then it springs from the Levitical cycle of St Mark's Gospel. The healing which is matched by St Mark with the calling of Levi is the healing of the withered hand. And this healing, as we have shown above (p. 160), is intimately connected with the text about David and the shewbread. After telling the scribes how David had entered the house of God and overriden the custom of the priests by taking shewbread, Christ proceeds immediately to enter the synagogue himself, and override the custom of the scribes by healing the withered hand. This is the Levitical healing sign, being the healing sign coupled with the call of Levi. But we see that as a Levitical sign it is negative. Through its relation to the saying about David and the Levitical priests, it is a sign of the abolition of Levitical privileges.

We are now in a position to understand what St Mark means by the discounting of Levi. Something very different, certainly, from what the Book of Numbers means by it. In Numbers the Levites are taken out of the list to be set by themselves on a higher plane of holiness. To speak of Levi and the Twelve would be like speaking of Israel and the nations. Whereas in the Gospel the Twelve are counted without Levi, because Levi as a separate people ceases to be. When Levi's privileges are distributed, his existence is distributed; all become Levitical, all become priests.

In fact Levi had never had a territory or a separate political existence. The Levites were settled among the lay tribes, and if they lost their privileges they would be merged with their neighbours. Persons of Levitical family were called by Christ, for example St Barnabas, and, says St Luke, a large company of the priests became obedient to the faith (Acts VI, 7). Such calls are typified by the call of the man named Levi in the Gospel. But these men are not called as forming a peculiar people among the saints, or as being privileged alone to receive what is now the holiest of all holy things, the bread of God. Levi is merged in a twelve-fold lay Israel, which is no longer lay, for it has all become Levitical. All are Levites. There is no one Levi among the twelve apostles.

We may begin to congratulate ourselves on having dealt with the relation between apostles, persons healed, and loaves or thousands. But there is still an aspect of the matter not yet touched, which threatens to be more elusive and harder to seize.

When we were discussing the relation of the thirteen persons healed to the twelve apostles, we were able to deal with the whole matter in a pattern of three lines or stages.

(a) Four men called and four persons healed.

(b) Levi called and one person healed.

(c) The Twelve called, including the four but excluding Levi, and in the sequel eight more persons healed, corresponding to the eight new apostolic names.

According to this pattern, it is only in (a) and (b) that the number of men called corresponds to the number of persons to be healed within the cycle which the calling initiates. When we reach (c) we reach a cycle in which three persons are in fact going to be healed, but the story of calling pays no attention to that; the number of men called is twelve, not three, and even the new names among those called are not three, but eight. After this the series of diminishing groups of healings continues to run on; two persons are healed in VII and one in VIII, one is healed in IX and one in X, but no corresponding small numbers of apostles are called.

It is true, certainly, that once the Twelve are called no more apostolic or quasi-apostolic persons are called; the exact equation between persons called and persons healed in each cycle is not kept up beyond the cycle of Levi. But it is not true, even so, that all numerical equivalence between the call-stories and the groups of healings within the several cycles breaks off after the cycle of Levi. It continues, in fact, in a modified form.

The number of persons called in the cycle following that of Levi is twelve, not three, but there is a group of three nevertheless specially marked out among the Twelve. The story of the institution of the Twelve is at the same time the story of the surnaming of Simon, James and John. In instituting the Twelve Christ gave a special place to his three chosen witnesses, the Stone and the two Sons of Thunder.

Within the cycle which the apostolic institution initiates, St Mark shows us what the special place of the three witnesses meant. They alone were to be taken to be witnesses to the resuscitation of Jairus's child. In showing this, St Mark also shows us something else—that the three witness-apostles are to be related to the three healings of their cycle, just as the four apostles first called were related to the four healings of theirs. It is the *third* healing of the three, to which the three chief apostles are made witnesses. In reading this, we recall a similar stroke of arithmetical emphasis: the fourth person healed in the group of four was carried in by *four* bearers to the house where Jesus healed him.

St Mark is not merely playing with numbers. The three healings in v represent the healing work of the three days from Good Friday to Easter Sunday. The evangelist is showing us that Christ, when in deference to Jewish usage he appointed three special witnesses and neither more nor less, was appointing them witnesses to his threefold work, the work of Friday, Saturday and Sunday, of crucifixion, lying entombed, and rising. So St Mark finds a place for the three alongside of the twelve.

In the cycle we have just been looking at, Christ institutes the Twelve that they may be with him, and that they may be sent on mission: but the sending on mission is in abeyance for the present; it does not actually happen within the cycle; only the being with him is as yet in force. Being with him, according to the evangelist's narrative, means seeing what he does and hearing what he says, being, in fact, witnesses to his words and acts. (It also means asking him questions.) And so the part of the three as special witnesses is appropriate to this cycle of St Mark's Gospel.

With the next cycle (VI) the 'being sent on mission' comes into force, and that means that the number *three* gives place to the number *two*. Three is the number of witnesses, but two is the conventional number of delegates or emissaries. The call-story of this cycle is concerned with all the Twelve, just as the call-story of the previous cycle was. But there the three witnesses were appointed at the head of the Twelve, and here all the Twelve are sent forth two by two. 'Two' stands for mission, just as 'three' stands for witness.

So far so good; but meanwhile what is happening to the parallel between apostolic numbers and numbers of persons healed? In the cycle which instituted the three witnesses there were also three healings; in the cycle which sends the apostles two by two there are not two healings, there are, indeed, no particularized healings at all; for this is that one anomalous cycle following the resurrection of Jairus's child and containing no healing narrative of the usual kind.

What it does contain is the feeding of five thousand. In the feeding of five thousand and the feeding of four thousand the theme of the twelve apostles on mission (sent two by two, that is) continues to be worked out. Through their twelve pairs of hands the world, both Jewish and Greek, receives the twelve mystical loaves Jesus breaks, and they it is whose creels gather the twelve-fold abundance of leavings out of which all mankind is evermore to be fed. Both the feedings of multitudes must be seen on the background of the apostolic mission in VI, 7–12, and until the second feeding has taken place there are no further scenes of apostolic mission or calling to distract our attention. Two cycles pass by without the usual apostolic scene for their opening (VII and VIII), a fact on which we have commented before (p. 95). As a consequence, St Mark's scheme of apostolic numbers and numbers healed has a chance to pull even again. In VI, 7–12 he put forward the apostolic number *two*, but there were no healings at all, let alone two healings, in that cycle. But in the next cycle the two healings duly turn up (the child of the Syrophoeness and the deaf stammerer) and as no apostolic calling has intervened, we may be allowed to pair them with the number *two* in VI, 7–12, for are they not the next healing actually recorded after the mission of the Twelve?

Once again, St Mark's scheme of numbers is no meaningless piece of mathematical elegance. The disciples sent by twos signify the mission to the world, and the two healings in VII are of all the healings in the book the two most concerned with the world-mission. The story of the Syrophoeness and her child tells us how the crumbs of Israelite bread are permitted to the Gentiles. This happens in the north-west (Phoenicia). In the pair to it, the Effatha miracle, Jesus has crossed to the opposite extreme, the south-east, to perform his mighty work in Greek Decapolis.

We have said that the theme of the Twelve on mission continues to work out through the two feedings of the multitudes, and so it runs over three short cycles (VI, VII, and VIII). The next cycle makes a fresh beginning, so far as the theme of apostolic mission and calling is concerned. Now this cycle is the cycle of the one healing; for in this cycle the constantly diminishing block of healings has at last shrunk to unity. The epileptic boy is healed alone. Does the number *one* have any corresponding prominence in the scene of apostolic calling with which the cycle opens?

The scene of apostolic calling to which we refer is the Transfiguration. But the Transfiguration is hardly separable from the discourses at Caesarea Philippi which are its prelude, and in these discourses the apostolic *one*, St Peter, takes the lead for the first time in an effective way by confessing Christ. In the Transfiguration the two other witnesses, James and John, accompany him; but it is Peter alone who speaks. But the significance of the one in relation to the Transfiguration is not rightly understood merely by observing that St Peter outshines his two companions by finding a voice, even if to no very good effect. The Transfiguration is not concerned with the singularity of St Peter among the three earthly witnesses; it is concerned with the singularity of Christ among the three heavenly witnesses to the truth of God. The three apostolic witnesses go up the mountain, and are confronted with three heavenly witnesses, Law (Moses), Prophecy

(Elijah) and Gospel (Jesus). And what they learn is that the three cannot be enshrined in parity side by side; Moses and Elijah pass away, and Jesus is authenticated as the one sufficient witness to the truth of God: 'This is my beloved Son, hear ye him.'

What is the relation of the uniqueness of the heavenly *one*, Jesus, to that of the earthly *one*, Peter? Through the oneness of Jesus the oneness of Peter is both revealed and abased. It is revealed: for the one Peter among the apostles and the one *prohistamenos* (afterwards bishop) in every Church is the sacramental expression of the one Christ. It is abased: for compared with Christ Peter is nothing, he is singular and first not by his merit but by the merit of Christ. If Peter confessed Christ, did he not also attack his teaching of the passion? If he ventured into the High Priest's courtyard, did not he also deny? It is no accident that the cycle of the Gospel which reveals Peter as the one is also the cycle which contains Christ's rebuke to his disciples for discussing who is senior or chief (IX, 33–37).

Let us now review the series we have been following:

Call of the four first disciples

(Call of Levi)

Surnaming of the three witnesses

(Mission two by two)

Earthly one and heavenly one.

I have placed in brackets the call scenes which initiate second halves of St Mark's double cycles, the halves which we have elsewhere called annexe cycles. If we leave these out, we may be struck by an interesting fact about the others. The four first called are Peter and Andrew, James and John. The three surnamed witnesses are Peter, James and John. The earthly or apostolic *one* is Peter. We have to do, that is, with a gradual diminution in a group of the same four names. The series is not perfectly regular, for there is no two. The four first called are reduced to the three witnesses, but there are no two consuls to whom the three witnesses are reduced, before they are reduced to the one leader. St Mark is obedient to history. Christ called four first, he surnamed three witnesses, he made one leader, but he made no pair of consuls.

He sent out all the Twelve two by two, but that is another matter.

Allowing for the gap (there is no two) we may compare the steadily diminishing group of the same four men with the steadily diminishing group of the same four healing themes:

1st double cycle	Simon Andrew; James John	Exorcism Restoration, Cleansing Restoration
2nd double cycle	Simon James John	Exorcism Cleansing Restoration
3rd double cycle	. . . . .	Exorcism Restoration
4th double cycle	Simon	Exorcism

(It may be forcing the point a little to make the *one* healing an exorcism, for it is a compound miracle, being a restoration also; but still the exorcisive character undoubtedly predominates; if we are to give it one name, it is an exorcism.)

The table we have written above does not prove that St Mark's imagination was highly elaborate; on the contrary, it proves that it was simple. The evangelist was content to allow the same pattern, the same form of order, to do double duty. The two sides of the parallel mean the same thing; they illustrate and explain one another. Why do the four healings condense towards unity in the successive groups? The unity towards which they are straining is Christ. The last healing in the series, the *one*, seems perfectly expressive, it seems to have everything. It is the expulsion of Satan, it is the quickening of the spiritual powers, it is health through falling dead and rising again, it is the salvation of the son of the father. But still it is a mere symbol, a mere fore-shewing; we must go forward into the passion and resurrection of Christ to find the substance of salvation.

It is the same with the narrowing of the apostolic group. Four (not to say twelve) are too many; only three are worthy or capable of the higher mysteries. Again three are too many; one alone can represent Majesty. But the one is not what he represents. No, he attacks the truth, he denies Truth Himself; he must be left behind weeping in the High Priest's court, while Christ goes on alone to save the world.

St Mark makes his meaning perfectly clear by repeating the pattern of the four, three and one in the passion. The first half of the last double cycle opens with the four, Peter, James, John and Andrew, questioning Jesus on the Mount of Olives, and receiving in answer his apocalypse. The second half of the double cycle begins with Jesus climbing the Mount of Olives again. But now the four are too many; he takes the three alone with him when he goes aside to pray. They could not watch, they could not supplicate, their flesh was weak, they fell into temptation, and when the armed men appeared they ran with the rest. Peter turned again and followed afar off into the High Priest's court; only the one was left now. And had Christ been acquitted Peter would have seemed to have done well. But Christ was condemned, his discredit soon spread to his follower, and Peter denied. So Christ went on alone; Simon the Cyrenian carried his cross for him, not Simon Peter, and the places to his left and his right were occupied not by the Sons of Zebedee who had asked to have them, but by thieves.

CHAPTER XV

TRIBAL SYMBOLISM

We come now to a chapter about which the author is in two minds whether it ought to be written or not. The conventional criticism of the sort of literary analysis this book attempts is, that it is impossible to know when we are pursuing the further refinements of a true exegesis, and when we are indulging in subjective, though perhaps 'ingenious' delusions. So far as the main part of this book is concerned, we are prepared to answer such criticism. The forms of St Mark's imagination which we have described give one another so much mutual support and play in so closely together and are so nearly related to the matter of his meaning, that they can look after themselves. But the subject of this present chapter has a marginal character which makes it a fair target for the criticism we have mentioned. For it opens up a realm of symbolism developing, indeed, out of the solid structure of the Marcan pattern, but spreading away into a fresh field. It seems possible to interpret the Gospel sufficiently without it, and it is not easy to find confirmation or support for it in the more evident parts of the symbolic structure. I shall therefore open up the question, do my best with it, and leave it to the reader's judgement. If he decides that this chapter would be better omitted, he has nearly half the author's mind on his side. All I beg is, that my indiscretion may not be tied like a stone round my neck, to drown me. It is only fastened with a single knot; if it is dead weight, please have the humanity to detach it, and then let me hope that I may yet swim to shore.

The question we have to consider arises out of the play St Mark makes with the name of Levi. He seems to square the general pattern of the Gospel by treating Levi the Son of Alphaeus as a symbol of Levi the patriarch or—which is virtually the same thing—of Levi the priestly tribe. And in so doing he gives the healing which he has paired with the call of Levi a specially Levitical significance. The cure of the withered hand, through its relation to the saying about David and the priests, is made to express the overriding and removal of Levitical privileges. The anointed prince, David, is set over against the anointed priest, Abiathar, and Abiathar gives way to David. It is often pointed out that Abimelech, not Abiathar, was the anointed priest when David took the shewbread; Abiathar was 'high priest' as yet only in that weaker sense familiar to St Mark's day, when the title was extended to the members of the high-priestly family. St Mark may be making an error, but if so, his error, like other people's, is the by-product of his intention. By putting Abiathar for Abimelech he makes the contrast between prince and priest absolutely typical—Abiathar became the high priest of David's reign. To say 'David and Abiathar' is like saying 'Zerubbabel and Joshua' or 'Judah and Levi'.

If, then, Levi the publican is made to sustain the role of Levi the Patriarch, and if St Mark's system turns on 'Levi and the Twelve' (lay patriarchs), the question arises, whether the Twelve are one by one identified with individual tribes or patriarchs also? Of course it would be all quite simple if the Twelve had borne the names Reuben, Simeon, Judah, Issachar, Zebulon and so forth. Then as Levi stands for Levi, Reuben might stand for Reuben, and so with the rest. But as it is, only two names of tribal patriarchs occur in the apostolic list, and one of those (to make it more difficult) comes twice. There are two Simeons or Simons (the names are really the same) and one Judah. Here is nothing but trouble; what are you to do with two Simeons, and how can you allow Iscariot to represent Messiah's own tribe? Judas may stand for Jewry, regarded as the people who sell their Saviour to the Gentiles. But that is a secondary point. A list of apostles should stand for the true Israel, the Israel of God, and the Messianic tribe is not well represented by Iscariot in such a company.

The apostles cannot be counted off against the tribal patriarchs on the score of their names, and it is fairly evident that they are not so counted off on any other grounds either. An interpreter who set out to prove that Bartholomew or James the Son of

Alphaeus stood for one tribe rather than another in St Mark's mind would be a trifler amusing himself with the demonstration of paradoxes.

Does not that close the question and end the chapter? Not quite. Another line of inquiry remains open. There are Levi and the Twelve, there are also the thirteen persons healed, and these persons are counted off against Levi and the Twelve. In the case of Levi himself, the healed person who corresponds to him is given a Levitical significance, as we have seen. It is possible, then, that St Mark gives a distinct tribal significance not to the apostles one by one, but to the healings one by one.

But surely, you may say, that does not mean anything. It is possible to give a Levitical significance to the sign of the withered hand because Levi had a significance, anyway; he was the priestly tribe. Reuben, perhaps, had a significance, being the first-born, and Judah, being the royal tribe, and then we all know the story of Joseph. But what is the significance of Zebulon or Gad, or any of the rest for that matter? If St Mark equated the persons healed with the tribal patriarchs he was indulging in the most frigid Rabbinical elaboration, and adding nothing whatever to the message of his Gospel.

Such an objection would be unanswerable, were it not that the Jews of St Mark's time and the century before seem to have had a taste for moralizing and allegorizing on the persons of the twelve tribal patriarchs. Much high spiritual doctrine gathered round what are to us barren names, and by running over them in order St Mark might hope to be put in mind of many matters of real importance.

In the heyday of the Maccabean Kingdom the author of the Book of Jubilees enlarged with much freedom on Genesis and part of Exodus, displaying by the way a knowledge of the characters and actions of Levi, Judah, Reuben and their brethren which may well astonish the modern reader. There already existed, it would seem, a 'Last Will and Testament' of Levi,[1] for the edification of the Jewish priesthood; and on the basis of it, and of the sort of lore which appears in Jubilees, someone—per-

[1] A fragment survives. See appendix to Charles's *Twelve Testaments*.

haps the author of Jubilees himself—composed a complete set of Testaments for all the Twelve Patriarchs. You would not think it could be done without insufferable monotony, and there is some monotony, certainly. But on the whole the work must be pronounced a great success. Making a most skilful use of the few scriptural phrases devoted to his several heroes, the author elaborates them into a gallery of Jewish types, the captain, the priest, the soldier, the farmer, the fisherman, the casuist, the penitent lustful, the penitent choleric, the penitent envious, and so on. The Testaments teach a safe and disciplined, but truly generous and amiable piety, and it is a commonplace to say that the spiritual teaching of Christ finds in some things its closest anticipation in their pages.

The book was as popular as it deserved to be, and was translated into Greek. It was known, probably in its Greek dress, to St Paul and St Matthew and other New Testament writers. I refer my readers to the late Dr. R. H. Charles's introductions for the proof of these facts. Since Dr. Charles wrote, a new evidence of the influence of the 'Testaments' has come to light. Dr. Arnold Meyer (*Das Raetsel des Jacobusbriefes*, Giessen, 1930) showed that the Epistle of St James is composed on a Twelve-Tribes basis, a fact fairly enough suggested by its exordium, 'Jacobus . . . to the Twelve Tribes . . . greeting'. On Dr. Meyer's view, the Christian writer is working from a Jewish 'Letter of Jacob' in Hebrew. I confess that I should like to see the experiment tried of dispensing with the Jewish 'Letter', and crediting a bilingual disciple of St James with the wit to allegorize St James for himself as a new Jacob writing to his twelve-fold family the Church. Such a disciple would need no other model than the Twelve Testaments themselves. But whether this view or Dr. Meyer's view is taken, the disjointed paragraphs of the Epistle are revealed as little homilies on the patriarchal names taken in due order.

Was St Mark acquainted with the *Twelve Testaments*? The peculiar quality and style of his writing make it less easy to answer. St Mark is not much given to verbal quotation, and verbal quotation is the scholar's favourite evidence for literary dependence. St Mark does not quote the Old Testament much either, but he is nourished on the substance of it, and so perfectly assimilates it that he can write it into the matter of his own sentences. St Matthew quotes more, but is he really more scriptural?

St Mark's dislike for writing out scripture citations is no evidence that he was ignorant of scripture, and his lack of verbal quotations from the Twelve Testaments is no evidence that he had not read them. And there are certain things in the Testaments which have a Marcan look. For example, Levi (the most Messianic person, so to speak, among the Twelve, in the view of the Jewish writer) anticipates the heavenly visions and ecstasies of his greatest descendant, Moses. And what is Levi's Sinai, his visionary mountain-top? Sirion or Hermon (it is the same thing). Now according to St Mark, the visions which Moses and Elijah had enjoyed on Sinai were renewed in Christ's presence on a high mountain-top, which, being reached from the region of Caesarea Philippi, is commonly presumed to be Mount Hermon. To take another point: the Testaments of Levi and Judah contain little apocalypses which carefully supplement one another. Levi informs his children how his great descendant (the idealized Maccabean High Priest) will introduce an age of gold. Judah touches on the same matters, in order to add that when the golden age has been established by Levitical virtue, his line (the house of David) will shoot again, to take over the lay principality as of old. Both Levi and Judah speak in an identical sense of the great Levitical person in the last times:

The heavens shall be opened, and from the temple of glory shall come upon him hallowing, with the Father's voice as from Abraham to Isaac; and the glory of the Most High shall be uttered over him, and the Spirit of understanding and of hallowing shall rest on him (Test. Lev. xviii, 6, 7).

The heavens shall be opened unto him, to pour out the Spirit, the blessing of the Holy Father (Test. Jud. xxiv, 2).

The text of the Testaments is uncertain, and it is possible to attack these verses as Christian interpolations based on the Marcan Baptism narrative (which the other evangelists obviously transcribe). But the Christian interpolator, if we are going to suppose him, must have been a man of unusual cunning. He saw that it was useless to interpolate the Testament of Levi without interpolating the Testament of Judah at the corresponding point; he saw that the Testament of Judah, since it is going over the same ground, ought to use more summary phrases. And, realizing that it would be too barefaced to write 'with the Father's voice in blessing on the only or beloved (*agapetos*) Son', he thought of the unobtrusively Jewish and scriptural paraphrase, 'with the Father's voice as from Abraham to Isaac', remembering that Isaac has the repeated description '*agapetos* son' in the story of Abraham's sacrifice: remembering also that it was by his sacrifice that Abraham earned a unique blessing which descended whole upon Isaac, and that it was at the sacrifice that he was spoken with out of heaven. This interpolator is the man for my money; if I am allowed to have him, exegetical problems of all kinds will yield to my touch like oiled locks to the master-key. But until the learned public has advanced several degrees in credulity, I despair of so much happiness, and make do with the alternative hypothesis that St Mark found the verses we have cited above in the Testaments, understood 'as from Abraham to Isaac' perfectly well, and decoded it into simple prose, as an expression of that ecstasy of divine sonship which seized Jesus at his Baptism.

There is, then, some *prima facie* evidence that St Mark knew the Twelve Testaments. But, we may go on to enquire, is there anything in the Testaments to suggest what we have decided to investigate—the tribal patriarchs in the role of sick persons healed by divine grace? Well, seven of the patriarchs are models of virtue and no sickness overtakes them. The remaining five are penitent sinners whose sicknesses both requited and expressed their sins. They were saved by God, usually at the intercession of Israel, who stands here, as it were, in the place of Christ. The lustful Reuben would have died of a plague of the loins, but for his father's intercession (T. Reub. i, 7). We may perhaps compare Mark v, 25-34. Wrathful Simeon's hand withered, because he put it forth against his brother Judah (T. Sim. ii, 12). It was restored through prayer. Cf. Mark III, 1-6. Judah, through pursuit of lucre, lost his children and would have died childless, had not his repentance and his father's prayers won acceptance (T. Jud. XIX, 2). We may think of Jairus. Gad's hatred so inflamed his liver, that he was diseased of it, and would have died but for Israel's prayers (T. Gad v, 9). Dan, the fifth sinner, was not physically plagued, but he preaches to his children from his own experience on spiritual blindness caused by wrath. And we may add that throughout the Testaments the allegorical treatment of over-mastering passions as possessing demons is commonplace. It is not only, then, that the Testaments present the picture of patriarchs sick and later healed. It is that their sicknesses, like those in the Gospel, represent sins.

We may conclude, then, that as the reading of the Twelve Testaments influenced St Mark's handling of the Baptism and Transfiguration narratives, so it influenced his handling of the Lord's healing mission, inclining him to treat it as a healing of the twelve-fold (or thirteen-fold) Israel. It by no means follows from this that the evangelist should particularize each person healed as this or that tribal patriarch; but it follows, perhaps, that it is worth our while looking to see whether he did so or not.

Whatever St Mark did, he did not sit down, as the writer of St James's epistle presumably did, to write his book in the form of concealed allegory on twelve or thirteen tribal names. The tribal symbolism of St Mark, if indeed he has any, is secondary and incidental. Nor does he start off with it. It arises as he proceeds, and weaves itself in with the other strands of his design. Let us trace it from the beginning and see how it grows (if it grows; but this form of speech becomes wearisome, and I trust that the reader will supply the qualifications henceforward for himself. We will write in ordinary positive style).

St Mark begins by telling us how Sim(e)on and three others were called, and how Simon's mother-in-law was healed in Simon's house, and three other persons in various places. So far nothing has happened to make us think of patriarchs or tribes at all. But when he goes on to tell us how Levi was called to the same discipleship and in the same manner and from beside the same shore, we do not need to be very learned to recall Jacob's oracle, 'Simeon and Levi are brethren' (Gen. XLIX, 5), the layman and the priest. We read on, and in the healing associated with Levi's call we find the subject of the Levitical priesthood and its privileges touched upon, when Christ acts after the example of David overriding the privileges of Abiathar.

So far we have nothing beyond the suggestion (a) Simeon and three other laymen, (b) Levi the priest, five persons in all, divided into two lots, the lay and the priestly. There were many ways of arranging the list of twelve tribes, but all of them placed Simeon and Levi among the first five. So the Bible-minded reader may well conceive the idea that he is dealing with the beginning of the tribal list, with the lay tribes and the priestly segregated from one another.

He reads on, and finds the place taken by the call of Simon and his friends in the first cycle of narrative, and by the call of Levi alone in the second cycle, occupied by the call of all the twelve together in the third cycle. Now he discovers the reason for the segregation of Levi from the four laymen: they are called among the twelve, he is not; no doubt the Twelve is a list of the lay tribes, with Joseph taken double. So the call of the Twelve helps to guide us along the line of thought we are pursuing; but there is one sort of guidance it fails to give us. The call of the four suggests that the group of four persons to be healed first may represent Simeon and three allied tribes; the call of Levi suggests that the one person to be healed next represents the tribe of Levi. The call of the Twelve is, in fact, going to be followed by a group of three healings, but it gives us no guidance at all for connecting these healings with any tribes rather than any others.

If such guidance is displaced from the call of the Twelve by more urgent matters, perhaps it is not displaced very far. Suppose we try the next paragraph. Here Satan is introduced under the less usual name of Beelzebul. Beel-Zebul is a compound name, 'Lord of the Dwelling', and the tribal name Zebulon is derived by scripture from the same root ZBL. 'Now', said Leah the

slighted wife, 'my husband will *dwell* with me, since I have
borne him a sixth son' (Gen. xxx, 20). St Mark, if he got so far
as to think about tribal allegory at all, cannot have missed the
derivation of Zebulon's name. It might still be supposed, however, that he used Beelzebul as an equivalent for 'Satan' without
reflecting on the derivation of it. It might be supposed, but only
so long as we keep our eyes averted from St Mark's text. If we
turn them in that direction we shall see that Christ's Beelzebul
riddles are a series of plays upon 'Lord of the Dwelling'. 'How
can Satan cast out Satan? If a *kingdom* be divided against itself,
that kingdom cannot stand' (so much for *Beel*, Lord). 'And if a
house be divided against itself, that house cannot stand' (so much
for 'House' *Zebul*). 'And if *Satan* is risen against himself and
divided, he cannot stand' (so much for *Beelzebul*). 'But no man
can enter into the *strong man's house* and spoil his goods, unless
he first bind the strong man, and then will he spoil his house' (so
much for the *Lord of the House*). The verbal clue to these riddles
was still well enough understood when St Matthew wrote: 'If
they have called the Lord of the house Beelzebul, how much more
his household?' (Matt. x, 25).

It is just worth recording that the Testament of Zebulon
contains a passage about unity and division which reminds us of
the Beelzebul riddles, although it does not play on Zebulon's
name as the riddles do. 'Observe the waters, and know that when
they flow together they sweep along stones, trees, earth and
other things; but if they are divided into many streams, the earth
swallows them up, and they become of no account. So shall ye
also be if ye be divided. Be not ye therefore divided into two
heads, for everything that the Lord made has but one head . . .
For I have learnt in the writings of my fathers that ye shall be
divided in Israel, and follow two kings' (T. Zeb. ix).

The healing which follows next after the riddles of Beelzebul
is the exorcism of Legion and, as we have said before, it illustrates the Beelzebul riddles point by point. 'If Satan be risen
against himself he cannot stand'—'Night and day the man was
crying and cutting himself to pieces with stones'. 'None can enter

the house of the strong man and plunder his stuff, unless he first binds the strong'.—'None could any longer bind him, even with a chain, for he had often been bound with fetters and chains, but the chains had been pulled in pieces by him and the fetters smashed, and none had strength to master him' until Jesus mastered him with a word. The general effect of the Beelzebul parables is to show that Christ's mastery of the many demons he exorcises is due to his having bound their 'lord'. In the episode of the Gerasene we see how Christ not only 'binds the strong', but disposes of a whole regiment of Beelzebul's host according to his pleasure.

So it may be a fair guess that Legion is the Zebulonite healing, being the next healing after the Beelzebul riddles, and closely united to them in sense. There is a further point which supports such a suggestion. When we were analysing IV–V (pp. 85 ff.) we showed that the stilling of the storm is a twin to the exorcism of Legion: both are regarded as examples of the mastery of rebellious 'breath' by Christ, and both are written in antitype to a single model, the exorcism in synagogue. Now the stilling of the storm may fairly be regarded as a Zebulonite story. It is the typical story about Christ sailing the sea; its antitype, the walking on the water, represents Christ not as sailor, but rather as the divine presence of Exodus, leading his people to safety. Zebulon, according to the 'Testaments', is the sailor or fisherman among the Twelve, just as Issachar is the husbandman, and he tells us in his Testament how he was saved at sea for his piety when others were lost. The Testament is building on Jacob's oracle, 'Zebulon shall dwell at the shore of the sea, and he shall be a beach for ships'. In St Mark's day it was probably held that the 'sea' to which Jacob refers was no other than the Sea of Galilee, since 'Zebulon and Naphtali' was an equivalent for 'Galilee'. Almost the only known Zebulonite hero was the prophet Jonah; his city Gath-hepher is expressly reckoned to Zebulon in Joshua XIX, 13. Jonah went a-sailing, and the adventure which befell him is the manifest literary model of the Marcan story.

'And the Lord raised a breath upon the sea, and the wave

became great on the sea, and the ship was in danger to be broken.
. . . But Jonas had gone down into the waist of the ship and lay
and slept. And the captain came to him and said, 'Why sleepest
thou? Arise and call upon thy God, that God may save us and
we perish not . . .' (Jonah showed them what to do, and) 'the sea
stayed from her surge, and the men feared the Lord with great
fear'.—'And there arises a great storm of wind, and the waves
beat into the ship, so that the ship began to fill. And he was in
the stern on the cushion sleeping. And they rouse him and say to
him, Rabbi, carest thou not that we perish? And he arose and
rebuked the wind . . . And the wind abated and there was a
great calm . . . And they feared a great fear . . .'

Perhaps it is fair to conclude, then, that the exorcism of the
Legion stands for the salvation of Zebulon and even that St
Mark's having such a thought in his mind influenced in some way
his management of his matter in IV–V.

The exorcism of Legion is the first of three healings in a group;
if the first is to be assigned to Zebulon, to what tribal names
should the other two be assigned? Let us look for our indication
in the beginning of the sequel to the story of Legion. In the case
of Legion, we found our indication in a strange proper name
(Beelzebul). Suppose, then, we take the next strange proper
name that meets us after the end of the story of the Gerasene.
We do not have to wait long. 'And when Jesus had crossed over
again in the ship to the other side much people gathered about
him. And he was by the sea when one of the rulers of synagogue
came to him, Jairus by name . . .' What can we connect with the
name 'Jairus'? Jairus, or Jair, is one of the minor judges in the
Book of Judges (Judges X, 3), and he is several times in scripture
said to be a Manassite. Not, you may say, the most famous name
among Manassites; but nevertheless of all Manassite names the most
appropriate to the present occasion, for it can be interpreted as 'JAH
awakens'. One of the most striking features of the Jairus story is
Christ's refusal to speak of the little girl as dead; she sleeps, for
she is to be awakened by the Lord. Jair was a judge of Israel; Jairus
is nothing quite so splendid, but at least he is a ruler of synagogue.

The tribal identification of Jairus and his daughter carries with it that of the woman who touched the Lord's garment. These two healings, that of the twelve-year-old girl and that of the woman twelve years afflicted, are the only two healings interwoven with one another in St Mark's narrative; and similarly Joseph is the only double tribe among the twelve. If the healing of Jairus's daughter is the healing of Manasseh, without doubt the healing of the woman is the healing of Ephraim.

But is it not an unbalanced sort of symbolism which gives the name of Jair as a badge to Manasseh, and no corresponding name as a badge to Ephraim? Yes; but there is in fact no need to accuse St Mark of such a fault. When we find the Manassite judge Jair appealing to Jesus, the name of Jesus receives a special sense from the connexion. For Jesus the Son of Nun, whom we call Joshua, was the great Judge of Israel from the tribe of Ephraim. We may recall what old Mattathias said in his exhortation to his sons: 'Jesus for fulfilling the word was made a judge in Israel' (I Macc. II, 55). According to Numbers, Jairus the Judge depends upon Jesus the Judge. 'Moses gave charge concerning' the colonists of Transjordania 'to Jesus'. If they fulfil their undertakings, said Moses, 'then ye shall give them the land of Gilead for a possession . . . And the children of Machir the son of Manasseh went to Gilead and took it . . . And Jair the son of Manasseh went and took the towns thereof' (Num. XXXII, 28–41). It is recorded in the Book of Jesus how Jesus confirmed the possession of Jair (Josh. XIII, 7–8, 30). And so to find Jairus appealing to Jesus in the Gospel seems scripturally appropriate.

We have seen that St. Mark's text suggests a play on the name of Jairus, interpreting it in the sense 'JAH awakens'. Equally it may be read as containing a play on the name of Jesus, interpreted as 'JAH is salvation'. Such, of course, is the interpretation of St Matthew: 'Thou shalt call his name Jesus, for it is he that shall save his people' (I, 21). Jairus himself says to Jesus, 'Come and lay thy hand upon her that she may be *saved*'. And, as they went towards Jairus's house for this purpose, a woman in the crowd 'having heard concerning *Jesus* . . .' said, 'If I but touch his garment I shall be *saved*'. She may be seen as making another such divination as the demoniac in the synagogue or blind Bartimeus made, when they took an omen from the name *Nazarene*. Jesus himself confirmed her divination. 'Thy faith', he said, 'hath *saved* thee.'

'Save' in connexion with healing appears first in III, 4, when Christ says that it is right to save life rather than to kill on Sabbath. He gives a principle broader than the instance it has to cover. He is not actually saving life when he heals the withered hand. We do not see him as saviour of life until Jairus calls upon him to prevent his daughter's death. This is really a matter of 'salvation', and the word naturally reappears. Having reappeared, it spreads into the context, and the woman uses it, as we have seen, although her life is in no danger. There are only two other instances at all of the verb in similar contexts; both are subsequent to the passage in v, and both are manifest and conscious echoes of it. In the next chapter many people repeat the woman's attempt 'to touch if it were but the border of his garment; and as many as touched', says the evangelist, 'were saved'. In x, 52 Jesus stops on his way for the blind beggar as here he does for the unclean woman, and condones, indeed praises his importunity in the same words: 'Thy faith hath saved thee.' Otherwise St Mark nowhere speaks of Christ's work as salvation, except in a passage where (*a*) it means rescue from death and (*b*) a play on the name of Jesus may be once more suspected. The High Priests and Scribes, seeing Jesus on the cross, said, jesting upon him (*empaizontes*): 'Others he saved, himself he cannot save. Let the Christ the King of Israel come down from the cross, that we may see and have faith.'

The parallel between Jesus for Ephraim and Jairus for Manasseh would be perfect, if the woman were the daughter of Jesus, as the girl is the daughter of Jairus. In a physical sense this is plainly not so, but St Mark does show us the woman as the 'daughter' of Christ's compassion, and presses the comparison between her and Jairus's daughter. 'Jesus said unto her, Daughter, thy faith hath saved thee; go in peace and be well of thy plague. While he yet spake there came from the ruler of synagogue's house some who say,

Thy daughter is dead; why troublest thou the Rabbi further? But Jesus, overhearing the word spoken, said to the ruler of synagogue, Fear not, only have faith'— faith will avail to save this daughter also. It is easily said that the forms of address, 'Son, daughter, father, mother', were too common as courtesy titles to sustain the interpretation we have proposed; but it was characteristic of Christ to mean what he said. 'Who is my mother?' we have lately read, 'who my brethren? Looking about on those who sat round him he said: Behold my mother and my brethren. For whoso doeth the will of God is my brother, sister, or mother' (III, 31–35).

The relation between the two daughters answers to the relation between Joseph's two sons, Ephraim and Manasseh. Manasseh came first, he was the firstborn, but Ephraim was put before him in the roll of tribes. In the same way Jairus's daughter is introduced into the narrative first, but the other 'daughter' intervenes, and comes above her in the list of the tribal healings. The point is neither formal nor trivial; the Christian evangelist, following the doctrine of St Paul, would see the divine preference for the less privileged son as a type of God's dealings with sinners and Pharisees, Gentiles and Jews.

The Old Testament story of the setting of Ephraim before Manasseh is highly dramatic. Joseph brought his two sons to old Israel for his blessing, exchanging their natural places and putting his firstborn on his left-hand side, so that when he faced Israel with them, the elder boy might receive the blessing of the old man's right hand. But, guided by God, Israel made a divination from the array in which Joseph and his two sons approached; he made as though Ephraim had been seriously given the right hand place with his father, and crossed his own hands in touching the boys. Moreover, he put the name of Ephraim before that of Manasseh in his verbal blessing. Joseph protested, but in vain (Genesis XLVIII). In Mark v the 'Manassite daughter' is first commended to Jesus, 'that he may come and lay his hand upon her'. But before this actually happens, the 'Ephraimite daughter' intrudes and, touching Jesus, makes contact with 'the Lord's Salvation'. The 'Manassite daughter' is touched second.

After blessing Joseph in the persons of his two sons, old Israel proceeded to bless him in his own name as chief among his twelve brethren (Genesis XLIX). 'Joseph', he says, 'is the son of a fruit-tree, a fruit-tree beside a fountain; his *daughters* run over the wall'. That is to say, Ephraim and Manasseh branch out in all directions. That the 'daughters' (branches) of the Joseph-tree mean Ephraim and Manasseh will be naturally supposed by anyone familiar with the equivalent passage in Moses's parallel series of blessings on the Twelve Tribes (Deut. XXXIII). Here Joseph is not a tree with two branches, but a bison with two horns, and the horns are said in so many words to be the myriads of Ephraim and the thousands of Manasseh.

We have made too many points. St. Mark is unlikely to have been thinking of all these things, but the more of them there are, the more likely he is to have thought of some of them. Before we become tempted into further elaborations, let us break off the allegory of Joseph and his sons, and cast a sober eye back over the journey we have hitherto made. We have plotted out some part of a tribal list. Is it a list which yields any intelligible order? We have got (*a*) Simeon and Levi, Simeon being supported by three more lay tribes, (*b*) Zebulon, (*c*) Ephraim and Manasseh.

This must surely be the very well-known form of list in which we write (1) the house of Leah, (2) the house of Rachel, (3) the houses of their handmaids. Writing the first two houses in order of seniority we get

LEAH:	Reuben
	Simeon
	Levi
	Judah
	Issachar
	Zebulon
RACHEL:	Ephraim ⎤
	Manasseh ⎦ Joseph
	Benjamin.

Benjamin for the present is *de trop:* we have written in his name to complete the House of Rachel.

There are two basic arrangements of the Twelve Tribes from which all other arrangements are derived. One of the two is that which we are attributing to St Mark. It puts the children of Leah first, those of Rachel second, and the four children of their hand-maids third. The other arrangement puts the tribes in the order of their patriarchs' births. That means interpolating the four sons of the handmaids between the name of Judah and that of Issachar in the list we have written above. Otherwise the list remains un-altered.

Of these two arrangements, which would most naturally appeal to St Mark? The former, obviously. For he is writing his Gospel, as we have seen (ch. VI), with a break after the eighth healing miracle, in such a way that the first eight miracles are to constitute a 'little Gospel' in themselves, prefiguring the whole of Christ's mission to the Jews, as far as his resurrection. In this little Gospel or octave the healings should signify the salvation of the Jews, that is, of the Israelites who are legitimate by natural descent. Now in the family of Jacob the sons of Leah and Rachel were legitimate by natural descent, whereas the children of the handmaids were legitimated by adoption, because their mothers 'bore them on the knees' of their mistresses Leah and Rachel (Gen. XXX, 3). Thus the four children of the handmaids are natural types of the Gentile Christians, grafted by adoption into God's Israel as St Paul constantly teaches. Therefore it will suit St Mark to use an order of counting the tribes which will give him nothing but sons of the true wives for the types of the persons healed in his little Gospel or octave, leaving the sons of the hand-maids for that subsequent part of his Gospel of which the pre-figurative sense foreshews the Gentile mission.

True enough, there is still a fly in the ointment—the little Gospel contains an octave of healings, whereas the two houses of patriarchs legitimate by natural right contain nine names, and so Benjamin is *de trop*. What to do with Benjamin is a problem which may wait its turn, and meanwhile we may contemplate the excellent fit of the eight names as far as Ephraim and Manasseh to St Mark's little Gospel. His little Gospel is an octave, because it ends with resurrection, the event of the eighth day. And (on this showing) it also ends with Joseph, for Ephraim and Manasseh are Joseph. And Joseph is himself a manifest type and token of the resurrection. Buried in an Egyptian prison and supposed dead by his kindred, he came upon the rest of the Twelve as alive from the grave in the splendour of his royal power, and they were troubled at his presence, for they had betrayed him; but he comforted them and told them not to fear.

If the reader can bear any more allegories upon the linked stories of the twelve-year-old girl and the woman twelve years sick, we will venture to indicate how appropriate they are to the person of Joseph as well as to the persons of Ephraim and Manasseh. The father, assured that his child merely sleeps and will return from the dead, puts us in mind of Jacob who so wrestled with his despair in the effort to believe that his son Joseph lived after all. Whereas the woman twelve years sick perfectly expresses the derivation of Joseph's name. Rachel makes a double word play: 'The Lord hath *taken away* (ASPH) my reproach; the Lord *add* (JSPH) to me a second son' (Gen. xxx, 23). The second of Rachel's sentences is not strictly about the birth of Joseph, it is a prayer for the birth of Benjamin. Joseph himself, then, is defined as the child by whose birth the Lord takes away a woman's reproach. And so a good MS. of the 'Testament of Joseph' contains the note that Joseph is named for the taking away of reproach. Rachel's 'reproach' was barrenness, and the disease Christ removes from the twelve years' sufferer is a disease directly causing barrenness in the most obvious way. Moreover, her disease was shameful, such as everyone would wish to hide—it was therefore doubly a 'reproach'. And Jesus took it away, not only by healing her, but by his gentleness in acknowledging her and blessing her as his daughter. The Testament of Joseph represents the patriarch in the character of 'the taker away of reproach', the man most tender of the honour of those thankless people with whom he had to do, and even, so far as was possible, of that impure woman who in the end was bold enough to *take hold of his garment.*

St Mark's sixth chapter, being piled full of images of Christ's death and resurrection, is 'Josephan' by that very fact; but there does also appear to be some positive and special influence of the Joseph-legend there. What prophet but Joseph would we choose to illustrate the maxim that a prophet is not without honour save in his own country and among his own kindred and household? —Joseph whose skill in dreams brought him the contempt of his brethren, and the viceroyalty of Egypt (Mark VI, 1–6). Or again, Joseph is the prophet whose inflexible uprightness concerning the purity of marriage brought him a prison and the hatred of an unchaste woman; and whose imprisonment came to an end at the king's birthday feast, at which—a strange feature, surely, in such a festivity—the king lifted one of his prisoners' heads from off him (Mark VI, 14–29).

The next scene of Joseph's life shows him feeding the fainting multitudes with a wonderful provision of bread (Mark VI, 30–44), in the course of which merciful activity he revealed himself to his brethren, as it were an apparition from the dead. They did not at first know him, and when he said to them, 'It is I, Joseph', they were *confounded* at his presence (St Mark uses the same word: 'They all saw him and were *confounded*', VI, 50). He needed to redouble his assurances before he could throw himself into their arms (Mark VI, 48–52).

Here are, the reader may justly complain, far too many allegories. Perhaps. But it is not surprising if tribal typology should exercise its greatest influence in the section concerned with Joseph and Ephraim (V, 21–VI, 52). For Joseph is the most Christ-like of the patriarchs, and the figure round which the 'Twelve Testaments' largely revolve; while the tribe of Ephraim has for its principal hero the great Jesus of the Old Testament. If the reader is in any doubt about the probability of a Christian evangelist's being much moved by the figure of Joseph, he should read the Twelve Testaments. Indeed a careful reading of Genesis might be enough to enlighten him. Anyhow, we are not going to ask him to believe that the rest of the Gospel contains any passage so saturated with patriarchal allegory, or anything near it.

So ends the octave of the sons of Leah and Rachel. How will St Mark go on from the point he has reached? Hitherto he has followed the order which sets the sons of the wives first and leaves those of the handmaids to the end, even though they were earlier born. If he is to continue with this order, he ought to set Benjamin in the ninth place, since he also belongs to the house of Rachel. But to do so would be to blur the division between the evangelist's 'little Gospel' and its sequel. The 'little Gospel' expresses Christ in Israel; in the sequel he goes to the Gentiles, that is to the handmaid tribes, grafted into the family of God by adoption and grace. Let Benjamin then be reserved until last, and for the day when Christ entered the land of Benjamin on which the Temple stood. To hold Benjamin over in this way is not arbitrary, because all the other patriarchs were born in close succession and in the twelve years during which Jacob served Laban, whereas Benjamin was born years after, when the whole family had migrated to the South (Gen. xxxv, 16). May not St Mark reserve the sign of Benjamin for the day when Jesus and the Twelve migrate to the South also? Rachel died in Benjamin, and in Benjamin Jesus will die.

Jesus dies in Benjamin: in the sphere, that is, of the fleshly Israel and of the legitimate heirs of Jacob, of whom Benjamin is the last. From the sign of Benjamin onwards (x, 46 ff.) Jesus is in the Holy City itself. Whereas his ministry to the handmaid tribes (VII–x, 31) covers precisely that part of the Gospel in which he visits Gentile areas: Tyre and Sidon (VII, 24–30), Decapolis (VII, 31–37). Caesarea Philippi (VIII, 27 ff.), and Peraea (x, 1–31.) If there is a part of the Gospel which prefigures the Gentile mission, it is surely this part. In fact the tribes are, it would seem, interpreted geographically from VII onwards, an interpretation which arises naturally enough once we begin to think of them as symbolizing 'the nations'.

The handmaid tribes are Gad, Asher, Dan and Naphtali. The portion of Gad had been middle Transjordan, or that part of the left bank of the river which extends from the Sea of Galilee southwards half-way to the Dead Sea. In Gospel times much of this was Decapolitan land; the only Decapolitan city mentioned by St Mark, Gerasa (v, 1, cf. 20) was in this region. Asher's portion lay along the back of Tyre and Sidon. Dan held a small territory round what, in St Mark's time, had become Caesarea Philippi; the 'city' of Dan was now a village a few miles from Caesarea. Naphtali stretched from the western border of Dan down the upper Jordan and the west side of the Galilean Lake; most of Jewish Galilee was Naphtalite. So for Gad, Asher, Dan and Naphtali we may use the contemporary equivalents Decapolis, neighbourhood of Tyre and Sidon, villages of Caesarea Philippi, and Galilee. The four healings in Mark vii–ix are connected with those four localities. The Syrophoenician exorcism is in the neighbourhood of Tyre and Sidon, the deaf mute is healed in Decapolis, the healing of the blind man is the stepping-stone to Caesarea Philippi, and the exorcism of the epileptic sends us back again to Jewish Galilee and in particular to Capernaum, which lay at the heart of the Naphtalite territory.

The Jewish character of the Naphtalite land may be felt to be an imperfection in St Mark's symbolism. If the four tribes are to symbolize the Gentile countries, it is inconvenient that one should be so Jewish. It is inconvenient, but it is not St Mark's fault, and he weakens the inconvenience as much as he can. In recording the passage through Naphtalite territory, the evangelist tells us that Christ was not at that time forwarding his mission to Galilee. 'And proceeding thence' (that is, from the healing of the epileptic) 'they passed through Galilee, and he would not have anyone to know it. For he was teaching his disciples . . .' No sooner are they on Peraean soil, than the crowds collect again, and 'as he was wont, he began again to teach them' (ix, 30, x, 1).

What order will St Mark follow in his arrangement of the four? Since the Leah-Rachel order has played a significant part in i–v, we may expect the same order in vii–ix: the children of Leah's handmaid will stand before those of Rachel's. And this is almost the inevitable order to use if we are going on to add a son of Rachel's own, Benjamin, at the end. And so we may expect

$$
\left.\begin{array}{l} \text{Gad} \\ \text{Asher} \end{array}\right\} \text{LEAH}
$$

$$
\left.\begin{array}{l} \text{Dan} \\ \text{Naphtali} \\ \text{Benjamin} \end{array}\right\} \text{RACHEL}
$$

This is the order St Mark gives us, except that he puts Asher before Gad, the younger before the elder, an order already instanced in the setting of Ephraim before Manasseh. There are strong reasons for this, which it is not difficult to appreciate. For the first handmaid sign must be the most evidently and emphatically Gentile in character, or we shall fail to grasp the transition from Jewish mission to a prefiguration of Gentile mission when we pass from the eighth sign (Jairus's daughter) to its successor. What, then, can we say beforehand about the most evidently Gentile healing? Can we not say that it must correspond, if possible, to the healing which Elijah wrought for the widow of Zarephath? When did crumbs from the children's table so obviously spill over the Israelite border for the benefit of Gentile dogs, as they did when Elijah both multiplied the widow's' bread and healed her child? The widow of Zarephath was 'a heathen, a Syrophoenician by race, from the borders of Tyre and Sidon'; the description St Mark gives of the Gentile mother fits Elijah's widow in each particular. Elijah gave her bread and healing; Jesus gives the Syrophoeness healing only, but he discusses it with her under the name of bread.

We are supposing two things—that the first 'handmaid' healing is to be antitypical to Elijah's miracle at Zarephath, and that the handmaid tribes are to be interpreted geographically. From these two suppositions taken together, it follows that Asher must be placed first of the four. For it is Asher (and not, for example, Gad) whose territory lies up against the back of Phoenicia. Asher is not merely the younger of Zilpah's two sons, he is the youngest of all the sons of either handmaid, and may therefore be viewed

337   Z

as the least considerable of all Jacob's children. If so, he is all the more appropriate to St Mark's purpose in ch. VII. For it is in the person of the daughter of Asher, the Syrophoeness, that St Mark designs to show how the least privileged are admitted to share the benefits of salvation. The Syrophoeness must stand in the highest possible contrast with Jairus. In status he is not merely an Israelite, he is a head of synagogue; she is a nameless Gentile woman. In tribal symbolism he represents Joseph the crowned among his brethren, and she the least of the half-legitimate patriarchs.

When we have recognized the general significance of the four tribes as standing for the Gentiles, the geographical placing of their healing signs, and the special significance of the tribe of Asher, have we, perhaps, exhausted the tribal symbolism of VII–IX? There is one further element of symbolism common to the four which we can hardly fail to observe. Surely the four handmaid tribes have something to do with the four thousands at the Gentile eucharist in VIII. We have already seen how closely the episode hangs upon the exorcism of the Syrophoenician child. If thousands = tribes, and if St Mark is treating four as the present representatives of all the Gentile thousands ultimately to be fed, this must have something to do with the fact that four handmaid-tribes stand for the recipients of the Gentile mission in the same part of his Gospel. So we may fairly say that the hand-maid tribes receive two different symbolizations side by side, (a) as four persons healed, (b) as four thousands fed. How elegantly, if so, the narrative of the four thousand is placed. The healings of the two children of Zilpah precede it, and the healings of the two children of Bilhah follow it.

We now turn to the detailed consideration of the four tribal signs. Has the Syrophoenician exorcism any Asherite features beside its geographical position? It is satisfactory to note that in the blessings of the tribes Asher alone is blessed with bread. Jacob says of him, 'Asher, his bread is fat' (Gen. XLIX, 20). It is very suitable, then, that the exorcism which constitutes the sign of Asher should be described as a gift of the children's bread; for

Israel gave bread to Asher his child. The point may not be important; but it is at least simple and clear.

Not so simple or so clear is the question of the Asherite character of VII, 1–23, the discourses on cleanness of hands. The discourses form a highly significant prelude to the Syrophoenician exorcism; so much at least is indubitable. The reason why the 'dogs' cannot share the 'children's table' is that the 'dogs' are unclean. The Pharisees practise supererogatory lustrations before their own meals, to be sure that they are rid of all defilement from Gentile contacts before they eat. When Christ attacks the necessity for such customs, he bids fair to remove the whole ground for the exclusion of the 'dogs' from the 'children's table'. The same process is carried farther when he gives the dogs the children's leavings in the exorcism which directly follows. The continuity of theme between discourse and exorcism cannot be doubted. But that will not of itself avail to prove that the discourse already has an 'Asherite' character. It may have, or it may not. The evidence that it has rests, for what it is worth, on the apparent echoes of the Testament of Asher which the discourse contains. The thought of the 'Testament' may be summarized as follows.

Moses blessed Asher under the name of Upright, interpreting AŠR (Happy) as JŠR (Upright). The blessing of Moses is, indeed, ambiguous. He blesses Asher last of the Twelve, and afterwards proceeds to a general blessing of Israel, and it is not clear where the division comes between the particular blessing and the general. We might put the stop before Deut. XXXIII, 25, or between 25 and 26; but the author of the Testaments evidently put it after 27, as his play on AŠR JŠR shows.[1] 'There is none like unto God, O Jeshuron' (child who art JŠR) is referred by him to Asher. 'Asher', then, speaks to his own children of uprightness in his Testament. But the uprightness of which he speaks is not formal correctness, but sincerity of heart, the virtue which determines a man's duty when legal precepts apparently conflict, and

---

[1] For this paranomasia, compare the naming of Joseph. 'She said, the Lord hath removed (ASPH) my reproach: and she called his name Joseph (JSPH), saying, The Lord add (JSPH) to me another son' (Gen. XXX, 23–24).

self-deception is therefore easiest. Asher compared unclean men to unclean beasts; but the unclean men of whom he spoke were neither the Gentiles, 'the dogs under the children's table', nor yet Israelites eating with hands unwashed. They were men who used the law to frustrate the law, and he gave many examples of insincere casuistry, where the principle at issue was the same as that in the corban-question discussed by Christ. As Mark VII is the *locus classicus* on casuistry in this Gospel, so the Testament of Asher is the *locus classicus* on cauistry in the Twelve Testaments. Asher uses against the false casuists the very same quotation from Isaiah which Christ applies to the Pharisees: 'Their heart is far from me, in vain do they worship me, teaching for doctrines the precepts of men.' Asher prophesies that in times to come men will fall into such evil ways; it might well seem to St Mark—it might well seem to Christ—that the patriarch had been foretelling the corrupter elements in first-century Pharisaism.

Asher's theme of the unclean beasts, the 'dogs', is presently taken up by Christ on Asher's own territory. Jacob had blessed Asher with bread, though he was only a child by adoption; and here is a woman who is not even that, but a 'Grecian' dog from Syria-Phoenicia, begging crumbs from the children's table; and Jesus accords them to her faith.

The dependence of Mark VII, 1–30 on the Testament of Asher is no better than a fair probability, and will scarcely stand on its own merits; it would not win acceptance except as part of a wider argument for St Mark's acquaintance with the 'Testaments'.

With or without the relation to the Testament of Asher, the Marcan sign of Asher is strongly characterized as Asherite; naturally enough, since it is made typical of the handmaid tribes and plays an important part in the whole tribal symbolism. There is no reason to expect the other three handmaid tribes to be so vigorously particularized. There is nothing at all evidently Gadite about the healing of the deaf stammerer, except the geography; but the geography is remarkable enough. After the exorcism of the gentile child, Jesus is described as passing in a single complex journey home to the Galilean Sea and on into Decapolis. Exactly what St Mark wrote, and exactly what he meant by his geographical expressions anyhow, is by no means clear. The hardest reading, and so perhaps the best, runs literally: 'And again departing from the territory of Tyre he went through Sidon, to the Sea of Galilee, amidst the territory of Decapolis.' It is easiest to suppose that St Mark's several geographical phrases represent simply the successive stages of a journey. What he means is: Jesus left the territory of Tyre, passed through Sidon, went to the Sea of Galilee, and plunged into the heart of Decapolis. Whereas if we join these phrases closely together, we get the extraordinary suggestion that Jesus passed from Tyre to the Sea of Galilee by going northwards to Sidon and making a great detour over Lebanon and Hermon and round through Philip's Tetrarchy, so as to strike the Galilean Lake 'in the midst of the borders of Decapolis', that is, at its south-eastern corner. It is hardly to be supposed that St Mark meant this; but even if he did, the result is the same: Christ passes in a single journey from the Tyrian region to Decapolis, from Asher to Gad. If St Mark desires to follow an Asher miracle with a Gad miracle, and to interpret the tribal names geographically, he will have to carry Christ from one extreme corner of the north Palestinian region to the other, without narrating anything that happens on the way. Apart from such an interest in the tribal sequence, it is difficult to explain the evangelist's so doing. There is nothing to parallel so long and featureless a leap across the map anywhere else in the Gospel.

The geographical placing of the sign of Dan is slightly ambiguous. At the end of the discussion in the boat concerning the leaven of the Pharisees and the miracles of bread, we read: 'He said unto them, Do ye not yet understand? And they came to Bethsaida. And they bring to him a blind man . . .' Is St Mark telling us that the voyage and the conversation ended in their arriving at Bethsaida, or he is telling us that upon their arriving at Bethsaida the blind man was brought? Probably the former. For Bethsaida, dignified with the splendid name of Julias, was no

village, whereas it is at a village that the blind man is healed
(VIII, 23). Moreover the name of Bethsaida is significant if considered as the terminus of the voyage. It emphasizes the parallel
between this voyage and a previous voyage. The one follows the
feeding of the five thousands, the other that of the four, in both
the disciples fail to understand concerning the loaves (VI, 52,
VIII, 16–21) and on both occasions their boat is making for
Bethsaida (VI, 45, VIII, 22). Nor is the name of Bethsaida unsug-
gestive in such contexts. It means 'Home of Provisioning' and so
contains an implied rebuke to the disciples for their lack of faith
in divine care, their failure to understand concerning the loaves,
their anxiety for bread. With 'Do you not yet understand?—
And they come to Bethsaida' we may compare a similar rebuke:
'It shall not be so among you . . . for the Son of Man himself is
come . . . to give his life a ransom for many—And they come to
Jericho.' Jericho, of which a former Jesus had prophesied that its
building would have to be ransomed by the life of the firstborn
(Josh. VI, 26, cf. I Kings XVI, 34). The notice about Bethsaida
and the notice about Jericho are, in fact, identically placed: they
stand just before the two healings of the blind, the 'appended
miracles' in successive cycles.

We may conclude, then, that the arrival at Bethsaida is rather
the end of the voyage than the occasion of the healing. The
healing follows in a village somewhere a little farther on—
farther in what direction? The end of the healing tells us. 'He
sent him home, saying, Tell no one in the village. And Jesus and
his disciples went forth into the villages around Caesarea Philippi.'
The final phrase suggests that the starting-point had been 'the
villages round Bethsaida'. In such a village, then, and on the road
to Caesarea, the blind man is healed. Bethsaida was Philip's lake-
side harbour, his Tiberias, and the gateway to his Caesarea. If
Caesarea is Dan, a miracle just beyond Bethsaida opens the way
to Dan, just as the similar miracle on the way out of Jericho later
opens the way to the Benjamite sanctuary of Jerusalem. At Jerusalem God was unworthily worshipped, but at Dan Satan had
been worshipped by mistake for God; there was the sanctuary of

the golden calf; in comment on that apostasy Dan prophesies to his children in his Testament, 'I know that Satan shall be your prince'. It is not inappropriate, therefore, that Peter should so confess Messiah on the Caesarean road as to commend apostasy from the truth of God, and be rebuked as the voice of Satan. 'Dan', Jacob had said, 'shall be a serpent in the road' (Gen. XLIX, 17). Jesus proceeds to preach upon fidelity and apostasy, and the rewards of each on the day of judgement. Judgement is the meaning of Dan's name, according to his birth-story.

To return to the healing miracle. It is on the road to Dan. Has it any Danite features? St Mark's whole pattern of healings requires a healing of the blind here; we have just witnessed an opening of ears, and an opening of eyes must follow it. But it is at least satisfactory to note that the only famous Danite, Samson, was blinded, and that in probable allusion to the fact, the Dan of the Testament moralizes to his children on spiritual blindness. That a spiritual allegory is in St Mark's mind is obvious from the context. Christ's expostulation to his disciples, 'Having eyes, see ye not?' is only a few lines back when the blind man is introduced in search of healing (VIII, 18, 22).

The geographical placing of the Naphtali sign is similar to that of its predecessor. It opens the road to Naphtalite Galilee and to Capernaum, just as the sign of Dan opened the way to Dan and Caesarea; or, again, as the sign of Benjamin is going to open the way into the Benjamite land and to Jerusalem. After exorcism of the epileptic they proceed to pass secretly through Galilee (IX, 30). The miracle takes place at the foot of the high mountain where Christ was transfigured. Since the high mountain is reached from Caesarea Philippi it is presumably Hermon, as we have said above (p. 321). The westerly foothills of Hermon are the head of the ancient Naphtalite land. The miracle at the foot of the Mount of Transfiguration may stand at the very gate of Naphtali.

We did not find the connexion between the name of Dan and the theme of sight and blindness very impressive. The connexion between Naphtali's name and the special character of the miracle under the mountain is considerably stronger. Naphtali receives this oracle from his father Jacob: 'Naphtali is a hind let loose; he giveth goodly words' (Gen. XLIX, 21). This means, says his 'Testament', that Naphtali is a swift and eloquent messenger on the errands of his father. How different is the son of the father who appeals to Christ beneath the mountain! So far is he from giving goodly words, that possession by evil powers makes him dumb. It is to be observed that there is a difference between this sufferer and the Decapolitan. The Decapolitan was a deaf man with speech difficulties, this is a dumb boy (IX, 17) whose deafness is only subsequently alluded to (IX, 25). So far as there is a difference between the two cases, the second is the more Naphtalite—the more concerned with ability to 'give goodly words'. When the boy has passed through Christ's hands, he is not only endowed with a fund of goodly words, he is also 'let loose' from a most violent spiritual oppression.

Naphtali's name means 'wrestling' interpreted in the sense of 'rivalry'. The very cure of the epileptic is a subject of contention; the disciples attempt to work it in order to triumph over Pharisaic criticism, but they cannot. The 'rivalry' in the story of Naphtali's birth is rivalry between the houses of Leah and Rachel for position in the twelve-fold family of Jacob (Gen. XXX, 8). The apostles are the twelve-fold family of the new Israel, and how do they occupy themselves on the road from the exorcism to Capernaum? They are at strife as to which is the greatest. The theme of strife and rivalry runs on (IX, 38–50) and recurs (X, 35–45).

We come last of all to the sign of Benjamin, the healing of Bartimeus's blindness. The first thing we meet is his situation and the second is his name. As for the situation, Jericho is the border of Benjamin to one coming over Jordan in the direction of Jerusalem. Then as to the name, it is one of three connected with healings, those of Simon and of Jairus being the other two. Both of these others have seemed to us tribally significant, so it is natural to ask whether Bartimeus is any less so. Bar-Timeus, the son of Timaeus, that is, of the Honourable, is carefully interpreted to his Greek readers by St Mark. Ben-Jamin is the only one of the patriarchal names having a similar form, for Ben- is in Hebrew what Bar- is in Aramaic. Benjamin's unhappy mother, dying in his birth, called him Benoni, 'Son of My Sorrow', but his father corrected the name to 'Benjamin', 'Son of the Right Hand', that is, of honour or fortune (Gen. xxxv, 18). That St Mark intends the play on Bartimeus, Benjamin is made all the more probable by the context. He has just told us how James and John have been refused their request for the places at *the right hand* and the left hand of glory, and so proceeds to describe how Christ grants the request of Bartimeus, the poor beggar; for whereas the two apostles had requested what no one ought to ask, Bartimeus had asked what Mercy will not refuse.

The nature of the healing is determined by its place in St Mark's cycle; a second opening of eyes matches the first, just as the second opening of ears has matched the first. It is superfluous to look for anything specially Benjamite about blindness.

The sign of Benjamin is the proper introduction to the whole topic of the Temple, which extends from xi, 11 to xiii, 14 and beyond. For the Temple stood upon Benjamite soil. But it would obviously be a waste of time to hunt for special Benjamin-themes wherever the Temple is in question. The evangelist who writes xi ff. has plenty to think about without fishing for detailed Benjamite typology. There is nevertheless one apparently Benjamite theme in the immediate sequel to Bartimeus's healing. King Saul was the principal hero of the Benjamites, and they continued to give his name to their children, as the case of the Apostle Paul bears witness. And the miraculous finding of the ass (Mark xi, 1–6) carries us to the history of Saul's anointing (I Sam. x, 2 ff.). We have discussed the Saul-typology of Mark xi and xiv above (p. 130 f.). There is a strong case for the evangelist's having the story of Saul in his head when he wrote those chapters. But there are sufficient reasons why he should have had it in mind anyhow. It squares with a Benjamite interpretation of Bartimeus, but it does not require it.

If we are trying to estimate the value of what this chapter contains, we shall do well to make a distinction between *tribal*

signatures and *tribal allegories*. The hypothesis we have set forth
stands or falls with the tribal signatures; it is not committed to
any one of the tribal allegories. The signatures are those marks
by which the evangelist distinguishes one tribal healing from
another. What are these signatures? The evangelist begins from
the most natural and the most obvious, actual tribal names.
Simon Peter and his companions stand for Simeon and his companions: Levi, son of Alphaeus, stands for Levi. From such a
simple form of signature St Mark advances to a slightly hidden
writing of the actual tribal name: Zebulon lurks in Beel-Zebul.
Then he goes on to use representative names: Jesus and Jairus
stand for Ephraim and Manasseh as Pericles for Athens or Caesar
for Rome. There is a special reason for such a type of signature
at this point in the relation of the name of Jesus to the tribe of
Ephraim. The evangelist does not carry the refinement of the use
of names any further; he breaks it off and uses a geographical
signature instead. In the last case, that of Benjamin, he fortifies
the geographical signature with a direct play on the patriarchal
name.

As for 'tribal allegories', it is perhaps incredible that the evangelist should trouble to identify his tribal persons by 'signatures'
unless he were going to make some allegorical use of them when
they were identified. And we might feel a moderate confidence
in certain of the allegories, for example those concerned with
Levi and Asher. But the trouble about allegory is that one does
not know where to draw the line; the material of Jewish allegory
is embarrassingly rich. It is easy to suggest what St Mark might
well have been thinking, but often impossible to decide what he
was thinking.

Dr. Tasker recently published a useful book under the title
The Old Testament in the New Testament. His title defines in a
very natural way the inquiry which the modern student makes.
He takes up the New Testament, and is surprised to find in it so
many shadows and allegories of the Old. He lays them bare and
analyses them. Not so, of course, the men of the New Testament
age. Their preoccupation was just the reverse. They searched for

the New Testament in the Old, and it was there that they found it. A primitive Christian evangelist looks into the Old Testament as into a magic mirror which gives him back the face of Christ and the form of the Church.

It is only by a serious grasp of this principle that it is possible to think intelligently about the subject-matter of this present chapter. Otherwise we must remain completely at the mercy of a whole sheaf of false questions. This, for example: 'But are you telling me that St Mark was attempting to convey all this tangle of Old Testament allusion and allegorical subtlety? If so, he was surely very unlucky, and not a little unreasonable. For he has certainly failed to make himself understood.' The right way to answer this question is, that what St Mark was attempting to convey was what he did convey, the portrait of Christ. How much of the Old Testament allusion he wished his first readers or hearers to understand is a point on which it is both unnecessary and impossible to dogmatize. But his primary purpose in allegorizing the Old Testament was not to make us follow his allegories, but to find Christ for himself, so that he could show him to us.

NOTE ON INTERPRETING THE TWELVE TESTAMENTS

The *Testaments of the Twelve Patriarchs* are available to the
English reader through the industry of Dr R. H. Charles.
Whether we take up the Corpus of the Pseudepigrapha or the
separate volume of the English text based on all the versions and
annotated, or the edition of the Greek versions, we are looking at
the Testaments through Charles's eyes. To read him now is to
marvel at his energy and critical skill, but to marvel no less at the
perversity of the interpretative principles accepted in his time.
Charles was the victim of his period. It was his misfortune to be
so placed that he could not grasp the pattern or meaning of the
work as a whole. It was his virtue to provide us with all the
materials we need for correcting his deficiencies.

To make a full list of Charles's false principles would be an
ungrateful proceeding, but it is necessary to mention a few of
them 'for the warning' (as it says in the *Arabian Nights*) 'of him
that would be admonished'. One of the most harmful is an
obsession with political interpretation. Sayings cast in the mould
of prophecy are constantly treated by Charles as detailed comment on contemporary, that is to say Maccabean, politics. This
is a rash proceeding, since the author of *Testaments* is speaking
through the mouths of the Twelve Patriarchs, and everything
referring to Biblical history since their time has to be thrown into
prophetic form. Again, it is always possible that the prophecy
may be genuinely prophetical, and refer neither to the Biblical
past nor to the Maccabean present, but to an ideal future. Charles's
political obsession refutes itself, for there is no Maccabean situation known to him which will accommodate all the political
references he supposes himself to find. Charles, undeterred,
disrupts the text of the Testaments and distributes it among
interpolators of various periods, so that all his imaginary political
arrows may find contemporary marks.

A second false principle is the theory of free fantasy. Charles sees the pseudepigraphical writers such as the author of *Testaments* as masquerading in Old Testament clothes and under Old Testament names in order to disguise their innovations. They build up their own apocalyptic fantasies under the guidance of their own insight and for the edification of their own times. They borrow and increase one another's stock, they quarry the Old Testament for materials, but always to serve their own designs. His theory deprived Dr Charles of what should be his guiding principles of interpretation. Such writers as the author of *Testaments* identified themselves with Biblical characters and plunged themselves into Biblical situations in the serious endeavour to make Scripture speak, or to obtain an oracle for their own times. What they give us is a sort of dramatized exposition and their thought is closely controlled by consistent exegesis, especially of certain basic texts. To understand the theology of the author of *Testaments* is to grasp these exegetical positions of his.

Lacking the guiding lines he might have learnt from his author's exegetical theology, Charles introduced *a priori* conceptions of his own, some of which hardly even make sense. For example, he introduced the conception of '*the* Messiah'. Every Israelite is supposed by him to be looking for a single saving and anointed person. Such a person may be looked for in the form of an anointed priest from the stock of Levi, or an anointed prince from the stock of Judah, but not both together. But why should this be so? The Old Testament records irrevocable covenants given by God to both Messiahs, both anointed stocks, the royal and the priestly, the Levitical and Davidic. And so a very natural form of Messianic speculation consists in asking, How will the great anointed priest of the last days be related to the great anointed prince of the last days? Will the Levitical or the Judaean Messiah appear first? And which will have the precedence in glory? It is in this form that the Messianic question is considered in the Twelve Testaments. But Charles is so convinced of his dogma about '*the* Messiah', that he forces the Testaments into the position of upholding a Levitical Messiah, and excluding a Judaean Messiah entirely. All the references to

the promised Son of David have then to be set aside as interpolations.

When we have cleared our minds of Charles's erroneous
principles we are rid of most of the reasons for which he con-
demns whole paragraphs, but we are still not finished with the
vexatious question of interpolation. For there are on any showing
many phrases in the Testaments which are manifest Christian
glosses; and apart from these, the state of the text throughout is
so bad and the evidence for it so discrepant, as to awaken the
suspicion of interpolation on a considerable scale. To take the two
points in order: it is not easy to be sure what the extent of the
Christian interpolations is. We find a sentence or a paragraph
which, as it stands, cannot be given a pre-Christian interpretation;
but alternative policies still lie before us. We can either give the
whole sentence or paragraph up, or we may attempt by excision
and restoration to recover a pre-Christian form of it. It may not
be at all clear which policy is the right one. And if it is not, then
we may find ourselves quoting as parts of the pre-Christian text
what we ought to have discarded as Christian interpolations.
Now to take the question of the bad state of the text in general:
suppose, for example, we were led to prefer the shorter readings
on the whole, we should thereby judge the longer readings to be
considerably interpolated. And might not our confidence then
be shaken in the shorter readings themselves? For a text so liable
to interpolation may have been interpolated already, before our
evidence for it begins.

It seems as though the most commonplace aids to confidence
desert us in the midst of our doubts. For in the ordinary way, we
repel suspicions of wholesale interpolation by appealing to the
principle that what is necessary to the substance and continuity
of the meaning must be genuine. But in many parts of the Testaments this principle helps us little, for they have neither the
continuity of narrative nor the continuity of argument. There
are piles of gnomic sayings, of oracular or hortatory remarks,
and it is hard to say which pieces, if any, are essential to the main
drift. The same difficulty besets us if we take longer units, the main

constituent parts out of which any one Testament is made up. Historical moralizing is followed by poetical exhortation, poetical exhortation by apocalyptic prophecy, and so on. The modern reader may see nothing but a haphazard sequence of different forms and topics. From the feeling that there are too many of them it is a short step to the suspicion that one or other of them has been interpolated. Here, we say, is a chapter or group of chapters which any Jewish sermonizer might have added. We should never have missed it if it had not been there, and the Testament (to our ear) reads better without it. What confidence can we have that it stood in the original text, or even (what is more to the purpose) in the text read by St Paul or St Mark?

The doubts and difficulties we have been ventilating are of a general scope and belong to a distant view of the subject. When we get to grips with it and interpret it as it comes, we find our way bit by bit and gradually recover our confidence. Interpretation is an art; it is an exercise of wit and not an application of general considerations. Whether or not a work is interpretable as a living unity can be found only by interpreting it. It cannot be found out beforehand by taking specimen soundings on selected pages, or by considering the general character of the work after a cursory reading of it.

Only a full scale essay in interpretation could vindicate the unity and genuineness of the Twelve Testaments, but even on the level of generalities some things can usefully be said. Let us take for example the difficulty presented by the miscellaneity and structurelessness of the several Testaments. It is not in fact true that we are left defenceless against the suggestion that this or that feature may just as easily as not be a spurious addition. We have a method for checking such wild surmises, the method of comparing the Testaments with one another. A single Testament may look like a shapeless miscellany of literary features and edifying topics. But what if we discover the same features and topics in the next Testament, or in the preceding one? It does not matter to us whether the author was aware that he was using one Testament as a model for another. It is enough if we can discover his habitual way of arranging a Testament. For we can feel confidence in the genuineness of features which find their place in such a habitual arrangement, however unconscious the author's habit may have been in so arranging them.

Twelve times a Testament is constructed before our eyes. If we cannot find out from so many examples how it is done, it reflects little credit on our wits. Comparison of one with another may teach other things besides the author's habitual sequence of topics or literary forms. It may equally well teach us how he went about the task of exploiting the Old Testament data concerning any given patriarch or tribe for the purposes of instruction or edification.

The study of literary form is an art much praised and discussed, but it is not always realized that the cogency of its results is in proportion to the narrowness of the field taken. Generalizations spread over magnificent areas like the Hellenistic philosophical homily or the Hellenistic literary epistle have certainly their own interest, and will often suggest something useful to the interpreter of a particular passage in a given writing. But to furnish suggestions is the most that such a study can do; it cannot furnish principles or rules, for any one philosophical preacher or epistolographer may depart at any point from the customs of his literary tribe. It is like a custom of dress or coiffure; it may be true that Abyssinians wear beards and bookmakers check suits, but such truths would never justify us in rejecting a beardless Ethiop or a bookmaker in a modest pin-stripe as manifest impostures. But if we narrow the field we get more binding conclusions. The most valuable exercise of form criticism is that which is exercised upon a number of comparable works from the same hand, say St Paul's genuine epistles, say the healing miracles in St Mark's Gospel, say the Twelve Testaments of the Patriarchs. Such a study admits us to the habitual working of a single mind. A writer may change his habits, but something will remain the same. In any case, we can study the process, degree and order of change.

We are principally interested just now in the Testaments of Levi and Judah, because in the chapter to which this note is appended, we founded an argument upon one point in the parallel between them. The Testament of Judah is the next successor to the Testament of Levi and was obviously composed on the model of it. We could show if we wished how the form which appears in *Levi* is sketched out in its predecessors, *Reuben* and *Simeon*. But that can wait for another occasion. The parallel of *Levi* and *Judah* is quite enough for the present.

Levi and Judah each begin by calling their sons about them to give them their last words. Then each patriarch proceeds to give the story of his achievements. We observe that Levi is credited with anticipating the glories of Moses and Aaron, his descendants, and Judah with a similar anticipation of David's acts (T. Levi I–X, T. Judah I–IX). Then Levi narrates the blameless history of his family affairs, and Judah the shameful history of his (T. Levi XI–XII, T. Judah X–XII). General homilies follow; Judah's is much longer, because he has the sad task of persuading his children not to follow their father's example (T. Levi XIII, T. Judah XIII–XX). After that we read warnings bearing on Biblical history: Levi warns his sons how the priesthood will in fact disgrace itself, and Judah gives a similar warning about the Davidic kings. Levi's warning introduces a scheme of chronology which, in the present state of the text, exercises the interpreters more that it enlightens the subject. Judah naturally omits the chronological feature, for it would be superfluous to repeat in terms of kingship a scheme already made out in terms of priesthood; not to mention the fact that a priestly chronology of Israel is feasible since the priesthood was continuous, a royal chronology impracticable because there were no kings most of the time (T. Levi XIV–XVII, T. Judah XXI–XXIII). After the almost unrelieved gloom of their historical predictions, both patriarchs utter brief apocalyses of final glory (T. Levi XVIII, T. Judah XXIV–XXV). Then there remains nothing more but their leave-takings and deaths (T. Levi XIX, T. Judah XXVI).

So much for the general parallel between the two Testaments. The particular parallel which we used on p. 321 concerned two corresponding texts from the two little apocalypses. The clue to the apocalypses and especially to the relation between them is the author's exegesis of Balaam's oracle in Numbers XXIV, 17. The oracle is of high importance in the author's eyes, because it is the most strikingly 'Messianic' text in the Books of Moses, and for the purpose of establishing any doctrine, a line of 'Moses' is worth a ream of 'the Prophets'. Balaam says: 'I see him, but not now; I behold him, but not nigh. There shall come forth a star out of Jacob, and a sceptre shall rise out of Israel; and it shall smite through the corners of Moab, and break down all the sons of Seth.' The author of *Testaments* interprets the star and the sceptre of different persons. The Star will be the great Levitical priest, the Sceptre the great Davidic king.

It seems to us that in so interpreting he misrepresents the meaning of a simple poetical parallelism, the sceptre being an equivalent expression for the star, and both referring to one person (or one dynasty, perhaps). But we must not imagine that he could not understand the conventions of the old Hebrew poetry. The parallelism of synonyms was perfectly well known and still used in his time. He would have told us, if we had asked him, that some parallelisms express the same thing under two forms, and others two distinct but parallel things, for example,

They are the myriads of Ephraim
And they are the thousands of Manasseh.

Some texts can be interpreted in either sense, if taken by themselves. Balaam's couplet, he would have said, is a case in point. In such cases we must appeal for a decision to other relevant texts, or to the general sense of scripture. Now scripture places the salvation of Israel in the priesthood and the kingdom. It is therefore right to conclude that Balaam spoke of both; his couplet expresses the parallel between two things, not one thing under two figures.

If 'star' and 'sceptre' expresses 'priesthood' and 'kingdom', which figure stands for which thing? Since it is obvious that 'sceptre' expresses kingship, it remains that 'star' should express priesthood. Nothing in the wording of Balaam's precious couplet is fortuitous. 'A star shall come forth.' Stars come forth in the heavens. 'A sceptre, or rod, shall arise', shall shoot up, that is, in the form of an ash-plant or the like out of the soil. For the province of the priesthood is heavenly, the province of the kingship is earthly. So Judah says in his Testament: 'To me God gave the things upon the earth, to Levi the things in heaven. As the heaven is higher than the earth, so is the priesthood of God higher than the earthly kingdom.'

Balaam may have been inspired against his will, but he was none the less inspired, and we must take notice of the order of his words. He speaks first of the star coming forth, and second of the sceptre arising. The author of *Testaments*, living in Maccabean times, thought he knew what that meant. The star was the priesthood, and one might understand it in either of two senses. Either Balaam had prophesied the ascendancy of the Maccabean House under the image of the star, or else he had focused his prediction more narrowly on the priest-king of that House who should fully achieve the saving work for which the House had been raised up by God. If one took the wider sense, one could actually see Balaam's star, for the Maccabean House already reigned. If one took the narrower sense, one at least knew where to look for the rising of the star, that is, somewhere in the reigning family; and his ascent was to be looked for soon.

Meanwhile Balaam's sceptre was totally invisible as yet, and one did not even know where to look for his rising, or from what stock he would spring; for what had become of the family of David? Who could tell? And if a Davidic prince should suddenly appear in the heyday of Maccabean power, he would seem very much *de trop*; for the Maccabean High Priest exercised all secular and military functions as well as his sacred office. The wise Balaam had understood these things perfectly, and so he had spoken of the arising of the sceptre as an altogether second and subsequent event. What he meant was, that after the world had been effectively subjected to God's kingdom by Levitical virtue, the rod of David would mysteriously shoot again and claim the functions of merely secular rule. When God's promises to David had been thus fulfilled, Israel would be complete. The present age would end, and the general resurrection of the righteous would introduce the age to come.

Such being the author's exegesis of Balaam's couplet, he puts short apocalypses into the mouths of Levi and Judah which are paired in the same way as Balaam's pair of lines. Levi utters an apocalypse of the star, and Judah caps it with an apocalypse of the sceptre. 'Then shall the Lord raise up a new priest,' says Levi . . . 'and his star shall arise in heaven as of a king, lighting up the light of knowledge as the sun lights up the day.' And Judah says: 'Then a branch shall go forth from me, and the sceptre of my kingdom shall shine out, and from your' (my children's) 'root shall arise a stem.' Levi describes the pacifying and hallowing of the earth by priestly effort, Judah shows how the return of David's line ushers in the end of all things.

The second apocalypse in effect continues the first; when we have read them both we have the complete picture. But the second does not simply resume the tale where the first left off, for in that case we might easily fail to see that the two had anything to do with one another. The second makes a short résumé of the first, and speaks briefly of the appearance of the star, before it goes on to its own proper theme, the shooting up of the sceptre. And the first throws out certain hints which the second develops. For example, Levi tells us how the priestly Messiah will bind the prince of demons, a useful but not a final riddance. Judah tells us that after the general resurrection the master demon will be thrown into the fire for ever. Levi ends his apocalypse with the somewhat unsatisfactory words: 'Then shall Abraham and Isaac and Jacob exult, and I will be glad, and all the holy ones shall clothe themselves with joy.' Are the patriarchs to have no other share in the Kingdom of God, beyond rejoicing in their sepulchres? Judah develops the point in his apocalyse: 'And after these things' (that is, after the establishment of David's throne), 'shall Abraham and Isaac and Jacob *arise unto life*, and my brethren and I shall be chiefs of the Tribes of Israel, Levi the first, I the second' and so forth.

The point which we made in the chapter to which this note

is appended (p. 321 above), was concerned with the résumé of the advent of the star with which the sceptre-apocalypse begins. We found a text in the apocalypse of Levi, and a résumé of it in the apocalypse of Judah, which St Mark appears to use in the narrative of Christ's baptism. At first sight it seemed an easy escape from such a conclusion to reverse the relation of dependence and suggest that the texts in the Testaments were Christian interpolations based on Mark. But we argued that the interpolator would have to be both cleverer and more deliberately fraudulent than we have any right to suppose, before he could do such a deed. For we should have to say that he was not content with the insertion of his Christian paragraph at an admittedly tempting point in the Testament of Levi. We should have to say that he also inserted a résumé of his own interpolation into a passage in the Testament of Judah which is itself a résumé of the Levi-passage he had interpolated. We have no right to suppose such things, and so (to put it otherwise) the pair of texts, one in the Testament of Levi and the other in the Testament of Judah, are genuine, and guarantee one another's soundness by their correspondence. Therefore, in all probability, St Mark really was acquainted with this pair of texts, and shows the effect of their influence in the wording of his Baptism narrative.

CHAPTER XVI

THE DATE OF WRITING

The purpose of this book is to understand how St Mark wrote, not to determine when he wrote; I do not pretend to know any more about first-century history than everyone picks up, and I have no qualifications for discussing chronology. But there are two pieces of evidence which emerge from the present study, one positive, the other negative in their bearing on the date at which the Gospel was composed.

The positive fact is the complete solidarity of the apocalyptic prophecy in XIII with the rest of the Gospel. What we have said about it in the course of this book amounts to a proof that the prophecy was cast into literary form by the evangelist himself for the place in which it stands. From this it follows that if we can determine the chronological point of view of the man who gave the prophecy its set form, we can roughly determine the date of the Gospel. If, for example, we can make up our minds whether the composer of the prophecy as a formal piece is looking forward to the fall of Jerusalem or looking back upon it, and from what supposed distance in time.

The negative fact is involved in the nature of the evangelist's process of composition. The formalization of the traditions about Christ takes place very largely in the evangelist's own mind and as he writes. It is therefore unnecessary to insert a great gulf of time for the formalization to take place in 'the mind of the Church'. We will now say a little about these two facts in order.

We have first, I suppose, to meet the old and outrageous principle that all true prophecies to be found in books ought to be treated as inventions made up after the event. Jersualem and the Temple fell; St Mark contains a prophecy of it; therefore St Mark was writing after the fall of Jerusalem. The maxim about true prophecies being all afterthoughts is sufficiently refuted by stating its contrary, that false prophecies always precede the events they misdescribe. If we take the two maxims side by side, we get the surprising joint conclusion (a) that people sometimes prophesy the future event; (b) that they are never right. The most hardened rationalist ought to admit that the human power of 'guessing' at the future has a 51 per cent chance of success, when it is a matter of guessing between simple alternatives (Will Oxford or Cambridge win the boat race? Will the Jews provoke the Romans into the violent suppression of the cultus and Temple within our lifetime, or will they not?)

To continue to talk the language of a mere rationalist—it is not as though we were claiming a 100 per cent success for the predictions which the literal sense of St Mark's Gospel contains. The fall of Jerusalem is not the only prediction. The evangelist's book also prophesies within the lifetime of some of Christ's hearers—say within seventy years at the most: it is unfair to suppose that the lifetimes of children are meant—the tribulation of Antichrist and the Advent of the Son of Man in glory. Three things are predicted for a date before A.D. 100 at the latest, and one of them happened within the time specified. So that, on the rationalist's calculation, we are only claiming a 33 per cent success for St Mark's predictions, and that is surely a modest allowance. Even if the rationalist rules out the Advent of the Son of Man as 'no serious historical prediction', the Tribulation of Antichrist remains. To prophesy the tribulation of Antichrist was to prophesy that an emperor would arise who took his conventional deification seriously and set about the systematic extermination of Christians and Jews. There was nothing politically unreasonable about such a prediction; it was, perhaps, as likely as not, on the evidence. If we say, then, that St Mark prophesied (a) the fall of Jerusalem and (b) the tribulation of Antichrist, both being reasonable political predictions, we can say that his prophecies were 50 per cent successful, which is just about what the rationalist ought to expect.

It is, indeed, to fly in the face of fact to suppose that the prediction of the fall of the Temple is based on political reasoning at all. The kind of reasoning on which it is based is written large in the Gospel. Since the true Temple is now Jesus Christ, in himself and in the Church his Body, the veil of the temple of Zerubbabel

and Herod is rent, and the divine presence gone forth. A long con-
tinuance of the empty shrine and of the superseded cultus is
unthinkable. They will be swept away. The fig, already withered,
will not stand for long a dead tree. There are, then, no sort of
difficulties about understanding why St Mark should have con-
fidently adhered to Christ's prediction of the fall of the Temple.

We are not obliged, then, to suppose that the Temple had fallen
when St Mark wrote, merely because he thinks fit to record
Christ's prediction of the event. The question is simply whether
St Mark appears to be looking forward to the fall of the Temple,
or looking back upon it. And when we say 'St Mark' we mean the
author of the prophetical passage in XIII in the form in which
it now stands. In trying to think sensibly about this question,
we have to distinguish two historical perspectives in XIII. The
events predicted are of course being looked at from the point of
view of Christ and his disciples sitting on the Mount of Olives
on the Wednesday afternoon before the Passion. But St Mark is
re-expressing Christ's prophecy under the impulse of his own
inspiration and for the benefit of his contemporaries. It is unlikely
that he will do so without betraying the point of view, the place
in history, from which he and his friends look at the course of
events which Christ had prophesied. What we have to do here is
to try to fix this second perspective point.

It has commonly been supposed that there is a third perspective
point to be reckoned with—that of St Mark's 'source'. Someone,
not St Mark, or, if you like, St Mark many years before the composition of the Gospel, had formulated the prophecy, and when
St Mark wrote his Gospel he incorporated it. We have, then, (a)
the perspective point of Christ on the Mount of Olives, (b) the
perspective point of St Mark's 'source', (c) the perspective point
of St Mark and of his composition of the Gospel. And it has often
been assumed that St Mark was so superficial an author that he
allowed (b), the perspective point of his source, to prevail, and
scarcely introduced his own at all. On such an assumption we can
obviously form no sound inference from the perspective point of
the prophecy to the date of St Mark's writing.

I will not discuss and refute the reasons which have led critics to assign the authorship of the prophetic passage to some shadowy figure standing behind St Mark. I do not have to discuss them, because the burden of proof lies with them, not with me. You cannot assume that a passage in a continuous book is a piece of old cloth patched on a new garment: you have to prove it. All I need to do is to show that the passage in question results from the imaginative process which produces the whole book, that it builds on what precedes and is built into what follows, and that it is the very stuff of the author's mind. I think I have shown these things (pp. 128, 135–141, 164–167 above), and all I can do here is to submit my expositions to the reader's judgement.

So we can keep our perspective points down to that of Christ and his disciples, and that of St Mark in the Holy Ghost. It is of the second that we have to treat here, but let it be understood that we take the first with complete seriousness. The prophecy is authentic. It is presupposed by the eschatological passages in the earliest of all Christian writings, I and II Thessalonians. Christ proclaimed himself Son of Man, and supported the prophecy of his advent with that context in which Daniel had set it. According to Daniel, to be the Son of Man is to be the supplanter of Antichrist. The roles are inseparable. Christ made no special apocalyptic predictions. He simply affirmed the old prophetic images as they stood, and left the decoding of them to the action of God in future events. He revealed what he himself was and what he was doing; his words and his actions interpreted one another. But the action which would interpret the prophetic words about Antichrist and Advent was not yet forthcoming.

What was forthcoming was the action which *prefigured* these things, and therefore it was necessary and fruitful to talk about them. Christ spoke of those still shadowy mysteries, those painted pictures on the clouds of prophecy, in order that the relation of his passion and resurrection to the end of all things might be understood, and to teach the lesson that the destiny of the Church was the re-enactment of his passion and resurrection.

He did not, in his human existence, know the day or the hour, and if we ask why, the history of his passion gives us the answer. If he had known 'the hour' in Gethsemane, his agony would not have been the agony of man. The unfixedness of the future is the human predicament. Nevertheless Christ saw the end of all things as not far removed. He had no human reasons for thinking otherwise; and his divine wisdom expressed itself in actualities, or in such shadows as they threw before them. It is no part of the incarnation of God that he should plot out the course of history for us beforehand. We have no particular interest in persuading ourselves that he distinguished between the fall of the Temple and the last agony of God's Israel.

What I have just written about Christ's prophecy is more like a confession of faith than a page of historical criticism. No harm, perhaps. If I were reading an historical argument like the one I am writing, and found the author however justifiably skirting round a point of faith, I should be continually asking myself, 'But what does the man believe?' So I have made my profession. Now to return to the matter in hand: can we determine the perspective point of St Mark in the prophetical discourse?

The fall of the Temple or city is not explicitly mentioned in the prophetical discourse at all. Christ declares, as he makes his way out of the Temple, that not one stone of it shall be left upon another. The prediction is isolated, and there are no conceivable indications by which we could determine St Mark's perspective point with regard to it. Presently, on the Mount of Olives, Christ unfolds a prophecy, in which there is some hope of fixing St Mark's perspective point: but the prophecy does not name the fall of the Temple.

Nevertheless, something equivalent to the fall of the Temple must be there, unless the evangelist is strangely incoherent. For, having heard the saying about the fall of the Temple, the disciples ask the question, 'When shall these things be, or what is the sign when these things are all about to be accomplished?' The disciples' question broadens the field of inquiry in much the same way as does their question in IV, 10. Having heard the parable of the sower, 'they asked him his parables' or riddles. So here, having heard that the Temple is to fall, they ask him when *these things* are to be, or what is the sign when these things are *all* about to be accomplished. They assume that the fall of the Temple is part of a larger complex of events, and it is about this that they ask.

We ought to suppose that Christ answers their question: that he tells them about the complex of events which includes the fall of the Temple. If St Mark can trust his readers to see where the fall of the temple fits into this complex of events he has every reason for not mentioning it explicitly, since he has already recorded Christ's oracle about it. But if the exhortation, 'Let him that readeth understand' (XIII, 14), does not evoke the response it demands, if the reader does not see where the fall of the Temple comes in, then Christ will not be seen to have answered that part of his disciples' question which bears upon the fall of the Temple.

The disciples ask for the 'sign when these things are all to be accomplished', and the first half of Christ's prophecy tells them of a time during which they must beware of misreading the signs. It is pretty clear that 'all these things' do not any of them begin until XIII, 14, the appearance of the 'Desolating Abomination'. 'All these things' are the Desolating Abomination, the Tribulation of Antichrist, and the Advent of the Son of Man. Where among these events are we to place the fall of the Temple?

We must place it in the appearance of the Desolating Abomination. 'But when ye shall see the desolating abomination standing where he ought not . . . then let the people in Judaea flee to the mountains.' It is here that we must place the fall of the Temple, for it is here alone that the Temple is mentioned at all. After a prophecy concerned with the state of the Church throughout the world (XIII, 6–13) we suddenly read of a heathenish or idolatrous outrage (for that is what 'abomination' means) planted in a spot where above all it ought not to be, and where it constitutes a special threat to the people in Judaea. It is fairly obvious that the spot is the Temple.

That is as much as to say that St Mark is interpreting Daniel's prophecy fairly literally. Daniel spoke of a desolating abomination to be set up in the Temple, and he meant an idolatrous altar or

image. The first application of his words had been to the forcible
hellenization of the Temple cult by Antiochus Epiphanes. Then, as
the Books of Maccabees inform us, the godly, after refusing com-
pliance with heathendom, had 'fled to the mountains' (I Macc.
II, 28, II Macc. V, 27). This, says the prophecy in Mark XIII, will
happen again.

But it does not seem that the Marcan prophecy simply recon-
stitutes the whole Maccabean picture. The Abomination had
'desolated' the Temple in the sense of causing the continuous
offering of the true worship to cease. But it had not desolated in
the sense of making the site look like a wild hilltop or an abandoned
ruin. The horror of the Abomination had lain precisely in the misuse of the still standing Temple courts. And it was possible for a
Christian prophet to view the coming of the future Antichrist in the
same terms. St Paul, interpreting the same prophecy of Christ as St
Mark interprets, speaks of 'the man of sin, the son of perdition, the
adversary and self-glorifier against all that is called divine or wor-
shipful, so that he seats himself in the temple of God, setting himself forth to be God'. (II Thess. II, 4). These words do not suggest
the destruction of the Temple, but the hideous misuse of it. St
Paul may well have believed that the Temple would in fact be
overthrown at a later stage of events, but he did not interpret the
planting of the desolating abomination in the Temple as the desolation of the Temple in the sense of its physical overthrow.

But such an interpretation was obviously possible, it is one
of the things that 'desolating abomination' could most naturally
mean. And such was St Mark's interpretation. It is stupid not to
interpret St Mark by St Mark, when the interpretation is in itself
perfectly natural. St Mark sees the triumphant and outrageous
self-deifying power as 'desolating', that is, utterly destroying
the Temple, and planting a heathen emblem, probably an image of
Antichrist himself, on the site. Such an interpretation of desolating abomination not only fits the words, it fits the political facts
of the day. The Romans had a supreme contempt for the Jews and
their 'superstition' and if Antichrist was to be a Roman Emperor,
he was more likely to impose his will on the Jews by razing the

Temple and building something opprobrious on the site, than by converting the hated edifice to the purposes of the imperial cult.

We conclude, then, that the appearance of the Desolating Abomination in XIII, 14 is equivalent to the overthrow of the Temple. We can now advance to our principal question, where the perspective point of the evangelist himself is to be placed, whether before XIII, 14 or after it.

The answer is 'Before'. XIII, 5-13 contains a comparatively long and detailed exhortation about the conduct of Christians during a disappointing period of serious but desultory persecution before the events connected with 'the end' begin. It would be strange indeed if St Mark should so much expand the mere prelude to the apocalyptic drama, unless that was where he and his contemporaries were, anxiously looking for the curtain to go up. After briefly rehearsing the last things in XIII, 14-27, he returns in 28 ff. to an exhortation addressed to men who are looking for the signs of the end. They cannot be given exact dates; what they are to look for is the unfolding of a process through stages, like the stages of the growth of the fig which forewarn us of summer.

The little that the evangelist does report of Christ's oracle about the Desolating Abomination suggests that it is still future to the evangelist, and not merely to the disciples on the Mount of Olives. Would St Mark have retained the words 'Pray that it be not in winter' if the matter were past praying for when he wrote? He might have done, but it is not so likely. For it is obvious that St Mark is not an evangelist who makes an attempt to report all the words of Christ he has heard. He is severely economical and uses only those that serve the purposes of his inspiration.

So we conclude that St Mark wrote before the fall of Jerusalem. If we could be sure that he was a careful and up-to-date historical observer, we might venture to guess how much before. We might ask ourselves whether the Jewish war was being fought when he wrote, and if so, what stage it had reached. As it is, I think these are fruitless questions.

Before the fall of Jerusalem, then, and after the outbreak of the Neronian persecution. The Bishop of Derby has written well in his commentary (p. 174) about the relation of St Mark's Gospel to martyrdom. Martyrdom, when the evangelist writes, is a recognized process with a pattern, of which Christ's passion is exhibited as the great exemplar. There is in particular a strong suggestion that St Peter has confessed Christ at the price of his life. So we may put the composition of the Gospel between A.D. 65 and 69, and we are lucky to be able to date it within five years.

There might, of course, be other considerations which outweighed the apparent evidence of the perspective point in Mark XIII and obliged us to accept a later date. More time, it has often been thought, would have to elapse between the Resurrection and the composition of the Gospel to allow the originally simple historical tradition to reach the degree of symbolical or theological formalization which the Gospel represents. When people make statements like this, there is no knowing what lurks behind them; perhaps the assumption, consciously or unconsciously held, that there was nothing supernatural about what happened in Galilee and Jerusalem round about the year 30, and nothing theologically surprising about the interpretation placed on the events by the chief participants in them. Any Christian interpreter must repudiate such an assumption once it is pulled out into the light and visibly expressed. But there are many who would still say that the original Gospel must have been fundamentally 'simple'.

What does the dogma of primitive simplicity mean? No doubt what Christ or his apostles began to say to neophytes had to be as simple as it could be made, and those to whom Christ or the apostles first spoke were neophytes, and so the Gospel as first uttered was simple. But the fundamental beliefs of the new faith were anything but simple. St Peter's beliefs were comparatively simple when he confessed Christ at Caesarea Philippi, but his simplicity did not satisfy Christ; by the time his feet were on the road from Peraea to Jerusalem the apostle's ideas were less simple, and after Easter and Pentecost they were not simple at all.

Naturally the process of reflection upon the paradoxical complex of things the faith contained took time, and indeed I do not see any signs of its being yet completed. It is possible to talk about degrees of theological maturity. But who will tell me that St Mark's theological maturity is greater than St Paul's? And St Paul was roughly a contemporary of St Peter's own. After all, no one is claiming that St Mark's Gospel is a pre-Pauline work, and I for my part am not claiming that it is unaffected by St Paul's thought and teaching.

Theological maturity is perhaps one thing, and the theological patterning of the traditions about Jesus is another. It may be argued that theological maturity ripened surprisingly fast, but that the simple factual memories of Christ's words and actions would have a strong power of resistance, a strong tendency to maintain their original outlines, and to withstand theological or symbolic patterning. It is therefore thought necessary to suppose a considerable time in which the process may take place. But the moral of our analysis is this, that the process of symbolical patterning, or whatever we choose to call it, takes place there and then as St Mark writes, and under the impulse of his inspiration. Theologically speaking, it is the work of the Holy Ghost, continuing the exposition of Christ which Christ had begun. To ask how long it took is to ask how long St Mark worked on his Gospel. What do you say? Days or weeks?

Naturally something is presupposed by St Mark's patterning of the tradition. But that something is not the pre-patterning of what he patterned by the community mind or any such mysterious agency. What is presupposed is a habitual way of handling anecdotes about Christ in sermons and instructions, and of relating them to Old Testament texts. St Mark himself had done plenty of it in the pulpit before he wrote his Gospel; who doubts it? He was already provided with a highly wrought form of thinking, an instrument which the Spirit chose to apply in a new way for the composition of his Gospel. But again, there is no need to postulate a great space of time for the development of the preaching art within the Church. It was a Jewish art in an advanced state of development, and it was taken over.

To a Christian mind, reverence for the evangelists and for their words can hardly seem too great, and yet the reverence rightly paid them may be misdirected, and the consequences of such misdirection have been at times serious. The evangelists ought to be, and have been, reverenced because they are inspired by God. In the heyday of Liberal Theology the inspiration of the evangelists was believed by Christian scholars, but with a pious and honourable agnosticism these men were willing to dispense with the hard-edged definitions of the past; they were content to be in doubt wherein the evangelists' inspiration lay. But if the nature of inspiration receded into mystery, there seemed all the more reason to grasp firmly what was clear. Whatever an inspired man might or might not be, one could not go wrong in seeing him as a good and truth-loving man. One would not expect to find him falling below one's own standard of integrity.

So far no error has slipped in. The error arises when the scholar begins to judge of the evangelists' integrity too nearly by the model of his own. Integrity is in a sense one thing everywhere, it is just the doing of a work as it requires to be done, and without admitting irrelevant motives. By such a definition a trustee and an historian and a statesman can have the same thing, integrity, each in his own sphere. But as soon as we wish to advance beyond abstract definition and to judge of any particular act whether it shows integrity or not, our judgement gets no help from the general definition. We cannot judge of the integrity of a banker except by understanding what the work of a banker is.

Now here was the liberal theologian's difficulty. He attributed integrity to the inspired man, but he was not clear what inspiration, or the function of an inspired man, was. He was ill-placed for judging the integrity of an evangelist by the function of an evangelist, and so it was virtually inevitable that he should plant an irrelevant standard upon him and judge him by the requirements of an alien function. Whose function? Most likely the scholar's own. He will take it that what would be integrity in him would be integrity in an evangelist. Now the scholar is an historian and critic, and if there is one thing which would not be integrity in him, it would be the symbolical or theological patterning of historical material. He is therefore most reluctant to attribute such patterning to the evangelist. The evangelist, he thinks, was an honest reporter, but of course the ray of modern historical scholarship had not shone upon his head, and so it is likely enough that he has reported other people's patternings and allegorizings in all innocence, taking them for simple history. If the modern scholar is an amiable man, he will like best to think that no one was to blame, no one consciously let down the standards of historical integrity. If there are 'symbolical elements' in the Gospels, it is no one's fault. One man made an allegory in all innocence, another with equal innocence mistook it for history. Or if that will not cover the facts, then we can say that unconsciously, and over a period of time, and in the course of many repetitions, historical tradition took on the shape and colour of theological belief.

What such a line of thought amounts to is invoking random accident to save the face of conscious intention. It is an amiable plan, but its effects on Gospel history are nothing short of calamitous. Accident is really nothing but a gap in the intelligible continuity of action. If we introduce plenty of accident, we shall have plenty of useful chasms in which to dump the load of undistributed blame; but we shall also have many open gaps between separate links of our historical evidence. If the Gospel tradition has submitted to a prolonged chaos of unrestricted accident, then we can scarcely hope to interpret it historically.

The hypothesis of unrestricted accident is unnecessary and (what is more to the point) untrue. We have to go back to the beginning and discover what the function of an evangelist is by understanding what he has done. Then we can respect his integrity by seeing that he discharges his function with singlemindedness. St Mark's function is not simply to report the life and works of Jesus, but to become the instrument of the Holy Ghost interpreting the life and works of Jesus. It was one divine mind which spoke in Galilee and which afterwards interpreted that speech through the evangelist. Our faith is the joint utterance of Jesus and the Holy Ghost.

The Christian historian is not a man who is at war with his own believing heart. He does not as an historian strip away or discard the work of the Spirit on which as a believer he is fed. The Christian historian differs from any other Christian chiefly by a special attachment to the time-series. He strips away, he discards nothing, but he assigns everything to its moment of occurrence. When he distinguishes between what Christ said in Galilee and the interpretation of that saying which Christ taught St Mark through the Holy Ghost, the distinction he draws is not one of truth but one of time. He is not dividing fiction from fact but the later from the earlier. To him as an historian St Mark's making the inspired interpretation is as much a fact as Christ's giving the original oracle; to him as a Christian the inspired comment is as true as the divine text.

It is nevertheless of deep concern to the Church to be able to make the time-distinction, and write the unconfused history of her origins. For such a task St Mark is in some ways our chief material. To write the history of Christ is very largely a matter of introducing the distinction we speak of into St Mark's work. We have to separate between the tradition on which he worked and the inspired labour he performed upon it. There is only one way to do this. We must first understand by direct study in what kind of mental or imaginative process his inspiration expressed itself. Then we can begin to see what St Mark does with the facts he presupposes, and what the facts he presupposes are.

What results from such a study? We find that the process of inspired interpretation is so powerful and so complete that it sufficiently accounts for the 'symbolical elements'. We do not need to presuppose an indefinite series of previous interpretative processes one imposed upon another. There is no difficulty in believing that the work St Mark performed was performed upon straightforward and first-hand memories of Christ; for example, St Peter's, as tradition on good ground upholds. It is not good sense to suppose that a few years after St Peter's death the Church would have allowed the form of the written gospel to be imposed upon her by any man who lacked a close personal acquaintance with the apostolic witness. The Church never underrated the importance of the apostles' words; and if ever there was a book which wove the gospel on an apostolic frame, it is St Mark's. Is it likely that the evangelist neglected as an authority what he built on as a symbol, the apostolate instituted by Christ?

INDEX OF SCRIPTURAL REFERENCES

Note.—Passages alluded to, but not cited, in the text will usually be found in this Index.

OLD TESTAMENT

APOCRYPHA AND PSEUDEPIGRAPHA

INDEX OF SCRIPTURAL REFERENCES

NEW TESTAMENT

Jerusalem   73, 81, 97, 117 f., 132, 146,
    151, 158, 160 ff., 184, 191 f.,
    209, 211, 215 f., 238, 335, 342,
    344, 366
  fall of   358 f., 365
  feasts at   211 ff.
  journey of Christ to   118, 158, 192,
    209, 335
  New J.   207
  problem of Johannine visitations of
    213 ff.
  theme of 8th Cycle   118
  way to   117 ff., 209, 230, 335, 366
Jesse, root of   105, 121, 237, 250
Jesus, son of Nun, see Joshua
JESUS CHRIST
  baptism   45, 60, 62, 66, 155 ff., 187,
    189, 215 f., 276
    vocation   60, 155
  sojourn in desert   59, 62, 66 ff., 156,
    189, 228, 277, 280 n.
  temptation
    in desert   60, 63, 66 ff., 156,
      228, 277, 280 n.
    by Peter   157, 214, 230, 280, 314,
      343
    in Gethsemane   157
  divine voice at baptism   60, 155,
    227 ff.
    at Transfiguration   51, 156, 227,
      229, 314
  ministry, mission   184, 209, 222, 246
    mission to Israel   79, 81, 183, 204,
      305, 332, 337
    to Gentiles   149, 188, 191, 335,
      337
    authenticated by signs   76 f., 102,
      272, 280 f.
  disciples, q.v.
  Galilean ministry, q.v.
  mastery of demons   81, 152, 235,
    325 f.
  rejection of   83, 99, 112, 147, 168,
    213, 236, 334
    followed by withdrawal   73, 77 f.,
      83, 118, 132 f., 146, 163, 190,
      219, 228
  besieged by crowds   73, 81, 92 f.,
    190, 300
  use of boat   73, 92 f., 240, 300
  preaching   106 f., 111 ff., 158, 190,
    219, 236

JESUS CHRIST (cont.)
  teaching q.v.
  discourses q.v.
  parables q.v.
  cornfield incident   72 ff., 82, 93,
    159 f., 233, 275 f., 302, 318
  conflict with scribes and Pharisees
    (see also scribe, Pharisee, con-
    troversy)   34 f., 71 ff., 81, 83,
    96 ff., 106, 123, 126, 132, 146 f.,
    152, 159 ff., 189, 192, 216, 232 ff.,
    270 ff.
  conflict with Sanhedrin   122 f., 132,
    165, 193, 216 ff., 232, 238 f.
  overrides   sabbath   law   71 ff.,
    158 f., 190, 233
  plot against him   159, 163, 188,
    213, 215
  his physical family   81, 97, 165, 240
  his spiritual family   81 ff., 190, 329 f.,
    333
  his table-fellowship   71 f., 81 f.
  confession of, see confession
  imposes silence, see secrecy
  journey to Jerusalem   118, 158, 192,
    209, 335
    problem of Johannine visitations
    213 ff.
  the rich man   116 f., 119, 124 f.,
    158, 170
  the good scribe   124 f.
  children   114 ff., 170
  triumphal entry   118, 120, 122,
    129 f., 160, 192, 217, 220, 238
  cleansing of Temple, see Temple
  withering of fig tree   36, 161 ff., 218
  fetching of ass   36, 109, 122, 129 ff.,
    161, 176, 238, 345
  finding of supper-room   36, 109,
    130 ff., 176, 217, 345
  the tribute-money   122, 170 f., 218 f.
  the widow's mite   126 f., 176
  anointing q.v.
  predicts his Passion, see under Passion
    sufferings of Church   136 ff., 150 f.
    (see also Apocalypse)
  last supper q.v.
  passion q.v.
  agony (see also Gethsemane)   128,
    134, 140 f., 157, 197, 200, 316,
    362
  betrayal   90, 137 f., 141, 204

Water, symbolism of 60, 63, 78
Week (*see also* Holy Week) 138, 145, 153
Wilderness, *see* Desert
Wind, *see* Spirit
Witness (*see also* Confession; Martyrdom; Three, the) 274, 371
  to miracles 36, 227
  Christ the sole true W. 231, 314
  Two, of Apocalypse 139, 270
  Three heavenly 313 f.
  of scripture 271
Women at the sepulchre 128, 134 f., 141, 169, 177 f.
World to come, the 49, 150, 179, 236

Zarephath 337
Zebedee, sons of (*see also* James, John) 34, 62, 68, 109
  request for thrones 118 ff., 129, 170, 316, 345
  Sons of Thunder 109, 311
Zebul (house) 324 f.
Zebulon 318 f., 324 ff., 331, 340
  Testament of 325
Zedekiah, false prophet 165
Zerubbabel 318, 359
Zilpah (*see* 'Handmaid' Tribes) 337 f.
Zion (*see also* Jerusalem, Temple) 161, 215